M000289940

Changing the
Game

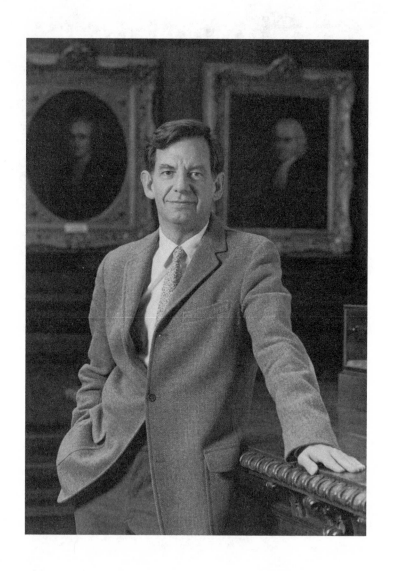

Changing the Game

William G. Bowen and the Challenges of American Higher Education

Nancy Weiss Malkiel

PRINCETON UNIVERSITY PRESS
PRINCETON & OXFORD

Copyright © 2023 by Princeton University Press

Princeton University Press is committed to the protection of copyright and the intellectual property our authors entrust to us. Copyright promotes the progress and integrity of knowledge. Thank you for supporting free speech and the global exchange of ideas by purchasing an authorized edition of this book. If you wish to reproduce or distribute any part of it in any form, please obtain permission.

Requests for permission to reproduce material from this work should be sent to permissions@press.princeton.edu

Published by Princeton University Press

41 William Street, Princeton, New Jersey 08540
99 Banbury Road, Oxford OX2 6JX
press.princeton.edu

All Rights Reserved

Library of Congress Cataloging-in-Publication Data

Names: Malkiel, Nancy Weiss, author.
Title: Changing the game : William G. Bowen and the challenges of American higher education / Nancy Weiss Malkiel.
Description: Princeton : Princeton University Press, [2023] | Includes bibliographical references and index.
Identifiers: LCCN 2022046724 (print) | LCCN 2022046725 (ebook) | ISBN 9780691247823 (hardback) | ISBN 9780691247816 (ebook)
Subjects: LCSH: Bowen, William G. | Princeton University—Presidents—Biography. | Andrew W. Mellon Foundation—Presidents—Biography. | College presidents—United States—Biography. | Endowments—Officials and employees—Biography. | Education, Higher—United States—History—20th century. | BISAC: BIOGRAPHY & AUTOBI-OGRAPHY / Educators | EDUCATION / Multicultural Education
Classification: LCC LD4605.B68 M35 2023 (print) | LCC LD4605.B68 (ebook) | DDC 378.749/65092 [B]—dc23/eng/20230411
LC record available at https://lccn.loc.gov/2022046724
LC ebook record available at https://lccn.loc.gov/2022046725

British Library Cataloging-in-Publication Data is available

Editorial: Eric Crahan, Peter Dougherty, and Whitney Rauenhorst
Production Editorial: Terri O'Prey
Jacket Design: Katie Osborne
Production: Erin Suydam
Publicity: Julia Haav and Kathryn Stevens
Copyeditor: Beth Gianfagna

Jacket photography by Robert Matthews, Office of Communications, Princeton University

This book has been composed in Sabon LT Std and Milano

Printed on acid-free paper. ∞

Printed in the United States of America

10 9 8 7 6 5 4 3 2 1

To Burt and Piper

Contents

Illustrations

Frontispiece: William G. Bowen. John W. H. Simpson photograph, 1981. ©
John W. H. Simpson. Office of the President Records: William G. Bowen,
AC187, Box 453, Princeton University Archives, Department of Rare
Books and Special Collections, Princeton University Library.

Following page 164

Albert A. Bowen. Photograph courtesy of Mary Ellen Bowen and Karen
Bowen.

Bernice Pommert Bowen and William G. Bowen. Photograph courtesy of
Mary Ellen Bowen and Karen Bowen.

Denison University Tennis Team. Scanned Images of Tennis Team from
1953 through 1955, RG09 Student Services, Series T Athletics, Format 90 Images, Folder "Coach with Tennis Players" (9T-90), Denison
University Archives & Special Collections, Granville, Ohio.

Mary Ellen Maxwell and William G. Bowen wedding. Photograph courtesy of Mary Ellen Bowen and Karen Bowen.

William G. Bowen. Orren Jack Turner photograph. RG PB Publications
& Biographical Information, Format 90 Images, Folder "Bowen, Wil-
liam G. Class of 1955" (P&B-90), Denison University Archives &
Special Collections, Granville, Ohio.

William G. Bowen and Robert F. Goheen. Marie E. Bellis photograph,
1971. Office of the President Records: William G. Bowen, AC187,
Box 451, Princeton University Archives, Department of Rare Books
and Special Collections, Princeton University Library.

William G. Bowen and his family, 10 Maclean Circle. Marie E. Bellis
photograph, 1971. Office of the President Records: William G. Bowen,
AC187, Box 453, Princeton University Archives, Department of Rare
Books and Special Collections, Princeton University Library.

Mary Ellen Bowen. Office of the President Records: William G. Bowen,
AC187, Box 451, Princeton University Archives, Department of Rare
Books and Special Collections, Princeton University Library.

William G. Bowen teaching a class in Economics 101 at Princeton. Office
of the President Records: William G. Bowen, AC187, Box 453, Princeton University Archives, Department of Rare Books and Special Collections, Princeton University Library.

William G. Bowen in the president's office at the Andrew W. Mellon
   Foundation. RG PB Publications & Biographical Information, Format
   90 Images, Folder "Bowen, William G. Class of 1955" (P&B-90),
   Denison University Archives & Special Collections, Granville, Ohio.
William G. Bowen at his retirement celebration at the Andrew W. Mellon
   Foundation. Andrea K. Dolloff photograph. Reproduced by permis-
   sion of Andrea K. Dolloff. Photograph provided by the Andrew W.
   Mellon Foundation.

Page 289

Derek Bok & William Bowen, by David Levine, 1998. © Matthew and
   Eve Levine.

Preface

As provost (1967–72) and president (1972–88) of Princeton University and president of the Andrew W. Mellon Foundation (1988–2006), and in the twenty books he authored, William G. Bowen confronted the central problems of American higher education. He tackled the critical issues of "cost disease," inclusion, affirmative action, college access, college completion, online learning—all the big, thorny problems that held American colleges and universities in their thrall in the half century from Bowen's assumption of administrative responsibility as provost at Princeton to his death in 2016. He took on the biggest challenges he could, and he attacked them with formidable tenacity, insight, and wisdom. It was not that he solved those problems—no one could—but through his efforts and pragmatic insights, they became more tractable, more malleable, more susceptible to solution than they had been before. Bowen's long history of addressing these issues shows us how vision, strategy, and political and organizational savvy can enable leaders to deal with pressing problems and elevate the stature and efficacy of major institutions.

Bill Bowen was arguably the most consequential leader in American higher education in the late twentieth and early twenty-first centuries.[1] He had a vision for higher education and a strategy for accomplishing that vision—not out of an existing playbook, not modeled on other institutions, but the product of his own invention. As provost of Princeton, working in close concert with President Robert F. Goheen, drawing on his own political and organizational sense, benefiting from the scale and collegiality of

---

1 As we shall see later, this is a common theme in contemporary assessments. See, for example, Brian Rosenberg, president of Macalester College: "Bill Bowen was the most important leader in higher education of the past 50 years." "Bill Bowen: Man of Achievement," *Chronicle of Higher Education*, Oct. 24, 2016, https://www.chronicle.com/article/bill-bowen-man-of-achievement, accessed Aug. 25, 2020.

the institution, he helped to craft a governance structure and a set of strategies to lessen the disruptions at Princeton during the period of intense tumult over race at home and the Vietnam War abroad that rocked so many colleges and universities. He pressed Goheen to embrace coeducation as critical to Princeton's future; he contributed in numerous ways to *The Education of Women at Princeton*, Gardner Patterson's highly analytical, data-driven study of the desirability and feasibility of coeducation; he worked to sell the proposal to admit undergraduate women to Princeton alumni; and once the trustees approved, he worked assiduously on the many details required to implement it successfully.

As president of Princeton, Bowen built on groundwork laid in the Goheen era and purposefully remade the university in multiple ways. His first priority, in his words, was "to increase the intellectual muscle of the faculty" through targeted recruiting and higher standards for external appointments and internal promotions. There was ample evidence of his success in raising the caliber of the faculty—Nobel prizes, elections to national academies, ability to go head to head with major universities in the United States and the United Kingdom in recruiting, evident growth in the intellectual stature of important departments.

Bowen's other most important priority, he said, was making the student body more diverse and more inclusive—active recruitment of Black students, early efforts to recruit Hispanic and Asian American students, the embrace of equal access in admissions for women and men.[2] Along with recruitment went efforts to refashion institutional structures to be more open and more welcoming to the students who were now enrolling. Those efforts manifested themselves in major changes in the operations of the university chapel, especially to make ceremonial convocations more ecumenical and more inclusive of students of many faiths. The efforts led also to a successful initiative to establish a Center for Jewish Life. They led to institutional support for the legal campaign to require the remaining all-male eating clubs to admit women. And they led, too,

2 "Hispanic" was the term used in the 1970s in Princeton reports. It was meant to encompass Mexican American (Chicano/Chicana) and Puerto Rican students.

to the development of a residential college system to provide an intellectual, cultural, social, and recreational home base for the increasingly diverse student population at the university. The Princeton that William G. Bowen inherited in 1972 was still struggling to shake off its historical identity as a very good liberal arts college for Protestant boys of good social standing, mainly from the mid-Atlantic and southern states. The Princeton he turned over to his successor, Harold T. Shapiro, in 1988 was far more diverse with a far stronger faculty and now had vaulted into the ranks of the world's great research universities.

That sounds like a lot about Princeton, the wary reader may think; unless one bleeds orange and black, why should one be that interested in Princeton? Princeton was in no way typical of American colleges and universities. It was smaller than its closest peers among private universities. It offered instruction limited to the arts and sciences and engineering, eschewing the full range of professional schools usually found in American universities. It focused on undergraduate education and had a very small graduate school, which it grew slowly over time. It had a single faculty who taught both undergraduate and graduate students. But for all of its uniqueness, a close examination of the Princeton case illustrates how an effective leader can take hold of an important institution and move, step by step, to confront the obstacles standing in the way of progress and transform it—to modernize it, to take it from very good to outstanding, to turn it into one of the leading examples of its kind in American society.

As president of the Andrew W. Mellon Foundation, Bowen then had the chance to apply things he had learned at Princeton to the larger educational world. Mellon gave him opportunities and resources to extend his vision broadly to American higher education. He doubled down on Mellon's historical investments in graduate education, liberal arts colleges, libraries, museums, and performing arts institutions, adding eastern Europe and South Africa to the foundation's traditional scope in the United States. He instituted new programs that had a major impact on higher education, notably JSTOR, the electronic journal storage project that transformed access to scholarly journals for faculty and students around the world, and the Mellon Mays—originally Mellon Minority—Undergraduate Fellowship Program, which has prepared hundreds of college students of color for teaching and administrative positions in the academy. As well, through his own persistence in persuading college and university presidents to hand over an unprecedented trove of student-level data, he created a massive database, College and Beyond, that opened new paths for social science research about issues profoundly important to colleges and universities: affirmative action, college athletics, and access and college completion for low-income and first-generation college students. Critics noted that Mellon devoted an unusual share of its resources to the president's personal research projects. While that was true, the data collection that Bowen directed was unique—such data had not been available before, and the scholarly work done using those data, first by Bowen and his colleagues and later by dozens of other researchers, illuminated subjects of critical importance to higher education.

Over the decades, Bowen steadily widened his field of vision. Originally focused on Princeton, he looked next to other elite private universities and liberal arts colleges—elite private universities because of his conviction that they carried outsize influence; liberal arts colleges because of his own formative experience at Denison. Later, he focused directly, both in his own scholarship and in the educational initiatives he promoted at ITHAKA, on public institutions. As we shall see, even before he made that pivot, however, his scholarship—especially on affirmative action and college athletics—was broadly meaningful to the public sector. With the examples of affirmative action and athletics especially in mind, William E. "Brit" Kirwan, former chancellor of the University System of Maryland, emphasized "the breadth and depth of the admiration and appreciation leaders in the public sector felt for Bill."[3]

Although not everything Bowen touched worked, and he was not always right in what he asserted, he had huge confidence in what he did and what he wrote. His friend Lawrence S. Bacow, president successively of Tufts and Harvard universities, described him

---

3 William E. "Brit" Kirwan, reader's report for Princeton University Press, June 2022.

as "unbelievably honest intellectually." Bowen was always open to testing his ideas, and he was well prepared to change his mind "in the face of data, evidence, a better argument."[4]

Following his retirement from Mellon, Bowen focused on technological solutions to the cost problems facing colleges and universities, in part through new scholarship, and especially through ITHAKA, the nonprofit organization he created with Mellon funding to do research and experiments to improve higher education, with a special focus on efforts to use digital learning to accelerate college completion and control the rising costs of education.

Just as Bowen's programmatic initiatives had a transformative effect on so many aspects of American higher education, so his scholarship in higher education pointed the way to using social science research to illuminate issues of central importance to colleges and universities. Explicating the cost structure and financial pressures on institutions of higher education was an important theme in his early publications. With William J. Baumol, he had articulated the concept of "cost disease," wherein colleges and universities, like performing arts institutions, would never be able to realize the savings of businesses that benefited from greater productivity and thus faced inexorable cost pressures that needed to be contended with to ensure their survival. Bowen was an early practitioner of the collection and analysis of data to understand important issues in higher education. As the economist of higher education and former president of the Spencer Foundation, Michael S. McPherson, has pointed out, Bowen's work "coincided with a remarkable era of increased data availability and dramatic improvement in analytical methods in the social sciences"—in other words, "innovations in research on higher education grew out of improvements in data and methods in labor economics."[5]

With the books growing out of College and Beyond and other specially curated databases—*The Shape of the River, The Game of Life, Reclaiming the Game, Equity and Excellence in American Higher Education, Crossing the Finish Line,* and *Higher Education*

---

4 Telephone interview with Lawrence S. Bacow, Sept. 3, 2020.
5 E-mail, Michael S. McPherson to Nancy Weiss Malkiel, Sept. 22, 2021.

in the Digital Age—Bowen made fundamental contributions to policies and practices at colleges and universities, to federal policy concerning affirmative action, and to further scholarship by labor economists and students of higher education seeking to do more sophisticated analysis of the important issues he raised. "A characteristic of [Bowen's] empirical work has been the use of relatively simple and intuitively understandable empirical methods with really high-quality data," McPherson said. Bowen made a notable contribution in "show[ing] other researchers the power of data" at a detailed student level.[6] Without using "sophisticated, fancy tools," the economist of higher education Catharine Bond Hill echoed, Bowen "collected the data" and "told the story."[7]

The economist of higher education Caroline Hoxby said that Bowen and McPherson seeded the notion that scholars could work on the economics of higher education, in part through their own pioneering work, and in part through the resources they invested to support other scholars—Bowen through Mellon grant money and the unique data sets he created; McPherson through grant money from the Spencer Foundation. Since then, there has been an explosion of work in the field, with many younger scholars attracted to doing research, with economic and sociological theory layered on data, and with access to a wealth of data—from the College Board, ACT, the National Student Clearinghouse, public college and university systems, the Internal Revenue Service—not previously available.[8] All of that, it can be posited, started with Bowen and his colleagues.

For all his impressive strengths as a leader in American higher education in the late twentieth and early twenty-first centuries, Bill Bowen was certainly not alone in his efforts to make the academy more effective. There would likely be universal agreement that in the mid-twentieth century, the preeminent leader in higher education was Clark Kerr, the first chancellor of the University of California at Berkeley (1952–58), president of the University of California

6 Ibid.
7 Telephone interview with Catharine Bond Hill, Feb. 1, 2022.
8 Telephone interview with Caroline Hoxby, Oct. 26, 2021.

(1958–67), member of the Carnegie Commission on Higher Education (1967–73), chair of the Carnegie Council on Policy Studies in Higher Education (1974–79), and author, among other books, of *The Uses of the University* (1963) and *The Blue and the Gold: A Personal Memoir of the University of California, 1949–1967* (2001, 2003). In Bowen's own generation, there were other formidable university presidents who commanded wide respect, among them Derek Bok at Harvard, Edward H. Levi and Hanna Holborn Gray at the University of Chicago, A. Whitney Griswold and Kingman Brewster at Yale, Frank Rhodes at Cornell, Richard Lyman and Donald Kennedy at Stanford, John Kemeny at Dartmouth, and Father Theodore Hesburgh at Notre Dame. Bok matched (perhaps more than matched) Bowen in terms of stature and influence, partly because people tended always to think of Harvard as a cut above other universities, but mainly by virtue of Bok's wisdom, his standing in the public arena, and his prolific writings about higher education. Still, Bowen stood out because of the range of his activity and impact: He played the key role in remaking Princeton into a university of the first rank; he led a major foundation in launching influential ventures for the public good; and he undertook scholarship grounded in voluminous new data not just to comment on aspects of higher education but to support fundamental changes in the ways colleges and universities did their most important work.

William G. Bowen had a tremendous influence on higher education through his accomplishments at Princeton, his contributions at Mellon, and his books. He strove throughout his life to universalize the efforts he had first tried out at Princeton, efforts that he wrote about with such passion, to make higher education more accessible and inclusive. As well, he made a profound impact in helping to choose leaders for colleges and universities throughout the United States (and he also identified and promoted important leaders for two Fortune 500 companies, both of them African American).

But the lessons in this book are broader than all of that, important and influential as it was. Bowen's insights and accomplishments are more generalizable, and in that sense, the book is about

leadership: how vision, strategy, and sophistication about governance influence the direction of key institutions in American society.
At a time when presidents, provosts, deans, and trustees of educational institutions have been struggling with major crises caused by
the COVID pandemic, racial and social unrest, cultural conflicts,
and economic challenges, Bowen's example provides important
guidance. Effective navigation of institutional crises, as this book
shows, begins with a vision. It then combines vision with strategy—
detailed, thoughtfully worked out, deliberately conceived to address the challenges at hand. It requires leadership—intelligent,
forward-looking, steady, even inspirational—leadership capable of
galvanizing the many constituencies so crucial to institutions. And
it requires the courage to address the toughest problems, no matter
how and where they present themselves and how difficult they are
to ameliorate. Reminding ourselves of the Bowen example provides
a playbook for addressing the pressing institutional crises of this
third decade of the twenty-first century.

Writing the history of the very recent past has its advantages as
well as its challenges. The advantages lie in access to the many individuals who participated in and can illuminate the matters at
hand. While the largest part of this book is deeply grounded in
archival sources, oral history interviews—with 230 individuals—
constitute a major part of my research. Of course, one needs always to be careful in assessing what one learns from interviews.
I have accepted as valid only those accounts that reinforce one another and/or that jibe with what I have learned from written sources.
I have chosen not to use information that cannot be corroborated,
arresting as that information might be. Where individuals have
asked to talk to me off the record, I have listened carefully to what
they have told me and I have tried faithfully to honor their requests,
so that I have neither told the stories they told me nor attributed
to them information also obtained from other sources.

The challenges of writing very recent history are magnified by
the ways in which history can change under you when you least
expect it. I used to tell my senior thesis advisees to be wary of choosing a topic where the narrative could be affected by the next day's
headlines. I offer two examples of ways in which headlines, if you
will, have changed the context for elements of my story.

As I wrote about Bill Bowen's signal contributions to our collective understanding of the benefits of affirmative action, in particular the ways in which he influenced United States Supreme Court decisions upholding affirmative action in *Regents of the University of California v. Bakke* and *Grutter v. Bollinger*, I could never have imagined that by the time this book went to press, the Supreme Court would be considering outlawing affirmative action in college and university admissions. Had he survived, Bowen would have been deeply engaged in mobilizing broad support for Harvard University and the University of North Carolina as they sought to sustain their long-standing admission practices, and he would have been working assiduously to persuade the court once again to uphold the legality of affirmative action.

Writing about the recent past can also present unique challenges when it comes to addressing uncomfortable topics. In chapter 11, I write about Bowen engaging during his early years as president in an affair with a woman undergraduate. Remarkably or not, the Princeton trustees did not require Bowen to relinquish his job. By contrast, in 2022, a different era in so many ways, Princeton fired a tenured faculty member for behavior related to his own affair with a woman undergraduate. Bowen clung to his conviction that his behavior was of a personal nature and had nothing to do with his professional standing and responsibilities. Whether or not that was a persuasive argument (and, other than Bowen himself, I found no one who believed that, even then), it would never hold water today. Changing awareness and expectations with respect to campus power dynamics and sexual relationships make this facet of Bowen's time at Princeton a necessary topic to address, much as many of my interviewees would have preferred that I not do so.

I need to make clear that I knew Bill Bowen almost from the moment I joined the Princeton faculty in 1969. It was unavoidable—because there was only a small handful of women faculty members at the time, having the president and provost know you came with the territory. Women were immediately recognizable, and we were in demand for all manner of university activities and service. Bill Bowen engaged me in university committee work, with increasing responsibility over the years: chairing the Governance Committee of the Council of the Princeton University Community, starting up the Women's Studies Program, serving as the first master (now called head) of Mathey College, one of the new freshman-sophomore residential colleges, and, in 1987, taking up an appointment as dean of the college, the dean responsible for undergraduate education, a role I filled for twenty-four years. When I returned to the faculty and to scholarship as a historian, Bill was an important source and reader for my book *"Keep the Damned Women Out": The Struggle for Coeducation*. My husband Burt (a long-standing colleague of Bill's in the economics department at Princeton) and I maintained a continuing friendship with Bill and his wife, Mary Ellen, with periodic dinners together in the kitchen at Bill's favorite haunt, the Homestead Inn in Hamilton Township. Burt and I attended the weddings of the Bowens' son David and daughter Karen as well as Mary Ellen and Bill's fiftieth anniversary weekend celebration, and Bill came to the ceremony for our wedding in the university chapel (Mary Ellen's absence visiting Karen in Belgium enabled him—in characteristic fashion—to skip the wedding luncheon on the grounds of what he described as a "data crisis" in the research project of the moment).

It will not be a surprise, then, that I admire Bill Bowen. I believe, however, that readers will see that I am not uncritical, and I hope that they will find my analysis balanced and appropriately grounded in the usual scholarly evidence and judgments rather than affected in any way by close association and friendship.

A final word: This is not an authorized biography, but I have benefited greatly from the generous cooperation of Mary Ellen, David, and Karen Bowen. My take on Bill Bowen will inevitably be different from theirs, but I hope they will respect that I have made an honest effort to portray a complicated human being who made groundbreaking contributions to Princeton University and to American higher education. I am not the first person to write about Bill Bowen—there are informative essays, for example, by his friends and colleagues Hanna Holborn Gray and Kevin Guthrie in *Ever the Leader: Selected Writings, 1995–2016*. But this is the first full, scholarly biography to be published.

Acknowledgments

Hundreds of people helped me construct this account of the life and career of William G. Bowen. The first is Princeton's president, Christopher L. Eisgruber, who saw to it, in consultation with the university's trustees, that Princeton's forty-year rule governing access to key records was changed to a thirty-year rule, a modification that made it possible for me undertake this project. Regrettably, the trustees of the Andrew W. Mellon Foundation declined to make an exception to their thirty-year rule, so it has been necessary to write about Bowen's Mellon years without access to those papers. Kevin M. Guthrie, in consultation with the trustees of ITHAKA, made available the minutes of the ITHAKA board from the organization's founding through Bowen's death. Bowen's voluminous correspondence from the years after he left Mellon is stored on the ITHAKA server. While it was not possible to see all of it, Johanna Brownell helpfully mined it for me to provide documentation for key moments in Bowen's last decade.

As always, archivists and librarians played an essential role in enabling my work. At Princeton Daniel J. Linke and his many colleagues in the university archives made their extraordinary holdings available to me over many months of research, concluding, as it happened, just before everything shut down because of COVID-19. I am grateful especially to Dan as I am, among others, to April C. Armstrong, Christa Cleeton, Amanda P. Ferrara, Brianna E. Garden, Sara J. Logue, Anne Marie Phillips, and Bilqees Sayed. At the Rockefeller Archive Center, Jack Meyers, Robert Clark, and Michele Beckerman found documents for me to compensate for research that could not be done in person, given the constraints of the pandemic. At Denison University, Bill Bowen's alma mater, Sasha Kim Griffin and Colleen Goodhart sent me important archival materials, including photographs I would not otherwise have seen. Similarly, Sherry Sheffield sent me a trove of useful materials from the Wyoming, Ohio, Historical Society—the town where Bill Bowen grew up.

At the Princeton University Investment Company (PRINCO), Andrew K. Golden and his colleagues Christine M. Amantia, Jennifer M. Birmingham, Michelle N. Cavallo, and Amanda Monte provided data I requested about the Princeton endowment.

So many individuals who participated in one way or another in Bill Bowen's life and career responded generously when I asked to talk to them. In all, I interviewed 230 people, sometimes more than once, and I corresponded further with some of them and mined materials they gave me, to understand as fully as I could the story I had to tell. A handful of people declined for their own particular reasons to talk to me, which I regret but respect. The names of the individuals I interviewed are cited frequently in the footnotes and are listed in the aggregate at the end of the book. My debt to them is enormous, as is my gratitude for their help.

Among them, I need to single out once again Mary Ellen, David, and Karen Bowen. As I have said in the preface, I have been the lucky beneficiary of their unparalleled generosity in speaking to me and providing materials for me. They could not have been more helpful or supportive. I am so grateful for their trust in me.

For ideas, opportunities, and materials of various sorts, I record also my thanks to William S. Anderson, Victoria Austin-Smith, Laurel M. Cantor, Alan Chimacoff, Kathleen Deignan, David P. Dobkin, Donald H. Fox, J. Lionel Gossman, Polly Winfrey Griffin, Elizabeth Hosny, Marc Lackritz, Julia Lee, Margaret Miller, Roger Montemayor, Daniel A. Notterman, Hilary A. Parker, Ushma S. Patel, Harvey S. Rosen, Iris G. Rubenstein, Beverly Sanford, Gregory Smith, Toni Turano, and Brooks Wrampelmeier. At Princeton, Judith L. Hanson, Kelly Lin-Kremer, Debora L. Macy, Max G. Siles, and Carla M. Zimowsk in the history department and Scott VanderVeer in the digital print center helped me with a host of technical and practical issues.

Noemi Benitah, Rick Glass, Kate Schofield, Mary Ellen Scully, Cindy Valush Sikora, Lesley Vannerson, and Lynn Warren will know their own particular contributions to enabling me to accomplish my research and writing while attending to the well-being of the canine side of the family.

One of the best parts of living and working in the academic world is the opportunity to enlist friends and colleagues of distinction to help with a scholarly venture of this sort. Lawrence S. Bacow, Eva Gossman, Hanna Holborn Gray, Eugene Y. Lowe Jr., Mary Patterson McPherson, W. Taylor Reveley III, Morton O. Schapiro, Harold T. Shapiro, James L. Shulman, and Shirley M. Tilghman have been generous enough to read and comment on the book in manuscript. Virginia A. Zakian has done the same for the chapter on biochemical sciences and molecular biology. As well, Kevin M. Guthrie has read the sections on ITHAKA. Their advice and wisdom have been priceless. Jonathan Cole, William E. "Brit" Kirwan, and Daniel H. Weiss, readers for Princeton University Press, provided a wonderful combination of enthusiastic support for publication and good ideas for further strengthening the text.

My editor at Princeton University Press, Peter J. Dougherty, was all in on this project from the moment I told him I wanted to write about Bill Bowen. Peter's expertise in higher education and his close personal and professional relationship with Bill Bowen made him the perfect person to shepherd this work from initial idea to published book. His unwavering encouragement lifted my spirits; his spot-on suggestions for improvement (always delivered with the gentlest touch) clearly strengthened the book. Peter is an incomparable editor and a great friend, and I could not be more fortunate to be one of his authors.

Also at Princeton University Press, Christie Henry invested more time and attention in this book than one might ever have expected from the director of a major press. A highly accomplished team took the book from manuscript to publication. I want to single out especially Terri O'Prey, the best imaginable production editor; Beth Gianfagna, my superb copyeditor; and Kathleen Strattan, who prepared an excellent index. Without missing a beat, Eric Crahan took over editorial responsibility for the book in the final stages before publication. Steven Lieberman, Elena K. Abbott, and Crystal Shelley contributed helpful readings.

Burt Malkiel, the love of my life for the past thirty-six years, is my biggest fan and best critic. While deeply engaged in his own book—the fiftieth anniversary edition of *A Random Walk Down Wall Street*—he has provided boundless encouragement and has insisted on creating the most supportive conditions for my work. He has read countless drafts of this book; he has talked through every problem, no matter how tough or how trivial; and he has sharpened every chapter, every page, through his excellent judgment, wise insights, and prodigious gifts as a writer. His love and partnership are the joy of my life.

This is the fifth book that Burt and I have dedicated to our beloved Miniature Schnauzer Piper. Piper died before the book could be published, but for everything she taught us about loving and living, her name rightly remains on the dedication page.

Princeton, New Jersey
June 2023

Part I

Preparation

1

Prologue

"I Have Very Serious Doubts" about the Princeton Presidency

On Friday, June 30, 1972, William Gordon Bowen, thirty-eight-year-old provost and professor of economics at Princeton University, took the oath of office as Princeton's seventeenth president. The ceremony, "simple" and "pompless," as a local newspaper put it, took place in the faculty room in Nassau Hall, the oldest building on the university campus.[1] The chair of the executive committee of the board of trustees, R. Manning Brown, chief executive of New York Life Insurance Company, presided; the oath was administered by Bowen's predecessor, Robert F. Goheen, still youthful at fifty-two, who was stepping down from the presidency after fifteen years of service. Some 250 invited guests packed the faculty room: trustees; senior officers of the university; representatives of the faculty, students, and alumni; local elected officials; and Bowen's family, staff members, and personal guests.[2] Goheen's immediate predecessor, Harold W. Dodds, was also in attendance; the two men together accounted for four decades of Princeton leadership. Portraits of Princeton's sixteen previous presidents looked down

---

1 "Princeton Gets 17th President . . . Pomplessly," *Trentonian* (Trenton, NJ), July 1, 1972, Bowen president, box 403, folder 7.

2 Dan D. Coyle, memorandum, "Installation of Princeton's William G. Bowen," June 27, 1972, Bowen president, box 403, folder 8.

from the wood-paneled walls, with, as Bowen noted in his remarks, "an occasional hint of skepticism in the eye."[3]

Bowen had been selected by the trustees in a relatively brief search process, since he was in so many ways such an obvious choice. It was a different search from the one that had produced Goheen fifteen years earlier. Then—as now—there had been a trustee search committee, which consulted closely with an elected faculty advisory committee. What was different then was the absence of an obvious choice. Looking back on the process a little more than a dozen years later, the members of the faculty committee told a slightly different story about how they came to their conclusion.[4] For the historian Joseph R. Strayer, the process was straightforward: Goheen was the faculty committee's first choice; the trustees interviewed him, liked him, and elected him. "If any university president was ever chosen by faculty action it was Goheen."[5] Professor of English Carlos Baker recalled that Goheen's name had come up early, but "then it disappeared in a welter of other names," only to resurface at the end of the process.[6] The physicist Allen Shenstone said that the faculty committee gave the trustees "the names of two men whom we were convinced would make a success as President of Princeton. These two were both very young, being Bob Goheen and McGeorge Bundy."[7]

The economist Richard A. Lester gave the fullest and most intriguing account (one that meshed most closely with the story as told by the chair of the trustee committee, Harold H. Helm).[8] After

3 News release, "William G. Bowen Remarks on the Occasion of his Installation as President of Princeton University," June 30, 1972, Bowen president, box 402, folder 4.

4 Stanley Kelley had asked for their recollections to inform the work of the Special Committee on the Structure of the University, which, he thought, might wish to say something about the process for selecting a new president. See, e.g., Stanley Kelley Jr. to Alan [sic] Shenstone, Feb. 20, 1969, Kelley Committee, box 1, folder 21.

5 Joseph R. Strayer, "Procedures of the Faculty Committee on the Choice of a New President, 1956–57," Bowen president, box 285, folder 3.

6 Carlos Baker to Stanley Kelley Jr., [Feb. 1969], Bowen president, box 285, folder 3.

7 A. G. Shenstone to Stanley Kelley Jr., Feb. 25, 1969, Bowen president, box 285, folder 3.

8 Memorandum, Harold H. Helm to Stanley Kelley, Mar. 27, 1969, Bowen president, box 285, folder 3. Helm recalled that the list of serious contenders came down to five names, of which Goheen was one. Goheen, he said, "had been on the faculty list as well as

some months of deliberation, the faculty committee focused on "about a half dozen" candidates; two men without Princeton connections were at the top of the list. In first place was Clark Kerr, at that time the first chancellor of the University of California, Berkeley; McGeorge Bundy, at that time dean of the faculty of arts and sciences at Harvard University, was second. Some members of the trustee committee met Kerr in Berkeley and asked if he would be interested enough in the Princeton presidency to travel to New York to meet with the full committee. Kerr agreed, and a date for the meeting was set. Shortly before the scheduled meeting, Kerr withdrew for personal reasons; his wife had made plain her resistance to leaving California. (She got her wish; in 1958, Kerr began a nine-year appointment as president of the University of California.)

The faculty committee focused next on Bundy, "but before any inquiry was made to him directly, the question was raised as to why Bundy was preferred over Bob Goheen, whose name was high on the remaining list." Bundy was the same age as Goheen—both were born in 1919. At first the sense had been that both men were too young for the presidency, but if the committee was prepared to be serious about Bundy, why not take a more careful look at Goheen?[9]

Fifteen years later, the search process bore some similarities to what had occurred in the Goheen search, but there were important differences, principally the fact that when the search began, the trustees already had the leading candidate in their sights. A trustee search committee, chaired by Manning Brown, began work in April 1971. The trustee committee consulted closely with elected faculty and student committees (the latter an innovation since the previous search). Beyond Bowen, the other most serious candidate was the dean of the graduate school, physics professor Aaron Lemonick, an undergraduate alumnus of the University of Pennsylvania

---

the trustees' list from the beginning but his junior position on the faculty and his age were responsible for his not having been given serious consideration at an earlier stage."

9 Richard A. Lester, "Informal Notes on the Operations of Faculty Committee on the Choice of a New President, 1956–57," Feb. 24, 1969, Bowen president, box 285, folder 3.

and a Princeton PhD in physics, who had taught at Haverford College before joining the Princeton faculty in 1961.[10]

But Bowen was the compelling favorite. He was an accomplished labor economist with special expertise in the economics of higher education. In five years as provost, he had provided essential leadership in modernizing the governance of the university and keeping the institution on an even keel as it grappled with such challenging issues as coeducation, racial integration, and the tumult surrounding controversies concerning apartheid in South Africa and the Vietnam War. Faculty colleagues told him that he was the obvious heir-apparent to Goheen and urged him to accept appointment to the presidency when it was offered.[11]

Bowen had—or chose to present—a different view. He repeatedly spelled out his reluctance in correspondence with those who regarded him as the obvious choice: "As I've said quietly to Bob Goheen and one or two other people, I have real doubts that whatever contribution I have to make to higher education can be made most effectively as president, with all that that job now entails. Accordingly, I've urged that the various search committees try hard to find someone whose comparative advantage matches the job requirements."[12] As well, "I have told Bob [Goheen] and others that I much prefer that someone other than me be found—I have real reservations about the match between the job and my own sense of what I want to do and what I can do best."[13] Bowen gave a detailed explanation for his resistance in a long letter to his faculty colleague, the distinguished philosopher Gregory Vlastos:

10 Telephone interview with Andrew P. Napolitano (one of the members of the student committee), Sept. 1, 2020; Dave Elkind, "Search for Next President Said to Focus on Bowen, Lemonick; Insider Expected," *Daily Princetonian*, Oct. 27, 1971, 1; David Elkind, "Seven-Month Screening," *Daily Princetonian*, Nov. 30, 1971, 1.

11 See, e.g., Sheldon [Hackney] to Bill [Bowen], Mar. 30, 1971; Gregory Vlastos to W. G. Bowen, Apr. 27, 1971, both in Bowen president, box 181, folder 10.

12 William G. Bowen to Joe [Joseph Kershaw], Apr. 5, 1971, Bowen president, box 181, folder 10. He made little dent in his friend's views. Kershaw wrote back: "In a nutshell, you will be dead wrong not to take it, and Princeton will be dead wrong not to offer it." Kershaw to Bowen, Apr. 8, 1971, Bowen president, box 181, folder 10.

13 William G. Bowen to Walt [Slocombe], Apr. 5, [1971], Bowen president, box 181, folder 10. See also Bowen to Jon Clark, Apr. 13, 1971; Bowen to Thomas H. Nimick Jr., Apr. 14, 1971, both in Bowen president, box 181, folder 10.

I have very serious doubts that whatever contribution I have to make to higher education can be made most effectively from the President's office. . . . I have urged all of my friends to think hard about other candidates. Perhaps I should add that my views on this subject are not recently developed but of long-standing. They are based, I think, not in any unwillingness to accept burdens, but in a fairly careful assessment of the nature of that job and of my own strengths and limitations. Thus, I hope a vigorous effort will be made to find someone who really fits the needs of the office, in terms of both abilities and predilections.[14]

When Bowen's close friend and colleague Stanley Kelley Jr., professor of politics and chair of the faculty search committee, talked with him about his candidacy, Bowen again appeared to push back. He made plain that the presidency was not a job he sought; he suggested that he was not ready to give up teaching and scholarship; he said that the search committee should look carefully at some talented outsiders, whom Bowen named. Bowen's own favorite candidate was Richard Lyman, provost (1967–70) and president (1970–80) of Stanford University, despite the fact that there was no reason to imagine that someone just named president of another university would contemplate a move to Princeton.[15]

In handwritten notes recorded in mid-September, Bowen spelled out at length the reasons why he thought that he and the presidency were not a good match. Given the job description for president, and given his own "abilities and interests," it was "highly unlikely that [he] could make as big a contribution in the long run as President as [he] could make as Provost." The key problem was the "growing 'public figure' aspect of the presidency." Moreover, there was another problem in terms of replacing himself as provost—"he could not name the same 'type' as Provost and thus both the president and

14 William G. Bowen to Gregory Vlastos, Apr. 30, [1971], Bowen president, box 181, folder 10.

15 Bowen oral history, June 25, 2009, 12–14; interview with Carol and Dennis Thompson, July 26, 2018, Cambridge, MA. Dennis Thompson was a member of the faculty committee.

the university would get much less help from that office than [they were] getting now." That meant that the university "could end up weaker in both president and provost than should be."[16]

And then there were Bowen's own proclivities: "There is real risk that WGB would try to do *all* parts of [the] presidency too thoroughly, with [the] result that he would wear out fast, become irascible, and not good at [the] job," which was "not viable for [the] long run." It was "especially not viable" because he would not enjoy the "'public figure' work." He liked teaching and research and having influence on policy. He was "not [a] natural public person."[17]

Moreover, there were personal costs. He would likely have to give up teaching Economics 101, which he did not want to do. The timing was not right for the family; his children were growing up; they were comfortable with the current patterns and rhythms of family life, and they liked living in the family home at 10 Maclean Circle, which the Bowens had designed and built.

He could continue as provost with a new president, "at least for [a] bit," but he was willing to consider the presidency if the trustees created a new position of chancellor to share some of the president's duties. The chancellor would chair the board of trustees, live in Lowrie House, the official university president's residence, and do "part of [the] public figure work."[18]

As unrealistic as this proposed division of duties may sound in retrospect, the idea was not original with Bowen. Such an arrangement—with a president running the internal affairs of the university and a chancellor running external relations and fund-raising—had been tried out more than once at some of Princeton's peer institutions. At the University of Chicago, Robert Maynard Hutchins served as president from 1929 to 1945, whereupon the office was divided, with Hutchins assuming the role of chancellor, which he held from 1945 to 1951, and the president, Ernest C. Colwell, clearly assuming a subsidiary role. Hutchins's successor, who served as chancellor from 1951 to 1960 without appointing a president, was

16 [William G. Bowen], untitled handwritten notes, Sept. 15, 1971, Bowen president, box 181, folder 10.
17 Ibid.
18 Ibid.

Lawrence A. Kimpton, who had served previously in several administrative roles. In January 1961, George Beadle, a geneticist at the California Institute of Technology, was elected chancellor at Chicago; that fall, he was elected president of the university, and the separate chancellor's position disappeared. At Northwestern, in 1970, the long-serving and very popular president J. Roscoe "Rocky" Miller became chancellor when the economist Robert Strotz, dean of the school of arts and sciences, was named president. When Strotz was succeeded by Arnold R. Weber in 1984, Strotz became chancellor, serving until 1990.[19]

How much Bowen knew about, or might have been thinking about, these models is not known. He clearly had his own ideas about Princeton, however. His friend and provost's office colleague, philosophy professor Paul Benacerraf, who seems to have listened to him talking all of this through, recorded his own notes on Bowen's thinking. A large percentage of the president's job would be "frustrating," with "results hard to assess"; much of the work would simply not be "enjoyable" for Bowen. Moreover, he would have to "surrender" a large part of what he really did enjoy about the provost's job: "significant oversight of institutional affairs at a detailed level." To whom would he entrust that work? A new provost? But such a person would need to be "strong and *independent*." The other senior academic officers? There were significant concerns no matter where one looked: The dean of the faculty, for example, "*need[ed] constant supervision*"; the dean of the college was "a problem." "If the structure developed in recent years is not to collapse (it seems heavily dependent upon the provost), adequate provision must be made—and *can* it be made? WGB's own tendency to be tortured at the sight of incompetence—particularly in his old bailiwick—would make him try to do the Provost's job as well, *with disastrous results*."[20]

---

19 I am indebted to Hanna Holborn Gray for much of this information. See also John W. Boyer, *The University of Chicago: A History* (Chicago: University of Chicago Press, 2015), 310–56.

20 P[aul] B[enacerraf], handwritten notes, Sept. 15, 1971, Bowen president, box 181, folder 10.

These themes carried over into Bowen's negotiations with the trustees. When he was first approached by Manning Brown on behalf of the search committee, he expressed concern about the "great diminution of his teaching activities as well as the impact upon his family life that the Presidency would entail." He told Brown that sharing the job with someone else struck him as "desirable," particularly with respect to "the ceremonial and other non-administrative responsibilities of the Presidency."[21] He proposed dividing the responsibilities of the president, such that someone else—Goheen, he hoped, might remain as chancellor—would take on the key external aspects of the job, chiefly alumni relations and fund-raising. But the presidency was not a job to be divided; Princeton had no precedent for a chancellor who would be, in effect, a co–chief executive; and Goheen had no interest in staying on. The trustees heard Bowen out, after which Brown finally persuaded him to embrace the presidency in full. The board announced Bowen's appointment on November 29, 1971.[22] "The choice . . . ," said the chair of the student newspaper, the *Daily Princetonian*, "was so obvious that approving it is like approving the sunrise."[23]

The national press covered all the expected points about Bowen's qualifications and preparation for the job but fixed on a special twist. Attending a meeting the previous spring on Hilton Head Island in South Carolina, Bowen saw a woman fall accidentally into a pond full of alligators, landing on top of one of them. Bowen hurried over and pulled her out of the water. The alligator, Bowen said, "was probably as scared as she was, but that seemed something you didn't want to leave to the alligator." The alligator rescue— a story Bowen may have embellished to his own advantage—

21 "Minutes of a Special Meeting of the Trustees of Princeton University," Nov. 29, 1971, Goheen, box 67, folder 8. See also [William G. Bowen], typescript, "Chairman or Chancellor," n.d., and [Bowen], handwritten notes, "RFG and MIT Model," n.d., Bowen president, box 463, unlabeled folder.

22 R. M. Brown Jr. to Members of the Princeton Family, Nov. 29, 1971; Princeton University news release, Nov. 29, 1971, both in Bowen president, box 402, folder 3. Dennis Thompson said that once the search committee started converging on Bowen, Bowen's tone "changed dramatically"; "sincere reluctance quickly turned into resolute ambition." Thompson interview.

23 Quoted in M. A. Farber, "Princeton Provost Named President," *New York Times*, Nov. 30, 1971, 49, Bowen president, box 402, folder 3.

featured prominently in news coverage of his appointment.[24] And it had staying power. In 1976, when a Princeton student, James Barron, a stringer for the *New York Times*, wrote a piece about Bowen for the newspaper, the alligator story made its way into the profile, where Barron asked if Bowen had encountered any more alligators since the Hilton Head rescue. Bowen assured him that he had not encountered any of the reptilian variety but left open the interpretation of the metaphorical alligators he had to deal with as he wrestled with the many challenges facing Princeton's president.[25]

There was great optimism about Bowen. No one doubted that he would provide strong leadership for Princeton. But there was no sense in June 1972 that the man who had just taken the oath as Princeton's seventeenth president would, in the decades to come, assume such a consequential role as a leader in American higher education in the late twentieth and early twenty-first centuries. Making sense of his significance depends, of course, on understanding his long presidency of Princeton (1972–88) and his even longer presidency of the Andrew W. Mellon Foundation (1988–2006). It depends also on assessing the impact of the books he authored about American higher education and the educational innovations he drove, first through the Mellon Foundation, and subsequently through ITHAKA, the educational institution he founded to explore ways of using technology to improve productivity in higher education. I will turn to all of that in due course. First, however, we need to understand Bill Bowen: who he was and how he became the individual who was elected the seventeenth president of Princeton University.

24 William K. Stevens, "Energetic Educator: William Gordon Bowen," "Man in the News," *New York Times*, Nov. 30, 1971, Bowen president, box 402, folder 3. See also Jonathan Daniels, "Sojourner's Scrapbook," *Island Packet* (Hilton Head, SC), Jan. 6, 1972, Bowen president, box 181, folder 1. The warning flag about possible embellishment comes from e-mail, Mary Ellen Bowen to Nancy Weiss Malkiel, Feb. 1, 2022.

25 James Barron, "A Student Eyes Princeton's Chief," *New York Times*, Jan. 25, 1976, https://www.nytimes.com/1976/01/25/archives/new-jersey-weekly-a-student-eyes-princetons-chief.html, accessed Apr. 18, 2022.

2

From Wyoming to Princeton

"He Will Probably Turn Up as One of Our Leading University Presidents"

Wyoming, Ohio

William Gordon Bowen was born in Jewish Hospital in Cincinnati on October 6, 1933. His father, Albert Andrew Bowen, and mother, Bernice Catherine Pommert Bowen, were natives of Indiana, Albert born on January 30, 1901, in Danville, a small town twenty miles west of Indianapolis, and Bernice on August 31, 1902, in South Bend. They married in October 1925. Both came from modest families. Albert's father, Joseph G. Bowen, had been a farm laborer and a garage man. Bernice's father, C. E. Pommert, was a co-owner of a barber shop in the Jefferson Hotel in South Bend and a manager of the Pythian building, an office building in the city. Bill was Albert and Bernice's first and only surviving child. A daughter, born the night of October 2, 1937, in Jewish Hospital, just before Bill's fourth birthday, survived only sixteen hours, succumbing to a lung disorder. The infant's birth and death were not discussed in later years in the family.[1]

1 *South Bend (IN) Tribune*, Oct. 22, 1925, 5, and Apr. 10, 1996, 15; Albert Andrew Bowen draft card, Ancestry.com, https://www.ancestry.com/imageviewer/collections/2238/images/44030_04_00, all courtesy of Roger Montemayor. State of Ohio, Department of Health, Department of Vital Statistics, "Certification of Birth, William Gordon Bowen," Oct. 6, 1933; "C. E. Pommert, 72, Dies Here after Week of Illness," undated, unidentified clipping, in scrapbook compiled by Bernice Bowen, Bowen personal; State of Ohio, Department of Health, Division of Vital Statistics, "Certificate of Death, Infant Bowen," Oct. 3, 1937; Ohio Department of Health, Division of Vital Statistics, "Certificate of

Albert Bowen sold cash registers for National Cash Register (NCR). He was already a thirteen-year veteran of the company when Bill was born, and he became the senior salesman in the region. He was often on the road, selling from the back of his station wagon, so Bernice, a homemaker, had principal responsibility for the young boy. When Bill was born, the Bowens lived in Cincinnati; by 1940, they had moved to Wyoming, a suburb of less than three square miles thirteen miles north/northeast of Cincinnati, with a population just under 4,500.[2] The family bought a modest house in a lower-middle-class neighborhood on the east side of town on the Springfield Pike, the highly traveled main commercial thoroughfare running south to north through the city. Built in 1926, 1116 Springfield Pike was a small, two-story house with two bedrooms and a bath upstairs, a living room, dining room, and small kitchen on the first floor, a small front porch, and a deep, narrow backyard. The garage was on the left at the end of the driveway, the steps to enter the house on the right. The house was very close to the Wyoming Avenue Elementary School, where Bill was enrolled in second grade in 1940–41. Even at the age of seven, he could walk to school, and he relished spending extra time after school pursuing additional assignments given by his teachers or engaging in sports on the Wyoming athletic fields, which were very near his house. His grades in elementary school were good; by high school, they were excellent.[3]

Bill and his friends played sports together, watched games on television at one or another family's home, went to the movies from time to time, played miniature golf, went on hayrides, went ice skating when the creek froze, participated in Y-Teens and after-school

Death, Albert Andrew Bowen," Jan. 11, 1951; interview with Mary Ellen Bowen, June 22, 2018, Princeton, NJ. The baby's death certificate lists the cause as atelectasis, the collapse of the lung, which may have been a function of premature birth, "a birth accident such as breathing in amniotic fluid," or "a congenital defect involving a malformation of the lungs or diaphragm." E-mail, Daniel A. Notterman, MD, to Nancy Weiss Malkiel, Jan. 23, 2020. It is worth noting that Albert Bowen died of a progressive lung disorder; whether there was any genetic connection between the two cannot be ascertained.

2 "Wyoming, Ohio," Wikipedia, https://en.m.wikipedia.org, accessed Oct. 17, 2020.

3 William G. Bowen, "Growth Record, Public Schools of Wyoming, Ohio," for grades 2 through 6, and "Wyoming High School Progress Report" for grades 7 through 12, Bowen personal.

clubs, and attended school dances after Friday night football games as well as the more formal junior and senior proms—all the stuff of ordinary teenage friendships in late 1940s–early 1950s small-town America. During the summers they played sports, took family trips, and held local jobs (in Bill's case, one summer, taking care of the Wyoming tennis courts). They knew each other very well; Wyoming High School was small (the graduating class in 1951 numbered forty-eight, almost evenly divided between boys and girls), and students were comfortable spending time together no matter whether their parents owned local businesses, worked for Proctor and Gamble, or held jobs in factories.[4] Inscriptions in the school yearbook in 1950, Bill's junior year, made plain both the ease of those relationships and the admiration his fellow students (his classmates in '51 as well as members of other classes) had for Bill Bowen. Bill was "a swell partner and friend," tennis teammate Howard Ryan penned. Harvey Mullaney called him "a real friend and a swell guy. Our class would be for the birds without you." Marilyn Easton wrote, "I've never seen anyone as active as you who still takes time to be friendly to everyone!" Dave Fleischer praised him for being "the spark that really keeps the juniors moving." The phraseology of the inscriptions was remarkably consistent: "a wonderful leader"; "a swell guy"; a "genius" with "a swell personality"; "a swell guy with lots of personality"; "a swell fellow." Don Bradson summed up the case: "an all-around boy and one of the best friends a fellow could have."[5]

Bill was both a strong student and a school leader. He was president of his junior and senior class, coeditor of the yearbook, and a member of the student council. As well, he was elected to the National Honor Society and the Cum Laude Society, and he ranked second in his class academically in his sophomore and junior years

---

4 Telephone interview with Richard Evans, Sept. 8, 2018; interview with Thomas D. Boyatt, June 24, 2018, Princeton, NJ (Evans and Boyatt were Bowen's classmates at Wyoming); interview with Mary Ellen Bowen, July 20, 2018, Princeton, NJ; Wyoming High School, "Sixty-Seventh Annual Commencement," June 6, 1951, program in scrapbook compiled by Bernice Bowen, Bowen personal; Wyoming High School, *The Round Table, 1951* (yearbook), Bowen personal.

5 Wyoming High School, *Mid-Century Roundup* [1950], Bowen personal.

and first in his senior year. While Bill played varsity basketball in his senior year, the sport at which he really excelled was tennis. He played first singles for Wyoming High School, which was the best high school team in the Ohio Valley in his senior year. In his junior year, he was the third-ranking player for boys under eighteen in the valley. In the fall of his senior year, he won the Northern Kentucky Junior Open Tennis Tournament and the Wyoming Invitational Tournament. That spring, he won the Ohio Valley first singles title and was the runner-up in the Ohio State singles tournament. It was no wonder that he was chosen "Best all-round Senior" by his graduating class.[6] His classmates, signing his yearbook, declared their confidence in his future: "I know that you will always be a winner in everything"; "I know you're going to go places."[7]

School was relatively simple and straightforward for Bill, but his home life was more complicated. With his strong academic and athletic interests, Bill had little in common with his mother and father. There were some organized family outings—for example, summer trips to a fishing camp on Mackinac Island between Michigan's Upper and Lower Peninsulas. But the ordinary, informal, easygoing daily interplay among parents and child was stunted, if not absent. With Albert on the road so much of the time for NCR, it was hard to find opportunities for the sorts of things fathers might do with young sons. Moreover, there were tensions between the parents; on at least one occasion when Bill was young, Bernice took him back to South Bend for an extended period.[8]

In Bill's junior year, he began dating Mary Ellen Maxwell, a classmate since fourth grade. Three-quarters of a century later, in the last weeks of his life, he told a caregiver what he said when he and

6 "Wyoming Senior Shines in 'All-Around' Role," Oct. 11, 1950, unidentified clipping; "Lockland, Wyoming Students Win Gardner Scholarships," May 17, 1951, unidentified clipping; undated photograph and typescript, Wyoming High School tennis team, probably 1950; and "Wyoming Netmen, Led by Bowen, Anticipate Winning Campaign," *Millcreek Valley News* (Lockland, OH), Mar. 29, 1951, all in scrapbook compiled by Bernice Bowen, Bowen personal; e-mail, Brooks Wrampelmeier (Wyoming '52) to Nancy Weiss Malkiel, Oct. 24, 2018; Wyoming High School, *The Round Table, 1951* (source of the quote).

7 Wyoming High School, *The Round Table, 1951.*

8 Interview with Mary Ellen Bowen, Sept. 19, 2018, Princeton, NJ.

Mary Ellen first got to know each other: "When I get big, I'm going to marry her."[9] Mary Ellen was born in Ashland, Kentucky; she and her family moved to Wyoming in 1942. The Maxwells lived on Reily Road, up in the hills in a more prosperous section of Wyoming. Mary Ellen's father, O. B., who had attended Miami University, worked for Armco Steel Corporation as a chemical engineer, first in Middletown, Ohio, and then in Ashland. He started a successful trucking company in Cincinnati in 1941, which led to the family's move to Wyoming. Outgoing and sociable, O. B. enjoyed games of gin rummy with friends at the local country club, along with fishing, hunting, and boating trips to Canada. Mary Ellen's mother, Ina Lee Maxwell, who had earned a degree from Western College for Women, managed the household and family and radiated warmth and sociability (later, Bill would tease that he married Mary Ellen for her mother). She, too, loved to play cards—bridge or gin rummy. O. B.'s family had lived in Ohio since the early 1800s. Ina's paternal grandparents had been farmers in Norway; her father, Thorwald Lee, a Norwegian sailor, resettled in Minneapolis in 1887 and with his brother opened a photography studio that "became one of the leading portrait studios in the Midwest." Mary Ellen had two older brothers and a younger sister, and their friends, and their parents' friends, were in and out of a lively, welcoming house. It was no wonder that Bill identified with the Maxwells, a family quite different from his own. He began spending a lot of time at Mary Ellen's house; she, by contrast, spent little time on the Springfield Pike and knew Bill's parents much less well than he knew hers.[10]

By Bill's senior year, Albert Bowen was very sick. He tried from time to time to attend Bill's sports competitions; one of Bill's friends remembered him huddling in the stands at a basketball game, bundled up in blankets.[11] By Thanksgiving he had fallen seriously ill

9 Interview with Jade Robinson, Aug. 6, 2021, Princeton, NJ.

10 Karen Lee Bowen, "Remembering the Maxwell and Lee Families," text and photographs in a soft-cover MS, May 2016, Bowen personal; interview with Mary Ellen Bowen, June 25, 2018, Princeton, NJ. The quote is from Karen Bowen, "The Lees of Minneapolis, Minnesota," in "Remembering the Maxwell and Lee Families."

11 Boyatt interview.

with lung disease, and he was hospitalized at Good Samaritan Hospital in Cincinnati shortly before Christmas in 1950. As family members tell it, Albert died of emphysema. Albert's death certificate described the primary cause of death as *cor pulmonale*, heart disease likely caused by pulmonary hypertension. The "antecedent cause" was said to be diffuse pulmonary fibrosis, probably sarcoidosis—a progressive lung disease in which thick bands of fibrous tissue form in the lung. As the lungs hardened, it became harder and harder for the heart to pump blood through them, leading, in the end, to heart failure, which caused Albert's death on January 11, 1951, less than three weeks before his fiftieth birthday.[12]

In later years, when the class of 1951 held reunions at Wyoming High School, Bill typically absented himself. Perhaps he was too busy; perhaps he was disinclined to participate in reunions. He also resisted allowing the high school to honor him, which it would have liked very much to do. Wyoming represented an important but complicated time in his life. Perhaps, as his classmate Richard Evans mused, he wanted those years to remain in his memory; perhaps he simply did not want to go back to Wyoming.[13]

Denison University

Bill had had his sights set on going east to college, but with Albert's death, leaving his mother alone in Ohio seemed untenable. Instead, with the intervention of the Wyoming High School principal, Bernard Shaw Bradbury, arrangements were made for him to enroll at Denison University, a fine liberal arts college in Granville, a village thirty-five miles east of Columbus, about a two-hour drive from Cincinnati. Bill knew about Denison, albeit at second hand; he had a friend from Wyoming who was in his freshman year there "and liked it very much," and the Denison tennis coach, English professor Tristram P. Coffin, knew about Bill's tennis prowess and was eager to have him on the Denison team. For the first three years of

12 Ohio Department of Health, Division of Vital Statistics, "Certificate of Death, Albert Andrew Bowen," Jan. 11, 1951; e-mail, Notterman to Malkiel; interview with Mary Ellen Bowen, June 22, 2018.
13 Evans interview.

Bill's college career, his mother worked in the purchasing department of the Drackett Company in Cincinnati, which developed and
sold leading consumer products such as Drano and Windex. In his
senior year, she took a job as a housemother in a women's dormitory at the University of Cincinnati. Her resources were very limited,
and she had no way of contributing financially to Bill's education.
A four-year scholarship from the Gardner Board and Carton
Company gave him money toward tuition, as well as paid summer
jobs.[14] Denison supplied a significant scholarship, and Bill had a
campus job all the years he was there—including, he said later,
"a good stint in the kitchen," where he "became best friends with
the cook" and therefore "ate very well in college."[15]

In later years, after Bernice retired, she moved back to South
Bend, where she had a sister. She visited Bill and Mary Ellen in
Princeton from time to time, but the family relationship was not
especially close, and Bill traveled to see her infrequently. His friend
Father Theodore Hesburgh, president of Notre Dame, sometimes
saw to her well-being on his behalf.

As it had been in high school, tennis became one of Bill's major
preoccupations in college. With his doubles partner Al Preucil (who
would be the best man in his wedding), Bill anchored Denison's tennis team, serving as captain for his junior and senior years. The
team compiled an outstanding record, winning the Ohio Athletic
Conference championship in both years, with Bill himself taking
top honors in singles and doubles.[16]

14 The quote is from Bowen oral history, June 9, 2009, 2. On the Gardner scholarship, see "Lockland, Wyoming Students Win Gardner Scholarships," May 17, 1951,
unidentified clipping; and photograph of first winners of the Gardner Scholarship Fund,
n.d., in scrapbook compiled by Bernice Bowen, Bowen personal. Years later Bowen noted
his "continuing sense of obligation to the Gardner family. The Gardner Board and Carton
Company scholarship that was given to me 26 years ago was critical in allowing me to go
to Denison and then later to Princeton." William G. Bowen to Ames Gardner Jr., Oct. 21,
1977, Bowen president, box 144, folder 11. See also telephone interview with Mimi Gardner
Gates, Nov. 2, 2021. On Bernice's employment at Drackett, see "Drackett Professional
Products," Reference for Business, https://www.referenceforbusiness.com/history2/53
/Drackett-Professional-Products.html, accessed Oct. 23, 2020.
    15 Bowen oral history, 2.
    16 Telephone interview with Alan G. Preucil, Aug. 28, 2018; telephone interview with
Richard G. Lugar, Aug. 22, 2018; telephone interview with William Y. Giles, Aug. 2, 2018;
telephone interview with David H. Bayley, July 31, 2018 (Preucil, Lugar, Giles, and Bayley

Coffin, Bowen's coach, said that at first glance, he gave no hint of being a star player:

> If you had wandered by the courts . . . you'd have seen a gangling boy with what was then an eccentric Aussie hat pulled tightly over large ears, wearing droopy shorts, with unorthodox strokes, big, slow feet, and a happy-looking grin.

"If you'd stuck around," Coffin continued,

> you'd have heard a steady stream of chatter, most of it explaining how well his opponent was hitting, how his own forehand was "off," and how lucky he had been to win the last point. If you'd stayed, you'd have discovered that the opponent's "nice shots" were insufficient, that the forehand was surprisingly effective for a stroke which was "off," and that luck had little to do with it.

Moreover, Coffin explained,

> You'd begin to realize that this gawky, slightly-built fellow knew exactly what he was about, was concentrating like mad through all the talk and smiles, and had no intention of losing to anybody at any time under any conditions. You'd also see he had the tools: a steady serve, a real touch on his volleys, a deadly backhand return, an accurate, reliable overhead, long arms and really quick hands. But most of all you would realize that he knew exactly what he could do with what he had, that he never tried anything that he wasn't sure of, and that he had not only discovered, but was thoroughly exploiting, his opponent's weaknesses, physical and psychological.

---

were all students who knew Bowen at Denison); William Gordon Bowen, Woodrow Wilson Fellowship application, Dec. 6, 1954, courtesy of the Woodrow Wilson National Fellowship Foundation; Ellen Foley James, "WGB from A to Z," *Princeton Alumni Weekly*, Jan. 25, 1972, 12, Bowen president, box 402, folder 1. Also see Tristram P. Coffin, letter of recommendation, Dec. 3, 1954, in the Bowen application.

Bowen and Preucil together, Coffin said, were "the best doubles team in Ohio and certainly the most intellectual tandem in the nation. Between them they received only two grades below A in four years of courses." "The present President of Princeton," Coffin said in 1972, "is very much the large-footed tennis player who came to Denison in 1951—winner in another game, to be sure," but a man "success has not spoiled at all."[17]

Beyond the tennis court, Bowen threw himself into the life of the campus: fraternity member and officer of Sigma Chi fraternity; member of the policymaking student-faculty council; member of Blue Key, the junior men's honorary society, and Omicron Delta Kappa, the senior men's honorary society; copresident of student government (a position shared, by long-standing college policy, with a female classmate); and co–head resident, with his roommate and lifelong friend David Bayley, of Curtis East, a freshman dormitory of 110 men.[18]

As a sophomore Bill lived at the Sigma Chi fraternity house, rooming with a junior and a senior. The junior, Chuck Curry, described Bill's daily routine this way: "He worked virtually every meal . . . in the kitchen, so he arose early. After breakfast, he was in class or the library; the same post-lunch, except on days when he had tennis practice or lunches. After the dinner meal, he went immediately to the library, where he rendezvoused with Mary Ellen. . . . At library closing, he escorted her back to her dorm, returned to the Sig house, deposited his books on top of his desk, changed into pajamas and went to sleep—a routine repeated virtually every class day."[19]

---

17 Tristram Potter Coffin essay [title missing] for Rutgers Football Program, Sept. 30, 1972, 10, Bowen president, box 402, folder 4. See also Coffin quoted in Thomas B. Martin, "A Proud Day for Denison: Bowen Becomes President of Princeton," *Denison Alumnus* 63 (February 1972): 4, Denison: "Bill is a fine athlete if you exclude his legs; he was slow on his feet. He was able to overcome that with his competitiveness, concentration, and unusually quick hands."

18 *The Adytum, 1952* (Denison yearbook), 108–9, 158; *1953*, 48, 49, 75, 100; *1954*, no pagination; *1955*, 94, 114, 115, 117, 123, 166, 176, all in Bowen personal; Preucil interview; Lugar interview; Giles interview; Bayley interview; Bowen, Woodrow Wilson Fellowship application; James, "WGB from A to Z," 12.

19 Chuck Curry, letter to the editor, *Denison Magazine* (Summer 2017): 11, Bowen personal.

Dave Bayley said that Bowen was a "problem-solver" who "had the capacity of seeing a problem, giving it thought, wanting to solve it—and getting himself out of the way of the solution." Normally, with Granville being a dry town, students who had alcohol in the dormitories kept it carefully hidden. But when things went awry, it was up to the head residents to intervene. An example: One night, around 10:00 or 10:30 p.m. in their shared suite in Curtis East, Bowen and Bayley heard a crash outside their door as a full bottle of gin hit the floor in the hallway. A flood of gin came in under the door. "Bill, what should we do?" Bayley asked. Bowen's response: "Nothing." And, in fact, the hallway was cleaned up by the next morning. In his response to Bayley, Bowen was imparting an important lesson: "Sometimes inaction is the proper course of action."[20] Making a related point about Bill's education in leadership, his Wyoming classmate Tom Boyatt put it this way: "Bill learned early on that it is much more effective if you can stay calm, be analytical, absorb the punches, and then punch back."[21]

In Bill's freshman year, Mary Ellen was a student at Sweet Briar College in Sweet Briar, Virginia, in the foothills of the Blue Ridge Mountains. Going to Sweet Briar had been the idea of Mary Ellen's father, O. B. Maxwell, but Mary Ellen herself quickly determined that she wanted to transfer to Denison. With the help of Dave Bayley's parents—his father, Frank, was a professor of philosophy and the dean of men during Bill and Dave's first three years at Denison—she submitted a successful transfer application and—coached by the Bayleys—made a persuasive case to her father. Once she arrived at Denison in her sophomore year, she and Bill often played bridge with the Bayleys.[22]

Social life at Denison meant going to basketball and football games, attending events at Bill's fraternity house, and cooking dinner at Mary Ellen's sorority house.[23] In the evenings, Mary Ellen and Bill frequented a particular study room in the library. Chuck Curry said that he could not study with Bill because "his focus . . .

20 Bayley interview.
21 Boyatt interview.
22 Interviews with Mary Ellen Bowen, June 25, July 20, 2018; Bayley interview.
23 Interview with Mary Ellen Bowen, July 20, 2018.

was so intense that his mannerisms—tapping his feet on the floor or fingers on the table—were so distracting that no one nearby could concentrate."[24] That concern did not dissuade Mary Ellen or Dave Bayley from studying with him. Bayley called their little study group the Friday Night Club—himself, Bill, Mary Ellen, and two other students who made a practice of going to the library on Friday nights, when there was hardly anyone else there. They were "really a straight arrow group," Bayley said. There was not much else to do on campus; "we studied, that's what we did."[25]

That said, Bill had a sense of humor—sometimes silly, sometimes goofy, but a sense of humor nonetheless. In their senior year, there was a fair on campus to benefit the United Way. An auction raffled off opportunities for students to do "goofy things for charity." Bill signed on to eat a raw egg in the middle of the dining hall. In a separate event, he offered competitors the chance to throw a pie at Dave, with the surprise winning contestant revealed to be Dave's mother, Connie Bayley, who took the pie from Bill and gleefully smashed it in Dave's face.[26]

Bill proved to be an extremely accomplished student. He routinely earned straight As, and by his junior year he was taking six courses each semester, up from the usual five. In his freshman year, the college reported to the Selective Service System that he ranked first among 133 men in his class; in his sophomore year, he ranked third out of 118. Sophomore year was when he first discovered economics, which became his major.[27] He wrote a five-hundred-page senior honors thesis on the Council of Economic Advisers, for which he read everything written by every member and interviewed all but one of the living members of the council since its inception in 1946. His interest, he said, was in understanding

24 Curry quoted in Alexander Gelfand, "Life Trustee: William G. Bowen '55, 1933–2016," *Denison Magazine* (Summer 2017): 67, Bowen personal.

25 Interview with Mary Ellen Bowen, July 20, 2018; Bayley interview.

26 Bayley interview.

27 Denison University, semester grade reports for William Bowen, first and second semesters, 1951–52 and 1952–53; first semester, 1953–54; Selective Service System College Student Certificate, June 9, 1952, June 8, 1953, Bowen personal; Denison University, permanent record of William Gordon Bowen, in Bowen, Woodrow Wilson Fellowship application. The Bowen quote is in the Woodrow Wilson application.

"the scope and proper relationship of economics to government," in particular, the role of "the technically trained economist . . . in governmental policy-making." A faculty member who saw him delivering the finished product recalled that he "appeared to be embarrassed by the size of it—it was gigantic." By the time Bowen graduated (again, at the top of his class), he had been elected to Phi Beta Kappa as a junior, earned honors in economics, and was headed to Princeton for graduate study in economics, supported by a Woodrow Wilson Fellowship (he also held a Danforth Fellowship, without funding).[28]

Denison made the critical difference in pointing Bill toward a PhD program. Neither of his parents had gone to college. As he wrote in his Woodrow Wilson Fellowship application, "My home is in a typical suburban business community in which sports and sales are the primary topics of conversation." Denison opened his eyes to the satisfactions of intellectual engagement. "It was during my freshman year in college that I first was exposed to the discussion of ideas." Philosophy, the history of western civilization, mathematics—these were stimulating new areas of intellectual inquiry. Economics "fascinated" him; "here was a new approach to problems the existence of which I had never even recognized. I began to think of mathematics not as an end, but as a tool to be used in solving economic problems." Courses in his junior year broadened his thinking still further. "I became more interested in philosophy, particularly modern social philosophy; general cultural problems such as the effect of ethnocentrism and materialism in our culture became paramount in my thinking. Just as I had come to conceive of mathematics as a tool, so now I began to consider economics as an instrument to be used in solving these broader problems."[29]

Initially interested in a career in business or law, Bill had decided by the beginning of his senior year, after a summer spent working in an industrial relations office, that he would shift gears, apply to

28 Bowen quoted in Woodrow Wilson Fellowship application. Leland J. Gordon, Bowen's thesis adviser, described the thesis in Martin, "A Proud Day for Denison," 4. The faculty member who saw Bowen delivering the thesis to the library was William Brasmer, professor of theater and film, quoted in ibid., 5.

29 Bowen quoted in Woodrow Wilson Fellowship application.

graduate school, earn a doctorate in economics, and teach at the college level. He thought he would love teaching and advising students and doing research, and he looked forward to the "free exchange of ideas with capable men in all fields." He said that he would also like to explore college administration, in which he had become interested through his service on the student-faculty council. All told, his experience at Denison, particularly the example of the Bayleys, whom he had come to know very well, convinced him that he would "enjoy living in a college community."[30]

Bowen's recommenders for the fellowship believed strongly in his promise as a teacher-scholar of the first rank. The president of Denison, A. Blair Knapp, described him as "unquestionably . . . our most outstanding student at the present time." His academic record was "magnificent"; he was an "outstanding . . . personality"; his leadership roles, discharged with "the same excellence of performance as . . . his academic pursuits," showed his "tact," "imagination," and perceptiveness. He was "a person of great charm and warmth, who commands both respect and confidence from students and faculty." He was sure to become "an eminent member of the profession."[31]

Bowen's thesis adviser, Leland J. Gordon, chair of the economics department, echoed Knapp's assessment. Bowen, he wrote, had a near-perfect academic record (he had one B in a core course as a first-term sophomore), confirming the faculty's judgment that he was "one of the most outstanding and promising students we have ever had." Bowen's history professor, Wyndham Southgate, who also served with him on the student-faculty council and came to know him well, said that Bowen's excellent academic record was "partly the result of an immense capacity for work and partly the result of his clear-headedness and ability to drive to the heart of a matter." His tennis coach, Tristram P. Coffin, put it this way: "An original and penetrating thinker, he has enlivened every class he has

30 Ibid.
31 A. Blair Knapp, letter of recommendation, Dec. 3, 1954, in Bowen, Woodrow Wilson Fellowship application.

been in with stimulating and argument-creating comments and observations."[32]

Mark Smith, then dean of men at Denison, provided a comprehensive summary of the case for Bowen. He wrote that it "would be difficult to think of a young man more suited than this one for graduate study and teaching in the social sciences." He continued,

> Even Bill's marvelous record in academics and activity here on the Denison campus is inadequate as an evaluation of him. He is a young man of driving but flexible intellect, of unquestionable integrity and moral strength. He possesses the kind of unusual skills of communication and leadership that are so badly needed in college teaching today. As co-president of the Campus Government Association, he has shown the same kind of originality and perspective that have characterized his academic work and engendered its excellence. As a member of his fraternity, he has shown not simply a strong interest in his fellows, but also unusual skill in leading them toward an unusual kind of intellectual curiosity. As a head resident in the men's dormitories he has further exhibited exceptional skills in dealing with college students on a very constructive plane.[33]

Most interesting, perhaps, were Wyndham Southgate's observations on Bowen as a person. He described Bowen's personality as "very different from that of the usual campus 'important figure.'" Bowen gave the initial impression, Southgate said, "of a rather naïve and youngish person straight from the farm." That was true, he thought, because Bowen had come from "a family of very limited means" and had grown up within "a rather narrow circle" before coming to college. But Bowen had "matured and developed

---

32 Letters of recommendation from Leland J. Gordon, Dec. 3, 1954; Wyndham Southgate, Dec. 14, 1954; Tristram P. Coffin, Dec. 3, 1954, all in Bowen, Woodrow Wilson Fellowship application.

33 Mark Smith, letter of recommendation, Dec. 7, 1954, in Bowen, Woodrow Wilson Fellowship application.

capabilities" at Denison in remarkable ways—still remaining, how-ever, "the same plain and likeable person he was at the start."[34]

Bill Bowen spent his years at Denison inventing himself, devel-oping the intellectual capacity and leadership skills that would serve him for the rest of his life. He had no template; his family experi-ence gave him little or no guidance or direction. Indeed, one can infer that his family experience served as a driving force, pushing him to become different from the family in which he had grown up. He was coming to define himself in opposition to the life he had known previously; it was clear that he wanted to be someone other than his father and mother, and that he would summon the energy and determination to make sure that that happened.

Economics at Princeton

Bowen chose Princeton because it had "by far the best program in labor economics of any of the major universities." Leland Gordon put him in touch with Richard A. Lester, the leading labor econo-mist at Princeton, and Lester "was very helpful in encouraging [him] to come." Robert F. Goheen, then the national director of the Wood-row Wilson Fellowships, pushed back; his marching orders from the board of the fellowship program were to spread Woodrow Wil-son Fellowships broadly among many universities rather than concentrating them at such institutions as Harvard, Yale, Prince-ton, Chicago, Columbia, and MIT, and he "did his best to convince [Bowen] to go to McGill." "The Princeton economists," Bowen re-called later, especially Richard Lester and Lester V. Chandler, then the department chair, "resisted that notion vigorously and they prevailed."[35]

Bowen arrived in Princeton in the summer of 1955. He lived in the Graduate College in his first year. The day he moved in, he walked across College Road to two graduate college tennis courts located very near his dormitory. There was a match in progress be-

34 Southgate letter of recommendation.
35 Bowen oral history, June 9, 2009, 3, 8. For Goheen's account, see Goheen oral history, Nov. 4, 2004, 4.

tween Goheen, who played there occasionally, and a Princeton classmate of Goheen's who taught at Rutgers. Bowen stood by the fence, watched the match, and introduced himself at its conclusion (he and Goheen had interacted previously around Bowen's Woodrow Wilson Fellowship, but they had never met). Bowen asked "how he could get a game of tennis." Goheen, who did not know Bowen's tennis history, "volunteered to play with him." The first time they scheduled a game, Goheen said, Bowen "just wiped me off the court." The two did play on occasion after that, usually doubles—given Bowen's strength as a player, singles were off the table. Goheen said later that meeting Bowen at the tennis court "began a friendship" that became "very meaningful" and "tremendously helpful" to him.[36]

While Bill got started on his PhD studies, Mary Ellen enrolled in a master's program in library science at Rutgers. The two married on August 25, 1956, at the Presbyterian Church of Wyoming, with a reception afterward at the Maxwells' country club. They then moved into 410-B Devereux Street in Princeton, a small unit in graduate housing in the Butler Tract, a complex of 250 units that had been built in 1946–47 to provide temporary accommodations for returning World War II veterans. The place had the look and feel of an army barracks. Originally intended to have a very brief lifespan, "the project," as it was commonly known, continued to house graduate students (as well as some junior faculty) for seventy years.[37]

Mary Ellen went to work in the library at Princeton Theological Seminary while Bill immersed himself in his work in the economics department.[38] At the outset, he was intimidated. It was a big step from Denison to Princeton. He felt insecure about his abilities, uncertain about whether he really belonged. "I guess the only time

36 Goheen oral history Nov. 4, 2004, 4. See also Bowen oral history, June 9, 2009, 8.
37 Karen Lee Bowen, "Mary Ellen Maxwell," in "Remembering the Maxwell and Lee Families"; "Butler Tract Demolition," https://facilities.princeton.edu/projects/butler-tract-demolition, accessed Oct. 24, 2020; interview with Mary Ellen Bowen, June 22, 2018; Princeton University, Faculty Biographical Records, "William Gordon Bowen," Sept. 17, 1956, Bowen president, box 402, folder 1.
38 "Close-Knit Home Life Enfolds President Bowen's Family," *Town Topics* (Princeton, NJ), Dec. 2, 1971, Bowen president, box 403, folder 7.

that I was really frightened, apprehensive as far as academics are concerned, is when I came here as a graduate student," he said.[39] He had wondered, he noted later, "what malevolent deities had conspired to make me the least competent, most confused, member of an entering class that, with my single exception, consisted entirely of paragons."[40] His "first and most lasting lesson," he said, was a "sense of what scholarship entailed; of what it meant to grapple with an idea, or a series of apparently conflicting, seemingly obscure ideas . . . and then finally to be rewarded by a flash of illumination." His professors taught him "that even neophytes, if they were sufficiently determined, could make headway with such materials"—and that "the entire process of studying and of learning was both wonderfully exhilarating and just plain fun."[41] From William J. Baumol he learned "that while it might take me a while to figure things out, by and large I could figure them out if I was patient enough and worked hard enough." From Baumol and from Jacob Viner he also learned "how important it was to say things clearly."[42] Years later, Bowen told Derek Bok, president of Harvard and one of Bowen's coauthors, that while he did not understand everything right away in graduate school, he learned that if he worked hard enough and long enough at something, it would become clear, so that he could finally figure it out.[43]

"I am enjoying my graduate work more than I had anticipated," Bowen reported in the spring of 1956 to the National Woodrow Wilson Fellowship Program. "I find the faculty friendly, stimulating and very willing to be of assistance. My fellow graduate students are challenging and congenial." He expected to take general examinations in the spring of 1957, embark on his thesis, and com-

39 Christopher Lu, "The Bowen Bio," in "William G. Bowen: Portrait of a President," *Daily Princetonian*, Jan. 6, 1988.

40 William G. Bowen, "A Quiet Confidence," commencement remarks, June 1977, in *Ever the Teacher: William G. Bowen's Writings as President of Princeton* (Princeton, NJ: Princeton University Press, 1987), 171.

41 William G. Bowen, "Reflections," commencement remarks, June 1987, in *Ever the Teacher*, 582.

42 Bowen oral history, June 9, 2009, 12.

43 Interview with Derek C. Bok, June 20, 2018, Cambridge, MA.

plete the degree by September 1958.[44] He met that schedule without difficulty. As the department of economics reported to the Woodrow Wilson Fellowship Program in June 1957, Bowen had earned the master's degree and had embarked on work toward the doctorate. He was, the department said, "one of several truly outstanding graduate students whom we have been fortunate enough to have at Princeton in the past two years. His work has been outstanding in every way."[45]

Bowen's field was labor economics, broadly construed. One of his principal instructors was the well-known labor economist Frederick H. (Fizz) Harbison, a Princeton PhD who had joined the Princeton faculty in the fall of 1955 to direct the Industrial Relations Section after a decade as a professor at the University of Chicago (going elsewhere and being hired back to Princeton was the normal trajectory for a highly talented Princeton PhD). Writing about Bowen in January 1957, he said, "Since 1945 I have had contact with approximately 150 graduate students in sociology or in economics who were interested in labor and industrial studies. Most of these students I knew at the University of Chicago, and four or five I have known since moving to Princeton last year. At his stage of development, Bowen is the best student I have ever had the opportunity to teach." It was "almost inevitable," Harbison predicted, that Bowen would "make very significant contributions to the advancement of knowledge in his field."[46]

Joining the Faculty

In October 1957, the economics department voted in favor of Bowen's appointment as a lecturer, for a term of three years, September 1958 through June 1961, the rank to be changed to assistant professor upon completion of his degree requirements. Hiring one

44 William G. Bowen report, Apr. 15, 1956, in Bowen, Woodrow Wilson Fellowship application.
45 William G. Bowen report, June 14, 1957, in Bowen, Woodrow Wilson Fellowship application.
46 Frederick H. Harbison recommendation to the Social Science Research Council, Jan. 9, 1957, William Bowen file, Faculty Files, box 724.

of its own students was an unusual move for the department; normally, such appointments went to new PhDs from top departments at other institutions, most commonly MIT, Harvard, and Chicago. Bowen had already published his first scholarly article, "The Balanced Budget Multiplier: A Suggestion for a More General Formulation," in the *Review of Economics and Statistics* in May 1957. The department expected him "to be a highly productive scholar" as well as "a really outstanding teacher and highly successful . . . lecturer, classroom teacher, and preceptor." By October 1958, Bowen had completed the thesis, qualified for the PhD, and been appointed an assistant professor of economics at Princeton.[47] Richard Quandt, who sat on his final public oral examination, said it was clear even then that Bowen was "the fair-haired boy of the department."[48] Along with the appointment to the faculty came the birth of the Bowens' first child, a son, David Alan, on August 30, and the family's move to a larger unit in the project, with a second bedroom, 414-B Devereux Street.[49]

Bowen made a strong and immediate impression on the department. Writing about him the following year, J. Douglas Brown, himself a labor economist then serving as dean of the faculty, said, "Mr. Bowen is one of the two or three best young labor economists with which I have been associated in thirty-five years at Princeton." Brown continued, "He combines a penetrating and subtle mind with a rare gift of communication, both oral and written. He has excellent judgment in interpreting exacting analysis. His character and personality support a humane understanding in a field which requires such understanding. He will go far in higher education, both in scholarship and in institutional leadership."[50] Writing again about Bowen for the John Simon Guggenheim Memorial Foundation in November 1959, Frederick Harbison elaborated on his earlier assessment. "Among the newer and younger

---

47 Princeton University faculty appointment form, Oct. 7, 1957, William Bowen file, Faculty Files, box 724.

48 Interview with Richard E. Quandt, July 18, 2018, Princeton, NJ.

49 Interview with Mary Ellen Bowen, June 22, 2018.

50 J. Douglas Brown recommendation, Nov. 20, 1959, William Bowen file, Faculty Files, box 724.

teachers in the Economics Department at Princeton," he said, "Bowen clearly ranks number one." Harbison appraised Bowen's forthcoming book, *The Wage-Price Issue: A Theoretical Analysis*, as "an outstanding contribution to knowledge in economics." Bowen's abilities as a scholar and as a teacher were "unusual and outstanding," Harbison said. And then Harbison made a prescient comment about what he regarded as Bowen's "unusual administrative skills": "In my judgment, he will probably turn up as one of our leading university presidents within the next twenty years."[51]

In late November 1960, the economics department put Bowen forward for promotion to associate professor with tenure, effective July 1, 1961, with a substantial salary raise in advance of the promotion proposed for February 1. Everything about the move was unusual. Bowen had recently turned twenty-seven years old. Assistant professors normally came up for tenure in the eleventh semester at Princeton; early tenure decisions usually meant consideration in the ninth semester. Bowen was only in his fifth semester as a faculty member at Princeton. He had not yet seen a graduate student in a class or seminar. But he was a stunning teacher of undergraduates, a remarkable achievement in a department where senior faculty did not ordinarily excel in (or devote themselves enthusiastically to) undergraduate instruction. "There is no one in the Department who can match him," the department asserted. "He is our most effective lecturer and no one surpasses him in the teaching of classes and precepts. In his teaching he is demanding, rigorous, orderly and popular."[52] As for scholarship, he had already turned his dissertation into a Princeton University Press book—*The Wage-Price Issue: A Theoretical Analysis*, published in January 1960—and he took up a different aspect of wage behavior in a monograph published that fall by the department's Industrial Relations Section, *Wage Behavior in the Postwar Period: An Empirical Analysis*. The department said in the case for Bowen's

---

51 Frederick Harbison recommendation to John Simon Guggenheim Foundation, Nov. 1959, William Bowen file, Faculty Files, box 724.

52 Princeton University faculty promotion form, Nov. 28, 1960, William Bowen file, Faculty Files, box 724.

promotion that it expected him "to become one of the most out-standing economists in America in his chosen fields."[53]

What the department did not say, but the confidential outside letters received by the dean of the faculty made plain, was that the early promotion came in response to outside offers. Bowen was already being courted actively by Yale and MIT, two of the departments that ranked higher than Princeton's. MIT in particular had what was widely considered to be the best economics department in the country, anchored by such luminaries as Paul Samuelson and Robert Solow, both of whom would later win the Nobel Prize. If Princeton wanted to keep Bowen, early promotion was an essential move.

Lloyd G. Reynolds, professor of economics at Yale, wrote, "I think the most sincere tribute I can give is that I tried twice to get Mr. Bowen to join our department here and was very sorry indeed that he decided to stay at Princeton." Praising Bowen's book, *The Wage-Price Issue*, Reynolds called it "an amazingly thorough and mature piece of work for a man beginning his professional career." Echoing Reynolds, Charles A. Myers, professor of industrial relations at the Massachusetts Institute of Technology, said, "We tried very hard to induce Bowen to come to M.I.T. following a visit here." Myers said that he considered Bowen "one of the brightest young men in the field of labor economics" and called *The Wage-Price Issue* "a first-rate contribution to the literature." Kenyon E. Poole at Northwestern had read Bowen's dissertation in manuscript and recommended that a revised version be published by Princeton University Press. Bowen stood, he said, "in the front rank of the theory-oriented younger labor economists." Albert Rees at the University of Chicago, himself a PhD student of Fizz Harbison, echoed his fellow writers, characterizing Bowen as "one of the most promising young labor economists in the country," "one of a very small group who are applying the techniques of formal economics to problems in the labor field."[54]

53 Ibid.; "Rank and Salary History, William Gordon Bowen, 1956–62," Bowen president, box 181, folder 2.

54 Lloyd G. Reynolds to J. Douglas Brown, Jan. 9, 1961; Charles A. Myers to Brown, Jan. 17, 1961; Kenyon E. Poole to Brown, Jan. 26, 1961; Albert Rees to Brown, Jan. 10,

With his promotion to tenure approved, Bowen established his place in the department and the university. The department gave him responsibility for Economics 101, "The Structure and Functioning of the National Economy," the introductory macroeconomics course. The course had not been very popular with undergraduates. Bowen quickly transformed it into one of the most compelling classes in the university, with an enrollment soon exceeding three hundred, then four hundred students. With eight hundred students in each entering class, Bowen taught a high proportion of Princeton undergraduates.

Bowen organized the course by giving one lecture a week, usually on policy issues that could be illuminated by the analytic techniques covered in the assigned readings. The lectures were "riveting," one of his students recalled—"interesting, clear, funny, and practical." Two weekly discussion classes focused on the basics of economic policy techniques. His objective was to show the relationship between contemporary policy issues and models describing how national output and employment were determined. For example, when the students were learning about Keynesian economics, Bowen was lecturing about the economic policy initiatives of President John F. Kennedy, the resistance to some of Kennedy's ideas, and what Keynesian economics had to say about whether Kennedy was right. As a discussion leader, Bowen had "a gift for encouraging thoughtful participation," drawing students out, patiently asking questions, Socratic-style, that enabled students to come to their own analysis rather than giving them answers directly. In course evaluations, students ranked him highly, with some students calling him "the best classroom teacher they have had in any course" at Princeton.[55]

1961, all attached to Princeton University faculty promotion form, Nov. 28, 1960, William Bowen file, Faculty Files, box 724.

55 I am indebted for this account to Burton G. Malkiel, who taught discussion classes in 101 when Bowen was in charge and inherited the course after Bowen became provost. See also the introductory lecture in 101: William G. Bowen, "Economics 101 . . . ," *Princeton Alumni Weekly*, Nov. 19, 1963, Bowen president, box 402, folder 2. On Bowen's effectiveness as a teacher, see the comments of the chair of the economics department, Richard A. Lester, in recommending Bowen's salary increase, in Department of Economics to the Dean of the Faculty, Dec. 3, 1962, William Bowen file, Faculty Files,

In terms of scholarship, Bowen accelerated the steady pace of publication he had begun as an assistant professor, but his reach became broader. Bowen's colleague, labor economist Orley Ashenfelter, said that his scholarship was "always current," "very connected to public policy interests at the time."[56] In early 1964, the Industrial Relations Section published his research report, *Economic Aspects of Education: Three Essays*, the section's third book on the economics of education. The three essays, written during Bowen's seven-month research leave in the United Kingdom in 1961–62, funded by the Social Science Research Council, addressed three discrete topics. The first appraised the methods used by economists "to estimate the returns from education." The second explored the policy implications of alternative methods of university finance in the United States and the United Kingdom. The third was a quantitative study of salary differentials among university faculty in Britain in three broad fields: arts, science, and technology.[57]

At the same time, Bowen went to work on a different, bigger project: a book with his senior colleague, William J. Baumol, on the economics of the performing arts. Baumol, more than a decade older than Bowen and one of the advisers for his PhD thesis, enlisted his younger colleague in the joint effort. The Twentieth Century Fund in New York had commissioned the two-year study. It was meant to show "the present condition and the prospects of the performing arts in the United States," with a focus on "the economic foundations of theatre, opera, orchestra, and dance to illuminate the place of the artist." Baumol and Bowen set out to "assemble and analyze figures on attendance, costs, box-office receipts and other sources of income, including contributions, for the performing arts."[58] Their findings, first aired at the annual meeting

---

box 724; e-mail, Marc Lackritz to Nancy Weiss Malkiel, Oct. 25, 2018 ("riveting"); telephone interview with Robert H. Rawson, Oct. 22, 2018; telephone interview with Philip Cannon, Jan. 24, 2019. Rawson and Cannon were Bowen's students in 101 in the early 1960s.

56 Interview with Orley C. Ashenfelter, Oct. 3, 2018, Princeton, NJ.

57 Frederick Harbison, foreword to Bowen, *Economic Aspects of Education: Three Essays*, v–vi.

58 "Bowen, William Gordon," *Current Biography* 34 (May 1973): 9, Bowen president, box 402, folder 1.

of the American Economic Association in December 1964 and published in the *American Economic Review* in 1965, saw full publication in 1966 in the book *Performing Arts: The Economic Dilemma.*[59] Baumol and Bowen spelled out in detail the economic pressures on performing arts organizations. Times were tough financially, and they were likely to get tougher. Income from ticket sales was hard pressed to stretch to cover costs. The basic issue was the impossibility of realizing productivity gains in the performing arts. It took four people to play a Haydn string quartet in the late 1700s, and it still took four people to play it two hundred years later. Wages for performing artists were going to have to rise with wages in general; in the absence of productivity gains, it was going to be harder and harder for the performing arts to make ends meet. The insight linked back to Bowen's work on wages, prices, and inflation, where he had documented the rapid increase in wages in the postwar period and explored the relationship of wages, productivity, and economic growth. In the performing arts, however, the usual relationship of wages and productivity did not apply. As Bowen would later illuminate, a similar economic dilemma described the relationship between costs and productivity in higher education.[60]

The theoretical contribution was Baumol's; the empirical work was done by Bowen. Baumol was clearly the senior member of the team by virtue of distinction and scholarly range, but Bowen more than held his own as an intellectual partner. And, as hard as Baumol worked, Bowen drove even harder, often calling his colleague

59 William J. Baumol and William G. Bowen, "On the Performing Arts: The Anatomy of Their Economic Problems," *Proceedings of the 77th Annual Meeting of the American Economic Association, American Economic Review* 55 (May 1965): 495–502; Baumol and Bowen, *Performing Arts: The Economic Dilemma* (New York: Twentieth Century Fund, 1966).

60 Baumol and Bowen, *Performing Arts*; Robert Lekachman, "What's Exploding Where?," *New York Times Book Review*, Jan. 8, 1967, Bowen president, box 402, folder 2; Howard Taubman, "Behind the Clouds," *New York Times*, Nov. 21, 1966, Bowen president, box 402, folder 2; William G. Bowen, *The Wage-Price Issue: A Theoretical Analysis* (Princeton, NJ: Princeton University Press, 1960); Bowen, *Wage Behavior in the Postwar Period: An Empirical Analysis* (Princeton, NJ: Industrial Relations Section, Department of Economics, Princeton University, 1960).

at eight o'clock in the morning to ask where the next chapter was.[61]
The shorthand label for the Baumol-Bowen insight was "cost dis-
ease." As we shall see, it would later come to define so much of
Bowen's approach to the problems of higher education.

In the immediate term, however, what was likely most consequential in terms of Bowen's future was a project for which he was
tapped by the president of Princeton, Robert F. Goheen. The university had committed to participate in "a comprehensive study of
relationships between universities and the federal government"
being conducted by the Carnegie Foundation for the Advancement
of Teaching. Each of the twenty-three participating universities had
agreed to undertake a self-study documenting its own involvement
with federal agencies and programs.[62] Instead of taking the year of
research leave to which he was entitled (a leave that was postponed
by a year), Bowen would be leading Princeton's self-study on a full-
time basis.[63]

Bowen completed the report in January 1962.[64] Beyond its stated
institutional purpose, it served to familiarize Bowen in great detail
with a set of interactions between the university and the federal
government that would turn out to be important to him when he
embarked on a full-time administrative career. As well, the report
signaled that Goheen had his eye on a newly tenured, very young
faculty member; Bowen's success in fulfilling Goheen's mandate
doubtless contributed to Goheen's sense that there might be new
career opportunities ahead for this particular professor.

61 The assessment of relative contributions comes from interview with Alan B.
Krueger, Sept. 14, 2018, Princeton, NJ. For the story about the 8:00 a.m. calls, I am
indebted to Burton G. Malkiel, who heard it from William Baumol.

62 Memorandum, Robert F. Goheen to Academic Deans, Chairmen of Departments,
Directors of Special Programs and Sections, Aug. 4, 1960, William Bowen file, Faculty
Files, box 724.

63 Memorandum, Robert F. Goheen to R. A. Mestres, Aug. 1, 1960, William Bowen
file, Faculty Files, box 724.

64 Memorandum, Robert F. Goheen to Chairmen of Departments, Heads of Sections
and Programs and Administrative Offices, Jan. 23, 1962; William G. Bowen, *The Federal
Government and Princeton University: A Report on the Effects of Princeton's Involve-
ments with the Federal Government on the Operations of the University* (Princeton, NJ:
Princeton University, Jan. 1962), both in Bowen federal government, box 1, folder 2.

With tenure, Bowen also saw more personal changes. The family moved out of the Butler apartments into Ferris-Thompson, the still–relatively new junior faculty housing complex. In 1964 a second child was born, a daughter, Karen Lee, on October 5.[65]

In December 1964, the economics department sent forward its recommendation that Bowen be promoted to full professor, effective July 1, 1965. Although the department did not mention it, at thirty-one, Bowen would be the second-youngest faculty member in the modern history of the university to be advanced to that rank. He continued to be a splendid lecturer, gifted in "clear, systematic explanation of the essence of complicated material and presentation of the essence in an interesting and challenging manner." He continued, too, to be a "most skilled classroom instructor," stimulating "widespread student participation while at the same time covering the essential material." He had begun teaching graduate students, both in the department (economics of labor) and the Woodrow Wilson School of Public and International Affairs (problems of economic stability and growth), and the students were impressed by "his mastery of the subject matter" and his "love of scholarship." In terms of his own scholarship, he had "made a fine scholarly reputation" in multiple fields: wages, labor force and unemployment, and the economics of education. His book with William Baumol on the economics of the performing arts was coming along. He was in demand as a consultant to nonprofit organizations and governmental councils. In sum, Bowen was doing everything one might expect of a highly successful young scholar.[66]

Within a year of Bowen's promotion to full professor, his life would take an entirely new turn when Goheen asked Bowen to join him in Nassau Hall as the first full-time provost of Princeton University.

65 Faculty information sheet, "William Gordon Bowen," Sept. 24, 1962, William Bowen file, Faculty Files, box 724; interview with Mary Ellen Bowen, June 25, 2018.

66 Bowen, *Current Biography*, 10; biographical information, Dr. William G. Bowen, n.d., Bowen president, box 404, folder 12; Princeton University faculty promotion form, Dec. 11, 1964, William Bowen file, Faculty Files, box 724 (source of the quotes).

Part II

Princeton

3

Becoming Provost

"Somebody to Handle a Lot of Important Duties"

In the spring of 1966, the Princeton trustees approved the establishment of a new senior administrative position to help the president lead an increasingly complex institution. For as long as anyone could remember, the senior administration had been very lean. Three men basically ran the university: the president, the dean of the faculty, and the financial vice president. Robert F. Goheen, J. Douglas Brown, and Ricardo Mestres, the incumbents in 1966, were the closest of colleagues and collaborators. It was often said that when the president had a problem to think through, he invited one or both of his colleagues to take a long walk. At the end of the walk, the problem had been solved, or a plan of action had been devised to tackle it.

That was a distinctively Princeton approach to administration, made possible in significant part because Princeton had eschewed the range of professional schools that characterized most universities in the United States. Princeton was small by comparison with its peers, and—unlike them—it retained a single faculty and a singular focus on the arts and sciences and the related professional schools of architecture, engineering, and public and international affairs. But the university, and the larger world in which it operated, had become increasingly complicated, and the challenges attendant on running the institution were very different by the mid-1960s than they had been even a decade earlier.

Goheen knew that some of his fellow university presidents had begun to appoint provosts "to be the number two person to them."[1] The historian Paul H. Buck had served as provost at Harvard from 1945 to 1953, a period when the president of the university, James Bryant Conant, was often absent in Washington, but the provostship had then lapsed, and Harvard did not revive the position until the 1990s.[2] But there were already enough examples of provosts among sister institutions in the 1960s—Yale, Columbia, Chicago, Stanford—to suggest that creating such a position might serve Princeton as well. Chicago, for example, had established its provostship in 1962, with the appointment of Edward Levi, dean of the law school, as second-in-command to the university's president, George Beadle. Levi's new post carried broad responsibility for academic administration, academic planning, faculty appointments, and budgetary matters involving academic affairs—as it turned out, a launching pad for Levi's appointment as president of the university in 1968.[3]

With Brown's retirement as dean of the faculty looming in 1967, Goheen thought that it would be a good idea to split the job into two parts—"Dean of the Faculty as Dean of the Faculty, but all the semi-presidential activities [Brown had been] carrying . . . would go to the Provost."[4] There was no single model that Goheen could look to—Edward Levi stood as an example of a strong provost, but as Geoffrey Kabaservice has pointed out, when Kingman Brewster became provost at Yale in 1960, the position commanded "little power, resources, or influence, and the office dealt mainly with buildings-and-grounds issues."[5] Goheen's idea, he said later, was that he "needed somebody to handle a lot of important duties," among them budget, priorities, and future planning, "somebody with whom [he] could talk about the most essential things in the university in a completely candid way, who shared [his] views and ideas."[6]

---

1 Goheen oral history, Nov. 4, 2004, 3.

2 I am indebted to Hanna Holborn Gray for this information.

3 John W. Boyer, *The University of Chicago: A History* (Chicago: University of Chicago Press, 2015), 357–58.

4 Goheen oral history, Nov. 4, 2004, 3.

5 Geoffrey Kabaservice, *The Guardians: Kingman Brewster, His Circle, and the Rise of the Liberal Establishment* (New York: Henry Holt, 2004), 154.

6 Goheen oral history, Nov. 4, 2004, 3.

Defining the Job

The trustees agreed that it would be useful for the president to have a provost to shoulder part of the load. The provost would be the general deputy to the president, the chief academic and budget officer of the university. He would have responsibility for setting academic priorities, developing and managing the university budget, and a long list of other functions.[7]

In consultation with the board, Goheen decided that the position would be filled initially by Brown. For his last year in office, Brown would carry both titles and both sets of responsibilities—an honorific designation as a gesture of respect for the extraordinary institutional service Brown had performed. At the same time, Goheen announced that the first full-time provost would be William G. Bowen, professor of economics, who would take up the post in the summer of 1967. Bowen was a highly accomplished teacher-scholar who had run the Industrial Relations Section on an interim basis and served as director of graduate studies in the Woodrow Wilson School. He brought an analytic ability that would increasingly be needed going forward. As well, he brought Goheen, who described himself as "not a money person," "real strength . . . with economics and dealing with financial issues." The arrangement paid appropriate homage to Brown, who had already been doing part of the provostial work in his role as dean, and it also gave Bowen a year to get ready for a major change in his professional life at Princeton.[8]

While Bowen was not averse to transitioning from academic research to university administration, he hesitated initially before accepting the appointment. He knew that one of the issues on the institutional agenda was coeducation, and he knew, too, that he and Goheen had different views about it. Goheen was still reluctant to embrace so dramatic a change; Bowen believed that in order to remain a university of the first rank, Princeton would have to admit women students. Bowen told Goheen that it might not be a good idea to move forward with the appointment with such a divergence

7 Princeton University news release, Apr. 5, 1966, Goheen, box 104, folder 4.
8 Ibid. The quotes are from Goheen oral history, Nov. 4, 2004, 3.

of views on so important an issue; he "wasn't sure it was workable to have someone in the provost position . . . who was known to have such a different view on the very sensitive . . . issue of co-education." Goheen responded, characteristically, "You should do your best to persuade me and . . . I'll do my best to persuade you and we'll just see how it comes out." Bowen smiled and said, "Bob, if I just give up on you I can always quit."[9]

The fifteen months between the announcement of Bowen's appointment and his assumption of the provost's position gave him and Goheen a chance to think through the contours of the job. In a long memorandum in January 1967, still six months before becoming provost, Bowen gave Goheen his most detailed thinking about the new job. "I think we are agreed," he wrote, "that in the Princeton context the Provost is to be primarily a policy-officer, with special responsibility for issues which affect several segments (or functions) of the University simultaneously and which are likely to have long-run implications." Bowen listed some of the current issues that he thought would qualify. It was an eclectic list, without apparent rhyme or reason in the kinds of issues included or in their ordering. The first concern was to identify "important new areas into which the University should move," as well as existing areas that ought to be dropped. After that came the relationship between the university and its neighbor, the Institute for Advanced Study, with particular reference to coordinating faculty appointments. Next Bowen listed tuition policy, teaching loads, teaching by graduate students, fringe benefits, the future of the computer center, the development of the library system, and the need to figure out how to collect and process all manner of data the administration needed to understand what was happening in various areas and set priorities going forward. All of these issues fell "in the spheres of other administrative officers," and many of them involved existing faculty committees. It would be up to the provost to bring together "the views of the relevant people" and to "com[e] up with proposals" for the president's consideration. "It is in this sense," Bowen said, "that the Provost is to be viewed as a general

9 Bowen oral history, June 9, 2009, 21, 14 (source of the quotes).

deputy to the President for purposes of policy formulation, planning, and coordination." As well, the provost would participate in "making specific decisions of importance," from personnel to "the construction of new buildings," and would familiarize himself with these matters so that he could act on behalf of the president when the president was away from the campus.[10]

Goheen penned his response in handwritten notes appended to Bowen's memo. He agreed with Bowen's list, but had two items to add: "oversight of certain university-wide activities that do not fall naturally under any of the deans or the financial vice-president"; and "recognition that certain university-wide issues of planning and coordination may be assigned to individual deans, rather than to Provost."[11]

Once the understanding with the president about his new job was settled, Bowen, on leave for the year with the support of a Ford Foundation Faculty Research Fellowship (he also held an Honorary McCosh Faculty Fellowship, "considered the highest honor Princeton can confer upon a faculty member in the social sciences and the humanities"), had important scholarly work to advance. He had published an edited volume of essays in 1965 titled *Labor and the National Economy*. His book with William J. Baumol, *Performing Arts: The Economic Dilemma*, was just out in 1966. Bowen had two other studies in progress that needed to be moved forward before he embarked on full-time administration. The more modest of the two was a brief report for the Carnegie Commission on Higher Education, *The Economics of the Major Private Universities*, prepared in the spring of 1967 and published in 1968. The more ambitious was a major study of labor force participation in partnership with his colleague T. Aldrich Finegan, an assistant professor of economics at Princeton who had gone on to take up a faculty post at Vanderbilt University. The study would be published in 1969 as a nine hundred–page book, *The Economics of Labor Force Participation*, a work still in print in 2023. The labor

10 Memorandum, William G. Bowen to Robert F. Goheen, Jan. 3, 1967, Goheen, box 104, folder 4.
11 Robert F. Goheen, notes on Bowen memo of Jan. 3, 1967, attached to ibid.

economist Alan Krueger said that it was econometrically sophisticated for its time—in 1969, "state of the art," "the most important treatment of labor force participation" then available in the literature.[12]

Bowen took up his new position in July 1967. His colleague, philosophy professor Paul Benacerraf, who joined him in the provost's office to work on coeducation, said that from that time forward, "he was in charge." Goheen gave Bowen the latitude to do what he thought was best, and Bowen "really took over the running of the institution." The general view was that Bowen had been made provost as the likely successor to Goheen.[13]

In March 1968, Bowen was ready to spell out his views on the most important relationship the provost had—save for his relationship with the president—in the senior administration. In a long memorandum to the president about the functions of the office of the provost and the office of the dean of the faculty, Bowen staked out his turf. Sharper and more focused than Bowen's January 1967 memo, this document laid out an expansive conception of the provost's role. The provost, he said, should have responsibility for making recommendations to the president in a list of areas previously the province of the dean. These included, most importantly, "authorization of 'slots' for the appointment of faculty and other teaching personnel"; "broad questions of teaching methods, leaves, and all other matters of this kind which have significant financial implications"; "general targets for salaries, including the establishment of salary pools"; and "numbers of courses offered." "The functions of the Dean of the Faculty," he said, needed to be "reconsidered," with an emphasis on filling authorized positions, reviewing recommendations to the Faculty Advisory Committee

---

12 The quote is from "Biographical Information, Dr. William G. Bowen," Mar. 24, 1970, Bowen president, box 404, folder 12. For the books cited above: Bowen, ed., *Labor and the National Economy* (New York: W. W. Norton, 1965); William J. Baumol and Bowen, *Performing Arts: The Economic Dilemma* (New York: Twentieth Century Fund, 1966); Bowen, *The Economics of the Major Private Universities* (Berkeley, CA: Carnegie Commission on Higher Education, 1968); Bowen and T. Aldrich Finegan, *The Economics of Labor Force Participation* (Princeton, NJ: Princeton University Press, 1969). Krueger's assessment is in interview with Alan B. Krueger, Sept. 14, 2018, Princeton, NJ.

13 Interview with Paul Benacerraf, July 17, 2018, Princeton, NJ.

on Appointments and Advancements "concerning members of the present academic staff"; seeing to the effective functioning and morale of the academic departments; recommending appointments of department chairs; and helping chairs sort out sticky personnel problems. As for allocation of resources, the role of the dean would be to help the provost in making recommendations to the president about the creation of new positions and the elimination of existing positions.[14] Basically, Bowen wanted to keep for himself all the big decisions such as priorities for growth while leaving the dean of the faculty with the full range of details involved in managing a faculty, from who got the better salary increases to who got the better housing.

We do not have Goheen's response, but we do know two things relevant to the rebalancing of responsibilities. The first is that Goheen's new dean of the faculty left after a year in the job. Robert R. Palmer, historian of early modern and modern Europe, with special emphasis on the French Revolution, had been a celebrated member of the Princeton faculty from 1936 to 1963, when he left to become dean of the faculty of arts and sciences at Washington University in St. Louis. Palmer had been in the deanship at Washington University for three years when Goheen persuaded him to come back to Princeton as J. Douglas Brown's successor. It was a coup by any measure: stunningly accomplished scholar, experienced dean, longtime Princeton faculty star—who better to succeed Brown to lead Princeton's faculty? But the job Goheen recruited Palmer to fill was not the same as the job in which he found himself. With changes in the purview of the deanship and tensions with the person and the office taking over duties Palmer might have been expected to discharge, deaning at Princeton turned out to be considerably less appealing than deaning at Washington University. After leaving the deanship, Palmer decamped for Yale, where he remained a faculty member until his retirement in 1977.

We also know that the structural realignment of duties put in place with the Bowen provostship has meant that over the past half

14 Memorandum, W. G. Bowen to R. F. Goheen, Mar. 7, 1968, Goheen, box 104, folder 4.

century, working relationships between the provost and the dean of the faculty have been highly person-dependent. Where the two individuals have collaborated effectively, indeed, where they have been good friends with strong mutual respect, it has been easy to work together to realize their shared goals of recruiting and supporting the best possible faculty. Where the personal relationships have been more competitive, however, the Bowen realignment has allowed the provost to dominate the dean in ways that make for tension and unhappiness at best, and for senior administrative turnover in the most difficult cases.[15]

Budgeting

Working through the relationship between the provost and the dean of the faculty was very important to the two protagonists and their immediate colleagues, but it was not obviously of great consequence to people outside those offices. What was of pressing moment, what was Bowen's most urgent responsibility as provost, was to establish a budgetary process to enable Princeton to make thoughtful decisions about resource allocation in an extremely difficult economic environment. Bowen was widely acknowledged as the expert on escalating university costs that were surpassing the growth of the universities' income (and far above the general rate of inflation), which he explicated in 1968 in *The Economics of the Major Private Universities*, his study for the Carnegie Commission on Higher Education. Here he made explicit the connection between higher education and his work with William Baumol on the performing arts: "[I]n every industry in which increases in productivity come more slowly than in the economy as a whole, cost per unit of product must be expected to increase relative to costs in general." In other words, cost disease was as much a concern for higher education as it was for the

---

15 My interpretation here is informed in part by e-mail correspondence with three colleagues: Robert C. Darnton, professor of history at Princeton (1968–2007), Oct. 30, 2020; David P. Dobkin, dean of the faculty (2003–14), Oct. 30, 2020; and Neil L. Rudenstine, provost (1977–88), Nov. 6, 2020.

performing arts.[16] Clark Kerr, a member of the commission who had just completed a decade as president of the University of California, labeled his insight "Bowen's Law" (it was also called "Bowen's Dilemma"): Costs per student at institutions like Princeton were rising at a rate of 7.5 percent a year, would likely triple in ten years, and thus threatened to price private universities out of the business of higher education.[17] Bowen needed to figure out how Princeton could navigate the most difficult financial circumstances any institution of higher education had seen since the Great Depression.

Creating an effective budgeting system meant, first, devising mechanisms to have a complete picture of the budget, with all requests for funds on the table at once so that they could be assessed in relation to one another and in the context of the total budget. In old-style budgeting, a full picture of the budget was hard to come by, and requests came forward piecemeal, such that each one was adjudicated without reference to other demands on resources, and before the full budget was known. Now, Bowen explained, Princeton was using procedures that made it possible for budget drafters "to view all of the University's needs and all of its resources at the same time. 'In earlier years we would have to make a decision on one part of the budget before we even knew what the rest of it would look like. Now we have projections of the whole budget far enough ahead so that we can weigh one thing against another.'"[18]

The second element of the new budgeting process was what Bowen called "a 'programmatic' approach to budgeting," where "items of expense" would be assessed in the context of "the basic objectives—the essential program—of the institution." That meant that a proposed allocation for graduate student housing, to take one example, would be evaluated not as part of the housing budget,

16 Bowen, *The Economics of the Major Private Universities*, 16, quoted in Roger L. Geiger, *Research and Relevant Knowledge: American Research Universities since World War II* (New York: Oxford University Press, 1993), 388n4.

17 Editor's note, William G. Bowen, "Paying for Princeton," *Princeton Alumni Weekly*, Nov. 18, 1969, 10.

18 William McCleery, "One University's Response to Today's Financial Crisis: Interview with William G. Bowen," *University: A Princeton Quarterly* 47 (Winter 1970–71), in *Princeton Alumni Weekly*, Dec. 15, 1970, 42.

but as part of the budget of the graduate school: Would an investment in graduate student housing be the first priority for the graduate school, or would it be preferable to put the additional money
into graduate fellowships?[19]

The third element of the new approach to budgeting involved
making "longer range projections of costs and income" than had
previously been employed; knowing what was likely to be coming
in terms of resources, especially if it boded ill for the future, would
drive clearer-headed, tougher budgetary decisions in the immediate term. Decisions regarding the current year's spending would be
considered in a context that took account of the long-run balance
between costs and income.[20]

The fourth element involved participation in the budget-setting
process by representatives of all segments of the university community through a Priorities Committee, chaired by the provost,
which made recommendations to the president for the next year's
budget. I will turn to the Priorities Committee later, in the context
of important changes in university governance that Bowen helped
to push forward.

What Princeton learned about budgeting was disseminated more
broadly through a Ford Foundation study of "the allocation and
use of resources in universities." Princeton had signed on to conduct the study in Bowen's second year as provost. It was carried
out in Bowen's office under the direction of Paul Benacerraf. The
study sought to help universities use resources more efficiently
through more accurate assessment of present and future costs of
budgetary proposals. It pointed up the importance of relating "proposed expenditures" to "anticipated benefits." It made plain the
link between the effectiveness of "various proposed allocations of
funds" and the effectiveness of "teaching and teaching methods."
It examined "scheduling methods, with the objective of making the
best possible use of the physical plant and of the time of both faculty and students." And it made the case for the design of an information system to allow each institution to have at hand the data

19 Ibid.
20 Ibid.

necessary to make decisions, as well as to understand the likely consequences of different policy decisions. While Benacerraf collected information from a wide variety of institutions, the work Bowen was doing at Princeton provided the major substantive and analytic underpinnings for the study.[21]

Coeducation

Budgeting probably accounted for 40 percent of Bowen's time in the provost's office. He estimated, years later, that he had spent 35 percent of his time working on the case for coeducation. He understood, as did Goheen, that the only way to move the trustees "to a thoughtful conclusion" on the matter was by mustering "real evidence," which meant "that a major research project was needed." And framing and executing a major research project was right up Bowen's alley. It was Bowen who identified the faculty member, Gardner Patterson, whom Goheen asked to undertake a careful analytic study of the desirability and feasibility of coeducation at Princeton. It was essential "to model how the addition of women to Princeton would work": Would talented high school women want to come to Princeton? What would they study? Where would they live and eat? What additional services would be required? What evidence could be mustered "for and against making the move"? And how had coeducation and coordinate education worked at other institutions? It was Bowen who worked hand in hand with Patterson at every turn to assist him in making the strongest possible data-driven case, in particular, producing in the provost's office the wealth of essential factual information. These data supported the conclusion that, because of the low marginal costs of adding women students, it was indeed feasible for Princeton to embark on coeducation. It was Bowen who ran interference for Goheen with the colorful campus figures who were most outspoken in their opposition to coeducation. Once Patterson's report was

21 Princeton University news release, Apr. 15, 1968, Bowen president, box 404, folder 11, mainly quoting Bowen. See the discussion of the Ford Foundation study, "Resource Allocation in Universities: A Demonstration Project at Princeton University," in McCleery, "One University's Response to Today's Financial Crisis," 42.

published, it was Bowen who led the team of administrators and faculty who fanned out across the country to talk with alumni about the case for coeducation, to hear and, as appropriate, rebut their objections to changing the university they loved. And once the trustees gave Goheen the green light to proceed with planning for coeducation, it was Bowen who marshaled the painstaking analysis to show exactly how, where, and at what rate Princeton could integrate women students into the campus. Later, as we shall see, regularizing the presence of women at Princeton became one of the linchpins of Bowen's commitment as president to making Princeton a more inclusive institution.[22]

Bowen's role with respect to coeducation illustrated the observation of the dean of students, Neil Rudenstine, about Bowen's influence in the administration: In weekly meetings of the president's cabinet, Rudenstine said, it was "obvious that Bill was the vital force." Goheen was fully engaged, but he "presided"; he "listened" carefully to what his colleagues around the table had to say, and when it was time to act, he "made decisions." But it was Bowen who "was driving the agenda."[23]

Race

It was the remaining quarter of Bowen's time in the provost's office that gave him the widest latitude to drive that agenda, to affect the strength and stability of the university at a time of great tumult in American higher education and, more broadly, in American society. So many colleges and universities came apart under the multiple pressures of the 1960s. Strongly influenced by the civil rights and Black Power movements, Black students, newly enrolled in significant numbers, engaged in often explosive demonstrations demanding the right to shape institutional policies and influence the distribution of institutional resources. The student movement, with

22 On Provost Bowen and coeducation, see Nancy Weiss Malkiel, *"Keep the Damned Women Out": The Struggle for Coeducation* (Princeton, NJ: Princeton University Press, 2016), chaps. 4, 5, 7, 9; Bowen oral history, June 9, 2009, 20–21 (source of the quotes); Goheen oral history, Oct. 26, 2004, 7.

23 Interview with Neil L. Rudenstine, July 22, 2018, New York City.

its advocacy of student engagement in institutional decision making, turned violent at institutions across the country. And the antiwar movement exploded with unprecedented ferocity to protest the
Johnson and Nixon administrations' escalation of American engagement in the war in Vietnam. All of these tensions had currency at Princeton. While Goheen set policy directions, Bowen took
key roles: pressing Goheen to act, guiding him toward the choices
Bowen believed to be wisest for Princeton, identifying faculty
members to play key roles, charting strategy, and executing policy
Goheen and the trustees embraced. All of that involved a mix of
forward motion and stability; how to strike the balance fell chiefly
to Bowen to figure out. I will turn now to elaborating some of the
challenges Goheen and Bowen faced and to illustrating how Bowen
influenced the university's ability to reshape itself to cope with the
new world in which it was operating.

It was Goheen who embraced what he regarded as the moral
imperative of bringing significant numbers of Black students to
Princeton. Through most of his life, he said later, he had been
"largely oblivious to the issue of race" in the United States. Watching the evolution of the civil rights movement in the South, learning from the Princeton undergraduate and graduate students who
had left the campus to work in the movement, he came to see, he
explained, "that we should do our utmost to increase the racial
diversity of the Princeton campus." Goheen instructed his director
of admission to seek able Black applicants, and he brought Carl A.
Fields from Teachers College to join the office of the dean of the
college, "the first black dean" at an Ivy League institution. Fields
"could understand what the University was about or for. He could
understand grievances, fears, and concerns of the black students.
And he could somewhat understand the blindness of us white
people to some of that experience."[24]

As the numbers of Black students on campus increased, so, too,
did their claim to right what they regarded as university policies in
need of correction. At other colleges and universities, confronta-
tions between Black students and their institutions spun out of

24 Goheen oral history, Oct. 26, 2004, 7–8.

control, with students occupying buildings and engaging in violent interactions with administrators, fellow students, and the police. Maintaining stability at Princeton depended on the good sense of the students and the ability of administrators to respond to protest in a measured fashion. Carl Fields was an essential part of that balancing act. So was Bill Bowen. Neil Rudenstine said that Bowen was the person he most relied on when there was a crisis. For all of Goheen's formidable strengths and integrity, he was "above the fray"—Bowen was "willing to be in the fray." He "had his finger on the pulse of what was happening and what was likely to happen." In the case of student protest, Rudenstine regarded Bowen as his most important colleague in charting a way forward that respected the intentions of the student demonstrators while safeguarding the integrity of the institution.[25]

Bowen had made it his business to establish good relationships with Black student leaders.[26] He believed—and worked through with them—that if they carried out the right kind of protest, it would be good for them and for the institution. Rudenstine turned to him for counsel when protests occurred. In 1971, for example, some 150 members of the self-styled Third World Coalition took over the reference room in Firestone Library at closing time and refused to leave. The issue was the university's plan to maintain the percentage of disadvantaged students in the next freshman class at 10 percent. Rudenstine called Bowen from the library; knowing that Bowen knew the students, he wanted to check his own instincts about how to proceed. Bowen came over, assessed the situation, and told Rudenstine that what the students wanted was to make a point, not to cause trouble. He advised Rudenstine to wait the students out—eventually (as they did after three hours, at 2:45 a.m., having first cleaned up the room) they would leave of their own volition.[27]

25 Rudenstine interview.
26 See, e.g., Jerome Davis, "Memorial Tribute," William G. Bowen Memorial Service, Princeton University Chapel, Dec. 11, 2016, courtesy of Jerome Davis.
27 Rudenstine interview; Mark Stevens, "150 Minority Students Sit-In at Firestone," *Daily Princetonian*, Mar. 15, 1971, 1, 5.

Jerome Davis '71, a graduating senior who had been president successively of the Association of Black Collegians and of the undergraduate student government, said later that "no one worked harder [than Bowen] to ameliorate the situation in the days following" the library "take-over" or "thought more about the long-range implications of this form of protest by minority students." Bowen, Davis said "went out of his way to talk to both groups [and] individual students about the reasons for the 'sit-in' and to explain the more complicated aspects of the problem from the University's point of view. Even those who did not agree with Mr. Bowen had to respect him for his exceptional ability and his overwhelming concern."[28]

In the case of the Black student takeover of the New South building on March 11, 1969, which focused on the issue of divestment from companies doing business in southern Africa, Bowen and Rudenstine together handled a more complicated situation. New South was the university hub for financial and administrative services; disrupting the ability of the various university business offices to conduct their work was a more sensitive matter than occupying the reference room in the library. About forty students, members of the Association of Black Collegians, occupied the building shortly after 7:00 a.m. and blocked the entrance of approximately one hundred university staff members who normally worked there.[29]

Goheen called in members of the Faculty Advisory Committee on Policy, together with Bowen and Rudenstine, to consider how to proceed. The president then issued a statement reminding the university community of the clear, well-publicized institutional policy with respect to protests and demonstrations, wherein the university would not condone actions that "block[ed] the legitimate activities of any person on the campus or in any University building or facility." "The seizure of the New South Building," he said, "places the students involved in it in clear violation of this University policy." The seriousness of the charges against them would be

---

28 Jerome Davis to [Ellen] James, Dec. 1971?/Jan. 1972?, courtesy of Jerome Davis.
29 Princeton University news release, Mar. 11, 1969, Bowen provost, box 23, folder 3.

"affected by how long they stay in violation of University policy, by their willingness to identify themselves and appear for hearings, and by how well they treat equipment, records, and other property in the New South Building." If they declined to come out voluntarily, the university would have to consider legal action—for example, by seeking a court order to force the students to vacate the building.[30]

There ensued lengthy negotiations and communications between the students and senior administrators, with Rudenstine going to New South to meet with the students and read them Goheen's statement. The students said they expected to be disciplined; they told Rudenstine that they were not messing up the building; in fact, they said, they were cleaning it up. There was no need to worry about the condition of the building or the integrity of the files. Their plan was to leave the building around 6:00 p.m. and, in a symbolic statement, walk single file up to the center of the campus. Proctors were unable to identify most of the students, which meant that discipline could only be focused on the leaders of the protest. In the end, those students who could be identified were placed on probation (that is, they were not expelled, and the penalties would remain on their records only for a specified length of time).[31]

It was Bowen who had to "pick up the pieces," fielding calls from alumni outraged that students they believed should be grateful to be at Princeton were disrupting the operations of the university, complaining that the discipline system had broken down, and arguing that the leaders of the protest should have been expelled from the university.[32]

30 "Statement by President Robert F. Goheen," Mar. 11, 1969, Bowen provost, box 23, folder 3.

31 Telephone conversation between Dean Rudenstine and Rod Hamilton from Provost Bowen's office, 11:20 a.m., as reported by E. D. Sullivan; ibid., 12:35 p.m.; report by telephone from Dean Sullivan to Provost Bowen, 5:40 p.m., Mar. 11, 1969; notes on Dean Rudenstine's meeting with Blacks at New South, Mar. 11, 1969, all in Bowen provost, box 23, folder 3.

32 Rudenstine interview.

In sum, just as Bowen played a key role in keeping the university from blowing up in tumultuous times, so too he effectively kept a lid on alumni protests so that they would not spin out of control. Maintaining that kind of balancing act—seeing to the long-run stability of the institution—would become a hallmark of Bowen's leadership of Princeton.

4

Using University Governance
to Manage Campus Tensions

"A Most Astute Capacity to Judge
What Was Needed"

Rethinking the Structure of the University

Bowen's emergence as the central leader in charting Princeton's way
forward amidst the tumult of the late 1960s grew out of his use of
university governance to manage tensions on the campus. On
May 2, 1968, a demonstration in front of Nassau Hall by some one
thousand students, organized by Students for a Democratic Society, called for the restructuring of university decision making "so
that those who live in the University and are most seriously affected
by the decisions which control its future, are themselves the ones
who make these decisions."[1] President Goheen, responding to the
demonstrators, voiced his approval of "a fresh and searching review of the decision-making processes of the University."[2]

It was an easy call; by comparison with the upheaval at sister
institutions, Princeton, by agreeing to a thorough-going study of
"questions of authority and decision-making," was embarking on

1 Quoted in Special Committee on the Structure of the University, "Interim Report,"
Nov. 18, 1968, 1, Kuhn, box 1, folder "Final Report." See also fact sheet, "The Governing
of Princeton University: Final Report of the Special Committee on the Structure of
Princeton University," Apr. 7, 1970, Kelley Committee, box 2, folder 25; and *Princeton
University, The President's Report, 1968–1969*, 10, Goheen, box 119, folder 9.
2 Robert F. Goheen remarks, May 2, 1968, Bowen provost, box 24, folder 1.

a much less fraught path, much more consistent with the deliberate, process-oriented style of the administration.[3] It followed logically from work already under way in the Faculty Advisory Committee on Policy, where Harold Kuhn, professor of economics and mathematics, had taken the lead in drafting a new document, "Students and the University," that would shortly be submitted to the faculty for approval.[4] Bowen played a big role behind the scenes in the production of the document and pressed Kuhn to "get on" with his drafting "and finish it." As well, Bowen strongly encouraged the president to embrace a process that had the promise of containing rather than escalating student protest.[5]

In presenting "Students and the University" to the faculty on May 6, Kuhn explained that the deliberation that had produced the document "was not undertaken as a reaction to demands or demonstrations but rather in recognition of the clear fact that the role of the student in the academic community deserved serious reconsideration and study." The document had gone through many drafts and had been developed in close consultation with the undergraduate student government. Its purpose was to "affirm those basic principles that underlie, and to state those policies and procedures that define, the rights and responsibilities of the student in the University."[6]

"Students and the University" proposed the establishment of two new student committee structures. One involved the creation of undergraduate departmental committees in each department, which would provide for regular contact between faculty and students

3 *Princeton University, The President's Report, 1968–1969.*

4 Kuhn oral history, 6–10.

5 Ibid., 7 (source of the quote), 9–10; interview with Neil L. Rudenstine, July 22, 2018, New York City.

6 [Harold Kuhn,] handwritten opening remarks, faculty meeting, May 6, 1968, Kuhn, box 2, folder "Students and the University." See also "Students and the University," draft, revised Dec. 12, 1967; and memorandum, "Students and the University: Policy Statements for Discussion," Faculty Advisory Committee on Policy and the President to Faculty, Undergraduate and Graduate Students, Feb. 5, 1968, both in Dean of Students, box 16, folder 7; memorandum, "Students and the University: Policy Statements," Faculty Advisory Committee on Policy and the President to Members of the Faculty, Apr. 8, 1968; and "Students and the University," final version approved by the faculty, Oct. 7, 1968, both in Kuhn, box 2, folder "Students and the University."

majoring in those subjects. Most consequential, perhaps, for the pressing issues of the day, the document proposed that the undergraduate student government constitute student committees to parallel the key standing committees of the faculty, and that the two sets of committees meet together—in effect, giving students membership on most of the major committees through which the faculty conducted its business.[7]

Council of the Princeton University Community

"Students and the University" won preliminary faculty endorsement in May and would ultimately be approved in its final form in October 1968. In the meantime, days after receiving the document in May, the faculty took up a second, much broader initiative concerning university governance. Again originating in the Faculty Advisory Committee on Policy, the new initiative involved the establishment of a special committee of faculty and students on the structure of the university. The charge of the committee sounded benign enough—"to examine and make recommendations on the lines of communication, the decision-making processes, and the exercise of responsibility in university affairs." In fact the committee was imagined as an antidote to the troubling strains of the times, strains that had begun to bedevil even Princeton.[8]

The committee would consist of eight elected faculty members and six students, at least two of whom would be graduate students. It would be chaired by a faculty member. The president or his representative would sit ex officio. The committee would work in cooperation with the administration and with a parallel ad hoc trustee committee established at the request of the president.[9] By the end of May, the committee had been constituted, and—at the initiative

7 Kuhn oral history, 14; "Student 'Bill of Rights,'" in *Princeton University Newsletter* (mimeograph), vol. 1, Oct. 31, 1968, Kuhn, box 2, folder "Students and the University."

8 Memorandum, "Proposed Special Committee on the Structure of the University," Faculty Advisory Committee on Policy and the President to the Faculty, May 10, 1968, Kelley Committee, box 1, folder 15. See also Kuhn oral history, 15–16.

9 Faculty Advisory Committee on Policy and the President to the Faculty, May 10, 1968.

of the provost—Stanley Kelley Jr., professor of politics, had agreed to serve as chair.[10]

The committee's objective, Kelley told its members, was "to satisfy ourselves that the arrangements for governing Princeton University—as modified in any way we may recommend—are reasonable, proper, or necessary, and that they are easily acceptable as such by the overwhelming majority of the members of the University community." They needed to take stock of "the way Princeton is governed now and what objections intelligent and disinterested observers could make." They would then focus on "those aspects of the governing of Princeton that are most controversial or that seem to us to have the most serious shortcomings." "Any remedies we may propose," Kelley continued, "must be *both* widely acceptable and able to bear thoughtful scrutiny in the light of relevant experience at Princeton and elsewhere."[11]

The committee convened in mid-June, held sixteen meetings before faculty and students dispersed for the summer, conducted research while members were away from the campus, and reconvened in the fall. It began with "a cram course in the present decision-making processes of the university"—extended sessions with senior administrators, who explained how different aspects of the institution worked, as well as with faculty members who described the functioning of their departments. The group considered the roles and responsibilities of different individuals and groups across the university and interrogated what could be done to strengthen the engagement and effectiveness of different constituencies.[12] It solicited opinions from all members of the university community, sent questionnaires to specific groups and individuals, conducted a survey of students and faculty, held open meetings to hear the views of members of the community, met with the parallel trustee

10 Bowen oral history, June 25, 2009, 7; memorandum, W. G. Bowen to R. F. Goheen, May 29, 1968, Goheen, box 79, folder 6.

11 Memorandum, Stanley Kelley Jr. to Members of the Committee, Sept. 16, 1968, Goheen, box 79, folder 6.

12 Memorandum, Robert F. Goheen to Trustees' Ad Hoc Committee on Communications and Governance, July 26, 1968, Goheen, box 79, folder 6 (source of the quote); minutes, Committee on the Structure of the University, June 19, 1968 (session with Wm. Bowen; Kelley on the politics department), Kelley Committee, box 3, folder 4.

committee, and read widely in relevant literature (especially on student unrest).[13]

Of necessity, given the president's other commitments, he attended only some of the meetings of the Kelley committee; the provost attended all of them.[14] As in the case of the Patterson committee on coeducation, Bowen had chosen Kelley to lead the effort, and he met with Kelley to work out procedures—for example, how the committee's surveys would be drawn up and who would be asked to do the drafting.[15] And at every stage of the deliberative process, as the committee produced drafts, especially of its final reports, Bowen commented in great detail on wording as well as substance. (Goheen did as well; normally, however, Bowen submitted his comments first, and Goheen wrote to Kelley that he agreed with what Bowen had said.)[16] Reflecting years later on his role, Bowen said, "I had a lot to do with the construction of the

13 Memorandum, Stanley Kelley Jr. to Members of the Committee, Sept. 16, 1968, Goheen, box 79, folder 6. For some of the solicitations of opinion, see, e.g., Kelley memos: to Graduate Students, Sept. 25, 1968; to Members of the Board of Trustees, Sept. 26, 1968; to Members of the Staff Council, Sept. 27, 1968; to Members of the Faculty, Sept. 27, 1968, all in Bowen provost, box 17, folder 6. On the meeting with the parallel trustee committee, see the minutes in memorandum, Dennis Gray to James F. Oates, Oct. 1, 1968, Kelley Committee, box 2, folder 12.

14 Memorandum, Robert F. Goheen to Trustees' Ad Hoc Committee on Communications and Governance, July 26, 1968, Goheen, box 79, folder 6. In response to notification of a scheduled meeting, Bowen typically penned a note to the president—e.g., "Bob, Are you going, or do you want me to go in your place? Bill," handwritten on memorandum, Stanley Kelley Jr. to Members of the Committee, received Sept. 17, 1968, Goheen, box 79, folder 6. At the same time, Goheen would ask Bowen to cover meetings he could not attend—see, e.g., note from Goheen to Bowen, Feb. 24, 1969, Goheen, box 79, folder 7. For an account from Bowen to Goheen of what transpired at a committee meeting Goheen did not attend, see, e.g., memorandum, Bowen to Goheen, Nov. 1, 1968, Goheen, box 79, folder 6.

15 "In suggesting this approach to the problem of the questionnaires, and in authorizing payment of his [the faculty member asked to take on the drafting] honorarium," Bowen wrote Goheen, "I hope I have not moved too far or too fast without your approval." Memorandum, W. G. Bowen to R. F. Goheen, Oct. 9, 1968, Goheen, box 79, folder 6. On Bowen choosing Kelley, see Bowen oral history, June 25, 2009, 7; Sept. 28, 2009, 6; Goheen oral history, Nov. 4, 2004, 11; Jan. 6, 2005, 1.

16 See, e.g., memorandum, Robert F. Goheen to Stanley Kelley Jr., Aug. 22, 1969, Kelley Committee, box 1, folder 11; memorandum, Goheen to Kelley, Feb. 12, 1970, Kelley Committee, box 1, folder 12.

CPUC. . . . I really do feel that I was a partner [with Kelley] in the construction of this machinery."[17]

In November 1968, the committee issued an interim report on its work thus far. The committee's analysis, the report said, pointed in "a clear direction—toward the desirability of bringing a much broader range of views and opinions to bear on many major matters of policy." Just how that would be accomplished required further deliberation on the part of the committee and would await its final report.[18]

That report came in two parts: the first, an initial targeted report in May 1969, proposing the establishment of a Council of the Princeton University Community, and the second, in April 1970, a longer, wide-ranging, final report on a number of specific aspects of university governance.[19] The theme throughout the two reports was broader, more open, more inclusive university governance, with greater participation on the part of students and faculty members. With the proposed changes, it would be "easier to raise issues, to get a hearing, to win the support of others, and to gain access to those formally responsible for making decisions."[20]

Accompanying the two reports were steps taken by the trustees after close consultation with the Kelley committee to increase the authority vested in undergraduate students and to diversify the membership of the board. With respect to the former, authority over student rules of conduct was delegated to students. This step built on important changes that had been spelled out in "Students and the University," wherein students were to take seats on most standing committees of the faculty; students would gain the power to

17 Bowen oral history, June 25, 2009, 7.
18 Special Committee on the Structure of the University to Members of the University Community, Nov. 18, 1968, Kuhn, box 1, folder "Final Report."
19 "A Proposal to Establish the Council of the Princeton University Community: A Report of the Special Committee on the Structure of the University," May 1969, Kelley Committee, box 2, folder 24. On the second report, "The Governing of Princeton University," see, e.g., Princeton University news release, Apr. 7, 1970, and fact sheet, "The Governing of Princeton University: Final Report of the Special Committee on the Structure of Princeton University," Apr. 7, 1970, both in Kelley Committee, box 2, folder 25.
20 Quoted in Princeton University news release, Apr. 7, 1970.

force reconsideration of an action taken by the faculty; and each academic department would establish an elected committee of undergraduates to participate in consideration of changes to strengthen the department's undergraduate program of study. As well, there would be a parallel committee elected from among graduate students in each department.[21] As for the trustees, again after consultation with the Kelley committee, the board voted in April 1969 to elect a graduating senior to a four-year term on the board; in June, the board approved a limit of ten years of service for charter trustees, who had previously served open-endedly, thus enabling "more frequent turnover in membership" and election of younger men ("in their 30's or 40's").[22]

The Council of the Princeton University Community—the most consequential of the Kelley committee's proposals—would be a multiconstituency deliberative body, with fifty elected representatives chosen from among undergraduates, graduate students, faculty, staff, and alumni. Seven senior administrators would sit by virtue of portfolio; the president—or, in his absence, the provost—would chair monthly meetings. To the best of its knowledge, the Kelley committee asserted, the council would be the most broadly representative deliberative body at any college or university. Its purview would be expansive: "The Council would have the authority to 'consider and investigate any question of University policy, any aspect of the governing of the University, and any general issue related to the welfare of the University.'" It could "recommend action to any decision-making body of the University or to any officer of the University." Had the council been in place, the report argued, "Many of the most controversial issues raised and debated at Princeton in the last two years . . . might have been brought to the Council for its consideration and recommendations." The council would be, in effect, "a permanent conference of the representatives of all the major groups of the University. There they

21 Ibid.; resolutions to be presented by the Special Committee on the Structure of the University for Faculty action at the Oct. 5, 1970 meeting of the Faculty, Office of the Clerk of the Faculty to the Members of the Faculty, Oct. 1, 1970, Kelley Committee, box 1, folder 12; *Princeton University, The President's Report, 1968–1969*, 19.
22 *Princeton University, The President's Report, 1968–1969*, 17.

could each raise problems that concern them and there they could be exposed to each other's views. The Council would afford an opportunity for them to find generally acceptable solutions to the common problems of the University community."[23] A more hard-headed way of looking at the CPUC, perhaps, was as "a buffering mechanism," a vehicle where issues could be aired thoroughly while the lid was kept on, without requiring action from the administration different from what the administration had in mind.[24]

The many constituencies—undergraduates, graduate students, faculty, trustees—that needed to approve the proposal from the Kelley committee did so in the spring of 1969; elections were held promptly, and the Council of the Princeton University Community and its standing committees were up and running in the fall.[25]

Princeton was not the only university to rethink governance structures in the late 1960s. At Stanford, for instance, the board of trustees was expanded by one-third, the new members to be trustees elected by the alumni, and faculty and students were granted representation to most board committees. As well, the university established an elected Faculty Senate and gave students new responsibilities in setting and enforcing rules of student conduct.[26]

But the Council of the Princeton University Community had a distinctive role and function. Created with Bowen's full engagement, the CPUC was a brilliant mechanism for bringing the university community together, for giving every constituency a voice, for managing, even taming, explosive issues by moving them into a contained, well-defined, multiconstituency deliberative structure. The CPUC also had the virtue of placing moderate students in a far stronger position relative to their more radical peers. They gained a strong voice in university decisions; groups like SDS had a harder time pulling in moderate students as a result. It was widely believed—probably correctly—that the CPUC and its committees

23 "A Proposal to Establish the Council of the Princeton University Community," 1.

24 I am indebted to Harold T. Shapiro for inspiring this formulation.

25 Faculty meeting minutes, May 26, June 2, Sept. 15, 1969, Dean of the Faculty, series 1, subseries 1B, box 1, folder 1.

26 Richard W. Lyman, *Stanford in Turmoil: Campus Unrest, 1966–1972* (Stanford, CA: Stanford University Press, 2009), 200.

held the university together at times of intense pressure and controversy, that they provided a critical safety valve that kept Princeton from blowing up, from coming apart, under the stressors that afflicted, and in many cases seriously damaged, so many colleges and universities in the late 1960s and early 1970s. The CPUC gave Princeton the infrastructure, the legitimacy, to arrive at decisions as a community. No other major universities—not Harvard, not Columbia, not Yale, not Berkeley—had the capacity to bring the community together to make pressing institutional decisions in an orderly way. The CPUC "didn't intrude on my responsibilities," Bowen reflected years later; "it helped me discharge them."[27]

Not only would the council itself play a central role in enabling the many constituencies in the university community to come together to think through the thorniest issues of the day. A group of standing committees of the council would permit broad participation in setting policy—more precisely, in making policy recommendations to the relevant bodies or individuals, but with the assumption that recommendations carefully arrived at in multi-constituency committees would have a compelling claim to become university policy. The principal committees, as spelled out in the charter of the council, were Rights and Rules, Governance, Priorities, Judicial, and Resources, each with broad scope to address pressing institutional issues.[28] The experience with two of those committees illustrates the significance of the new structure.

The first, the Priorities Committee, chaired by the provost, became the vehicle for setting the university budget. A group of undergraduate students, graduate students, faculty, staff, and alumni, together with cognizant administrators, met in intensive sessions over a several-month period in the fall to listen to and evaluate requests for funding from every part of the university community. This was the group to recommend tuition increases, faculty salary pools, money for additional faculty positions, graduate and under-

27 Bowen oral history, June 25, 2009, 8. For the observations on empowerment of moderate students and the critical role of the CPUC in giving Princeton the infrastructure for community decision making, see Rudenstine interview.

28 "A Proposal to Establish the Council of the Princeton University Community," 1, 8–14.

graduate student financial aid, allocations for the library, and new expenditures in response to specific proposals from entities across the institution. The committee was effective because its members worked very hard and because individuals came to understand quickly (with very few exceptions) that they needed to function with a university-wide view instead of representing their particular constituency. Bowen and other administrators listened carefully to the many different views around the table instead of short-circuiting the discussion to impose their own preferences. And Bowen had great skill in giving everyone his and her say while guiding the group to the right conclusions. Technically, the Priorities Committee made recommendations to the president, who made recommendations to the trustees; in fact, because the committee worked so well, the president and the trustees typically endorsed their recommendations. An intensively participatory process made for better decisions, and made, as well, for decisions that could be more broadly accepted in the larger university community.

There was another interpretation of the Priorities Committee, less favorable, but no less credible: The committee gave the appearance of open, participatory democracy and controlled dissent while allowing a fairly centralized planning authority to proceed without undue objection. In either case, the committee provided a teaching mechanism that attempted to make the whole university better understand the reasoning behind major budgetary decisions. It is no wonder that the Priorities Committee became one of the Princeton innovations most often copied at other colleges and universities.[29]

Strengthening university budgeting practices was no abstract intellectual exercise. Colleges and universities were under intense financial pressure in the late 1960s and early 1970s. Income was down (especially federal support for sponsored research, but also including income from the endowment, private gifts, and foundation and government grants other than sponsored research); costs

29 William McCleery, "One University's Response to Today's Financial Crisis: Interview with William G. Bowen," *University: A Princeton Quarterly* 47 (Winter 1970–71), in *Princeton Alumni Weekly*, Dec. 15, 1970, 43–46.

were up. Deficits were common. The Priorities Committee called it "a new depression in higher education."[30] For Princeton, that meant $1 million in the red in 1969–70, with a projected $2.5 million deficit in 1970–71. Aggressive budget-cutting reduced the shortfall for 1970–71 to $1.5 million. Had the Priorities Committee not recommended major budget cuts for 1971–72, the deficit might have ballooned further. (As it turned out, there was a surplus in 1971–72 of $32,000.)[31] Princeton's approach to budgeting through the priorities process set it apart from other institutions, such that the American Council on Education distributed four thousand copies of the 1971 Priorities Committee report "to serve as a model to other colleges and universities."[32] The cost-cutting at Princeton would continue into the 1970s under Bowen's successors in the provost's office. Wrestling with an unforgiving budget became the leitmotif for the university, as it was for so many other private institutions of higher education.

The second example of CPUC committees in action had to do with the Judicial Committee. In early March 1970, President Nixon's secretary of the interior, Walter J. Hickel, came to the campus to deliver a public speech as part of a Princeton University Conference on "Ecology and Politics in America's Environmental Crisis." The talk, which took place in Jadwin Gymnasium, was disrupted by undergraduates, graduate students, and others not affiliated with the university, who shouted, chanted, and set off noise devices and fireworks that forced cancellation of the discussion that was scheduled to follow the lecture. The students were charged with violating the University Policy on Campus Protests and Demonstrations, a policy adopted by the faculty and the undergraduate student government in February 1969. Because the case involved a major disruption where the students charged were graduate students as well as undergraduates, it was heard by the still-new Judicial Com-

30 "'A New Depression in Higher Education': The Report of the Priorities Committee to the President," *Princeton Alumni Weekly*, Feb. 16, 1971, 8, 10–11.
31 "The Crunch Is Here," *Princeton Alumni Weekly*, Feb. 16, 1971, 6–7; *Princeton University, The President's Report*, Oct. 1971, 20, Goheen, box 119, folder 12; Princeton University news release, Sept. 12, 1972, Bowen president, box 212, folder 3.
32 *Princeton University, The President's Report*, Oct. 1971, 15.

mittee, the first major case to come before that body. The committee assigned disciplinary penalties to eleven undergraduates and one graduate student, who appealed the penalties to the provost, who had been designated by the president to handle the appeal in his place, since Goheen had been the presiding officer in Jadwin and had warned the students to cease the disruption or risk disciplinary action. At the end of April, after reviewing the students' demand that the case be dismissed, Bowen upheld the charges as well as the penalties, with two modifications. "It has become something of a sport," he said, "to mock the traditional values of the university, to downgrade the importance of maintaining various freedoms, including the freedom of discourse, on the ground that we are living in a time when there are pressing social and political problems which cannot be solved by discourse alone. I regard this attitude as short-sighted and self-defeating. The more controversial and divisive the issues, the greater the need to protect this fundamental right of everyone to hear speakers of all persuasions, to question them, and to make up his or her own mind."[33] Within days, actions on the part of the Nixon administration would make "Hickel heckling" and the right to be heard on campus seem almost a quaint relic of a distant past.

Vietnam

The Vietnam War posed huge challenges to colleges and universities. Some institutions found ways to respect and manage the intense campus protests that erupted in the late 1960s and early 1970s in response to highly provocative actions taken by the Johnson and Nixon administrations in Vietnam and Cambodia. At other institutions, buildings were occupied and parts of campuses literally set ablaze, with local police and National Guardsmen forcibly clearing buildings, clubbing and jailing students, and, in extreme cases, shooting and killing them. What determined in which category an

33 Princeton University Newsletter, Apr. 4, 1970; Princeton University news release, Apr. 25, 1970; Princeton University Newsletter, Apr. 27, 1970 (source of the quote), all in Bowen provost, box 21, folder 9; "Report to the President by the Provost for the Year Ended June 30, 1970," Goheen, box 104, folder 4.

institution would fall? On the one hand, principled moral leadership on the part of the president, which Robert F. Goheen surely provided at Princeton. And on the other hand, a clear sense of strategy for how to manage the highly explosive environment, strategy that fell, in the case of Princeton, significantly to William G. Bowen.

Like students at so many colleges and universities in the 1960s, Princeton students were deeply disturbed by American involvement in the war in Vietnam, a war in which it was difficult to discern a clear national interest, a war in which their contemporaries—indeed, their friends and classmates—were being drafted and killed, a war in which repeated American bombing was killing untold numbers of noncombatants and destroying so much of the countryside in Vietnam and later in Cambodia. Distressed by the escalation of the war by presidents Johnson and Nixon, Princeton students—together with faculty members—staged antiwar protests on campus and took part in massive demonstrations in such cities as Washington, DC; New York; and San Francisco.[34]

Local irritants also fueled antiwar sentiment on campus. The university had for the better part of a decade leased a building on a parcel of campus land to the Institute for Defense Analyses for its communications research division. Neither a creature of the federal government nor of the universities, IDA was "an independent corporation" that had been set up to give the federal government "objective analyses of the complex problems affecting the national defense." Princeton was one of a dozen universities to serve IDA as corporate member institutions. No matter that the institutional ties between the university and IDA were tenuous, or that corporate sponsorship of IDA did not make Princeton complicit in defense-related research. Students saw IDA as a symbol of the war that did not belong on their campus. Beginning in 1967, SDS students staged protests, blocking the entrance to the IDA building, and on one occasion, knocking out the dean of students, which resulted in arrests by the police and significant publicity.[35] In November 1967,

34 Allen J. Matusow, *The Unraveling of America: A History of Liberalism in the 1960s* (New York: Harper & Row, 1984), 318–30.

35 Statement by Princeton Students for a Democratic Society, Oct. 23, 1967; Princeton University and IDA, presentation by President Goheen, Oct. 31, 1967 (source of the quote),

seeking to clarify the university's relationship to IDA, the faculty established a committee of seven faculty members, led by Stanley Kelley Jr.; the provost and the chair of the University Research Board served ex officio. Reporting in March 1968, the committee urged that Princeton take joint action with other members of IDA to remove universities from any role in the institute's management or activities.[36] In June, IDA was reorganized to become a corporation of individual members, without institutional sponsors; Princeton severed its institutional ties with IDA, and Goheen left the IDA board in November. Yet Princeton students persisted for many months in staging demonstrations to block entry to the IDA building.[37]

More consequential than the IDA protests were mass actions taken on campus to express opposition to the war. Princeton, like many other campuses, staged a moratorium on October 15, 1969, to engage in discussion of American policy in Vietnam.[38] On November 13, at the call of the president, the faculty, the undergraduate student government, and other groups, there convened an unprecedented, six-hour community assembly in Jadwin Gymnasium, chaired by trustee John Doar, "to provide an opportunity for members of the University community to come together to discuss the issue of American participation in the war in Vietnam." More than three thousand voting participants were present when the evening began, with another four hundred non-voting guests. A number of resolutions were put forward for debate and action. The results were to be communicated to the Nixon administration in an effort to influence national policy.[39]

both in Dean of Students, box 10, folder 19; Edward R. Weidlein III, "On the Campus: 'IDA' Sit-In," *Princeton Alumni Weekly*, Nov. 7, 1967, 6; "University News: 'IDA' Report," *Princeton Alumni Weekly*, Apr. 16, 1968, 5.

36 "University News: 'IDA' Report," *Princeton Alumni Weekly*, Apr. 16, 1968, 5; statement by President Robert F. Goheen, May 1, 1968, Bowen provost, box 24, folder 1.

37 Princeton University news release, Apr. 23, 1969, Bowen provost, box 24, folder 1.

38 Statement by President Robert F. Goheen regarding October 15th "Moratorium," Sept. 25, 1969, Goheen, box 136, folder 1; Faculty Advisory Committee on Policy to Members of the Faculty, Oct. 8, 1969, Bowen provost, box 24, folder 8; Princeton University Newsletter, Oct. 15, 1969, Goheen, box 136, folder 1.

39 Letter to Members of the University Community, Oct. 29, 1969, Bowen provost, box 24, folder 4 (source of the quote); Robert F. Goheen to the *Daily Princetonian*,

On April 30, 1970, President Nixon announced that he had sent two thousand American troops into Cambodia, thus significantly widening American involvement in the war in Southeast Asia. Four days later, Ohio National Guardsmen fatally shot four student antiwar protesters at Kent State University. Campuses around the country exploded in protest, with student strikes at hundreds of colleges and universities. Other schools, though not formally on strike, ended the academic year abruptly, with final examinations postponed or canceled. Ten days after Kent State, two Black students were killed at Jackson State University in Mississippi under circumstances similar to those at Kent State.[40] Events in Cambodia and at Kent State and Jackson State significantly widened support for the antiwar movement, and moderate and even conservative students joined in the outrage of their more liberal and radical peers. President Nixon stoked the flames by publicly deriding student protesters "blowing up the campuses" as "bums."[41]

At Princeton, Nixon's widening of the war into Cambodia, together with the resumption of large-scale bombing in North Vietnam, prompted a call for an emergency meeting in the university chapel on the night of Thursday, April 30. Bowen, on his way to California for board meetings at the Center for Advanced Study in the Behavioral Sciences in Palo Alto, did what he would do again and again in difficult situations over the years: identify faculty members who could help; make sure that they would show up; ask individuals, where appropriate, to speak up for the right point of view; and indeed—again where appropriate—literally manage the

Nov. 6, 1969, Goheen, box 135, folder 6; Princeton University Newsletter, Nov. 11, 1969, Bowen provost, box 24, folder 4; "Princeton Vietnam Assembly," Nov. 13, 1969, Kelley Committee, box 7, folder 9; [Goheen,] "Remarks at Princeton Vietnam Assembly," Nov. 13, 1969, Goheen, box 135, folder 6; "A Summary of the Princeton Vietnam Assembly," Nov. 20, 1969, Bowen provost, box 24, folder 4; "Princeton Vietnam Assembly," Princeton Alumni Weekly, Nov. 25, 1969, 10, 11.

40 Jonathan Schell, The Time of Illusion (New York: Alfred A. Knopf, 1976), 90–102; William E. Leuchtenburg, A Troubled Feast: American Society since 1945 (Boston: Little, Brown, 1973; updated ed., 1983), 244–46; Irwin Unger, The Movement: A History of the American New Left, 1959–1972 (New York: Dodd, Mead, 1974), 185–88; John Morton Blum, Years of Discord: American Politics and Society, 1961–1974 (New York: W. W. Norton, 1991), 367–70.

41 Nixon is quoted in Schell, The Time of Illusion, p. 97.

discussion. In this case, he spent the hours before his departure for California alerting faculty leaders and selected administrators to the chapel meeting and calling on them "to encourage sensible people to come" to the meeting. As well, he spoke to the director of campus security, asking that he and his colleagues be present and ready to respond to whatever might ensue. "As of the moment," he told Goheen, "I am guardedly optimistic that no dire actions will result from the meeting," adding, however, that "any large group, under emotional harangues, is somewhat unpredictable and a cause for concern."[42]

Some 2,500 people, most of them undergraduates, crowded into the chapel. The upshot of the evening was a decision "to call a 'strike' to protest the escalation of the war, pending action of an Assembly of the whole University community called for Monday afternoon."[43] Following a series of campus meetings over the weekend, the Council of the Princeton University Community met in Alexander Hall, the largest auditorium on campus, in a special seven-hour session on Sunday, May 3. Here was the signal test for Bowen and Kelley's faith in the structure of governance as a means for Princeton to weather the disruptions caused by highly destabilizing external developments. The CPUC recommended revised arrangements for end-of-term academic work (recognizing that May 4 would be the last day of classes, with the two-week reading period beginning on May 5), so that students who wished to do so could suspend normal academic activities to devote their full attention to protesting the war. Students could waive further course requirements and gain credit on the basis of work done thus far, or could postpone exams and papers until the fall. Students who wished to do so could complete the semester as scheduled. At the same time, the council recommended a rearrangement of the academic calendar for 1970–71 to institute a two-week recess immediately preceding the November elections, so that students who wished to do so could campaign in local and congressional elections, an effort

42 Memorandum, W. G. Bowen to R. F. Goheen, Apr. 30, 1970, Goheen, box 120, folder 4.

43 Lawrence Stone, "Princeton in the Nation's Service," n.d. [1970], 2, Kelley Committee, box 8, folder 8.

to channel strong concerns about the war into "effective political action." With a general meeting of the university community called for 1:00 p.m. on Monday, May 4, in Jadwin Gym, the council urged the broadest possible attendance.[44]

With some five thousand people in attendance and Stuart Hampshire, the widely respected professor of philosophy, in the chair, the general meeting on Monday adopted the council's recommendations, encouraged widespread efforts to communicate campus views against the war, and urged especially that students, faculty, and staff campaign vigorously to defeat Nixon administration supporters in the coming congressional elections.[45] Holding such a meeting was a risk, Neil Rudenstine reflected; so was allowing a vote on whether Princeton should go on strike. It was Goheen's and Bowen's genius to trust the process to work.[46]

In a series of hours-long, unusually well-attended faculty meetings over four afternoons and evenings, the faculty approved the revision in end-of-term arrangements and the change in the fall academic calendar proposed by the CPUC, and it also debated and approved a number of resolutions about the war: expressing outrage at administration policy and calling for the withdrawal of American forces from Southeast Asia; supporting the student-initiated strike against the war; deploring the killing of students at Kent State by National Guardsmen; calling for a review of university policy on accepting funds from the Department of Defense for sponsored research; endorsing efforts to terminate university relations with the Reserve Officers Training Corps (ROTC); and supporting the initiative of President Goheen in seeking to vacate the lease of the Institute for Defense Analyses.[47] (Goheen announced

44 Princeton University news release, May 4, 1970, Goheen, box 120, folder 4 (source of the quote); "Statement and Recommendations by Its Executive Committee to the Council of the Princeton University Community," May 3, 1970, Kelley Committee, box 7, folder 9.

45 "Report of the Assembly of the Princeton University Community," May 4, 1970; Robert F. Goheen to Members of the Board of Trustees, May 5, 1970, both in Goheen, box 120, folder 4.

46 Rudenstine interview.

47 "Resolution Adopted by the Faculty," May 4, 1970, Kelley Committee, box 8, folder 8; "Major Actions Taken: Faculty Meeting of May 4, 5, 6, and 7, 1970," Goheen, box 120, folder 4; "Abstract of Minutes and Summary of Actions Taken, Faculty

in September that IDA had found land on which to erect a new building.)[48]

Some of this was tough to take for members of the faculty who believed that it was entirely appropriate for individual faculty members to take political positions, but not at all appropriate for the university as an institution to commit to a political stand. All of it was tough to take for many Princeton alumni, a large number of whom were Republicans who were fully supportive of the Nixon administration's actions, and who were skeptical of, if not downright opposed to, the activities on campus. In a talk at reunions, "The Princeton Strike: Princeton in the Nation's Service," Frederick H. Harbison, an economics professor and a member of the class of 1934 who was well known to hold conservative views, sought to reassure his fellow alumni that what was going on at Princeton was not in fact a strike (an action with which he was fully familiar as a labor economist). The students were making no demands of faculty, administrators, or trustees. No one was stopping them from completing their academic work. Rather, what the university had seen in recent weeks was "a *mobilization of concern* over national policy, particularly as it relates to the war in Indochina," together with "a deep university-wide *expression of responsibility to serve*" the nation. The "problems facing the nation are grave," he said, and "members of the Princeton University community are anxious to do something to solve them."[49]

And in a speech at the alumni association meeting during reunions, the senior class president, Stuart Dill, explained his classmates' decision to forgo the usual commencement-related festivities, including marching in the P-Rade, the annual extravaganza in which thousands of alumni and their families paraded through the campus, the younger alumni in class costumes, the older in specially

---

Meetings, May 4, 5, 6, 7, 11, and 12, 1970," Dean of the Faculty, series 1, subseries 1B, box 1, folder 1; Princeton University Newsletter, May 11, 1970, Bowen provost, box 24, folder 2.

48 Luther Munford, "Goheen Says IDA Has Found Land for Move," *Daily Princetonian*, Sept. 11, 1970, Dean of Students, box 10, folder 20.

49 Frederick H. Harbison, "The Princeton 'Strike': In the Nation's Service?," *Princeton Alumni Weekly*, June 30, 1970, 8.

designed class blazers, waving banners and balloons, joined by marching bands, bagpipers, vehicles festooned in orange and black, bicyclists and unicyclists, animals caged or walking under their own steam, and other supporting characters. "Our actions today, as well as the entire strike effort, should not be interpreted as anti-alumni or anti-Princeton. In fact, our class is probably as proud to be a part of Princeton as any other class present here today." The senior class had "chosen this time to demonstrate not against Princeton or its alumni but against certain national policies and their tragic consequences." They were "repudiat[ing] our nation's foreign policy," which had caused "the wanton destruction of the Vietnamese people and their homeland," and had "grossly distorted" the United States's "sense of priorities, diverting attention and necessary resources from pressing domestic needs." "We have not lost faith in our nation or in our university. In fact, our faith is strengthened by our resolve that both our nation and our university can be made more humane."[50]

Bill Bowen was in the midst of all of the major flashpoints that challenged and transformed Princeton in the late 1960s and early 1970s. Figuring out how to manage these tensions became a central part of his portfolio, not by virtue of assignment, but because he had a gift for thinking strategically about constructive ways of responding to the pressures roiling colleges and universities. Foreseeing the range of troubles that might ensue and thinking through the policies that needed to be put in place to address them enabled Bowen to position Princeton to roll with the challenges to come. With the right governance structure in place, with the right regulations, with the right processes established to deal with an incident when it arose, with the faculty behind the administration, Princeton had the ability to withstand the pressures that disrupted so many of its fellow institutions.

"The center held" at Princeton, Rudenstine reflected later, "because, first, Bob Goheen was a steady, wise president of enormous integrity; and second, Bill Bowen was an extraordinary, tal-

---

50 Stuart Dill, "Urgent Business," *Princeton Alumni Weekly*, June 30, 1970, 9.

ented, and engaged provost."[51] Much of Princeton's success in riding out the turmoil of the times can be attributed to Bowen's cool-headedness, strong analytic capacity, and keen sense of how best to position the institution to thrive. As Rudenstine characterized it, Bowen had "the most astute capacity" of anyone he knew "to judge what was needed" and "to come to the right conclusion about what to do." Bowen, Rudenstine said, "really understood the politics of universities" and understood, as well, "the key values that had to be protected." It was an unusual combination among university administrators of the day.[52]

Bowen also knew when to step out front and when to stand back and let the president lead. Goheen was visibly and actively in charge at all the critical moments: He chaired the big meetings in the wake of Cambodia and Kent State, for example—the CPUC meeting and the sequence of faculty meetings throughout the week. He was, Rudenstine reflected, "so willing to be out there in a way [Nathan] Pusey [at Harvard] and [Grayson] Kirk [at Columbia] never were." That was a visibility and engagement that Bowen strongly encouraged.[53]

Looking back years later, Bowen said that he had "contribut[ed] to institutional steadiness" and had helped the institution "weather some rather tough storms." He had "played a part," he said, "along with many others, in helping the university stay on a steady course through really trying days and through days that knocked a lot of institutions off of a steady course." In fact, he, more than any other senior administrator, charted Princeton's path in a way that held the university together in the face of the intense challenges of the times.[54]

---

51 Rudenstine oral history, 27.
52 Rudenstine interview.
53 Ibid.
54 Bowen oral history, June 9, 2009, 18–19. On Bowen's singular role, see also Rudenstine interview.

5

New Man in the President's Office

"A Juggler Who Keeps All the Balls in the Air"

The Bowen presidency began formally with a reaffirmation of the oath of office at the university's opening exercises on September 10, 1972.[1] In his address, Bowen spoke (not surprisingly, perhaps, for a new president just finding his footing) in generalities, almost platitudes: The university, he said, was *"a center of learning."* The key ingredient in the climate of learning, the process of learning, was excellence: excellence as a goal, excellence as a fundamental commitment.[2] To the faculty the next day, Bowen made a similar point. The university, he said, should "continue to stand primarily for two things": the first, "a commitment to excellence, pure and unabashed, without qualification or embarrassment, in all that we do"; the second, "the close integration of undergraduate teaching, graduate teaching, and research."[3] But these were more than platitudes. Bowen made these themes the centerpiece of his presidency. He told his last dean of admission at Princeton, Anthony Cummings, that "you pull places up" by virtue of will and effort, and he insisted on excellence and the highest possible quality in everything he did as president.[4] There would be no better illustration of these com-

1 Dan D. Coyle, memorandum, "Princeton's 227th Year—President William G. Bowen," Sept. 10, 1972, Bowen president, box 403, folder 8.
2 "The Address of President William G. Bowen at the Opening Exercises for Princeton University's 227th Year," Sept. 10, 1972, Bowen president, box 403, folder 8.
3 WGB notes for meeting of the faculty, Sept. 11, 1972, Bowen president, box 283, folder 1.
4 Interview with Anthony M. Cummings, Mar. 22, 2019, Princeton, NJ.

mitments than Bowen's strong efforts to increase the "intellectual muscle" of the faculty.[5]

Assembling the New Administration

First, though, Bowen needed to put an administrative team in place to help him run the institution. Unlike any Princeton president before him (or any other president of an Ivy League institution), he made a deliberate effort to find women he could appoint.[6] Most of the candidates proposed to him would have been too junior for senior posts, but Bowen had one that he wanted to pursue. He tried unsuccessfully to bring to Princeton Hanna Holborn Gray, then a professor of history at the University of Chicago. The instinct was on the mark: Gray was about to embark on a meteoric administrative career as dean of the college of arts and sciences at Northwestern University, provost and acting president at Yale, and president for fifteen years at Chicago, the first woman to serve as president of a major university in the United States. But Bowen's approach, coming just before Gray's appointment at Northwestern, was ham-handed and ill-timed (she, however, thought it was amusing). He took Gray to lunch, where, as she tells it, they had "a vigorous and enjoyable discussion about all kinds of issues." Then, "out of the blue," Bowen asked whether she "might consider an administrative position at Princeton." She declined, thanking him for his interest, whereupon he said, "Oh, what a shame. We need some *older* people in my administration." Gray, just forty-one, was all of three years older than Bowen. Yet, as she said later, she always thought of him as older, "because of his wisdom and his commanding habit of authority."[7]

5 Bowen oral history, Sept. 18, 2009, 25; Sept. 28, 2009, 12.

6 William G. Bowen to Patricia Graham, Jan. 26, 1972; Bowen to Phyllis Zetlin Boring, Feb. 4, 1972; Bowen to Ruth Silva, Feb. 4, 1972; Margaret D. Wilson to Caroline Mercer, Feb. 28, 1972; Elga Wasserman to Bowen, Mar. 21, 1972, all in Bowen president, box 48, folder 2.

7 Hanna Holborn Gray, "Afterword: William G. Bowen," in Kevin M. Guthrie, ed., *Ever the Leader: Selected Writings, 1995–2016, William G. Bowen* (Princeton, NJ: Princeton University Press, 2018), 313.

For provost Bowen chose Sheldon Hackney, an accomplished historian of the American South; a fabled teacher; a native of Birmingham, Alabama; a Navy man; and a graduate of Vanderbilt with a doctorate from Yale. Cool, laid back, ironic—in personal style, that is, Bowen's opposite—Hackney was a fiercely competitive tennis player who could easily hold his own on the other side of the net in playing Bowen. He was a man very much of Bowen's generation (just two months younger than the new president). "I chose him," Bowen later told an interviewer, "because, first of all, I thought he was exceptionally talented, not only as a scholar and teacher—he was terrific in those roles—but also he had very good leadership qualities, and his manner . . . was sufficiently different from mine to provide a nice complementarity of styles."[8]

The dean of the faculty position would open up in Bowen's second year as president, with the retirement from that post of the economist Richard A. Lester. Bowen announced that he would then move the dean of the graduate school, physicist Aaron Lemonick, into Lester's position. Warm, passionate, deeply committed to Princeton's mission of teaching and scholarship, Lemonick was the other insider who had been taken seriously as a candidate for president. Ten years older than Bowen and Hackney, he would be the first Jew in a senior academic post at Princeton.[9]

The dean of the college, Edward D. Sullivan, professor of Romance languages and literatures, had been appointed by the trustees to a second five-year term, beginning July 1, 1971, but Bowen had other ideas. Looking five to ten years ahead, he had concluded that it was "time for a change," he told Sullivan. It was important "to establish the principle that good people can do these adm[inistrative] jobs for a time and then can renew themselves in teaching and res[earch]." Bowen gave Sullivan a year's leave and appointed him to an honorific professorship, the Avalon Foundation Chair in the Humanities, and, within two years, to the chairmanship of the university's Council of the Humanities.[10] Having

8 Bowen oral history, Sept. 18, 2009, 16.

9 Princeton University news release, Jan. 19, 1972, Bowen president, box 48, folder 2.

10 Typescript, RFG [Robert F. Goheen], "Board Meeting, Reelection of Dean Sullivan," April [1971]; handwritten note, Richard A. Lester to Robert F. Goheen, Jan. 5, 1972, both

Sullivan give up the deanship allowed Bowen to move Neil Rudenstine from dean of students to dean of the college. Five years later, in 1977, Bowen named Rudenstine provost.[11]

And Bowen made good on his determination to appoint women to the senior administrative ranks. To succeed Rudenstine as dean of students in 1972, he brought to Princeton Adele Smith Simmons, a Radcliffe graduate with a PhD in African history from Oxford who was serving as dean of Jackson College at Tufts University.[12] And in 1977 Bowen executed what appeared to be a double coup by appointing two women academic deans, the first such appointments (save for Hanna Gray) in the Ivy League: for the graduate school, Nina Garsoian, a Byzantine historian on the faculty at Columbia University, and for the college, Joan Stern Girgus, a psychologist serving as dean of the division of social science at City College of the City University of New York.[13] While Garsoian—clearly not well-matched to an administrative post—left after two years, Girgus served for a decade, whereupon Bowen appointed another woman, professor of history Nancy J. Weiss, to succeed her.

As well, Bowen succeeded in his desire to bring to Princeton a highly experienced senior woman administrator who would embody unique wisdom and gravitas. The woman in question was Mary Ingraham (Polly) Bunting, who, after her retirement from the presidency of Radcliffe College in 1972, accepted Bowen's invitation to come to Princeton for three years as assistant to the president for special projects. (President Goheen had asked in 1970 that

in Bowen president, box 302, folder 4; William G. Bowen, "Aide Memoire," Jan. 10, 1972, Faculty Files, Edward D. Sullivan file; Bowen, handwritten notes, "Conversation with Ed Sullivan" ("time for a change"; "good people"), n.d. [Jan. 10, 1972], Bowen president, box 302, folder 4.

11 Hackney had left Princeton in 1975 to become president of Tulane University and was succeeded by the labor economist Albert Rees, but the fit was not a comfortable one for Rees, and he returned to the faculty after two years (soon thereafter, he left Princeton to take up the presidency of the Alfred P. Sloan Foundation), creating a vacancy that Rudenstine quickly filled. Princeton University news releases, Feb. 3, 25, 1977; Alfred P. Sloan Foundation news release, Mar. 9, 1979, all in Bowen president, box 299, folder 5.

12 William G. Bowen to Department Chairmen et al., Apr. 15, 1972, Bowen president, box 48, folder 2.

13 Virginia Kays Creesy, "Princeton Portrait: Dean Nina G. Garsoian," *Princeton Alumni Weekly*, Feb. 7, 1977, 12; and "Princeton Portrait: Dean Joan S. Girgus," May 16, 1977, 12.

Bunting join the Princeton board, but she had declined on the grounds that the confusion and complexity surrounding the failure of the proposal to merge Radcliffe with Harvard left her more than fully occupied in Cambridge.)[14] Bunting set up a program in continuing education, advised Bowen about a range of educational issues, gave moral and practical support to women faculty and staff, and provided counsel and wisdom on a host of other issues. By bringing someone of Bunting's stature to the university, Bowen conveyed a powerful message: Princeton had to move forward, and change—orderly, constructive change—was coming.[15]

Of all of Bowen's appointments, Neil Rudenstine would prove to be the most important. As different as they were in personality, background, and outlook on the world, the two men came to the same conclusions and shared fundamental values and beliefs—about universities, what it would take to protect them and keep them whole, how to ensure not only their survival but their flourishing. They were prepared to work hard—very hard—to do everything necessary to accomplish that goal. They thought alike, reasoned similarly, analyzed problems and situations similarly, and assessed people similarly. They had forged a close working relationship when Bowen was provost and Rudenstine dean of students. "We hit it off right from the beginning," Bowen later told an interviewer. "It was obvious to me that this was an exceedingly able person who could help us tremendously in an area where we really needed help because student life issues were so gripping and so challenging in . . . that whole time of turbulence. So we just became both close colleagues and good friends from that day until today."[16] Rudenstine, he said, was "simply outstanding, brilliant, as the dean of students"; he was "so steady, so intelligent. . . . He always responded thoughtfully to whatever transpired."[17] As we have seen, Rudenstine took a similar view of Bowen, whom he

14 Mary Ingraham Bunting to Robert F. Goheen, Apr. 28, 1970; Goheen to Bunting, May 15, 1970, both in Goheen, box 69, folder 3.
15 Elaine Yaffe, *Mary Ingraham Bunting: Her Two Lives* (Savannah, GA: Frederic C. Beil, 2005), 273–80.
16 Bowen oral history, June 9, 2009, 16–17.
17 Ibid., June 25, 2009, 3.

called "an extraordinary, talented and engaged provost"; he later told an interviewer that their connection had grown and deepened during his service as dean of the college. From the time Bowen invited Rudenstine to be provost, the collaboration grew "even closer."[18] Bowen called Rudenstine "without doubt, my closest steady colleague" during the two decades they worked together in the Princeton administration.[19]

Bowen said that "Princeton hit the proverbial home run when Neil Rudenstine moved into the provost job," and he characterized Rudenstine as "the ablest academic administrator I have ever known." Rudenstine, he elaborated, "just saw around corners when a lot of people didn't even realize there was a corner there, and he could parse out the pros and cons of any issue very quickly, very rigorously, and he had superb judgment plus patience, a remarkable ability to deal with people of all kinds, and, of course, a deep understanding of what the educational purpose of the university was. So he was terrific. It was the best single appointment, certainly, that I made."[20]

Bowen had full confidence in Rudenstine to make the right decisions, to act for him and for the institution, to execute the most sensitive and difficult assignments, to take on the most intractable challenges, as Bowen himself would have done. "It was often said," Bowen remarked, "that Princeton was able to accomplish a lot during the years that we worked together . . . because it had in effect two presidents and two provosts. We saw our roles as really interchangeable, and when there was something that normally would have been the provost's responsibility that I could do better or I was able to do, available to do, I did it, and when there was something that might have been the president's role that he could do, he did it. We almost never went to a meeting together. We divided up the world, and if one of us was there, that was enough, because we had, I think, a very clear view of what the other one was thinking."[21]

18 Rudenstine oral history, 27–28.
19 Bowen oral history, June 9, 2009, 16.
20 Ibid., Sept. 18, 2009, 18.
21 Ibid., 18–19.

In the words of Eugene Y. Lowe Jr., trustee and later dean of students, the two men "complemented each other" and could "anticipate each other" in remarkable ways. The partnership was "legendary," Bowen's assistant and later vice president for public affairs, Robert K. Durkee, said; Bowen had "absolute confidence" in Rudenstine's judgment. The two were "a great team," Richard R. Spies, whom Bowen brought into the provost's office, reflected; there was "great complementarity" between them, and Rudenstine had an unusual gift for translating Bowen's guidance into terms that other colleagues could understand and act on. Indeed, as Joan Girgus pointed out, Rudenstine was the only person among Bowen's fellow cabinet members whom he would allow "to manage a situation completely on his own."[22]

When substantive questions came to the president's cabinet, they had generally been talked through first by Bowen and Rudenstine. When difficult issues arose—trying to negotiate an agreement with a group of eating clubs, for example, or thinking through the university's position on sexual harassment—Bowen invariably turned to Rudenstine to take them on. When Bowen—always so sure of himself, almost always right—made a mistake, whether a mistake about people, or a mistake about how to handle a situation, he could be slow to acknowledge that he had been wrong. Rudenstine had an almost unique ability to persuade him to think again, to reconsider his judgment.[23] And Rudenstine had the ear of the faculty; he forged strong relationships with senior professors, especially in the humanities and social sciences, and he was very well informed about departmental aspirations and concerns. Invariably, as faculty members knew, what they told Rudenstine would be reported reliably to Bowen.[24]

22 Interview with Eugene Y. Lowe Jr., Nov. 6, 2018, Evanston, IL; interview with Richard R. Spies, July 24, 2018, Princeton, NJ; interview with Robert K. Durkee, July 9, 2018, Princeton, NJ; interview with Joan S. Girgus, Sept. 12, 2018, Princeton, NJ.
    23 Spies interview.
    24 Interview with Stanley N. Katz, July 18, 2018, Princeton, NJ.

Running the Place "like It Was His Small Town"

The pace of work in the new administration was extraordinary. Bowen himself worked all the time, usually at lightning speed, and he expected his colleagues to keep up with him. He was like "a juggler" who "keeps all the balls in the air," his executive assistant, Marcia H. Snowden, said—"involved in everything," from the "grand scheme" to the smallest details.[25] Ruth J. Simmons, who began at Princeton as a residential college director of studies and later filled other roles in the central administration, commented that Bowen had made "a lasting impression" on her by seeming "to be everywhere at the same time," "walking through the campus, paying attention to small things"—a "powerful symbol" of a president "being involved across the campus, put[ting] his hands into everything," an approach Simmons herself adopted when she became president of Smith College and, later, Brown University.[26] Richard Spies was finishing his PhD in economics when Bowen brought him into the provost's office in 1971 to do a study of rising costs in selective colleges; when Bowen became president, he asked Spies to stay on as Hackney's numbers person. Bowen had a way, Spies observed, of "intensifying every conversation," of making the person he was talking to "feel that it was the most important thing in the world to get this right"—"and the most important thing for *you* to get it right." There was no issue, Spies said, that was "too small to get that intense treatment from Bill."[27]

One of Bowen's trustees, Nancy Peretsman, said that he "ran the place like it was his small town." He was into everything; he knew everything that was going on, and he believed—possibly correctly—that he could do any job in the university at least as well as the incumbent.[28] Bowen's first dean of admission, Timothy Callard, said that the president's drive and intensity, his commitment to excellence, inspired his colleagues to work harder, strive to do better,

---

25 Interview with Marcia H. Snowden, June 25, 2018, Lawrenceville, NJ.
26 Interview with Ruth J. Simmons, Oct. 4, 2019, Princeton, NJ.
27 Spies interview.
28 Interview with Nancy Peretsman, Aug. 13, 2018, New York City.

and reach for higher standards.[29] For Bowen's assistant Carol Herring, who was in charge of research for annual reports, speeches,
and other writing projects, working for Bowen was like "getting
another college education."[30] Herring's successor, Georgia Elliott,
said that Bowen's effusive praise for her writing motivated her to
work that much harder.[31]

As Bowen's colleagues learned, he had some mantras that expressed his sense of how to do business. From his Princeton economics professor Jacob Viner came the insight that "there is no
limit to the amount of nonsense one can propound if one is thinking
alone." The oft-repeated observation "people come in packages"
meant that one needed to appreciate strengths and discount or compensate for weaknesses. "Doubts increase" signaled that uncertainty
about a person's qualifications should be resolved by passing on an
appointment. "Press on" meant to persist in the work at hand.
And "madness!" meant, simply, that—an idea or a situation made
little or no sense.

Bowen went home every night for dinner with Mary Ellen and
the children. It was an easy trip; Walter Lowrie House, the president's residence, was at 83 Stockton Street, just a half mile down
Nassau Street from Nassau Hall. There was family conversation of
the usual sort—each of the children was asked what happened in
his or her day, and Bowen told stories about people and situations
he had encountered. But the dinner table involved much more than
casual conversation. Bowen wanted Mary Ellen's reactions and advice on difficult challenges—Shelby Cullom Davis and Concerned
Alumni of Princeton; eating club issues; the brief he was preparing
for the United States Supreme Court in the *Bakke* case on the use
of race as a factor in college and university admissions. He would
"talk through what he was wrestling with," his son, David, said.
Mary Ellen was a "trusted adviser," and he wanted to know what
she thought. "Do you agree? Am I missing something? What do you
think I should do?"[32]

29 Telephone interview with Timothy C. Callard, June 18, 2018.
30 Interview with Carol P. Herring, Oct. 23, 2018, Princeton, NJ.
31 Telephone interview with Georgia Elliott, Sept. 7, 2019.
32 Interview with David Bowen, Sept. 29, 2018, Princeton, NJ.

Bowen then normally returned to the office after dinner to tackle more work. He would be on the phone to colleagues late at night and early in the morning. "Did I catch you at a bad time?" he might be gracious enough to ask when he phoned late in the evening or on weekends.[33] The early morning calls came at 6:30 or 7:00 a.m., so early that some of the wives talked with Mary Ellen to establish a no-calls-before-8:00 a.m. rule for weekend mornings to protect some semblance of family time for staff, especially those who had young children.[34] At a tribute to Bowen (more likely a roast) on his departure from Princeton, Marcia Snowden reported, tongue in cheek, that telephone records showed that she and Carl Wartenburg (then assistant to the president) had received phone calls from Bowen before 8:00 a.m. on fifty-one of the fifty-two previous Sundays—the only exception on a Sunday when Bowen was on Samothrace, a Greek island in the northern Aegean Sea, and miscalculated the time difference.[35]

Nor did Bowen have a good sense of the need of his colleagues to prepare for and observe holidays. He knew when it was Christmas Eve (or was prompted by Mary Ellen to know)—and to show up at the homes of selected administrators and faculty members to deliver bottles of wine as Christmas gifts. And yet he was oblivious enough to call his president's office researcher-speechwriter Georgia Elliott one Christmas Eve with his usual request—"Could you get me . . ." She told him, "I have two pies in the oven. I'll get to it first thing Monday morning."[36] On another Christmas Eve when Bowen was at the Mellon Foundation, he and the economist Allen Sanderson were in the foundation's Princeton office, sorting through data. It got to be dinnertime, and Sanderson was looking at his watch. "Do you have to be somewhere?" Bowen asked him, oblivious to the date. Go home and be with your family, Bowen

33 Snowden interview. See also telephone interview with Louise H. Bessire, June 11, 2019.
34 Durkee interview; Marcia Snowden in "Administrative Staff Council tribute to William G. Bowen and Neil L. Rudenstine," Jan. 5, 1988, tape courtesy of Marcia Snowden.
35 Administrative Staff Council tribute.
36 Elliott interview.

urged. Two hours later, Bowen showed up at the Sandersons' home, a bottle of champagne in hand.[37]

The atmosphere in One Nassau Hall lightened up, literally as well as figuratively. In place of the dark leather-and-mahogany men's club style of the Goheen era, the president's office was painted white, with modern furniture, modern art, and fabric sculptures (one a moose head, another an octopus) made by Karen Bowen.[38] As hard as Bowen pushed his staff to work, he also joked with them, traded stories with them, and created a familial (if highly intense) atmosphere. He made it his business to take care of them. If someone fell ill, he would do everything he could to find the right doctor.[39] If someone was celebrating a birthday or a wedding anniversary, he would deliver a bottle of wine or champagne. All of that led staff members to feel a great sense of loyalty to him; as Princeton's first general counsel, Thomas H. Wright Jr., put it, "You wanted to be on the team and pull your weight."[40] But there were limits to caretaking. Once two women in the office quickly exited the bathroom in the suite, alarmed by the presence of a frighteningly large cockroach. Bowen came along—"What's the matter, ladies? I'll take care of it." But as soon as he went into the bathroom, he came back out, slamming the door, guarding it with outstretched arms, and exclaiming, "Call Public Safety!"[41]

Bowen was intense, but he was informal: informal in dress, informal in behavior, informal in interactions with his colleagues. His office notwithstanding, there was no pretense about him. In his

37 Telephone interview with Michael S. McPherson, Aug. 20, 2020.

38 "The University: Changing of the Guard," *Princeton Alumni Weekly*, Sept. 26, 1972, 8.

39 When the university photographer, John W. H. Simpson '66, survived a terrible automobile accident that landed him in the critical-care unit of the Burn Center at Crozer-Chester Medical Center in Chester, PA, Bowen called the center weekly during his three-month stay to check on his progress. And when Simpson came home for weekends from a second hospital, Bowen came to his house for an extended visit, "just talking." John W. H. Simpson, letter to the editor, *Princeton Alumni Weekly*, Feb. 10, 1988, 3.

40 Interview with Thomas H. Wright Jr., June 29, 2018, Princeton, NJ. On Bowen's kindness to members of the staff, see also interview with Judith B. Walzer, July 5, 2018, Princeton, NJ; interview with Van Zandt Williams Jr., July 12, 2018, Princeton, NJ; Callard interview.

41 Interview with Lee T. Nolan, June 27, 2018, Princeton, NJ.

words, he "work[ed] and liv[ed] simple."[42] His "usual uniform" was a navy blazer and gray pants, which he bought at Jos. A. Banks. Mary Ellen Bowen remembered him once buying a suit at Harry Ballot, generally regarded as the third-tier men's shop in Princeton (Robert Goheen bought his suits at the first-tier shop, Langrock's), and later one at Brooks Brothers.[43]

Bowen's cars were a prime example of living simple—"always . . . inexpensive," always "driven . . . for a long time." His first car during his time in the president's office was "an ancient Dodge Dart." Its successor: a similarly unpretentious Chevrolet, affectionately dubbed "Mr. Chevy." The Dodge was in terrible shape, to the point where the floor in the back seat had rusted through, and the back door could not be opened from the inside. Cynthia Nitta, one of the students who lived with the Bowens in Lowrie House, sometimes got a ride to campus with Bowen. She was "startled," she said, "by how basic his transportation was." Bowen was perfectly comfortable transporting trustees in the Dodge. (One of them, Poss Parham, remembered it as an "ancient little rattletrap.") David Bowen recalled his embarrassment in 1979 at being asked to take the Dodge to drive an honorary degree recipient from the honorary degrees dinner at Lowrie House to lodgings in town. One morning, Anthony J. Maruca, vice president for administration, who understood Italian, heard two Italian groundskeepers outside Nassau Hall commenting on Bowen's car. "Why do you suppose the president drives such a pile of junk?" one of them asked. "Maybe they don't pay him any better than they pay us!" the other responded.[44]

A third example of living simple: Bowen's catholic taste in food. Frederick H. Borsch, Bowen's dean of the chapel, told the story of encountering Bowen at the Burger King on Nassau Street. Burger

---

42 Quoted in David Bowen, remarks at memorial service for William G. Bowen, Princeton University Chapel, Dec. 11, 2016, courtesy of David Bowen.

43 E-mail, Mary Ellen Bowen to Nancy W. Malkiel, Aug. 6, 2021.

44 David Bowen, remarks at memorial service; William G. Bowen, *Lessons Learned: Reflections of a University President* (Princeton, NJ: Princeton University Press, 2011), 83n11 (source of the quotes); e-mail, James C. Parham Jr. to Nancy W. Malkiel, July 16, 2018; telephone interview with Cynthia Nitta, Aug. 31, 2019.

King was the first fast food chain to come to Princeton, and "not a few faculty" and townspeople had vowed that they would never frequent the establishment. That made Borsch more than diffident about being seen there. "There was a day, however—something like 1:45 in the afternoon when this Dean of the Chapel was walking by hungry and lured by the smell of the french fries," he recalled. "I peered in, hoping not to see anyone who would recognize me. I rather slinked down the long passage to place my order, relieved that I knew no one. But, while contemplating what I might have, I felt this finger in the middle of my back—a finger, I learned as I turned, belonging to the President of the University."[45]

What was in no way simple was Bowen's relationship with the university tennis courts. As often as possible, he spent lunch hours playing tennis with faculty colleagues. Sheldon Hackney noted Bowen's extraordinary powers of concentration. "What really amazes me is his ability to come to a tennis game with a clear mind, fresh out of a long and difficult meeting, and to completely slip out of his other roles for that hour. Unlike me, he doesn't carry his problems with him to the court." Charles Westoff, professor of sociology and later director of the Office of Population Research, was a good friend and frequent opponent. "The guy has an uncanny sense of where you're going to hit the ball," he said of Bowen. "There's something subliminal about it, and even he can't explain how he can predict, with almost 90 percent accuracy, whether I'm going to hit to his left or his right. His radar is always clicking, so that he knows what's going on around him, even in the next court."[46]

Bowen hated to lose and expected to win; one frequent partner, history professor Robert Tignor, said that "if he regularly lost to somebody, he'd take that person off his schedule."[47] The more Bowen complimented his opponent ("beautiful shot," "great shot"), the more it meant that he was winning. The legendary basketball coach Pete Carril was on an adjacent court one day when Bowen

45 Typescript, Frederick H. Borsch, Bill Bowen family service homily, Princeton University Chapel, Oct. 26, 2016, courtesy of Hanns Kuttner.

46 Hackney and Westoff quoted in Ellen Foley James, "WGB from A to Z," *Princeton Alumni Weekly*, Jan. 25, 1972, 12–13, Bowen president, box 402, folder 1.

47 Interview with Robert L. Tignor, Sept. 24, 2019, Princeton, NJ.

was playing Westoff. Westoff hit the ball out and called it in. Ten minutes later, he did the same thing. Bowen said, "Nice shot, Charlie. Unbelievable. How'd you ever get that one?" Bowen beat Westoff 6–0, 6–1.[48]

Bowen was intent on continuing to teach undergraduates. Having to give up Economics 101 was part of the reason he had hesitated about accepting the presidency. While he relinquished the lectures, he insisted on teaching a class section in the course every year that he was president, save for the brief period in the 1980s when he was in the midst of the most intense travel for A Campaign for Princeton. Michele Warman '82 recalled the Bowen playbook in the classroom: calling on students without prior warning with carefully sequenced questions to encourage them to explicate the issues at hand; close reading and commenting on their written work; class Christmas parties at Lowrie House.[49] Bowen relished the interaction with students; he stayed in touch with many of them through their careers at Princeton and, for some, well beyond that. The *New York Times* featured him as one of a "Rare Species: College Chiefs Who Teach." "I do it," he told the reporter, "for the most selfish reason—I enjoy it."[50] By showing that teaching undergraduates was an important part of the work of the Princeton president, Bowen created a model for his successors in the office, all of whom have continued to teach. His example extended beyond Princeton; he "created a model for the rest of us to emulate," Morton Schapiro, president successively of Williams College and Northwestern University, reflected. "As I prepare my syllabus . . . while writing a new preface for the paperback edition of my latest book . . . I give all the credit to Bill for being able to teach and publish while being an administrator of the highest

<hr>

48 Telephone interview with Peter J. Carril, July 17, 2018 ("beautiful shot," "great shot"); interview with Charles F. Westoff, July 3, 2018, Princeton, NJ; interview with James Wickenden, June 22, 2018, Princeton, NJ. The Bowen-Westoff story was recounted by Carril at the Administrative Staff Council tribute.

49 Telephone interview with Michele Warman, Mar. 18, 2022.

50 Kathryn Sullivan, "Rare Species: College Chiefs Who Teach," *New York Times*, Apr. 24, 1983, https://www.nytimes.com/1983/04/24/education/higher-education-rare-species-college-chiefs-who-teach.html, accessed Apr. 20, 2022.

order. While I clearly am no Bill Bowen—nobody is—he is the reason some of us try so hard."[51]

Of necessity, like most presidents, Bowen traveled all the time—early on in his tenure in the office, he spoke at fifteen to twenty alumni events a year; when the capital campaign was in full swing, the pace picked up, divided between lunches or dinners with small groups of prospects and fund-raising calls to close deals with the most important donors. He routinely left items (usually of clothing) behind; Lee T. Nolan, who served for many years as the receptionist in the president's office, had a standing relationship with a men's store on Nassau Street that carried Bowen's sizes and could replace a missing shirt or raincoat on short notice.[52] (Decades later, working on one of many books to be published by Princeton University Press, he left his laptop, containing the manuscript, in a taxi. Luckily, the next passenger retrieved it and called him to arrange to return it to him.)[53] On the way home from his travels, whether on the plane, in the airport, or in a car, Bowen spent the time in transit dictating letters of thanks and follow-up. The same was true when the Bowens went to their house in Avalon on the Jersey Shore: Mary Ellen drove, and Bill spent the time dictating. Members of his staff marveled at his ability to use the dictating machine to produce clear, well-organized prose.[54]

When Bowen spoke, he was a master at commanding an audience: focused, intent, expert at presenting his argument, interspersing humor with the case for Princeton. He thrived in question-and-answer settings—he "relished the give and take of the platform" and had a "stunning command of detail" as well as an "amazing store of knowledge," which he used to excellent effect.[55] He loved to tell stories. A favorite, which he recounted frequently, came from

51 E-mail, Morton O. Schapiro to Nancy Weiss Malkiel, Dec. 27, 2021.
52 Nolan interview. At the Administrative Staff Council tribute, Marcia Snowden (only partly tongue in cheek) listed all the lost items she had tried to find for Bowen, from raincoats to briefcases and dictating machines.
53 I am indebted to Peter J. Dougherty for this story.
54 Durkee interview.
55 Ibid.

his friend Ezra Zilkha, an Iraqi-born Babylonian Jew, the scion of a Middle Eastern banking family who built a second life in New York as a financier, investor, and philanthropist. Zilkha, who was also a Princeton parent, liked to tell the story of "the condemned prisoner who was asked by the sultan if he had a last wish. The prisoner said that if he were given a year's reprieve, he could make the sultan's favorite black horse talk. So the sultan reprieved him for a year, and as the prisoner returned to fetch his clothes from the jail, his friends asked how it was that he had been set free. He told them the reason the sultan had reprieved him, and they asked how it was possible for him to accomplish this. He replied, 'Well, in one year I could die naturally, the sultan could die, the horse could die, or, who knows, I might make the black horse talk.' That is the reason I am in favor of improvising," Zilkha said. "Time, if we use it, might make us adapt and maybe, who knows, find solutions." Zilkha added a Princeton riff to the story: "The Princetons of this world must be preserved and encouraged, for in places like Princeton it is possible that we might educate people who could make the black horse talk."[56]

If anyone could have made the black horse talk, it would have been Bowen. He was focused, intent, deeply immersed in the details of everything at Princeton, able to analyze virtually any situation and propose a credible course of action. It seemed to knowledgeable observers—and this was only a modest exaggeration—that he knew everything and could make anything happen. His longtime friend and trustee W. Michael Blumenthal, chair and chief executive officer of Bendix, secretary of the treasury in the Carter administration, and subsequently chair and chief executive officer of Burroughs Corporation and Unisys, described Bowen this way: "My impression of him is that he had his finger . . . in every pie and I think ears on everything that was going on in the university, and if he didn't do it directly, he had spies that did it for him. I think

<hr>

56 Ezra K. Zilkha with Ken Emerson, *From Baghdad to Boardrooms: My Family's Odyssey* (self-published, 1999), 174.

nothing was happening at Princeton while Bill was there that Bill wasn't aware of."[57]

How Bowen would exercise those habits became clear as he addressed his highest priorities for Princeton: building the intellectual strength of the faculty and making the university more inclusive and welcoming to a more diverse population of faculty and students.

---

[57] Blumenthal oral history, 32.

6

Building Intellectual Muscle

"Making Princeton Stronger in Terms of Scholarship and Teaching"

Bowen talked at length about his objectives as president in a series of oral history interviews done two decades after he left office. "Building intellectual muscle was number one," he declared. "The most important goal always for me," he elaborated, was to "make Princeton a stronger place in terms of its scholarship, in terms of its teaching capacities at both graduate and undergraduate levels." While Princeton was clearly first or second in the country in departments like math or physics, there were many others that were less distinguished. Bowen was determined to change that by "strengthening the faculty . . . and recruiting absolutely top people from all over the world who would sustain great departments like mathematics and build great departments where there weren't great departments, molecular biology being the most dramatic example."[1]

Building the faculty, he thought, was "the most important single job" he had. "I felt that from the first day, and I felt it the last day I was in the president's office. And so I spent an enormous amount of time on faculty development, faculty recruitment, faculty retention."[2] In his first year in office, he told the *Daily Princetonian* that he was spending 20 to 30 percent of his time wooing

---

1 Bowen oral history, Sept. 18, 2009, 25. On "intellectual muscle," see also Sept. 28, 2009, 12.
2 Bowen oral history, June 25, 2009, 20–21.

top academic talent, a proportion that would certainly increase over the years. It was, he said, "the most important" segment of his time.[3] Bowen made essentially the same point at his last faculty meeting. The minutes record, "The President said that his greatest satisfaction had been working with the Faculty, in attracting and promoting outstanding individuals to its ranks, and in participating in the never-ending task of building a faculty."[4]

Building the faculty was by no means unique to Princeton. The historian of education Roger L. Geiger has noted that just in the period 1969–74, "the average public Research 1 university added 250 faculty (18 percent), and the private ones added 400 (55 percent)."[5] What Bowen was doing was not that different from what was going on at Princeton's peer institutions, but his activity allows us to see up close in granular detail how the process of faculty building at a leading university actually worked.

Faculty Recruitment

Bowen knew exactly the kind of talent he was looking for: "I had . . . a pretty clear view of what kinds of people we wanted to recruit . . . people who were not only great individually, but could attract other able people. I think sometimes it's not understood that having outstanding faculty leadership is crucial with the other faculty in the department." ". . . I just felt it was so central," he continued, "because if you had good leadership in key departments, everything was possible. If you didn't, nothing was possible. So I took tremendously seriously working directly with chairmen and directly with faculty on faculty recruitment. It was a very satisfying role, and it was something, actually, that I was good at, and it paid off tremendously for Princeton." Bowen's formula for success was, in short: "recruiting the right leadership in the absolutely

3 Bowen quoted in Kerry North, "Bowen Woos Academic Talent, Recruits Professors," *Daily Princetonian*, Nov. 15, 1972, p. 1.

4 Faculty meeting minutes, Jan. 4, 1988, Dean of the Faculty, series 1, Faculty Meetings and Minutes, subseries 1A, vol. 35.

5 Roger L. Geiger, *American Higher Education since World War II: A History* (Princeton, NJ: Princeton University Press, 2019), 262.

pivotal fields . . . and giving the leadership the resources and the support that they need to build and do their work."[6]

At a time of constrained budgets, amassing those resources was not easy to do. It meant, Bowen said later, "using whatever resources we could get—obtained by economies or whatever."[7] While financial stringency pushed the dean of the faculty to institute tenure flow plans, showing each department the number of tenure appointments it could make in the foreseeable future, Bowen himself created a competitive target of opportunity program, with separate resources available to departments that identified truly exceptional candidates for appointment. He had dual objectives: to find outstanding scholars and to increase the diversity of the faculty. The point was to build "excellence and diversity" through appointments that would "promise a significant and continuing lift to the teaching, research, and general intellectual leadership in a department . . . and for the University community as a whole." There would be special attention to women and minority candidates. (The target of opportunity program had to be suspended for a time in the 1970s in the face of extraordinary pressures on the budget.)[8]

The payoff was considerable. Bowen thought that the humanities needed a particular boost, and boosted they were with the appointments in the 1970s of the prolific scholar of nineteenth- and twentieth-century European literature Victor Brombert, "the most distinguished 'modernist' working today in French in America," recruited from Yale, in comparative literature and Romance

6 Bowen oral history, June 25, 2009, 25, 21, 28.

7 Ibid., Sept. 28, 2009, 12.

8 Re tenure flow plans, see, e.g., Aaron Lemonick, sample staffing authorization memorandum for 1976–77, Dec. 18, 1975, Bowen president, box 212, folder 6; memoranda re tenure flow revisions, Lemonick to Chairmen of Departments and Directors of Programs, Sept. 15, 1976, Sept. 20, 1977, both in Rees and Rudenstine provost, box 83, folder 7; Sept. 20, 1978, Rees and Rudenstine provost, box 88, folder 9; Sept. 19, 1985, Dean of the Faculty, series 4, box 140. Re the target of opportunity program, see memorandum, William G. Bowen to Lyman Spitzer, July 29, 1975, Bowen president, box 8, folder 3; memorandum, Bowen to Chairmen of Departments and Directors of Interdepartmental Programs, Oct. 26, 1972; memorandum, Richard A. Lester to the Priorities Committee, Oct. 10, 1972 (source of the quote), all in Bowen president, box 91, folder 2. The Lemonick staffing memorandum cited above speaks about the suspension of the target of opportunity program in 1974–75.

languages and literatures;[9] along with the equally prolific Lionel Gossman, a scholar of wide range focusing especially on the history, theory, and practice of historiography, recruited from Johns Hopkins, also in Romance languages and literatures.[10] The invitation to come to Princeton, Brombert said later, was an "offer which I could not resist." It opened "an exciting new opportunity, a renewal for me." He had declined many offers from other prestigious institutions, but Princeton was different; "I sensed that here one could pursue teaching and learning in a climate of joy."[11]

There were other appointments to bolster the faculty in literature: Samuel Hynes, scholar of Yeats, Auden, and Edwardian literature, recruited from Northwestern, in English;[12] and also in English, Alvin Kernan, a distinguished specialist in the English Renaissance, whom Bowen recruited from Yale to succeed Aaron Lemonick as dean of the graduate school, who then reverted to the English faculty after five years in the dean's office. A Princeton humanist who spent a weekend in New Haven after Kernan's hiring wrote to Bowen, "I can assure you that you have broken many hearts there by appointing Kernan as Dean of the Graduate School. Everywhere I turned at Yale I heard only raves about him not only as a scholar ... but also as a humane practitioner of the humanities."[13]

In area studies, Bowen landed two eminent social scientists: Bernard Lewis, widely regarded as the leading historian of the Near East in the English-speaking world, indeed, in the view of many,

9 Memorandum, Karl D. Uitti to President Bowen et al., Mar. 13, 1973 (source of the quote); memorandum, Robert Fagles to President Bowen et al., Mar. 14, 1973, both in Bowen president, box 91, folder 2; Princeton University news release, Nov. 19, 1973, Bowen president, box 402, folder 5.

10 "Recommendations of the President to the Committee on the Curriculum," Oct. 23, 1975; Lionel Gossman to William G. Bowen, Feb. 4, 1976, Bowen president, box 19, folder 8; "Major Personnel Recommendations and Reports of the Committee on the Curriculum," Apr. 16, 1986. These reports are in the minutes of Princeton trustee meetings, which can be accessed online through the Princeton University Archives.

11 Brombert oral history, 5.

12 "Recommendations of the President to the Committee on the Curriculum," May 16, 1975.

13 Princeton University news release, Nov. 9, 1972, Bowen president, box 402, folder 4; A[lbert J.] Sonnenfeld to W. G. Bowen, Nov. 28, 1972, Bowen president, box 19, folder 8.

the "most outstanding orientalist," the "leading Islamist" in the world, and Charles Issawi, the renowned authority on the economics of the Near East and North Africa, recruited from the University of London and Columbia, respectively, who together vaulted Near Eastern studies to international distinction.[14] History was another department that needed strengthening. The work had begun late in the Goheen era, with the recruitment from the University of California at Berkeley of the eminent European intellectual historian Carl E. Schorske. Now the department attracted the dazzling early modern European social and cultural historian Natalie Zemon Davis, also from Berkeley, who, together with Lawrence Stone and Robert Darnton, already on the faculty, would make Princeton *the* place to do early modern European history. The second new appointee in the late 1970s was Stanley N. Katz, taking up a new chair in American law and liberty, coming from the University of Chicago law school, who, it was believed, would strengthen and stabilize American history, long regarded as the weaker side of the department.

In the 1980s, as the constraint on resources eased, there were more star appointments, notably the medievalist Peter Brown, recruited from Berkeley to the history department, and the novelist Toni Morrison, author of *Beloved* and *Song of Solomon* (a future winner of the Nobel Prize in Literature), coming from SUNY-Albany to the Council of the Humanities.[15] The humanities were further strengthened by the appointments of Sandra M. Gilbert (from the University of California at Davis), Margaret Doody (from Berkeley), and Elaine Showalter (from Rutgers), who together made the English department a leading force in feminist literary

14 Re Lewis: Cable, William G. Bowen to Bernard Lewis, Dec. 13, 1973; Princeton University news release, Sept. 5, 1974, both in Bowen president, box 296, folder 2. Re Issawi: A. L. Udovitch to Charles Issawi, July 25, 1974, and Princeton University news release, Apr. 20, 1975, both in Faculty Files, Charles Issawi file. The quote about Lewis as "the most outstanding orientalist" is in E. Kedourie to Aaron Lemonick, Nov. 27, 1973, Faculty Files, Bernard Lewis, second file. The quote about "leading Islamist" is in S. D. Gotein to Lemonick, Nov. 27, 1973, Faculty Files, Bernard Lewis, second file.

15 "Princeton Notebook: Toni Morrison Named to Goheen Chair," *Princeton Alumni Weekly*, Nov. 25, 1987, 11.

criticism.[16] In the social sciences, the most striking appointments were in economics: the macroeconomist and public policy analyst Joseph E. Stiglitz (another future Nobelist) from Oxford, regarded as one of the leading economists of his time; the microeconomic theorist Hugo Sonnenschein, hired from Northwestern; the theorist of financial markets Sanford J. Grossman from the University of Chicago; the macroeconomic policy specialist Ben Bernanke (later chair of the Federal Reserve and Nobel Prize winner) from Stanford; the game theorist Avinash K. Dixit from the University of Warwick; and Angus S. Deaton, the analyst of consumption, poverty, and welfare (another future Nobel winner) from the University of Bristol.[17]

As for already-top departments, Bowen's plan was to make new appointments that built on existing strength. Mathematics was a case in point. It was, Bowen said, "the best in the world," and he "was determined that was what it was going to remain. So whenever there was an opportunity to add an outstanding person, I was always right there. We would find the resources, we would talk with the people."[18] During Bowen's presidency, the department added Charles Fefferman, the brilliant young scholar of mathematical analysis (he was appointed a full professor at the age of twenty-five, the youngest person to hold that title at Princeton), from the University of Chicago; the multitalented theorist John H. Conway from Cambridge; the applied mathematician Andrew J. Majda from Berkeley; the arithmetic geometer Gerd Faltings from Gesamthochschule Wuppertal; and the number theorist Andrew J. Wiles from Harvard, who would win international recognition for proving Fermat's Last Theorem.[19] Philosophy, another example of an out-

16 "Major Personnel Recommendations and Reports of the Committee on the Curriculum," Oct. 25, 1984 (Gilbert); Mar. 21, 1980 (Doody); May 18, 1984 (Showalter).

17 "Major Personnel Recommendations and Reports of the Committee on the Curriculum," June 11, 1979 (Stiglitz); June 7, 1976 (Sonnenschein); Mar. 15, 1985 (Grossman, Bernanke); Dec. 12, 1980 (Dixit); Jan. 22, 1983 (Deaton).

18 Bowen oral history, June 25, 2009, 21–22.

19 Kerry North, "Bowen Announces New Faculty Hirings," *Daily Princetonian*, Nov. 11, 1972; "The University," *Princeton Alumni Weekly*, Dec. 5, 1972, 6 (both Fefferman); "Major Personnel Recommendations and Reports of the Committee on the Curriculum," Mar. 13, 1987 (Conway); Jan. 19, 1985 (Majda); June 4, 1984 (Faltings); Apr. 17, 1982 (Wiles).

standing department, was bolstered by the appointments of the powerful analytic philosopher Saul Kripke, coming from Rockefeller University; Michael Frede, a towering figure in ancient philosophy, from Berkeley; John M. Cooper, another expert in ancient philosophy, from the University of Pittsburgh; and Bas C. van Fraassen, the philosopher of science and epistemology, from the University of Toronto and the University of Southern California.[20] Physics, similarly, added the condensed matter theorist Philip W. Anderson from Cambridge University (a future Nobel Prize winner), the pulsar astrophysicist Joseph H. Taylor from the University of Massachusetts (another Nobelist), and the young mathematical and theoretical physicist Edward Witten from the Harvard Society of Fellows, whose exceptional accomplishments in string theory, quantum gravity, and a range of other fields have been recognized with numerous international awards.[21]

There were so many other star appointments: in biology, for example, Robert M. May, a world-renowned mathematical ecologist from the University of Sydney, who would later become president of the Royal Society and chief scientific adviser to the government of the United Kingdom; and Peter R. Grant from the University of Michigan, who, with his wife Rosemary Grant, would win an extraordinary array of prizes for their outstanding work in evolutionary biology, including, most recently, the Kyoto Prize in basic sciences. In electrical engineering and computer science, Bruce W. Arden, a specialist in computer science, came from the University of Michigan, and, from Bell Labs, Daniel C. Tsui, a specialist in experimental solid-state physics who would win the Nobel Prize in Physics.[22]

20 "Major Personnel Recommendations and Reports of the Committee on the Curriculum," June 6, 1977 (Kripke); Mar. 20, 1981 (Cooper); "Recommendations of the President to the Committee on the Curriculum," Oct. 23, 1975 (Frede); Apr. 11, 1981 (van Fraassen). Bowen on philosophy: Bowen oral history, June 25, 2009, 28.

21 "Recommendations of the President to the Committee on the Curriculum," May 16, 1975 (Anderson); "Major Personnel Recommendations and Reports of the Committee on the Curriculum," Apr. 19, 1980 (Taylor, Witten).

22 "The University," *Princeton Alumni Weekly*, Dec. 5, 1972, 6 (May, Arden); "Major Personnel Recommendations and Reports of the Committee on the Curriculum," Dec. 14, 1984 (Grant); Oct. 22, 1981 (Tsui).

In making these appointments, "I was looking first of all," Bowen explained, "for outstanding intellectual leadership. I was looking for people who would continue to be at the edges [by which he meant forefront] of their subjects, not people who were in any danger of going to sleep. I mean, intellectual vitality was enormously important. But then there was more to it than that. We also needed, in any number of spots, people with real leadership ability. People who were not only good themselves, but who would know how to build a department—build a team."[23] Bowen found them. For example, Robert Sedgewick, a specialist in the mathematical analysis of algorithms and algorithm animation, from Brown University; Robert E. Tarjan, from Bell Labs and New York University, known for his pioneering work in graph theory algorithms and data structures; and David P. Dobkin, from the University of Arizona, who worked in computational geometry and computer graphics, would become the nucleus of a freestanding computer science department.[24] And the intellectual firepower for the new department of molecular biology would come from a group of stellar appointments: Bowen recruited Arnold J. Levine (from SUNY-Stony Brook), a specialist in molecular genetics who, with colleagues, had discovered the p53 suppressor gene, one of the most frequently mutated genes in cancer; and Thomas E. Shenk (also Stony Brook), a broad-ranging microbiologist and virologist who would make major contributions to understanding human cytomegalovirus replication and pathogenesis. Levine, in turn, recruited Shirley M. Tilghman (University of Pennsylvania / Fox Chase Cancer Center), a molecular geneticist, who, with others, had cloned the first mammalian gene; James R. Broach (Stony Brook), a leader in the field of yeast genomics; and Thomas J. Silhavy (National Cancer Institute), a bacterial geneticist known for his work on protein secretion, membrane biogenesis, and signal transduction.[25]

23 Bowen oral history, June 25, 2009, 21.

24 "Major Personnel Recommendations and Reports of the Committee on the Curriculum," Mar. 15, 1985 (Sedgewick); Jan. 19, 1985 (Tarjan); Dec. 12, 1980 (Dobkin).

25 "Major Personnel Recommendations and Reports of the Committee on the Curriculum," Jan. 22, 1983 (Levine, Shenk); Jan. 18, 1986 (Tilghman); Oct. 28, 1983 (Broach); Apr. 13, 1984 (Silhavy).

Bowen participated personally in these appointments in multiple ways. The first was in his formal role as chair of the Faculty Advisory Committee on Appointments and Advancements, known colloquially as the committee of three (with four voting faculty members), the body that made recommendations to the president on all outside appointments and promotions from inside the university to tenured faculty positions. The Princeton system was different from that at most other universities, where the president was more distant, or totally removed, from the appointments process. At other institutions, provosts might chair appointments committees, or might receive and act on recommendations from committees that reported to deans who reported to the provost. Or external committees assembled for the purpose of reviewing individual appointments—ad hoc committees, as they were known at some institutions—might report directly to the president or provost, who would then act on the recommendations.

What was different about the Princeton system was, first, that one elected faculty committee acted on all proposals for external appointments and internal promotions alike, which gave the faculty a direct role in appointments at the highest level; and, second, that the president, as chair of the committee, participated fully in the committee's deliberations. The committee consisted initially of four elected department chairs, one from each of the four academic divisions of the university, along with the provost, and the deans of the faculty, graduate school, and college. (The nickname for the committee—committee of three—dated from a time when science and engineering were part of the same division.) Later, beginning in 1981, in an expression of faculty power unusual in the Bowen presidency, the faculty voted, despite the reservations of the president, to revise the elected membership of the committee to include six faculty members, only two of whom had to be chairs—opening the way for the election to the committee of the first women and Black faculty members before women and Blacks began to be appointed as department chairs.

Bowen took an active role in leading the discussion around the table, asking pointed questions reminiscent of his Socratic teaching method. "I was a very activist chairman," he said later.

"I spent . . . a great deal of time reading folders, going over materials, soliciting advice, testimony, and guiding the deliberations of the faculty who served on that committee. They were advisory to the president. But we never reached a point where they gave me advice I couldn't take, and it was in part because I'd played a role in shaping the advice they gave me."[26] The president's full participation in the deliberations concerning each candidate meant that Princeton was generally able to avoid the fraught situations at other universities where a president or provost not previously involved in the process turned down recommendations for appointment or promotion that came from faculty committees or divisional deans.

Bowen saw the work of the committee of three as "a collaborative enterprise." He recalled the adage of the longtime dean of the faculty, J. Douglas Brown, about faculty appointments: "Doubts increase." What that meant was that "if you have doubts about somebody, if you're not sure this is really the right person, the likelihood is that those doubts will grow over time"—or, as Brown so often put it, "When in doubt, do without." And that is what the committee did under Bowen's leadership. "We turned away any number of recommendations because we just didn't think they were of the right quality. I remember vividly one department coming in with a proposal to appoint someone from outside, and it didn't really look quite right to me. The department persisted, and said, 'Well, this person is better than anyone we have now.' And I said, well, that might be true, but not good enough."[27] As for recommendations for internal promotions, he pressed for the same high standards: Was this the very best person in the field? Did the outside letters sing? If the person were not already at Princeton, would the department be trying to recruit him or her from somewhere else?[28]

Bowen set out intentionally to raise standards for faculty appointments, which involved a "deliberate decision to reduce the number of tenure awards." As he explained, "I thought that the

26 Bowen oral history, June 25, 2009, 22.
27 Ibid., 22–23.
28 Interview with John V. Fleming, Mar. 25, 2019, Princeton, NJ.

standard had to go up, and that one reason it was so important not to give tenure to too many people was you wanted to keep room for other new people to come in. I remember very well students and parents and others complaining that some very popular teacher was not given tenure, and I said, well, my goal is to increase the number of such complaints."[29] Ideally, what Bowen wanted were distinguished scholars who could also teach.

Equally, if not more, important were the informal ways in which Bowen contributed to the recruitment of faculty he wanted to attract to Princeton. Some examples illustrate the many ways in which he involved himself. When Victor Brombert and his wife, Beth, came to Princeton from New Haven to look at housing, Bowen took them around to see what was available.[30] When Charles Issawi was first trying to make up his mind about whether to leave Columbia for Princeton, Bowen went out of his way to offer Issawi any and all assistance and to come to see him at the home of the chair of Near Eastern studies, L. Carl Brown, when Issawi and his wife, Janina, visited the campus. ("Knowing how busy you are," Issawi wrote Bowen, "I deeply appreciate the interest you have shown in me and the time you have taken to make Janina and me feel that we would be welcome and useful members of the Princeton community.") Later, as a second attempt to hire Issawi was making progress, Bowen stayed in touch, making sure the Issawis knew that he was fully aware of the state of the negotiations, and conveying how much he wanted them to come to Princeton.[31] Bowen set out to communicate to these faculty members their importance to the university—and to him. In offering Bernard Lewis his professorship, for example, he told Lewis, "I can imagine nothing more important to Princeton, and to our work in Near Eastern Studies, than your coming here."[32]

29 Bowen oral history, June 25, 2009, 23.
30 Interview with Victor and Beth Brombert, Aug. 20, 2018, Princeton, NJ.
31 Charles Issawi to William G. Bowen, Dec. 22, 1972 (source of the quote), Feb. 5, 1973, Dec. 14, 1974; Bowen to Issawi, Dec. 13, 1974, all in Faculty Files, Charles Issawi file.
32 Cable, William G. Bowen to Bernard Lewis, Dec. 13, 1973, Bowen president, box 296, folder 2.

When Ben and Anna Bernanke came to town in the course of his negotiations with the economics department, Bowen entertained them briefly at Lowrie House and took them to dinner at the Homestead Inn in Hamilton Township, where Bowen routinely claimed the single table in the kitchen.[33] With an offer from the history department, Stanley Katz, then teaching in the law school at the University of Chicago, came to Princeton for an exploratory weekend to talk to Bowen and Aaron Lemonick about his most pressing concern—the need to give up his law school teaching. There was a practical solution, Katz told Lemonick: a joint appointment with the law school at the University of Pennsylvania. Lemonick said that was impossible. When Katz arrived at the president's office, he told Bowen he could save him some time, since Lemonick had told him that he could not teach simultaneously at Penn, which meant that he would not be coming to Princeton. Bowen marched Katz back to Lemonick's office and said, "Aaron, there isn't anything wrong with Stan teaching at Penn, is there?"—leaving Lemonick to respond that there certainly wasn't. When Katz accepted the Princeton offer, Bowen sent him a gift with a personal message: "Congratulations on coming to Princeton."[34]

When Elaine Showalter, then teaching at Rutgers, received an offer from Harvard that she was inclined to take, Bowen called her into his office on a Saturday morning, made her some coffee, and talked to her at length about why, instead, she should accept an offer from Princeton. He was "warm, welcoming, friendly, direct," she recalled—quite a contrast to the Harvard administration. His "humanity," she said, "made the difference—it made a huge impression." Shortly after she left Bowen's office, she accepted the Princeton offer.[35]

Economics, of course, presented a special case, where Bowen's involvement in recruitments could have outsize influence. To Hugo Sonnenschein, he sent a handwritten letter: "Your appointment here was endorsed unanimously and enthusiastically by a group that

33 Telephone interview with Ben Bernanke, Oct. 11, 2019.
34 Interview with Stanley N. Katz, July 18, 2018, Princeton, NJ.
35 Telephone interview with Elaine Showalter, Aug. 22, 2019.

prides itself on setting the highest standards. For my own part, I am convinced that you can make a major contribution here; and I know that your wife would receive the warmest of welcomes from the entire University community."[36] Sonnenschein recalled the impact on his decision to accept the offer of the time he and his wife, Beth, spent with Bowen in the president's office. Sensing that the reservations about the move were Beth's, not Hugo's, Bowen spoke directly to her. He told her about Charlie Feffer-man, who had just been appointed to the math department—and said that Hugo was of Fefferman's caliber, that he belonged at a place like Princeton. Bowen "had an amazing touch," Sonnen-schein said, making his case "with a kind of modesty," not "with a sledgehammer."[37] After Sonnenschein came to Princeton, he and Bowen coordinated Bowen's intervention in the effort to recruit Joseph Stiglitz to the economics department. Later, Stephen Gold-feld, chair of the department, wrote of Bowen's role in recruiting Sanford Grossman and Ben Bernanke: "The superb quality of these two appointments clearly raised the stature of the Depart-ment in the eyes of our envious competitors. While the members of the Department are aware and appreciative of your role in recruit-ing Grossman and Bernanke, only you and I are aware of the truly extraordinary efforts that you made."[38]

The recruitment of the distinguished novelist Toni Morrison, car-ried out mainly by Ruth Simmons, at that point associate dean of the faculty and director of the Program in African American Stud-ies, was the last big coup of Bowen's presidency. Bowen had given Simmons a $10,000 grant to use to strengthen African American studies. The money came from the Wallace Foundation (*Reader's Digest*), where he was a member of the board. One of the things Simmons did with the grant was to invite Toni Morrison to give a

36 William G. Bowen to Hugo Sonnenschein, Apr. 8, 1976, courtesy of Hugo F. Sonnenschein.

37 Telephone interview with Hugo F. Sonnenschein, Jan. 31, 2020.

38 Ibid.; Hugo Sonnenschein to William G. Bowen, Dec. 4, 1978, and memoran-dum, Bowen to Sonnenschein, Dec. 8, 1978, both in Bowen president, box 12, folder 8; memorandum, Stephen H. Goldfeld to Bowen, June 26, 1985, Bowen president, box 13, folder 1.

reading on campus. There followed an explicit recruitment. Bowen wrote to Morrison in September 1987, first to congratulate her "on the simply splendid review" of her latest novel, *Beloved*, in the *New York Times Book Review*, and then to follow up on her visit to the campus the previous week, when the two had talked. Morrison, at that point holding an Albert Schweitzer chair at the State University of New York at Albany, would win the Pulitzer Prize for *Beloved* the following spring and the Nobel Prize in Literature in 1993. "Having now had an opportunity to gather together the threads of your conversations with different people (as I promised I would)," Bowen wrote, "I am more convinced than ever that we are heading in exactly the right direction. Neil [Rudenstine], Aaron [Lemonick], and I met this morning to organize the next stages of the process of extending a formal invitation to you. We are optimistic that that can happen within, say, two weeks. I will then write a formal letter outlining what we would like to propose." He was eager, he said, for her to be able to come to a final decision about Princeton in early October. "There is nothing more important to me, or to Princeton, than bringing these discussions to an emphatically affirmative conclusion." Where to place a distinguished creative writer posed some jurisdictional challenges on the campus. Bowen arranged for Morrison to hold a new chair, the Robert F. Goheen Professorship in the Humanities, and to be appointed to the Council of the Humanities, arrangements that brought her to Princeton in 1988–89.[39] "Nothing stood in his way when he saw a good idea," Ruth Simmons commented. He had "incredible political skill"—he was "like an old-line politician." Every problem, every hurdle, had a solution, a solution he was singularly able to devise.[40]

While presidents at other institutions may have engaged in a full court press to recruit individual faculty members (one thinks, for example, of Derek Bok flying to California to persuade Dennis Thompson, on leave from Princeton at the Center for Advanced

39 Interview with Ruth J. Simmons, Oct. 4, 2019, Princeton, NJ; William G. Bowen to Toni Morrison, Sept. 14, 1987, Morrison, box 71, folder 2.

40 Simmons interview.

Study in the Behavioral Sciences, to accept Harvard's offer to build a new program in ethics and the professions), the extent of Bowen's personal engagement was simply unusual.

Tending to the Faculty

Bowen's close personal interactions with prospective faculty members carried over to faculty members already at Princeton. Some of those connections were intellectual. After Bowen read Robert Darnton's book *The Great Cat Massacre*, he wrote Darnton a letter about it and then used the book in his annual report in the context of the need to understand otherness. Bowen "took the book in, made sense of it, and used it in his own way," Darnton said. It made Darnton feel that he "mattered to the head of the institution"— which made the institution feel "quite personal" to him.[41]

Some of Bowen's interventions had to do with health. When English professor Daniel Seltzer suffered a heart attack, Bowen wrote to say that he wanted to do anything he could to help—in particular, to "address any financial problems caused by this attack."[42] When Dennis Thompson was in the hospital with osteomyelitis, Bowen used his presidential contingency fund to pay for a private room, came over for a visit, and called on commencement morning to see how Thompson was doing.[43] When Edward Sullivan had a stroke in Europe, Bowen arranged for a special plane to get him home.[44] When the art historian John Shearman's wife committed suicide, Bowen took time away from the office to do what he could to care for Shearman and his family.[45]

When Robert and Susan Darnton's daughter was born in the Netherlands during a year they spent at the Netherlands Institute for Advanced Study, they learned that the hospital costs would not be covered by their medical insurance. "Somehow, Bill found out

41 Telephone interview with Robert C. Darnton, Aug. 26, 2019.
42 William G. Bowen to Daniel Seltzer, Mar. 27, 1978, Bowen president, box 306, folder 3.
43 Interview with Carol and Dennis Thompson, July 26, 2018, Cambridge, MA.
44 Brombert interview.
45 Fleming interview.

about that, and we received a payment from the president's contingency fund."[46] Learning that John Fleming was under a lot of stress because of the need to care for his severely handicapped brother in New Mexico, Bowen called to ask if there was anything he could do—"I have a fund I could use to send you to New Mexico if it would help." Bowen "did that with dozens of people," Fleming reflected. He was like a "shepherd" to his faculty flock.[47]

And any time a faculty member or administrator needed to see a doctor, Bowen made the necessary referral or connection, either in Princeton or in New York, where he had a range of specialists at his command.

Other Bowen interventions came when faculty had family members who appeared to be in trouble. When Bowen learned that Victor and Beth Brombert's son, Mark, seemed to have disappeared while on a cruise in Venezuela, he insisted on contacting the American embassy in Caracas to check on his welfare.[48] Lionel Gossman's parents, in their early eighties, traveled with a group from Glasgow for a holiday in Spain. When they were due to return, Gossman got a phone call from his cousin who had gone to the airport in Glasgow to pick them up and take them home: They were not on the plane. Gossman "called the last hotel they were supposed to have been staying at," but "they had checked out." Decades later, the story of what happened next was still vivid in Gossman's mind:

> I was obviously now very alarmed. But what to do? Then Eva [Gossman's wife] said: "Go and see President Bowen." This struck me as an outlandish suggestion. Go and see the University President about a personal problem which he had nothing to do with and which had absolutely no connection with his activities or responsibilities as a university president! But I was desperate. I had no idea what could be done or what steps I could take to locate my elderly parents, or indeed what had happened to them. So I went to see Bowen and told him

---

46 E-mail, Robert Darnton to Nancy Weiss Malkiel, Aug. 26, 2019.
47 Fleming interview.
48 Brombert interview.

the story. Not only did he listen carefully and express his sympathy, he got into action right away. Exploring the amazing Princeton alumni network, he came up with an alum who was the U.S. consul in a town moderately close to the place where my parents had last lodged. The consul immediately went there and learned that my mother (who suffered from quite serious emphysema) was in the hospital and that my father was wandering around the little town in a daze. Not only did he locate my parents, he visited my mother in the hospital, saw to it that my father was put up somewhere, and . . . arranged for them to fly back home once my mother was released from the hospital. I have never forgotten this. I truly do not think many university presidents would have responded so immediately and generously to a personal problem of a member of their faculty or taken the initiative to intervene and do whatever could be done to resolve it.[49]

Still other interventions on Bowen's part involved simple gestures of hospitality and friendship. There were invitations to dinner, at the Chinese restaurant A Kitchen in Kendall Park, or at the Homestead Inn. There were croquet parties on the lawn at Lowrie House in the summer, designed to introduce new faculty members to department chairs and other established faculty members and administrators, parties combining food, drink, and competition, with the winner claiming a stuffed fabric creation (often an octopus) fashioned by Bowen's daughter, Karen.[50] Each year on Christmas Eve, Bowen would show up at the homes of faculty members of his choosing to deliver bottles of wine. "That was amazing" Robert Darnton thought, "that the president of the university would spend Christmas Eve doing that and would make that kind of gesture."[51]

49 E-mail, J. Lionel Gossman to Nancy Weiss Malkiel, Aug. 9, 2018.

50 Interview with Robert C. Gunning, Aug. 26, 2019, Princeton, NJ. I am indebted to Mary Ellen Bowen for the description of the croquet parties.

51 Darnton interview; interview with Henry S. Bienen, Nov. 5, 2018, Chicago; Fleming interview; interview with Robert L. Tignor, Sept. 24, 2019, Princeton, NJ.

Bowen was a master at cultivating his faculty. Some of the cultivation involved explicit instruction in how the university worked. Elaine Showalter recalled his invitations to her in her first year on the faculty—for example, to an alumni gathering in Palm Beach, along with other members of the faculty, an opportunity, she thought, that was designed to familiarize her with the alumni network, alumni loyalty, to expose her to "the whole structure of the university" so that she would understand how it worked. On other occasions, after events on campus, Bowen would talk to her about what she had seen, give her background information, and explain what things meant. He conveyed a highly detailed sense of how the university worked, an experience she found to be engaging and motivating.[52]

Bowen's cultivation of faculty often happened through strategically planned communication, especially handwritten notes. The story line about him was that he wrote handwritten thank you notes for thank you notes. One set of messages congratulated members of the faculty on promotions. To Edward Tufte, for example, on his promotion to tenure, he wrote: "Now that the Trustees have acted formally, I want to add a note of warm, personal congratulations on your promotion. I could not be more pleased! There is much to be accomplished in both the Politics Department and the Woodrow Wilson School, and I look forward with real anticipation to your role in both efforts. We are fortunate to have you!"[53] To Sean Wilentz, promoted to associate professor of history, Bowen wrote, "All of us involved in this decision believe that you will be a major long-term contributor to American history at Princeton."[54]

To Dennis Thompson, upon his promotion to full professor, Bowen wrote to say "how absolutely delighted I [was] with your promotion." "I can think of few meetings [of the committee on appointments and advancements] which I have chaired this year that have been more satisfactory than the session of the 'C3' at which

52 Showalter interview.

53 William G. Bowen to Edward Tufte, Apr. 22, 1974, Bowen president, box 303, folder 4.

54 William G. Bowen to Sean Wilentz, Apr. 21, 1985, Bowen president, box 304, folder 7.

your promotion was supported. I was especially pleased by the shared feeling that your general contributions to the life of the University had to count greatly, along with your teaching and scholarship. These are not easy times for us, as I hardly need to tell you, and I think it is no exaggeration to say that how well we come through this period is going to depend a lot on people like you. We are very fortunate to have you, and it is right and proper that full rank be conferred now."[55]

Bowen wrote, too, to congratulate faculty members appointed to endowed chairs. To his economics department colleague Richard E. Quandt, he wrote, "It is an unusual and very special privilege for me to inform you that I shall be recommending to the Board of Trustees at its January meeting that you be named the first incumbent of the Hughes-Rogers Professorship in Economics." "The assignment of this chair to you is meant to represent, in at least a small way, the great confidence so many of us have in you as a scholar, as a teacher, and as a colleague. These days, perhaps more than ever, we count on that small number of people who care about the University at large as well as about their own work, and I count you as a critical member of this small group." "We are very fortunate to have you."[56] To Val Fitch, who would later win the Nobel Prize in Physics, Bowen wrote, "It is a special privilege for me to tell you that at its last meeting the Curriculum Committee of the Board of Trustees accepted my recommendation that you be named to the Cyrus Fogg Brackett Professorship of Physics," "one of the most distinguished professorships in the sciences at Princeton." "In assigning this chair to you we mean to suggest, in at least a small way, the great confidence we have in you as a scientist, as a teacher and as a colleague."[57]

55 William G. Bowen to Dennis Thompson, Apr. 25, 1975, Bowen president, box 303, folder 1. See also Bowen to T. M. Scanlon, whom he had taught in Economics 101, May 15, 1977, Bowen president, box 300, folder 5.

56 William G. Bowen to Richard E. Quandt, Dec. 23, 1975, Bowen president, box 58, folder 1. See also the similar letter to A. Walton Litz, named Holmes Professor of Belles-Lettres, on Mar. 8, 1977, Bowen president, box 58, folder 2.

57 William G. Bowen to Val Fitch, Dec. 23, 1975, Bowen president, box 58, folder 1. For a similar letter to Sam Treiman about the Eugene Higgins Professorship of Physics, see Bowen to Sam B. Treiman, Mar. 8, 1977, Bowen president, box 58, folder 2.

When faculty members made what Bowen considered to be especially effective statements in meetings, Bowen sent notes—usually handwritten—of appreciation. This practice fit with Bowen's careful strategy of managing meetings—when difficult issues were coming up for discussion, he planned in advance whom to line up to speak, sometimes even in what order, so that concerns could be aired fully while the meeting would be guided to the right conclusion. Allowing the discussion to unfold in an orderly fashion was one part of the method; managing it—indirectly—to come out in the right place was the other. The strategy also involved careful efforts to get the right people—enough of the right people—to come to meetings. Leaving to chance who would attend and who would speak were just not part of the presidential playbook.

To the astrophysicist Martin Schwarzschild Bowen wrote, "Just a brief note . . . to express my appreciation—and admiration—for your statement at the end of the last CPUC meeting concerning the responsibility of elected members of the CPUC to represent themselves rather than any constituency. As you know, this is something that I feel very strongly."[58] To Stanley Kelley: "Just a quick note, written en route to La Guardia, to thank you for your *excellent* statement at yesterday's meeting. It directed attention where it should go, explained the *real* consequences of [the proposal under debate]—and raised my spirits!"[59] To John Gager, professor of religion: "Just a quick note . . . to thank you again for your *excellent* statement at yesterday's meeting. You conveyed just the right tone, I thought, and I wish only that more of the rest of the discussion had been up to the standard you set." "And the issues are *so* complex *and so important*."[60]

58 William G. Bowen to Martin Schwarzschild, Nov. 22, 1978, Bowen president, box 300, folder 9.

59 William G. Bowen to Stanley Kelley Jr., Apr. 7, 1981, Bowen president, box 283, folder 7.

60 William G. Bowen to John Gager, Apr. 7, 1981, Bowen president, box 283, folder 7. On similar themes, see the raft of handwritten notes Bowen wrote on May 19, 1981, to faculty members who had spoken at the special faculty meeting on May 16, 1981, addressing proposals to alter the rules of eligibility for election to the Committee of Three: Bowen to Arthur Wightman, Peter Kenen, Douglas Arnold, all in Bowen president, box 283, folder 7; and Bowen to Dennis Thompson, May 19, 1981, Bowen president, box

When faculty members won external recognition, Bowen was right there with his own congratulations. When the historian Carl Schorske won the Pulitzer Prize for his book *Fin-de-Siècle Vienna*, Bowen wrote: "It is particularly encouraging to see an outstanding teacher, and a warm friend, recognized for the outstanding quality of his scholarship. What splendid news for all of us!"[61] But the stakes did not have to be at the level of a major award. In a letter to the Dostoevsky biographer Joseph Frank, Bowen complimented Frank on the "excellent review" of his latest volume in the *New York Times Book Review*. "It is nice to see such a well-deserved accolade."[62]

When Bowen heard students praise their teachers, he passed the compliments along. To the philosopher Richard Rorty, he wrote: "As I was walking to my office early this morning, I met a student coming out of Commons. He looked even more disheveled than the norm, and I asked him how he was getting along. He replied: 'Oh, fine now; I have been up all night finishing a paper for Professor Rorty's course.' He went on to say that yours was the most interesting and stimulating course he has ever taken."[63]

Retirements from the faculty brought heartfelt thanks from Bowen for the faculty member's long and effective service. To Carlos Baker of the English department, he wrote to convey his personal thanks "for all that you have done for Princeton over the years"—naming Baker's "contribution . . . as a scholar, as a teacher . . . as a loyal departmental chairman . . . as our Chief Marshal, and, most importantly of all, as a valued colleague and friend of so many of us."[64] To the historian Joseph R. Strayer, he wrote to express his "deep appreciation for everything you have done for

---

303, folder 1. On the issues at hand, see faculty meeting minutes, Apr. 6, May 4, 1981, Bowen president, box 284, folder 4.

61 William G. Bowen to Carl E. Schorske, Apr. 20, 1981, Bowen president, box 300, folder 8.

62 William G. Bowen to Joseph N. Frank, Jan. 19, 1984, Bowen president, box 291, folder 9. On another "splendid review" in the *New York Times Book Review*, see also Bowen to Bernard Lewis, July 23, 1985, Bowen president, box 296, folder 2.

63 William G. Bowen to Richard Rorty, May 14, 1979, Bowen president, box 299, folder 9.

64 William G. Bowen to Carlos H. Baker, June 13, 1977, Bowen president, box 286, folder 11.

Princeton in 43 years of teaching and writing here": "You continue
to represent what Princeton must continue to stand for."[65] To Martin Schwarzschild, he wrote: "I want to add a word of personal
thanks to you for all that you have done for Princeton, in so many
capacities, over the last 32 years." In addition to the students he
had taught and his extraordinary contributions to his field, ". . . you
have meant an enormous amount to the University generally, and
certainly to me, through your consistent efforts to bring good sense
to our deliberations." "I hope you have at least some sense of how
important you have been to us."[66]

And when faculty members Bowen considered especially valuable were being recruited by other institutions, he went all out to
retain them. In a letter to Hugo Sonnenschein, who had multiple
offers over the years of faculty and administrative positions, he
counseled patience—there would be many opportunities "to reshift
the balance of your activities," and it was worth waiting for the
right institution and moment. (What he did not say, Sonnenschein
said, was just as important: Are you really ready for this next level
of responsibility? Is this institution of Princeton quality?) Bowen
added, "My proudest achievement is the quality of the faculty I've
brought to Princeton." He knew, Sonnenschein said, "how important it was for faculty to hear that."[67]

Dennis Thompson was the target of Harvard's recruitment efforts to build a new program in ethics and the professions. The
first offer came in 1979. Bowen tried hard to influence the decision:
"We do not want to badger you, or impose on you," he wrote,
"but we care so much about this decision that we want to make
that clear—as well as to be sure you are aware of how extraordinarily important you *and* Carol are to us—as professional colleagues, of course, but also as friends." Given Thompson's "abilities
and predilections," Bowen said, he thought that Princeton "can
offer an exceptional setting for outstanding work and much satis-

65 William G. Bowen to Joseph R. Strayer, June 6, 1973, Bowen president, box 302,
folder 2.
66 William G. Bowen to Martin Schwarzschild, June 14, 1979, Bowen president, box
300, folder 9.
67 Sonnenschein interview.

faction—a good place to really settle in and leave a deep imprint."[68] Thompson turned down the Harvard offer. Bowen responded with an invitation to dinner at Lutèce, then regarded as one of the truly exceptional restaurants in New York City, to celebrate the decision. The Thompsons were "interest[ed] in fine dining," and they had never been to Lutèce before. The experience "both impressed and touched us," Carol Thompson recalled. "Not only did we enjoy the great food, but we had the chance to become much better acquainted with the Bowens."[69]

To economics professor Burton G. Malkiel, who was being recruited to the deanship of the School of Organization and Management at Yale, Bowen sent a long, handwritten letter: "In thinking back on our conversation, I worry that my deeply-felt disappointment at the prospect of losing you may have led me to be less gracious than I should have been. If so, please forgive me— and please recognize that the cause is my deep attachment to you, my respect for *all* that you do for Princeton, and my sense of your unique qualities. For all of these reasons, and others, I cannot suppress the hope that you and Judy will still decide to stay at Princeton."[70]

While it is impossible to quantify the impact Bowen had on the quality of the Princeton faculty, there is no doubt that he succeeded admirably in his goal of building intellectual muscle. Robert Darnton, one of the brightest stars of the history department, called him "a tremendous force for creating a [topflight] university." The faculty had the sense, Darnton said, that the administration was "pushing the faculty to do better, to recruit better people to appoint, to stretch themselves."[71] A notoriously tough critic, the astrophysicist Jeremiah Ostriker, who was well known for pushing relentlessly for the highest standards of quality for students as well as faculty, spoke to the point months before Bowen's departure in his

68 William G. Bowen to Dennis Thompson, Apr. 21, 1979, Bowen president, box 303, folder 1.

69 E-mail, Carol Thompson to Nancy Weiss Malkiel, Jan. 11, 2022.

70 William G. Bowen to Burton G. Malkiel, Feb. 2, 1981, Bowen president, box 12, folder 9.

71 Darnton interview.

confidential report as department chair. He told Bowen that he wanted to express his "gratitude for the enormous, and carefully wrought, changes made here during your 20-year tenure as Provost and President." Ostriker contrasted Princeton as he knew it when he arrived in 1965 and the Princeton Bowen had built two decades later: "I remember describing Princeton to outside friends as 'the geometric mean between a somewhat sleepy boys school and a real university.' The balance has changed. Put simply, none of Princeton's former virtues (that I recognized as such) have been lost as we moved to a position as one of the world's leading universities. That you were able to achieve this, while keeping peace with those constituencies who liked it all as it was, I consider miraculous."[72]

Throughout, Bowen commanded the respect of the faculty. They respected his "dedication and drive," his analytic skills, and his "orderly, rational decision making." But more than anything, they respected his intelligence—his ability to excel in the terrain in which they operated.[73] As one senior professor put it early on in his presidency, "Bowen may be the smartest man on the faculty, and that's unusual for a university president. One cannot help but be impressed that this is a man who is learning, always learning, and just beginning to realize his potential."[74]

72 Jeremiah Ostriker, "Confidential Report to the President," Department of Astrophysical Sciences, July 14, 1987, Bowen president, box 8, folder 4.

73 Joyce Rechtschaffen, "Success Marks Bowen's First Year as President," *Daily Princetonian*, Oct. 22, 1973, 1.

74 Quoted in Richard K. Rein, "Bowen's First Year," *Princeton Alumni Weekly*, May 15, 1973, 14, Bowen president, box 181, folder 5.

7

An Initial Failure

Grappling with Molecular Biology,
"the Most Exciting Frontier of Science We Will See"

Strengthening the faculty involved identifying outstanding individuals who would add luster to their departments and likely jump-start a set of additional recruitments, the sum total of which would result in a demonstrable increase in quality. It was expensive, since the university had to put its resources and persuasive power behind the recruitments. But it was a known process, within the ordinary parameters of faculty hiring; the only real difference was how high one set one's sights.

Making a bet on building a new area of academic inquiry was a different proposition. It was much more expensive and much harder to get it right. Identifying a new field to invest in required good intellectual taste and canny judgment and timing; it required excellent leadership, a core faculty, and resources sufficient to support the wide range of infrastructure—offices, laboratory space and equipment, library resources, teaching spaces—necessary to develop academic strength in a new field.

The Bowen administration was deeply constrained in making such a bet. The 1970s could not have been more unpromising for major new investments in the academic enterprise. Resources were incredibly tight. In October 1973, the Organization of Petroleum Exporting Companies (OPEC) declared an oil embargo targeted at nations that had supported Israel during the Yom Kippur War. By the time the embargo was lifted five months later, oil prices in the

United States had skyrocketed. Energy costs, spiraling out of control, had thrown college and university budgets into deficit. To make matters worse, food prices were also rising sharply. The general level of wages began to rise rapidly as well, and economic activity began to suffer. The stagflation of the remainder of the decade, with an unprecedented combination of high inflation and high unemployment, deepened the budgetary crisis. Belt-tightening was the order of the day. Annual reports of the Priorities Committee documented deficits of as much as $500,000 to $1.5 million. The university was prepared to tolerate modest deficits on occasion, but recurring shortfalls of these proportions were unsustainable. The result was often painful budget cuts, targeted as well as across the board, in the interest of balancing the budget.[1] At the same time, tuition and fees grew markedly, typically increasing by double digits in the 1970s and early 1980s, a rate of increase moderated only when the economy turned around and the capital campaign began to yield results in the 1980s.

Table 7.1 shows increases in tuition and fees in the Bowen era in the context of increases in the Consumer Price Index. The percentage increase in tuition and fees over the six years 1976–77 through 1981–82 was 59.3 (compared with Yale's 59.1, Harvard's 61.7, and Stanford's 66.4). For the five years 1983–84 through 1987–88, it was 31.0. By comparison, the percentage increase in the general level of prices, as measured by the CPI, in the first six-year period was 48.7; in the second five-year period, it was 13.5 percent.[2]

In addition to budgetary pressures, there was no growth in the stock market in the 1970s; it was only in the 1980s that markets started to soar. Princeton's endowment—a small percentage of

1 Princeton University, "Report of the Priorities Committee to the President, Recommendations Concerning the Budget, 1977–78 through 1987–88," in possession of Nancy Weiss Malkiel.

2 The Princeton data for 1976–77 through 1981–82 come from Princeton University, "Report of the Priorities Committee to the President, Recommendations Concerning the Budget for 1982–83," Jan. 8, 1982, 19, in possession of Nancy Weiss Malkiel. The data for 1982–83 through 1987–88 come from the annual reports of the Priorities Committee, also in possession of Nancy Weiss Malkiel. CPI comes from US Bureau of Labor Statistics, Databases, Tables & Calculators by Subject, CPI for All Urban Consumers, https://data.bls.gov, accessed May 2, 2022.

TABLE 7.1. TUITION AND FEES AND THE CPI IN THE BOWEN ERA

	Tuition and fees		Consumer price index
1976–77	$6,275	1977	58.5
1977–78	$6,695	1978	62.5
1978–79	$7,217	1979	68.3
1979–80	$7,811	1980	77.8
1980–81	$8,761	1981	87.0
1981–82	$9,994	1982	94.3
1982–83	$11,468	1983	97.8
1983–84	$12,910	1984	101.9
1984–85	$13,930	1985	105.5
1985–86	$14,940	1986	109.6
1986–87	$15,980	1987	111.2
1987–88	$16,918	1988	115.7

which could be spent to support annual operating costs—fared accordingly. The endowment totaled $449.5 million in 1971. In 1977 it was valued at $470.3 million. It ended the decade at $658.7 million.[3]

This was no climate in which to take on major new initiatives. That said, early in his presidency, Bowen had authorized "quiet" investigations of the role that Princeton could play in some of the professions. In the spring of 1974, he commissioned a study of legal education at Princeton—not so much to assess whether to establish a law school, which everyone recognized to be an outsize proposition, but rather to imagine what distinctive contributions Princeton might make through a program in legal education apart from a law school, perhaps in some relationship to the Woodrow Wilson School of Public and International Affairs.[4] The provost, Sheldon Hackney, led the effort, working with the new dean of the Woodrow Wilson School, Donald E. Stokes '51, professor of politics Dennis F. Thompson, and D. Robert Owen '52, a New York lawyer at the firm of Patterson, Belknap & Webb who had

3 June 30 closing market value, attached to e-mail, Andrew K. Golden to Nancy Weiss Malkiel, May 4, 2022.
4 Minutes of meeting of the Board of Trustees, Princeton University, June 10, 1974, 2–3, Princeton trustees.

prosecuted celebrated civil rights cases in the South for the United States Department of Justice in the 1960s. That October, Bowen described the inquiry to the trustees as "low-keyed" and "slow paced."[5] With Hackney's departure in the summer of 1975 to take up the presidency of Tulane University, Stokes assumed leadership of the investigation.[6] A long report, submitted in the fall of 1975, spelled out models of a law program that could be established at Princeton, including an institute for legal studies, a public service law school, and a full-service law school. But the likely costs were prohibitive—a base projection of at least $50 million in initial capital requirements, surely at the low end of the actual investment required. The report concluded that "with the University under financial siege," it was not a time when the educational issues at stake could receive the appropriate consideration. The report therefore proposed "to put a semi-colon in the decades-long discussion of a law program at Princeton"—in other words, to table the issue for the foreseeable future.[7] In November, the trustee executive committee affirmed "the importance of the educational issues involved" but concluded that "the serious financial constraints now facing Princeton . . . would make it inappropriate to try to pursue this set of questions under present circumstances."[8] In short, there was no chance of moving to implement even the most appealing initiatives in a new field in the budgetary climate in which the university was operating.

The Collapse of Biochemical Sciences

The matter of the life sciences was a different proposition. Unlike legal education, the life sciences were not a departure from what Princeton had done before. They were squarely in the arts and

5 Ibid., Oct. 18, 1974, 3.

6 Ibid., June 9, 1975, 3.

7 Ibid., Oct. 1975, 3–4; "Princeton and Legal Education: A Preliminary Survey," Oct. 13, 1975, in minutes of meeting of the Board of Trustees, Princeton University, Oct. 1975, appendix A-1.

8 "Statement Concerning Legal Education at Princeton," Nov. 17, 1975, in minutes of meeting of the Board of Trustees, Princeton University, Oct. 1975, appendix A-2, Princeton trustees.

sciences—disciplines, in Bowen's words, that were "central to the mission of the University as now defined."[9] But figuring out what to do in the life sciences was another matter. Thinking about initiatives in the field of law was a comfortable proposition for a social scientist president and social scientist provost. Imagining what might be contemplated in the life sciences was a more challenging stretch. Princeton knew how to handle some fields in the hard sciences—physics, astrophysics, and mathematics had long flourished there at the highest level of quality, and there was external validation—Nobel Prizes and other awards—to affirm Princeton's distinction in those fields. But there was no comparable surefootedness in the life sciences. Focused as it was on the arts and sciences, Princeton had never had a medical school. When Lewis Thomas '33, physician, cell biologist, dean of the medical schools of Yale and New York University, president and chancellor of Memorial Sloan-Kettering Cancer Center in New York, and National Book Award–winning author, won the Woodrow Wilson Award in 1981, an award given annually to an undergraduate alumnus for "distinguished achievement in the nation's service," he devoted his remarks at Alumni Day to explicating the importance of Princeton's decision to eschew medical education. Not having a medical school, he said, was a "spectacularly intelligent achievement." Without such a school (the same was true of the law), there was "more room for thinking on a campus like Princeton's," where "the paths [were] not jammed by people running from place to place aswamp in facts, bulging with facts, dropping facts around at every turn like solid, indisposable waste." It was "easier, in such a place," he said, "to learn about learning, and to acquire a regard for the ambiguity of knowledge"—"to form the habit of asking questions rather than giving answers."[10]

Thomas was by no means the only proponent of the absence of such a professional school; it was widely recognized as a matter of institutional pride and relief. Medical schools were hugely expensive;

9 Bowen quoted in ibid.

10 William G. Bowen citation for Lewis Thomas, Alumni Day, Feb. 21, 1981; Thomas's remarks on receiving the Woodrow Wilson Award, Alumni Day, [Feb. 21, 1981], Bowen president, box 161, folder 7.

at a time when university finances were so severely stressed, medical schools, and their associated hospitals, greatly intensified budget crises. Bowen hung on his wall a photograph taken with a group of fellow presidents, an image captured when only one man—Bowen himself—was smiling. The oft-recited caption: "Why is this man smiling? He's the only one without a medical school."[11]

Whether there was any role for Princeton to play in medical education, was, nevertheless, a question that was investigated frequently. George P. Berry, dean of the Harvard Medical School and a longtime trustee who then spent some years as a special assistant in Nassau Hall, had studied the question for President Goheen. It had again been investigated "quietly" and "careful[ly]" by Polly Bunting in the early 1970s in her capacity as special assistant to President Bowen. The conclusion was to set the idea aside and essentially affirm the status quo.[12]

For all the advantages of the absence of a medical school, it made it harder to achieve real quality in the life sciences. The bench of life scientists in the institution was shallower than it might have been otherwise. As Bowen pointed out later, chemistry and biology had some "outstanding" individual faculty members, "but never the concentrated strength evident in math, physics, and astrophysics."[13] Nor did Princeton have facilities to support excellent work in the area. There were three departments in the life sciences—chemistry, biology, and biochemical sciences, with faculty members spread out among three buildings: on the upper campus, Frick Chemical Laboratory (1929) and on the lower campus, Moffett Biological Laboratory (1960) and Guyot Hall, built in 1909 to house biology and geology. Even in the most modern of these buildings, Moffett, facilities were inadequate. Moreover, there was no sure way of locating natural colleagues near one another, and distance made it difficult to share equipment.[14] Nor was there lab space to hire new

11 William G. Bowen, *Lessons Learned: Reflections of a University President* (Princeton, NJ: Princeton University Press, 2011), 80n7.
12 Minutes of meeting of the Board of Trustees, Princeton University, June 10, 1974, 2, Princeton trustees.
13 Bowen, *Lessons Learned*, 74.
14 I am indebted to Virginia A. Zakian for these observations.

faculty. Even if funding had been available for new facilities, it was not clear where new space should be located—up campus, in close proximity to chemistry, or down campus, near biology? Nor was it clear where faculty appointments, if shared between biochemistry and biology or chemistry, would best be lodged.

Without direct personal knowledge of the life sciences, Bowen needed to listen to people he trusted, faculty on the ground as well as distinguished outsiders. He was being bombarded with appeals for support, predicated on an assumption he could hear but not easily validate: Biochemical sciences represented the future of the life sciences, he was told, and Princeton needed to make a big bet on developing work in the field. A big bet, it is worth underscoring, at a moment when Bowen could barely pay for the academic enterprise Princeton had already built.

At the outset of his tenure as president, in the early to mid-1970s, Bowen had on the faculty in biochemical sciences (as the field was then called) two highly disruptive senior biochemists, Jacques Fresco and Charles Gilvarg, who, as we shall see, threatened repeatedly to blow up the whole enterprise. He also had a remarkable constellation of talent—among the best, if not the best, young scientists in biochemical sciences in the country: Bruce Alberts, Ulrich Laemmli, Harold Weintraub, Marc Kirschner, Arnold Levine. Had they remained and grown to scientific maturity at Princeton, the university would have had one of the most distinguished groups of faculty members in the field. But these young men left Princeton in the 1970s for better opportunities, motivated to go by the departures of their talented colleagues, the difficulty of working with the two senior men in the field, and—perhaps more than anything else—what they perceived to be the unwillingness of the university to invest in them and to provide the facilities necessary to develop their science. As we have seen, Bowen was constrained by extremely tight budgets—it was difficult, if not impossible, to imagine finding the resources to grow an expensive new field. He was limited, too, the biochemists believed, in that he seemed not to appreciate the great potential of the science, or the great promise of the young scientists he had on the faculty, or the fact that early capital investments could pay off handsomely for Princeton. (Bowen did acknowledge, however, in an interview in 1974, that Princeton had "some exceptionally able young faculty members in biochemistry, in biology, in chemistry.")[15] By the latter years of his presidency, however, he changed course, clearly appreciating that Princeton had to develop a strong presence in what had evolved from biochemistry to molecular biology. He then raised the necessary funds, recruited excellent faculty leadership, and invested in an impressive new building.

Princeton's decision to pursue scholarship and teaching in biochemical sciences dated to 1961, when President Robert F. Goheen announced the inauguration of a new doctoral program, to be directed by Arthur B. Pardee, a distinguished senior biochemist Princeton had just recruited from the University of California at Berkeley. Bridging chemistry and biology, biochemical sciences focused on the study of the chemistry of living things. There was biochemical work in progress on the part of eight faculty members in chemistry and biology, and new laboratories had been constructed for them in each department's facilities.[16] By his own choice, Pardee stepped down as chair in 1965; he had been notably unsuccessful as a leader of the new venture, and he did not want to continue to have administrative responsibility for the program. Chemistry professor Charles Gilvarg succeeded Pardee in directing the program.

In 1970 biochemical sciences was elevated to departmental status, with undergraduate as well as graduate student degree programs, and fourteen participating faculty members drawn from chemistry and biology. Gilvarg was appointed to chair the new department. Already there were two outstanding young men on the faculty: Bruce M. Alberts, an associate professor originally appointed in chemistry, and Arnold J. Levine, an assistant professor originally appointed in biology.[17]

15 Bowen quoted in William McCleery, " 'Good' Problems (& a 'Bad' One) on a University President's Mind," *University: A Princeton Quarterly* (Fall 1974), in *Princeton Alumni Weekly*, Dec. 3, 1974, 20.

16 Princeton University news release, May 29, 1961, Faculty Files, Arthur Pardee file. I am indebted to Virginia A. Zakian for the description of biochemistry.

17 Princeton University news release, Apr. 20, 1970, Faculty Files, Arthur Pardee file.

There was controversy almost from the outset. In late February 1972, with two faculty members, Max Burger and Noboru Sueoka, planning to leave,[18] and "signs of trouble with respect to the funding of graduate students," President Goheen appointed an advisory committee on the future of biochemistry, chaired by then-dean of the graduate school, physicist Aaron Lemonick, whom Bowen had named dean of the faculty-designate to succeed Richard A. Lester in 1973. Lemonick would report formally for the committee in the early fall of 1972, but in late summer, he gave Bowen a confidential account of what he had learned, with much more detail about people than would appear in the final report. After lengthy conversations with members of the biochemistry department, along with a number of biologists and chemists, Lemonick said, he found "that we apparently had here a department whose birth and subsequent career had made for personal and professional rifts, bad feelings and burnt bridges between itself and its neighboring departments, Chemistry and Biology." "There also seems," he said, "to be among a large fraction of the members of this department a rather abnormal lack of respect for the personal character, professional excellence, and administrative skill of others in the department and in neighboring departments."[19]

What he heard, Lemonick said, "added up to an indictment in one way or another of the entire senior faculty of the department with the exception of Bruce Alberts." Gilvarg, to whom the leadership had been entrusted, "was characterized as an honest, unimaginative, insensitive steamroller whose administration had alienated all the young people. He was said to be a scientist of no particular reputation who has burnt all his bridges to the Chemistry Department and who constantly alienates Biology by treating them with hostility and lack of regard." Gilvarg's senior colleague, Jacques Fresco, was "referred to as one of the steamroller twins,

18 Princeton University, Dean of the Faculty, "Increases and Decreases in the Tenured Faculty, 1972–73–1976–77," in "Report of the Committee on the Curriculum to the Board of Trustees," Dec. 10, 1976, in minutes of meeting of the Board of Trustees, Princeton University, Jan. 22, 1977, appendix E-3, Princeton trustees.

19 Memorandum, Aaron Lemonick to William G. Bowen, Aug. 28, 1972, Bowen president, box 8, folder 6.

as a self-serving politician with a bad scientific reputation who is a violent table-pounder, a vicious disrupter, a divisive and corrosive influence." Another senior man, Robert Langridge, was "reputed to be a total disappointment, a diletante [*sic*]" who had "failed completely to live up to expectations." Arthur Pardee was "very much respected," with an "excellent scientific reputation," but "administratively is not considered to be one who sticks long enough or is interested enough in administration to help run the department or to set its course." Indeed, Pardee himself told Lemonick that "for too long he had ignored signs that Biochemistry was headed for disaster and that Biochemistry at Princeton, which was on its way to respectability and standing, has suddenly deteriorated and has the potential for simply deteriorating further at the present time." Bruce Alberts, on the other hand, was "universally respected and is considered to have great scientific potential," though there were "some serious doubts . . . about his administrative abilities."[20]

The "personal animus" among the chemists in the department "grew out of rancor both before and after the creation of the Department of Biochemistry," such that the chair of the chemistry department told Lemonick that he thought the department would "refuse" joint appointments for Gilvarg and Fresco "even if they wanted them." "The rift with Biology," Lemonick said, "is somewhat harder to understand since the 'Biology' type Biochemists hold joint appointments." Gilvarg thought that the biologists had "seduced" the young biochemists "into a discontent with the Biochemistry Department."[21]

Lemonick gave Bowen the gist of what he had learned from a visit by the external advisory council to the biochemistry department, and he conveyed his own recommendations for how best to proceed. It was "very important" that biochemistry and biology— "the core of the Life Sciences"—"be strong at Princeton." "To the best of anyone's ability to predict, the Biological Sciences should prove to be the exciting forefront field over the immediate future."

20 Ibid.
21 Ibid.

Toward that end, Lemonick thought, biochemistry and biology should be brought together in a single department, a "federate[d]" arrangement with two "semi-autonomous sections," with an overarching administrative structure that would nurture and support the strong young biochemists and provide a shot in the arm for the "somewhat sleepy" biologists while "modulating the belligerence and narrow focus of the Biochemistry Department." The federated department of biology and biochemistry would be chaired by the highly respected evolutionary biologist John Bonner, whose "soothing thoughtfulness and gentle persuasive ability to bring people together are vital to the enterprise." There would be associate chairs for each section, Alberts for biochemistry, biology's to be identified. As for facilities, Lemonick said that he was "more and more convinced that while we cannot promise a building without finding the money for it, that finding money for it be one of our higher priority projects. I believe that the new Department would suffer as has Biochemistry under the present conditions of physical separation and substandard space in Moffett" Biological Laboratory. "I am persuaded that very much is lost if there is not the possibility of easy, informal contact in corridors, lounges, seminar rooms, offices and laboratories. I am also persuaded that we may have a serious morale problem which will affect our ability to attract or hold faculty of the quality we want unless they perceive a commitment by the administration to work toward a new building."[22]

With that, Lemonick clearly diagnosed the problems that were crippling the nascent biochemistry effort at Princeton, and he laid out a reasonable plan for moving forward—marginalizing the personalities who were sabotaging the young department, creating structures to allow quality to emerge and grow, making a new building a high priority for the university. That is not the direction Bowen embraced. Instead, he made choices that drove away the talented faculty around whom he should have wanted to build. He defaulted repeatedly to the leadership of the two individuals—Gilvarg and Fresco—whom everyone knew to be toxic to the flourishing of biochemistry. He also declined (or was forced by the

22 Ibid.

budgetary climate to decline) for too many years to make an institutional commitment to finding the resources for a new building; and he let pass (or was forced to let pass) for too many years real opportunities to recruit the kind of top-quality leadership that—with adequate resources and institutional backing—could have vaulted Princeton to the forefront of the life sciences in the United States. Understanding that torturous history provides a difficult lesson in the many ways in which institutions can fail to avail themselves of fairly clear paths to significant growth and improvement.

Probably the most striking missed opportunity involved the recruitment of Roy Vagelos to chair the department of biochemistry. Vagelos, a highly respected biochemist with a medical degree from Columbia, was in the midst of a successful run chairing the department of biological chemistry at the Washington University School of Medicine in St. Louis. The biochemists, Alberts said, were "wildly enthusiastic about him"; the consensus was that "he was probably the best man for Princeton of anyone in the entire country." And it looked very much as though Princeton might have a real shot at attracting him.[23] Vagelos thought that "preclinical medical education" was going to move from medical schools to universities; while the medical school at Washington University was first-rate, he did not believe that science on the main campus—indeed, the main campus as a whole—was up to that standard. As well, Vagelos had grown up in Westfield, New Jersey, and he was receptive to coming back east so that he could be closer to his aging parents.[24]

Alberts—chairing biochemistry briefly between the long-running chairmanships of Gilvarg and Fresco—had taken the lead in recruiting Vagelos, with Levine fully involved as well. Vagelos had visited the campus; had engaged in extensive conversations with Alberts, Levine, and Fresco, as well as with Lemonick; and was coming back to meet with Bowen in April 1973. Despite assurances from Lemonick, however, he was "skeptical about the future commitment of Princeton to biochemistry," and he wanted to hear directly from

23 Memorandum, Bruce Alberts to William Bowen, Mar. 8, 1973, Bowen president, box 8, folder 6.

24 Memorandum, Aaron Lemonick to William G. Bowen and F. Sheldon Hackney, Apr. 11, 1973, Bowen president, box 8, folder 6.

Bowen about what he could expect in terms of new positions and a new building.[25]

Lemonick briefed Bowen before his meeting with Vagelos. Vagelos, he confirmed, was "concerned about what he takes to be our ambivalence with respect to the building"—he wanted to know "how much money has already been earmarked," how far along the university was in terms of planning, what size building was contemplated, what the university would provide in terms of equipment, and what time frame was contemplated for construction. As for faculty, he wanted to know how many positions the department could expect to have, how many of them could be tenured, and whether the university's tenure limits could be exceeded for "a person of unusual quality." He had questions, too, about graduate student support, the renovation of his own laboratory space, and plans to accommodate a second full professor appointment before the new building was completed.[26]

Vagelos came to see Bowen and Hackney on April 11. After the meeting, he and Lemonick talked at greater length. Vagelos told Lemonick that Princeton could not expect to "keep its best Biochemists if they don't sense a firm commitment to a building," and he expressed surprise that Bowen, who seemed to put a "high priority" on such a building, was "not willing to promise" it. He talked about what he would want to see in an offer letter: a salary no lower than his medical school salary, as well as specific commitments on the building (he said "he could not come unless the probabilities of the building were high"), the schedule of increases that would be allowed in the size of the department, graduate student support, funds for instrumentation, and funds for renovation of his interim laboratory space in Moffett. And he said that if an offer were to be made, he would want to receive it by the end of the academic year. If everything were to be in good order, he would plan to join the faculty for the fall of 1974.[27]

25 Memorandum, Alberts to Bowen, Mar. 8, 1973.

26 Memorandum, Aaron Lemonick to William G. Bowen, Mar. 21, 1973, Bowen president, box 8, folder 6.

27 Memorandum, Lemonick to Bowen and Hackney, Apr. 11, 1973.

Lemonick wrote back on May 7. He began with a strong af-
firmation of institutional support for biochemistry: "All of us in
the central administration are strongly committed to our efforts
in the Biochemical Sciences and to its development. We feel that
you can be the keystone of this development and, for this reason,
we would like you to come to Princeton as Professor of Biochemical Sciences and Chairman of that department."[28] Then came
the details, which complicated the clarity of the opening statement. Vagelos had asked for a firm offer letter in the spring of 1973;
Lemonick explained that such a letter could not come until the
appointment had been reviewed and recommended to the president by the Faculty Advisory Committee on Appointments and
Advancements. That would require outside letters from biochemists around the country; to solicit those letters, Lemonick would
need Vagelos to release him from Vagelos's insistence on the strict
confidentiality of his discussions with Princeton.[29]

As for salary, putting Vagelos at the top of Princeton's salary
scale, and adding summer salary and an administrative override
for chairing the department, would enable Princeton to exceed
slightly the salary Vagelos could expect at Washington University.
Lemonick made the commitments Vagelos had asked for with
respect to renovation of Vagelos's laboratory and funds for instrumentation, and he spelled out the university's policies on
graduate student support. With respect to the building, Lemonick
wrote that Bowen had asked him to tell Vagelos "that this building has highest priority." Bowen was "committed to give fully of
his time and energy" to raise the necessary funds. "With the active support of the right chairman, he is optimistic that funds
can be raised but he cautions that plainly no one can guarantee
success with absolute certainty." With "some sizeable fraction of
the full amount" required in hand, Bowen would recommend to
the board of trustees "that a building be started." As for the size
of the department, fifteen positions were authorized, ten of which

28 Aaron Lemonick to P. Roy Vagelos, May 7, 1973, Bowen president, box 8, folder 6.
29 Ibid.

could be tenured. Under certain circumstances, the size might grow to eighteen.[30]

Three weeks later, Bowen himself wrote to Vagelos. Vagelos had told Alberts and Lemonick that he was concerned about the university's commitment to the building. Bowen recapitulated the assurances he had already given through Lemonick: The building was "at the top of our fund-raising priorities," and he was "fully prepared to commit [his] own time and energy in the search for the resources to make it a reality." The university had identified the site and undertaken preliminary architectural plans; the university's $125 million capital campaign included $20 million for the life sciences, $12 million of which would be for the new building. Bowen was prepared to ask the trustees to "advance funds against pledges for the building if we find donors prepared to make long-term commitments," and he was prepared, too, to recommend moving ahead with the building "when a sizeable fraction of the funding is assured."[31]

The problem, Bowen said, was that donors would likely want to invest in the project only after they were assured of the faculty leadership to bring the department to full fruition. But Vagelos did not want to commit to Princeton without the assurance of a building. "Whereas you are reluctant to commit yourself to the development of biochemical sciences at a place lacking the requisite physical facilities," Bowen wrote, "potential donors are likely to be reluctant to invest funds in physical facilities at a place where the availability of the right human resources is not yet assured."[32]

Bowen's message to Vagelos could so easily have been phrased more affirmatively: "You come to Princeton, and I will make sure we get the money for the building"—a simple declarative statement that would not have promised more than Bowen had already said he was prepared to commit, but would have been couched in a manner likely to be much more persuasive than Bowen's intricate equivocations. Instead, the letter Bowen sent stood as a convoluted

30 Ibid.
31 William G. Bowen to P. Roy Vagelos, May 29, 1973, Bowen president, box 8, folder 6.
32 Ibid.

effort at reassurance, a suggestion that Vagelos trust Princeton's good intentions, and a plea that Vagelos join in resolving the dilemma. For Vagelos, that was not enough; he wanted a stronger commitment from Bowen, and he turned down the offer.[33] In 1975 he moved back to New Jersey to head the pharmaceutical research laboratories at Merck, Sharp & Dohme in Rahway, an appointment that led eventually to his elevation to the positions of president, chief executive officer, and chair of Merck & Co. in the mid-1980s.

The failed Vagelos recruitment prefigured the grave difficulties biochemistry would face throughout the 1970s.[34] One by one, talented faculty departed. After Max Burger and Noboru Sueoka, Arthur Pardee resigned in 1975 to join the faculty of the Dana-Farber Cancer Institute and Harvard Medical School.[35] Bruce Alberts left for the University of California at San Francisco in 1976. By 1978, Ulrich Laemmli decamped for the University of Geneva in his native Switzerland, Harold Weintraub left for the Fred Hutchinson Cancer Research Center at the University of Washington, and Marc Kirschner for the University of California at San Francisco.[36] The last to go was Arnie Levine, who left in 1979 to chair a new department of microbiology at the State University of New York at Stony Brook.[37] In the end, only Gilvarg and Fresco remained, along with Jane Flint, who joined the department as an assistant professor in 1977.

Throughout the departures—and the efforts to prevent them from happening—were some common themes. One was Princeton's seeming blindness to the quality of the talent it had. In the mid-

33 Telephone interview with Bruce Alberts, Aug. 27, 2020.

34 For a contemporary account, see James E. Neuger, "Death of a Department: Biochemistry's Legacy; Cleaning Up the Debris," *Daily Princetonian*, Mar. 3, 1983.

35 Arthur B. Pardee to William G. Bowen, Jan. 30, 1975, Faculty Files, Arthur Pardee file.

36 "Major Personnel Recommendations and Reports of the Committee on the Curriculum," May 5, 1978, in minutes of meeting of the Board of Trustees, Princeton University, June 5, 1978, appendix D-2, Princeton trustees; telephone interview with Marc Kirschner, Aug. 5, 2020; Alberts interview.

37 "Major Personnel Recommendations and Reports of the Committee on the Curriculum," May 11, 1979, in minutes of meeting of the Board of Trustees, Princeton University, June 11, 1979, appendix C-1, Princeton trustees.

1970s the external advisory council for biochemistry told Bowen that he had the best young people in the field, and that Princeton would lose them if it did not put up a building and invest in the development of the department. Levine recalled the administration's response: Bowen told the council that it would be very hard to raise the money to build a building; Lemonick said that the young faculty members ought to be grateful to be together at Princeton.[38] From the inside, Alberts—later president of the National Academy of Sciences—tried to persuade Bowen of "how critical and central the new field of molecular biology would be"—and of the rare opportunity presented by the extraordinary group of young faculty assembled at Princeton. Looking back years later, he remembered Bowen's response this way: "Look, every department thinks they're important. German thinks they're important. French thinks they're important. Go win some Nobel Prizes and then I'll know you're important."[39] Before Kirschner accepted an offer from UCSF, he had an offer from Stanford—clearly superior to Princeton in biological sciences—at twice his Princeton salary. He went to talk to Lemonick about it. Years later, he recalled Lemonick's response— "deeply offensive" to him—this way: "Marc, that's Stanford, this is Princeton. You have to decide where you want to be."[40]

The second theme was what critics considered to be the reactive nature of the institutional effort in biochemistry. The university failed to understand how important the field would turn out to be. So instead of a carefully articulated, comprehensive, long-range plan for moving forward in the life sciences, Princeton responded piecemeal, crisis by crisis, trying to avert further damage.[41] The threatened departure of Alberts prompted an institutional commitment of $5 million in the fall of 1975 to build a new module for biochemistry up campus on William Street, to be connected by a bridge to Frick Chemical Laboratory. Its timing, Bowen said,

38 Interview with Arnold J. Levine, Aug. 7, 2018, Princeton, NJ.
39 Alberts interview.
40 Kirschner interview.
41 On the absence of a long-range plan and the responses in "crisis" mode, see memorandum, Arnold J. Levine to Aaron Lemonick, June 26, 1978, Bowen president, box 316, folder 2.

"may well depend on whether Professor Alberts chooses to stay or to go."[42]

The money, it was hoped, might come from the government of Saudi Arabia. King Faisal had promised a gift to Princeton, but he died before it could be consummated. His son, Prince Sa'ud Bin Faisal '64, the Saudi minister of state for foreign affairs, took up the matter in his stead. The conversations were a matter of some delicacy. On the Saudi side, the gift could not be understood to come directly from the Faisal family or from the government; instead, it was to be funneled through the University of Riyadh as part of a proposed collaborative effort in the life sciences between the two universities. On the Princeton side, the most pressing concern involved the complexities of Saudi policies with respect to Jews and women; the university wanted assurances that there would be no strings attached to the proposed gift, no discrimination in its administration. Bowen was careful to review the prospective gift with the Hillel rabbi, Edward Feld, as well as with Jewish leaders outside the university and the members of the biochemistry department, eleven of twelve of them Jewish, to make sure they were comfortable about taking the money (as Levine recalled, Bowen invited them all to Lowrie House to discuss it; the faculty told him to take the money).[43] Were the discussions with Saudi Arabia to proceed too slowly (in fact, it took five years for them to come to

42 Memorandum, William G. Bowen to the files, Oct. 15, 1975, Bowen president, box 316, folder 1.

43 Telephone interview with Gerald W. Parsky, Jan. 22, 2019; Levine interview; telephone interview with Edward Feld, Sept. 5, 2019; Feld to William G. Bowen, Nov. 6, 1975, and Bowen to Feld, Nov. 14, 1975, Bowen president, box 210, folder 1; "Princeton Notebook: $5 Million from Saudi Arabia," *Princeton Alumni Weekly*, Mar. 24, 1980, 12, in Bowen president, box 403, folder 2; memorandum, WGB to the files, n.d., Bowen president, box 463, unlabeled folder; minutes of meeting of the Board of Trustees, Princeton University, Oct. 24, 1975, 3, Oct. 22, 1976, 2–3, Jan. 26, 1980, 2; Executive Committee minutes, Nov. 14, 1975, 2, in minutes of meeting of the Board of Trustees, Princeton University, Jan. 24, 1976; Executive Committee minutes, Nov. 17, 1978, 3, in minutes of meeting of the Board of Trustees, Princeton University, Jan. 20, 1979, appendix C-1, all in Princeton trustees; Princeton University news release, Mar. 3, 1980, with attached agreement, dated Mar. 2, "Arrangements for Cooperation and Support in the Life Sciences," Bowen president, box 43, folder 11; [Bowen,] "The Saudi Gazette," Mar. 1980; Bowen to Prince Saud Al Faisal Al Saud, Mar. 10, 1980; Bowen to Mansour Al-Turki, Mar. 7, 1980; memorandum, N. L. Rudenstine to Edward C. Cox, Sept. 3, 1980, all in Bowen president, box 241, folder 7.

fruition) or come to naught, Bowen said, "the University is now prepared to commit up to $5 million of capital funds raised in conjunction with the $125 million campaign, these funds to be used for some combination of new construction and renovation at Frick. The purpose would be to see if such an expenditure, combined with some internal rearrangements of space, might not enable us to house all the biochemists currently on our staff at and around Frick." It was "only because of the importance we attach to Biochemistry, and to keeping good people here," Bowen added, "that we are willing to make what is for us an extraordinary commitment under present financial circumstances."[44]

Bowen told the executive committee of the board in December 1975 that the effort to hold Alberts at Princeton had failed. He urged that the $5 million commitment to biochemistry "be reaffirmed notwithstanding" Alberts's loss "in order to hold the rest of the faculty in this area, and to ensure that Princeton would continue to play a strong role in this crucial area of teaching and scholarship." The executive committee voted to reaffirm the commitment.[45] In January 1977, the university announced plans to construct a new $5 million building on William Street adjacent to Frick to allow for consolidation of biochemical sciences in one location.[46]

From one point of view, Bowen's actions were slow and hesitant, taken too late and too modestly in a vain attempt to keep Bruce Alberts at Princeton. From another point of view, at a time of severe constraints on finances, Bowen's willingness to commit $5 million from capital funds raised in the campaign was a major move, an affirmation of the importance of building a credible biochemistry effort at Princeton.

Funding was only one part of the rub. The other main problem was leadership. It was widely understood that Fresco and Gilvarg were destructive influences whose daily interactions with other

44 Memorandum, Bowen to the files, Oct. 15, 1975.

45 Executive Committee minutes, Dec. 12, 1975, 2, in minutes of meeting of the Board of Trustees, Princeton University, Jan. 24, 1976, appendix A-1, Princeton trustees.

46 Princeton University news release, Jan. 11, 1977, Bowen president, box 316, folder 2.

faculty were driving good people away and standing in the way of recruiting excellent new talent.[47] But Bowen was reluctant to jettison them or isolate them, as he eventually had to do. Why he continued to listen to Fresco for as long as he did is an open question; perhaps he had no choice, given the difficulty of finding a new chair and the costs of making a significant break. Moreover, Fresco had undeniably made important contributions to the department—he, along with Gilvarg and Pardee, had started recruiting junior faculty members who would become real stars. Perhaps Bowen was more comfortable with Fresco than he should have been—the two had been neighbors on Maclean Circle, and they got along well, which gave Fresco more influence with Bowen than he might otherwise have had.[48]

Harold Weintraub's account to Lemonick of his decision to leave Princeton addressed the corrosive effects that Fresco and Gilvarg had on the department. Fresco, then chairing biochemistry (1974–80), was much too rigid about what Weintraub taught, whether one could rotate courses, whether one could use outside awards to relieve teaching. "Jack is not a leader, is not highly respected in the field, does not lead the department anywhere," Weintraub said. There was "a serious serenity problem in the department": "Jack in his frenzy and in his moralistic righteous outlook just makes the department seethe all the time"; "Jack and Charlie are still the forces in the department," which "keeps the department in a turbulence constantly." "In the final analysis, unless we can neutralize the effect of Charlie and Jack . . . we will continue to disintegrate."[49]

The issue of the chairmanship—the need to neutralize Fresco and Gilvarg, the fruitless effort to recruit an outsider to lead the department—was a constant preoccupation. Roy Vagelos recalled a moment when he and James D. Watson, director of Cold Spring

47 E-mail, Neil Rudenstine to Nancy Weiss Malkiel, Jan. 27, 2021; interview with John Hopfield, Oct. 24, 2019, Princeton, NJ.

48 Levine interview; interview with Edward C. Cox, Aug. 26, 2019, Princeton, NJ.

49 Aaron Lemonick, conversation [with Harold Weintraub], Sept. 17, 1977, attached to handwritten note, Lemonick to W. G. Bowen, received Sept. 26, 1977, Bowen president, box 8, folder 7.

Harbor Laboratory, who shared the Nobel Prize in Physiology or Medicine in 1962 for his work in discovering the three-dimensional structure of DNA, came to Princeton as part of an advisory council of experts to review biochemistry. After meeting for a couple of days, they asked to have dinner with Bowen. They met at Lahiere's, a French restaurant on Witherspoon Street not far from Nassau Hall. They told Bowen that the faculty assembled at Princeton were extremely strong, but that they needed new space and new leadership. Bowen responded defensively—he did not have a checkbook, and there was nothing he could do. Watson reached across the table, grabbed Bowen's tie, and said, heatedly, "Do you realize you're going to lose these guys?"[50]

In August 1978, Watson resigned from the biochemistry advisory council. "I do so," he told Bowen, "because I believe it is not only ineffective, but probably does positive harm in giving you the feeling that we can effectively help to solve the very real problems which have long bedeviled your potentially excellent Biochemistry Department. But as long as Jacques Fresco is your Chairman, I doubt that you will be able to attract any first-class scientist to put his trust in Princeton's future."[51]

The next month, Bowen announced that Lemonick, working with an advisory group of faculty members drawn from other departments, would lead an external search for a new chair.[52] In May 1979, Lemonick reported to Bowen on the failed effort. He had tried to recruit Gary Felsenfeld from the Laboratory of Molecular Biology at the National Institutes of Health, but Felsenfeld refused. What to do? Seven excellent people had departed in seven years: Burger, Sueoka, Pardee, Alberts, Kirschner, Weintraub, Levine. Fresco's "intensity and compulsiveness seem to make membership in his Department an enormous trial." "The personnel situation in Biochemistry," he told Bowen, "seems to be as close to a nadir as it could possibly get short of total dissolution." After extensive consultation, Lemonick in May 1979 recommended disbanding

50 Interview with P. Roy Vagelos, Oct. 1, 2018, Bedminster, NJ.
51 J. D. Watson to William Bowen, Aug. 22, 1978, Bowen president, box 8, folder 7.
52 Memorandum, William G. Bowen to Aaron Lemonick, Sept. 23, 1978, Bowen president, box 8, folder 7.

biochemistry and combining its components with biology and chemistry.[53] In June, Bowen told the trustees that "continuing difficulties" in biochemistry were "the most troublesome academic situation in the University at the moment."[54]

By October, after further consultation, however, Lemonick had changed his mind. As he told the trustees, putting biochemistry back in biology was "not the best course of action." He emphasized the desperate need to find new leadership for biochemistry.[55] In November 1979, Lemonick and Bowen asked Walter Kauzmann of the chemistry department to take the chairmanship of biochemistry for the final two years before his retirement from the faculty, an appointment announced in December. While Kauzmann led the department, he would run a search for a new chair.[56]

Under Kauzmann's leadership, offers were made to Charles Cantor at Columbia, David Prescott at the University of Colorado at Boulder, and Aaron Shatkin at the Roche Institute of Molecular Biology in Nutley, New Jersey, later at Rutgers University. All of them refused. As his second year in the chairmanship approached its conclusion, Kauzmann was working once again on recruiting Gary Felsenfeld from NIH. Bowen got the board to agree to a private commitment of $15–$16 million in additional funds for biochemistry (that would allow for doubling the size of the existing research and teaching facilities and significant investments in new faculty hiring) if the candidate accepted.[57] At the same time, planning was under way to put the biochemistry department into re-

53 Memorandum, Aaron Lemonick to William G. Bowen, May 17, 1979, Bowen president, box 8, folder 7; "Report of the Committee on the Curriculum to the Board of Trustees," May 11, 1979, 2, in minutes of meeting of the Board of Trustees, Princeton University, June 11, 1979, appendix C-1, Princeton trustees.

54 Minutes of meeting of the Board of Trustees, Princeton University, June 11, 1979, 4, Princeton trustees.

55 "Report of the Committee on the Curriculum to the Board of Trustees," Oct. 18, 1979, 1, in minutes of meeting of the Board of Trustees, Princeton University, Oct. 19, 1979, appendix D-1, Princeton trustees.

56 Memorandum, Aaron Lemonick to W. G. Bowen, Nov. 28, 1979; memorandum, Bowen to Members of the Department of Biochemical Sciences, Dec. 10, 1979, Bowen president, box 1, folder 8.

57 Minutes of meeting of the Board of Trustees, Princeton University, June 8, 1981, 2–3, Princeton trustees; memorandum, Aaron Lemonick to William G. Bowen, Mar. 16, 1982, Bowen president, box 1, folder 8.

ceivership under a special committee chaired by George A. Miller, professor of psychology.[58]

In March 1982 Bowen met with Roy Vagelos in his office at Merck to discuss biochemistry. Vagelos advised Bowen not to press Felsenfeld too hard. If he wanted to come, he should do it with some enthusiasm. He might be looking for reasons to say no. Suppose Felsenfeld didn't come? Vagelos said that he "considers Fresco in particular, and Fresco and Gilvarg together, as major problems. He said that Fresco was without any question a dominant negative factor in our equation. Thus, whatever can be done to 'wall off' Fresco and Gilvarg would be all to the good." Vagelos thought the plan for receivership was "excellent." It would be received well outside, a sign "that we were prepared to deal with the Fresco/Gilvarg problem." Vagelos believed that Princeton could still attract the necessary leadership. Princeton continued to need to search for a first-rate outside appointment. It was "essential" he told Bowen, "that we do excellently in this field. It will not do to settle for a 'B+' solution."[59]

The Rise of Molecular Biology

The appointment of the Special Committee on Biochemistry was announced in April 1982.[60] The committee had three responsibilities: oversee the work of the department of biochemical sciences; provide advice on the organization of the life sciences for the longer term; and make recommendations about the continuing search for strong faculty leadership.[61]

---

58 Memorandum, Lemonick to Bowen, Mar. 16, 1982; "Report of the Committee on the Curriculum to the Board of Trustees," Mar. 19, 1982, 1–2, in minutes of meeting of the Board of Trustees, Princeton University, Apr. 17, 1982, appendix C-1; memorandum, Bowen to Members of the Biochemical Sciences Department, Apr. 5, 1982, in minutes of meeting of the Board of Trustees, Princeton University, Apr. 17, 1982, appendix C-2, all in Princeton trustees.

59 Memorandum, William G. Bowen to the files, Mar. 18, 1982, Bowen president, box 8, folder 8.

60 Memorandum, William G. Bowen to Chairmen of Departments and Directors of Programs, Apr. 6, 1982, with attached memorandum, Bowen to Members of the Biochemical Sciences Department, Apr. 5, 1982, Bowen president, box 8, folder 8.

61 Memorandum, Aaron Lemonick to William G. Bowen, Apr. 13, 1983, Bowen president, box 8, folder 9.

In June, the special committee made an interim report. It had four general recommendations. The first was to create a program in molecular biology, followed shortly by a department, and reorganize the biological sciences such that Fresco and Gilvarg would be based outside the new entity. This recommendation—focusing on molecular biology instead of biochemistry—made clear the ways in which the science had evolved and the determination to signal that Princeton was ready to embrace a more modern field of inquiry. Unlike biochemistry, where studies were carried out not in cells but in extracts made from cells, molecular biology involved studies carried out in cells or in whole organisms. Its methods, such as DNA cloning and recombinant DNA technology, enabled scientists to understand biological events at the molecular level.[62]

The second suggestion of the special committee was to "commit the University to an aggressive program of growth in the biological sciences." As we have seen, the university had once boasted a stunning collection of young faculty in the field and had been well on the way to having a first-class department but had allowed the group to disintegrate. Princeton was not close to keeping pace with other universities in the biological sciences. "The continuing instability of the program in biochemistry is merely a symptom of the general neglect of biology," the report said. It was essential to remedy that. The third recommendation was to "start immediately to plan another building." Moffett and Frick needed badly to be renovated, and there was simply not enough space for the kind of science molecular biologists would want to do. And the final advice was to "convene an ad hoc Advisory Council" of eminent molecular biologists, who would give specific guidance in the development of a proposal for the creation of a program.[63]

In September, Bowen had personal conversations with Fresco and Gilvarg. The meetings were difficult and contentious. Bowen

62 Special Committee on Biochemistry, "Interim Report, 5 April–18 June 1982," Bowen president, box 8, folder 8. Once again, I am indebted to Virginia A. Zakian for the description of the science.

63 Special Committee on Biochemistry, "Interim Report" (source of the quotes); minutes of meeting of the Executive Committee, Sept. 24, 1982, 3, in minutes of meeting of the Trustees of Princeton University, Oct. 22, 1982, appendix A-1.

rehearsed the special committee's proposal for a program in molecular biology and explained the recommendation that Fresco and Gilvarg not be included (the plan was that they would remain in the biochemistry department). Neither of them liked what he heard. Fresco was "enraged" and "humiliated."[64] Gilvarg was "calm," but took the opportunity to make sure Bowen knew that he had a much higher standing in the world of biochemistry than Fresco.[65]

In January 1983, Bowen sent the trustees a long working paper as background for a special meeting about molecular biology. The paper was prepared by the biologist Robert M. May, chair of the University Research Board, along with Lemonick, Rudenstine, and Bowen. May had joined the Princeton faculty in 1973. He was a scientific powerhouse who dominated so many fields in biology— mathematical biology and ecology chief among them. In 1988 he would leave Princeton for Oxford, and he would later become chief scientific adviser to the government of the United Kingdom and president of the Royal Society. May's working paper addressed the evolution of the relevant scientific fields; Princeton's organizational history in the life sciences; the recommendation to establish a program in molecular biology, which could become a department; the faculty size needed for a successful program; the facilities required and the arguments for a location on the upper campus versus one down the hill; alternative building plans; and implications for fundraising. Bowen told the trustees that he had made major progress in the effort to recruit new faculty leadership and expected to be able to propose by the time of the board meeting the appointment of a chair and another senior appointment. "The individuals with whom we are discussing possible appointments seem to us to be absolutely outstanding, with a record of both scientific accomplishment and leadership ability."[66]

---

64 Memorandum, William G. Bowen to Aaron Lemonick and Neil Rudenstine, Sept. 29, 1982 (re Fresco), Bowen president, box 8, folder 8.

65 Ibid. (re Gilvarg). On the arrangements for biochemistry after the establishment of the molecular biology department, see memorandum, Aaron Lemonick to William G. Bowen, Apr. 13, 1983.

66 Memorandum, William G. Bowen to Members of the Board of Trustees, Jan. 14, 1983, Bowen president, box 16, folder 2.

By the time of the special meeting, Bowen told the trustees about Arnold Levine and Thomas Shenk, who would provide the new leadership necessary to make molecular biology succeed at Princeton. Bowen had been personally involved in the recruitment. He knew Levine from his time at Princeton in the 1970s, so those conversations flowed naturally. But he did not know Shenk, and the way he proceeded illustrated very well how good he was at the art of persuasion. When Shenk was at the university to give a seminar about his work, Bowen invited him to his office in Nassau Hall to talk about the future of molecular biology at Princeton and asked Shenk to think about whether he might have a role in it. In a subsequent visit, on a weekend, Bowen, alone in his office, made Shenk a cup of coffee and talked to him about Princeton. He told Shenk that they had something in common—both of them had gone to college at small midwestern universities (Bowen at Denison, Shenk at the University of Detroit). Bowen said that in coming to Princeton years earlier, he had wondered whether he would fit in, and he asked Shenk whether he was having similar concerns. Bowen's assurance—"you'll fit in just fine"—Shenk said, made him feel comfortable about something that had been making him feel insecure.[67]

Throughout the recruitment, Bowen asked Levine and Shenk what they would need to be successful in making a go of molecular biology at Princeton. His response to their answers was invariably: "We can make that happen." There was never any pushback; indeed, at every stage, Shenk said, "Bowen did more for us than he had promised."[68]

Levine, forty-three years old, professor of microbiology and chair of the department at the State University of New York at Stony Brook, was widely regarded as an outstanding scholar and teacher, "a world-class molecular biologist" of "highest quality and great originality."[69] As Bruce Alberts and George Khoury, chief of the

---

67 Levine interview; interview with Thomas E. Shenk, July 31, 2018, Princeton, NJ; Cox interview.

68 Shenk interview.

69 The quotes are from Princeton University news release, Jan. 27, 1983, Bowen president, box 15, folder 7.

laboratory of molecular virology at the National Cancer Institute at NIH, attested, Levine had the personality, energy, enthusiasm, scientific taste, and organizational ability to build a topflight department; he had done that at Stony Brook, and he was eager to come back to Princeton and do it again. Shenk, thirty-six, was Levine's most outstanding hire at Stony Brook, who had been described as "one of the newest and brightest stars in the firmament of molecular biology." Khoury characterized Shenk as "*the* outstanding young molecular biologist in this country today." "If I were building a department," Khoury said, "he would be the single candidate I would most avidly seek." If Princeton succeeded in recruiting Levine and Shenk together, Alberts said, "you will have scored a major coup."[70]

Following the board meeting, Bowen announced the appointments of Levine and Shenk "as part of a major initiative to expand and improve [Princeton's] teaching and research programs in the life sciences." "In all of our consultations," he said, "there was widespread agreement that molecular biology is one of the most exciting and important scientific frontiers. There was also widespread agreement that Princeton must take strong action if it is to play a leadership role in this field."[71] As he elaborated later, "We are persuaded that this is perhaps the most exciting frontier of science we will see certainly for a number of years, offering tremendous possibilities for understanding the nature of life itself. It seems to us critically important that Princeton as a center of learning in the most fundamental subjects be strong in this field."[72] Toward that end, molecular biology would begin as a program in 1983–84 and become a department in 1984–85. There would be a major new building project behind Moffett, and funding would also be provided to renovate facilities in chemistry to make the separate module (Hoyt Laboratory), previously devoted to biochemistry,

70 WGB presentation to special meeting on molecular biology, Jan. 21, 1983 (Khoury and Alberts quotes); Princeton University news release, Jan. 27, 1983 ("newest and brightest stars"), both in Bowen president, box 15, folder 7.

71 Princeton University news release, Jan. 27, 1983.

72 Bowen quoted in "Princeton Notebook: $46 Million R$_x$ for the Life Sciences," *Princeton Alumni Weekly*, Feb. 9, 1983, 23.

workable for that department. Levine had been promised nineteen full-time equivalents to build a stellar faculty. There would be a big increase in funds sought for these purposes in A Campaign for Princeton—$46 million, up from the $24 million already incorporated within the objectives of the anticipated $275 million campaign.[73]

Levine and Shenk moved quickly to recruit senior as well as junior faculty. They would bring candidates to Bowen's office for a meeting in which he would share his vision of what Princeton was seeking to accomplish. It was "always the case," Shenk recalled, that candidates "were much more impressed and excited after they met him" than they had been before.[74]

Corporations and individuals endowed chairs for Levine, Shenk, and other senior members of the new department. Construction of the new building, south of Moffett Laboratory, proceeded under the joint direction of the architect Robert Venturi and the firm Payette, experts in the design of scientific laboratories. (Venturi, who had previously been engaged to design Gordon Wu Hall and to renovate the dining rooms of commons to form Rockefeller and Mathey Colleges, called Bowen "my Medici.")[75] Bowen persuaded trustee Laurance Rockefeller, funder of so many critical ventures at Princeton, to make the lead gift of $10 million to name the building for his friend Lewis Thomas, whose board he was chairing at Memorial Sloan-Kettering Cancer Center. In August 1984, when bricks of the wrong color and the wrong texture arrived from the manufacturer in Salt Lake City, it put the whole project at risk: The wrong bricks would ruin the aesthetics of Venturi's design. Princeton had millions of dollars invested and a tight construction schedule, with no time to spare. Bowen called trustee John Kenefick, vice chair of the executive committee of the board and chair and chief executive officer of the Union Pacific Railroad, to see if he could help. He finally found Kenefick in his private railroad car in Los Angeles, where he was watching his niece compete in the sum-

73 Princeton University news release, Jan. 27, 1983.

74 Shenk interview.

75 Fred A. Bernstein, "Robert Venturi Dies at 93," *New York Times*, Sept. 20, 2018, B15.

mer Olympics. Kenefick tried first to reach the president of the brick company, who declined to speak to him. Angered, Kenefick "did some quick research" and learned that the brick company "was a subsidiary of another corporation whose chairman he knew well." He spoke to his friend, and the president of the brick manufacturer quickly called to apologize. The manufacturer set other projects aside and fired a new set of bricks for the laboratory, and Kenefick arranged to have them shipped by rail to Princeton. Lewis Thomas Laboratory was dedicated on April 18, 1986.[76] When Bill Bowen really wanted to accomplish something, he got it done.

What had changed to make all of this happen? First, the approach Princeton had taken through the 1970s—essentially, and of necessity, to build biochemistry on the cheap—had clearly failed. One after another, the talented faculty members in biochemistry had left the university, driven away by the deeply flawed leadership of Gilvarg and Fresco, the lack of institutional commitment to facilities adequate to a workable initiative in biochemistry, and the sense—justified or not—that Bowen really didn't "get" biochemistry or care very much if it thrived. The effort to recruit first-class leadership from the outside foundered for the same reasons. Once biochemistry was essentially reduced to Gilvarg and Fresco, the university had a choice: let biochemistry die, or contemplate a radically different approach.

Second, the financial situation began to turn around. Annual budgets came into balance, external financial pressures eased, and

76 Minutes of meeting of the Board of Trustees of Princeton University, June 6, 1983, 3; Oct. 29, 1983, 4; minutes of a special meeting of the Executive Committee, Princeton University, Aug. 3, 1983, 1, in minutes of meeting of the Board of Trustees of Princeton University, Oct. 29, 1983, appendix B-1; "Major Personnel Recommendations and Reports of the Committee on the Curriculum," Oct. 28, 1983, in minutes of meeting of the Board of Trustees of Princeton University, Oct. 29, 1983, appendix D-2; minutes of meeting of the Board of Trustees of Princeton University, Oct. 26, 1984, 6; minutes of meeting of the Board of Trustees of Princeton University, Apr. 19, 1986, 1; minutes, Committee on Plans and Resources, Feb. 14, 1986, 1, in minutes of meeting of the Board of Trustees of Princeton University, Apr. 19, 1986, appendix E, all in Princeton trustees; "The Bowen Legacy: A Close-up Review of His Vision and Accomplishments," *Princeton Alumni Weekly*, Dec. 23, 1987, 9–10 (source of the quotes); William G. Bowen, "A Campaign for Princeton: Reflections," Oct. 24, 1986, Bowen president, box 252, folder 4; Levine interview; Shenk interview.

with a major capital campaign on the horizon, it became possible for the first time in the Bowen presidency to imagine investing in molecular biology on a scale sufficient to build a high-quality enterprise worthy of the university.

Had Bowen's own worldview changed, or did the change in external circumstances enable him finally to act on what he had known and understood all along? Bowen said later, as he was leaving Princeton, "I didn't understand as early as I should have how very difficult it was going to be to strengthen Princeton in the life sciences. And I think I did not understand soon enough what an extraordinary commitment was going to be required if we were going to get anywhere."[77] He later elaborated: "The most serious misjudgment we made was to think that a gradual, incremental effort would work. For some years, we kept approving modest numbers of new appointments, mostly at the junior level, and making equally modest investments in renovating facilities. We enjoyed some success in identifying and attracting talented young faculty members. But we never managed to 'get to scale' and the frustrations that bedeviled all of us led some of the ablest young scientists to take positions elsewhere. We kept turning over positions with little net gain."[78]

Bowen's assessment supports the view of the people who believe that he knew that he had missed the opportunity to build around the talent assembled at Princeton in the 1970s—that he was embarrassed by what Princeton had allowed to slip through its grasp and was determined, when he could, to rectify the situation. Some cite the influence on him of George Khoury of NIH, a Princetonian in the class of 1965. Bowen knew Khoury, knew how devoted he was to Princeton, and reached out to him for advice. Khoury told Bowen that he could not let Princeton's failure to establish a significant presence in molecular biology go on any longer, a message that had a significant impact on Bowen's thinking. The two men talked at length about what was needed and what Princeton could afford to do to make a statement in the field. Khoury told Bowen

77 "Bowen Speaks Out on Bowen," *Daily Princetonian*, Jan. 6, 1988, 9.
78 Bowen, *Lessons Learned*, 74.

that Levine and Shenk would provide the leadership that Princeton needed, and he worked very hard to help to recruit them.[79]

Neil Rudenstine argued that the economic constraints of the 1970s explained what Bowen could and could not do. "We had no extra money to spare—certainly not enough to build a new major lab and add a whole department of FTEs [full-time equivalents]." And there were other pressing needs—computer science, for example, and a wholesale, multimillion-dollar renovation of Frick Laboratory for chemistry—"all of them expensive," none of which could be attended to in any serious way, "because we simply did not have the resources." "We had to find ways, if possible," Rudenstine said, "to somehow make do while waiting for the moment when we could count on a reasonable economy, launch a campaign, and garner the necessary resources."[80]

Biology professor Edward C. Cox, who chaired biochemical sciences for a time and chaired the biology department for a decade, beginning in 1977, agreed with Rudenstine that the university could not find the resources needed to compete in biochemistry in the 1970s, but he also raised the question of whether it really cared about finding those resources. At one point in the 1970s Bowen asked Cox to find a new chair for biochemistry. Cox spent two years in a fruitless search, trying ten or twelve people and failing in every case. He recalled that Charles Cantor at Columbia, to whom an offer of the chairmanship was made, told Bowen in "blunt, even rude" terms that Princeton was not even close to what it needed to invest to make a go of biochemistry. Cox never could figure out, he said, "why Bowen did not see this more clearly sooner," why he did not listen to outside experts or pay closer attention to advisory council reports from smart, disinterested people. Was Bowen not listening? Was he attending to other priorities? Was he hamstrung by the economy? Was he worried about the strength of the endowment? It was never clear to Cox what the obstacles were. But Bowen

---

79 Levine interview; Shenk interview; Cox interview; Bowen, *Lessons Learned*, 75. Hugo Sonnenschein thought that molecular biology was a signal example of Bowen's ability to engage in self-criticism; he knew he had missed a shot, and he would not miss it again. Telephone interview with Hugo F. Sonnenschein, Jan. 31, 2020.
80 E-mail, Neil Rudenstine to Nancy Weiss Malkiel, Jan. 27, 2021.

finally turned around and did what was necessary to build the field.[81]

Years later, addressing the question how Princeton had missed the opportunity it had in the 1970s to create a distinguished department, Bowen acknowledged that the university had not realized the talent it had, nor how much of its competitive future would depend on upgrading the scientific enterprise in what would become a critically important field. The lesson Bowen drew was that "once you make a mistake, you can make an investment and fix it." In short, Princeton, being Princeton, could afford to make a mistake and then move aggressively to recoup—because of its strengths, the university could acknowledge its error and mobilize the donors and resources to catch up and join the top tier of institutions in the field.[82]

81 Cox interview.
82 Telephone interview with Mark S. Schlissel, Sept. 30, 2019.

8

Inclusion—Gender and Race

"Making the Place Much More Inclusive
in All Respects"

"Building intellectual muscle" was Bowen's first priority as president of Princeton. The second priority, he said later, was "making the place much more inclusive in all respects, less homogeneous." That meant coeducation, "the recruitment of minority students," and efforts to make the university "more welcoming to Jewish students." "Those," he said, "were all critically important elements of inclusiveness, which I thought was a very, very high priority."[1] Inclusiveness meant creating a richer, more varied community; "we're only going to learn," Bowen asserted, "if we're a community of people from different backgrounds, different perspectives."[2]

In a letter to an alumnus in the spring of his first year as president, Bowen explained how that worked. "I think there is widespread agreement," he wrote, "that the presence of a significant number of women and minority students during the last several years has added new perspectives to our classrooms and, perhaps more importantly, has expanded the outlooks and broadened the views of a great many members of the University community." There was more work to do, he said, "as we continue to look for ways of enabling and encouraging students who are different from each other to learn from each other. But already a good deal of learning of this kind has been and is occurring at Princeton; indeed,

1 Bowen oral history, Sept. 18, 2009, 25–26.
2 Ibid., Sept. 28, 2009, 13.

without a milieu that promised real diversity we could not attract as many outstanding students of *all* races and both sexes as come to us at present."[3]

At opening exercises in September 1977, Bowen laid out his views to the university community: "The learning environment is a far richer one," he said, "when it contains not only individuals who come from cities and rural areas, from different economic backgrounds, from different regions and countries, and who represent a wide array of academic and extracurricular talents and interests, but also women as well as men, and students who come from a wide variety of religious and cultural backgrounds and who bring with them various senses of what it is like to grow up as a member of a racial or ethnic minority in America." That kind of setting, he said, offered students "unprecedented opportunities" to "learn from [their] differences" and to "reexamine [their] most deeply held assumptions" about themselves and their world.[4]

Bowen spoke later about the roots of what an interviewer characterized as his passion "for equity and fairness." "It goes back in part, I think," he said, "to the way I grew up and to the fact that I myself was a beneficiary of other people's passion for fairness and opportunity and excellence." He noted, first, that he had come "from a family of very modest circumstances, and it was thanks to the generosity of a great many people and the belief of a great many people that I was able to get the education that I did and then ultimately to lead the life that I was privileged to lead." He noted, too, that he "had been blessed all my life with friends of every background and persuasion." Because of the diversity in the student body at Wyoming High School, he had "always had African American friends." As well, he had "a woman partner as a doubles player" in tennis in high school, and his "major partner in mathematics" at Denison was a Korean woman. "And so I had just had the

3 William G. Bowen to Howard C. Anderson, Mar. 16, 1973, Bowen president, box 97, folder 1.

4 William G. Bowen, "Diversity: The Opportunities and the Obligations," opening exercises address, Sept. 1977, in *Ever the Teacher: William G. Bowen's Writings as President of Princeton* (Princeton, NJ: Princeton University Press, 1987), 380.

opportunities—not everyone does—to see firsthand the benefits of diversity."[5]

Decades after Bowen left the Princeton presidency, his close friend Jerome Davis of the class of 1971—president of the Association of Black Collegians, president of the undergraduate student government, Rhodes Scholar, Princeton's first Black alumni trustee—put Bowen's commitment this way: "It seemed that . . . Bill made it his business to advocate for those not historically recognized to be 'worthy of Princeton'—initially women, blacks and browns; and later, among others, students from low income families lacking a tradition of higher education."[6]

I turn now to two examples of that advocacy in the areas of gender and race. The next chapter will focus on two other examples of Bowen's efforts to make Princeton "much more inclusive" in religion and residential life.

Gender

Bowen, of course, had been the driving force behind coeducation in the Goheen administration. As we have seen, he worked hard to appoint women to senior positions in his administration and to recruit senior women to the faculty. He also modeled his commitments in his own behavior, as when he turned down membership in the Nassau Club on Mercer Street adjacent to the campus, membership extended to every Princeton president, on the grounds that the club excluded women as members.[7]

Bowen's ascension to the presidency came in the fourth year of coeducation, a time when the numbers of women students were pushing up against the de facto cap that had been accepted as part of the putative bargain with alumni when coeducation was first instituted. The deal was to keep the number of men in each entering class constant at eight hundred, the number that had been enrolled

5 Bowen oral history, Sept. 28, 2009, 17.

6 Jerome Davis, memorial tribute, William G. Bowen Memorial Service, Princeton University Chapel, Dec. 11, 2016, courtesy of Jerome Davis.

7 William G. Bowen to W. Irving Harris, June 18, 1983, Bowen president, box 146, folder 13.

before coeducation; the number of women would move upward as increases in dormitory capacity permitted. The problems with this plan became clearer each year. The credentials of women applicants as a group far surpassed those of men, so that the cutoff in terms of quality—academic and nonacademic—for admitting women was at a much higher level than that for men. Women were excelling both in the classroom and beyond, especially in athletics, so that there was every reason to want more of them. And the laws were changing, at both the federal and state levels, so that it seemed clear that it would soon be against the law to discriminate against women in the admission process.

A commission appointed by President Goheen in the winter of 1970 to review undergraduate education at Princeton recommended in the spring of 1973 that Princeton abandon quotas based on sex and adopt a policy of equal access for men and women. The faculty voted for it unanimously; the undergraduate student government favored it by a lopsided margin, as did the alumni council executive committee. Led by Bowen and Manning Brown, chair of the trustee executive committee, the trustees took up the question of equal access in the fall of 1973. To understand the intentions of the trustees who made the decision for coeducation in 1969, they took testimony from Goheen; from Harold Helm, an emeritus trustee who had chaired the trustee committee that had recommended coeducation; and from Jeremiah Finch, secretary to the board at the time of the decision. They heard from lawyers about current legal requirements and likely changes in the legal environment going forward. They concluded that the board in 1969 could not have meant to bind successor boards of trustees; that the assurance of continuing to admit eight hundred men expressed an understanding, not a formal commitment; and that it was incumbent on the current board to make decisions for Princeton in light of changing conditions. Strongly encouraged by Bowen, the board voted in January 1974 for equal access, effective with the admitted class of 1978.[8]

8 Nancy Weiss Malkiel, *"Keep the Damned Women Out": The Struggle for Coeducation* (Princeton, NJ: Princeton University Press, 2016), 288–92.

In 1980 Bowen devoted his annual president's report to the subject of coeducation. Faculty members attested to the many positive effects of having women students at Princeton. Suzanne Keller, professor of sociology and the first woman to be tenured at Princeton, remarked on the change in "the style of the university": There was "a freer spirit," with "more wit, humor, less pretentiousness . . . more innovation, more insouciance."[9] Edward D. Sullivan, professor of Romance languages and literatures, dean of the college from 1966 to 1972 and later chair of the humanities council, said, "This university is, in my view infinitely richer, more varied, more intellectually interesting, more warmly human than it ever was before 1969, however much I enjoyed the Princeton that I first knew in 1946." Charles C. Gillispie, professor of history and director of the program in history and philosophy of science, said, "I have no doubt that [coeducation] is the best thing that has happened to Princeton since 1746."[10]

Hitherto skeptical alumni had been won over as well. It was one thing to be opposed to coeducation in the abstract; it was a different situation when daughters and granddaughters eagerly seized the opportunity to enroll. And women students themselves, with their credentials and accomplishments, easily made the case for the wisdom of Princeton's new direction. "It seemed to me," Bowen told John William Ward, the president of Amherst College, who had asked about alumni reactions to coeducation at Princeton, "that many people who were against coeducation 'in principle' would not be against real live women students when they saw them—and when they saw how impressive they were."[11] After hearing Laurie Watson '73 speak on a panel in the early months of coeducation,

9 Quoted in William McCleery, *Conversations on the Character of Princeton* (Princeton, NJ: Princeton University, 1986), 58.

10 Quoted in William G. Bowen, *Princeton University, Report of the President, April 1980: Coeducation at Princeton*, 18, published in *Princeton Alumni Weekly*, Apr. 21, 1980. The material in this paragraph was previously published in Malkiel, *"Keep the Damned Women Out,"* 302.

11 William G. Bowen to John William Ward, Nov. 10, 1972, Bowen president, box 104, folder 14.

an alumnus told Bowen, "It was easy for me to be against coeducation; it is impossible for me to be against Laurie Watson!"[12]

By the close of the 1970s, Princeton had seen its first woman
valedictorian as well as its first woman Latin salutatorian, both in
1975. In 1977, the first year that women were eligible for the
Rhodes competition, a Princeton woman was among the thirty-two
scholars named. Two women were elected to serve as young alumni
trustees, and two women who were mothers, daughters, and sisters
of Princetonians were named to terms as charter trustees. (There
had been an unrealized effort in the last years of the Goheen presidency to find a "lady trustee.") Four women—including future
United States Supreme Court Justice Sonia Sotomayor '76—had
won the M. Taylor Pyne Honor Prize, the highest general distinction the university conferred on undergraduates. Five women had
been elected class presidents. The first woman had been elected
chair of the campus newspaper, the *Daily Princetonian*, and another
future United States Supreme Court justice, Elena Kagan '81, had
handled football reporting and become editorial chair of the paper.
Two of the eating clubs had elected women presidents.[13]

And coeducation had encouraged larger numbers of qualified applicants to apply to Princeton. All told, from 1968–69 (for the
class of 1973) to 1978–79 (for the class of 1983), the total number

12 I am indebted to William G. Bowen for this story. The material in this paragraph
was previously published in Malkiel, *"Keep the Damned Women Out,"* 302–3.

13 Emily Buchanan, "On the Campus: Coeducation's Tenth," *Princeton Alumni
Weekly*, Dec. 3, 1979, 17; Catherine Keyser, *Transforming the Tiger: A Celebration of
Undergraduate Women at Princeton University* (Princeton, NJ: Princeton University,
2001), 76; *Report of the Steering Committee on Undergraduate Women's Leadership*
(Princeton, NJ: Princeton University, Mar. 2011), 25–28; "New Trustee Peretsman '76
Targets Academic Pressure," *Daily Princetonian*, June 4, 1976, 1. On efforts in the
Goheen years to find a "lady trustee," see, e.g., memorandum, A. J. Maruca to Robert F.
Goheen, Apr. 27, 1970 (suggesting Joan Ganz Cooney); Goheen to Mary Ingraham
Bunting, May 15, 1970 (inquiring about Ruth Schachter Morgenthau); Bunting to
Goheen, May 26, 1970; memorandum, Goheen to Henry F. Bessire, May 28, 1970 (re
Elsie Hillman); memorandum, Goheen to the Committee on Governance, June 2, 1970;
Gen Fraiman to Goheen, May 9, 1971 (declining to be a candidate); Goheen to Fraiman,
May 17, 1971, all in Goheen, box 69, folder 3. Except for the "lady trustee," the
material in this paragraph was previously published in Malkiel, *"Keep the Damned
Women Out,"* 303.

of applicants rose by 82 percent. And there was a marked increase in the quality of the pool.[14]

Significant progress had also been made in appointing women to the Princeton faculty. In 1969–70 Princeton had one tenured woman faculty member, two women assistant professors, and seventeen women teaching as lecturers and instructors (most frequently in foreign languages). In 1979–80 Princeton had 10 tenured women, 40 women assistant professors, and 35 women teaching as lecturers and instructors—that out of a total faculty of 371 tenured professors, 196 assistant professors, and 122 lecturers and instructors. And, as we have seen, women had been appointed to the senior administrative ranks as dean of students, dean of the graduate school, and dean of the college.[15]

As for equal access, it was not nearly as disruptive as critics had feared in terms of changing the ratio of undergraduate men to women. The number of women crept up slowly, and equal access proved to be more important in the near term as a statement of institutional policy than as an instrument for genuine change in the composition of the undergraduate student body. Princeton reached the threshold of 40 percent women in 1990. Only in 2010 did it approach a 50–50 male-female ratio.[16]

As the numbers of women students and faculty increased, so did the pressure to make women and gender part of the Princeton curriculum. The decade of the 1970s saw the emergence of women's studies as a field of scholarly study in American colleges and universities. By December 1970 more than 100 courses in women's studies had been created nationally; by 1980 there were some 20,000 courses and 350 programs. Cornell established a women's

14 Bowen, *Coeducation at Princeton*, 6, 8–9. Previously published in Malkiel, *"Keep the Damned Women Out,"* 304.

15 Bowen, *Coeducation at Princeton*, 20–21. On Bowen's efforts to identify candidates, see, e.g., William G. Bowen to Patricia Graham, Jan. 26, 1972, and Bowen to Elga R. Wasserman, Jan. 26, 1972, both in Bowen president, box 48, folder 2. This material was previously published in Malkiel, *"Keep the Damned Women Out,"* 304.

16 Princeton University Registrar's Office.

studies program in 1972, Dartmouth in 1978, Yale in 1979, Harvard—the last in the Ivy League—in 1986.[17]

It was difficult to persuade male faculty members that gender was an appropriate area for study. Many male professors regarded women's studies with skepticism or outright hostility. It was often thought to be frivolous, faddish, political, a movement based on women's desire for representation rather than a commitment to serious intellectual inquiry. The initial strategy of the small group of women faculty members at Princeton who were interested in the study of gender was to encourage students to approach department chairs to ask that they offer courses relating to gender. Such courses were offered occasionally in departments including sociology, politics, history, psychology, and English. But making a commitment to regular course offerings about gender meant hiring scholars who studied gender, and most departments had other hiring priorities. Moreover, some assistant professors whose research was related to gender failed to win reappointment or promotion to tenure— evidence, it was claimed, that specializing in the study of gender would be toxic to a woman's academic career. Under the imprimatur of the dean of the faculty, Aaron Lemonick, some of the tenured women faculty members met with selected department chairs to suggest how the university might make better progress in appointing women faculty and offering courses related to gender, but their efforts met with relatively little enthusiasm.

At the same time, students made it clear that they wanted to study gender. From 1975 to 1980, more than two hundred senior theses were written on topics that would fall under the rubric of women's studies.[18] In 1979 a new group called WHEN—Women's Studies Hiring, Education Network—was organized at the women's center to press for the establishment of an undergraduate certifi-

17 Catharine R. Stimpson with Nina Kressner Cobb, *Women's Studies in the United States: A Report to the Ford Foundation* (New York: Ford Foundation, 1986), 4. The discussion that follows of women's studies was previously published in Malkiel, *"Keep the Damned Women Out,"* 296–99.

18 Margaret M. Keenan, "The Controversy over Women's Studies: And the Related Issue of Whether Princeton Is Hiring and Tenuring Enough Women Faculty Members Come to the Fore as the University Marks the 10th Anniversary of Coeducation," *Princeton Alumni Weekly*, Apr. 21, 1980, 13, cited in Keyser, *Transforming the Tiger*, 47.

cate program in women's studies and for the promotion to tenure of more female faculty members.[19] Impatient with the very slow progress on women's studies, women students affiliated with the women's center threatened a march on Nassau Hall.

Lemonick and the dean of the college, Joan Girgus, fully supported by Bowen and provost Neil Rudenstine, responded in the winter of 1979–80 by appointing an ad hoc committee of senior faculty members to advise on whether women's studies belonged in the Princeton curriculum. The committee was made up of four senior women faculty members who studied gender (it was considered too risky for junior women faculty, many of whom had scholarly interests in gender, to be identified publicly with the effort), and four prominent male faculty members who, if they were persuaded in committee of the importance of studying gender, could help make a case for the establishment of an undergraduate certificate program. The undergraduate student government selected seven women students to serve on the committee. History professor Nancy J. Weiss, though not herself a scholar who studied gender, was appointed chair.

The committee read widely in the field, consulted outside experts, studied course syllabi and program descriptions from other institutions, and solicited the views of undergraduates, graduate students, and faculty members. It made an inventory of women's studies courses that had been offered at Princeton and considered the proposal for a program prepared by WHEN. It considered how gender issues might be incorporated into regular course offerings in the various departments. In the end, the group agreed unanimously that the study of gender was an important new intellectual venture, fundamentally interdisciplinary, that raised questions that were recasting the basic assumptions of the disciplines, and that it should be "an integral part of a Princeton education in the 1980s."[20]

---

19 Elena Kagan, "The Women's Center: Gaining a New Identity amidst Controversy," and Kagan, "Karp Leads Women's Center with Chutzpah, Aggressiveness," both in *Daily Princetonian* supplement, "Women at Princeton: The First Ten Years," Nov. 1979, S-1, S-7.

20 "Report of the Ad Hoc Committee on the Future of Women's Studies," Princeton University, May 1980, in possession of Nancy Weiss Malkiel.

The ad hoc committee report was completed in May 1980. In January 1981, at an unusually well-attended faculty meeting, the proposal for an interdisciplinary undergraduate certificate program was approved overwhelmingly. The program began in 1981–82 under Weiss's temporary leadership. With Bowen's full support, the first appointed director, anthropologist Kay Barbara Warren, took office in 1982–83.

In Bowen's penultimate year as president, the words of the university's alma mater, "Old Nassau," were finally changed to reflect the fact that Princeton was coeducational. For almost two decades Princeton women had sung the alma mater as it was written in the nineteenth century:

> Tune every heart and every voice.
> Bid every care withdraw;
> Let all with one accord rejoice,
> In praise of Old Nassau.
>
> In praise of Old Nassau my boys,
> Hurrah! Hurrah! Hurrah!
> Her sons will give, while they shall live,
> Three cheers for Old Nassau.

The question of updating the lyrics had come up from time to time, but the university had been resistant. As the Keeper of Princetoniana Frederic E. Fox wrote to one correspondent who had advocated change, the reference to "boys" and "sons" was "generic"—as was the case with similar wording in the "Star-Spangled Banner" and "America," it should be understood as "embrac[ing] all mankind."[21]

The university's stance began to change in the fall of 1986, when Janet Sarbanes '89, daughter of Senator Paul Sarbanes '54 and sister of John Peter Sarbanes '84 and Pyne Prize winner Michael Sarbanes

---

21 Frederic E. Fox to Mrs. Earl Kreder, June 28, 1977, in Donald H. Fox, *The Old Familiar Places: The Life and Letters of Frederic E. Fox, the Spirit of Princeton,* vol. 1: *January 1975–August 1978* (La Crosse, WI: Fox Head Press, 2016), 319–20.

'86, wrote a column about "Old Nassau" for the *Daily Princetonian*. "I had sung 'Old Nassau' many times before I came to Princeton," she said. "But I never really heard the words until I was actually a student here, and wanted to sing along with everyone else about my new school with a hopeful devotion. I realized all of a sudden that I couldn't throw myself wholeheartedly into the singing of 'Old Nassau,' because there was no place for women—for me—in its lyrics. It seemed incredible that a co-ed school could condone, tolerate, or even ignore the exclusive nature of its school song."[22]

The *Princetonian* followed up with an editorial calling for "Old Nassau" to be made "an alma mater for *all* Princetonians."[23] The undergraduate student government passed a resolution urging that new wording replace the male references in the chorus. The executive committee of the alumni council appointed an ad hoc committee to propose specific changes. The new wording involved replacing five words:

In praise of Old Nassau we sing,
Hurrah! Hurrah! Hurrah!
Our hearts will give, while we shall live,
Three cheers for Old Nassau.

"Old Nassau was written to be inclusive for the Princeton of its day; these changes in lyric allow it to be inclusive for today's Princeton," Bowen said in announcing the trustee action approving the change.[24] Congratulating Sarbanes, he wrote, "My hope is that the change will be accepted gracefully and will serve its purpose: to allow all Princetonians to join together in celebrating their university."[25]

22 Sarbanes quoted in "Princeton Notebook: Lyrics of 'Old Nassau' Brought Up to Date," *Princeton Alumni Weekly*, Mar. 11, 1987, 13.

23 Ibid.

24 Princeton University news release, Feb. 26, 1987, Bowen president, box 372, folder 2.

25 William G. Bowen to Janet M. Sarbanes, Mar. 3, 1987, Bowen president, box 372, folder 2.

Race

Bowen's efforts to make Princeton more inclusive in terms of race built on the efforts launched in the Goheen administration. The objective was to bring more Black—and later Hispanic—students to the university, to support them through counseling and programming, and to integrate African American studies into the curriculum. What was different about Bowen's role with respect to race, however, was his emergence as a respected national spokesman for affirmative action.

When Robert F. Goheen assumed the presidency of Princeton in 1957, he took up the leadership of an institution generally regarded as wealthy, conservative, elitist, and snobbish, a characterization popularized in the famous novel by F. Scott Fitzgerald, *This Side of Paradise*. Fitzgerald, who had matriculated in the class of 1917 but failed to graduate, called Princeton "the pleasantest country club in America," an image reinforced in campus social life, which was dominated by the eating clubs, the private facilities where juniors and seniors ate, drank, and partied.[26]

The university had a long history of racial discrimination, dating back especially to the presidency of Woodrow Wilson; as well, it had a strong historical association with white students from the South, so that it was widely known as the northernmost southern university. And it had a notoriously racist, anti-Semitic director of admission, Radcliffe Heermance, who served from 1922 to 1950, thereby ensuring that Princeton would make very little progress toward racial diversity. Princeton enrolled its first Black student only in 1945. In the fall of 1960, in the entering class of 1964, there was only one Black student. The record was not much better at Harvard, with nine, or Yale, with five—universities that were much less southern than Princeton, and that had significantly larger entering classes.[27]

---

26 Fitzgerald quoted in James Axtell, *The Making of Princeton University: From Woodrow Wilson to the Present* (Princeton, NJ: Princeton University Press, 2006), 117 (see also 119).

27 Jerome Karabel, *The Chosen: The Hidden History of Admission and Exclusion at Harvard, Yale, and Princeton* (Boston: Houghton Mifflin, 2005), 379. On Heermance, see 123–24. On the history of racial discrimination in Princeton admissions, see chap. 8.

In the fall of 1961, again, one Black student matriculated in the freshman class at Princeton.[28] As the national context changed in terms of the urgency of civil rights, so, too, did the university begin to evolve. In 1962–63, when E. Alden Dunham took up the post of director of admission, Princeton first publicly stated an interest in recruiting qualified Black students. Numbers of applicants and matriculants increased slowly during the Dunham years. Princeton in the 1960s enrolled freshman classes of eight hundred students. Five Blacks matriculated in the freshman class in 1963–64. The next year, the number of matriculants increased to twelve. By 1965 Princeton had sixteen Blacks in the freshman class; in 1966, the number inched up to eighteen. In 1967–68, with yet another new director of admission, Jack Osander, strong pressure from the newly constituted Association of Black Collegians, and racial violence in American cities, recruitment of Black students became a real institutional priority, and the number of Black freshmen in 1968–69 rose to forty-four. Not only was the university intent on recruiting Blacks; in 1968–69, for the first time, it began to recruit Mexican Americans, Puerto Ricans, and Native Americans, and it "expanded its efforts to recruit more 'disadvantaged' whites."[29]

Over time, the Black applicant pool grew significantly, and the admission office extended its efforts to identify and recruit "disadvantaged students from other minority cultures" in addition to Blacks.[30] Active recruitment was necessary, as Bowen explained, because of "the history of this country and of Princeton." As well, Princeton wanted a critical mass of minority students to enable them to "feel like regular students and not objects of curiosity," a critical mass large enough to permit "the diversity of experience and viewpoint *within*" the population of minority students, "as well as

---

28 Ibid., p. 392.

29 "Enrollment, January 1973," and Timothy C. Callard, "The Admission of Minority Students, 1958–1972," in "Background Material for Trustee Student Life Committee Meeting," Jan. 19, 1973, Bowen president, box 78, folder 3; Karabel, *The Chosen*, 315, 393–98 (the quote is from 398).

30 Timothy C. Callard and Franklin D. Moore, "Minority Admissions," in "Background Material for Trustee Student Life Committee Meeting," Oct. 21, 1976, Bowen president, box 79, folder 1.

within the University at large, that is so important educationally."[31] Progress was slow but real; before Bowen became president, there had been eleven Black seniors in the class of 1968 and thirty-six in the class of 1972. Now there were forty-eight Black seniors in the class of 1973 and ninety-three in the class of 1976.[32]

Outside the classroom Black students participated in the newly established Third World Center, which opened in 1971–72 as a place where students from several ethnic groups could gather for shared intellectual, cultural, and social activities.[33] Previously an athletic field house, the center stood at the corner of Olden and Prospect Streets, next to the engineering quadrangle at the furthest end of the rows of eating clubs that lined the street. An expansion of the facility in the early 1970s added a multipurpose room that permitted holding a much wider range of functions at the TWC. In terms of housing and dining, Black students gravitated to Wilson and Princeton Inn Colleges (later Forbes), the two university-sponsored residential colleges that had been established as alternatives to the eating clubs. Beyond the campus, Black students took an active role especially in Community House, which offered tutoring and counseling programs for Black youths in the town of Princeton.[34] The first Black student served as president of the undergraduate student government in 1970; the first Black student was elected a young alumni trustee in 1971. Black students were selected as Rhodes Scholars in 1971 and 1977.

The record with respect to Black faculty also suggested an upward trajectory, but the numbers were much smaller. In 1969–70 there had been three Black faculty in the professorial ranks and

31 William G. Bowen to Howard C. Anderson, Mar. 16, 1973, Bowen president, box 97, folder 1.
32 "Enrollment, January 1973," and Timothy C. Callard, "The Admission of Minority Students, 1958–1972," in "Background Material for Trustee Student Life Committee Meeting," Jan. 19, 1973; "Enrollment Statistics as of July 3, 1976," in "Background Material for Trustee Student Life Committee Meeting," Oct. 21, 1976.
33 Conrad Snowden, "The Third World Center," in "Background Material for Trustee Student Life Committee Meeting," Jan. 19, 1973; "The Third World Center," memorandum, Snowden to Adele Simmons, Oct. 7, 1976, in "Background Material for Trustee Student Life Committee Meeting," Oct. 21, 1976.
34 Joseph F. Moore, "The Social Life of Black Students," in "Background Material for Trustee Student Life Committee Meeting," Jan. 19, 1973.

Bill Bowen was the son and only surviving child of **Albert A. Bowen**, a native of Indiana who sold cash registers for National Cash Register. Albert was already a veteran of the company when Bill was born, and he became NCR's senior regional salesman. He was often on the road, selling from the back of his station wagon. In 1940 Albert moved the family from Cincinnati to a modest house in the nearby suburb of Wyoming, Ohio. By Bill's senior year in high school, Albert was very sick. In December 1950, he died of heart failure, provoked by a progressive lung disease.

With Albert on the road so much of the time, Bill's mother, **Bernice Pommert Bowen,** carried the lion's share of the responsibility for raising the young boy. After Albert died, Bernice worked first in the purchasing department of the Drackett Company in Cincinnati, and later as a housemother in a women's dormitory at the University of Cincinnati. When she retired, she moved back to her birthplace, South Bend, Indiana. Bernice visited the Bowens in Princeton from time to time, but the family relationship was not especially close, and Bill traveled to see her infrequently. His friend Father Theodore Hesburgh, president of Notre Dame, sometimes saw to her well-being on his behalf.

Bill excelled at tennis in high school. He played first singles for Wyoming High School, which was the best high school team in the Ohio Valley in his senior year, and he won two regional tournaments. He then played for four years on the highly successful **tennis team at Denison University**, which won the Ohio Athletic Conference in his junior and senior years, with Bill serving as captain and taking top honors in singles and doubles. Bill is in the back row, second from right, flanked by his coach, English professor Tristram P. Coffin, and his doubles partner, Alan G. Preucil, who later served as best man in Bill and Mary Ellen's wedding.

Bill and Mary Ellen Maxwell first met in fourth grade, when the Maxwell family moved to Wyoming from Ashland, Kentucky. Mary Ellen's parents, O. B. Maxwell and Ina Lee, lived in a more prosperous section of Wyoming. Mary Ellen had two older brothers and a younger sister, and the siblings, their friends, and their parents' friends were in and out of a lively, welcoming house. Mary Ellen and Bill started dating seriously as juniors in high school, and the relationship deepened during their college years at Denison. **They married on August 25, 1956, at the Presbyterian Church of Wyoming,** with a reception afterward at the Maxwells' country club.

Upon completing his PhD in economics at Princeton in 1958, Bowen joined the faculty in the department of economics. Hiring its own PhDs was unusual for the department, but Bowen was an unusual talent, and the department prized both his growing body of scholarship in labor economics and his unusual effectiveness as a lecturer and class instructor. With competing offers from other top-ranked departments, Bowen was promoted to associate professor with tenure in 1961. In 1965 he was promoted to full professor, the second-youngest faculty member in the modern history of the university to be advanced to that rank. **This photograph, likely from 1960, shows Bowen as a young faculty member.**

In 1967 Bowen became the first full-time provost of the university. He played a key role in rethinking university governance. He pressed President Goheen to embrace undergraduate coeducation and participated actively in its implementation. He instituted a new budgeting system. And he contributed importantly to holding the institution together amidst the turmoil of the late 1960s. When Goheen announced in 1971 that he would retire from the Princeton presidency the following spring, Bowen was the leading candidate to succeed him. After a short search, the trustees elected Bowen the seventeenth president of Princeton. **Here he appears with Goheen at the press conference following the announcement of his appointment in November 1971.**

With Bowen's election to the presidency, the Bowens moved from the family home they had designed and built at 10 Maclean Circle into Walter Lowrie House, the official residence of the university president. The move would change the normal rhythms of family life, especially for Mary Ellen and the children, David, born in 1958, and Karen, born in 1964. Mary Ellen now had responsibility both for the organization of family life and for all the official entertaining that took place in the house. David, now a high school student, could still enjoy some independence and maintain familiar routines. For Karen, about to turn eight, the changes were more striking. With Mary Ellen and Bill often away from the house, the Bowens each year employed a university student to live in Lowrie House and keep Karen company. Here **the family is pictured at 10 Maclean Circle** after Bowen's election. In the other photograph, **Mary Ellen appears in one of her early portraits.**

Bowen was a spectacularly effective teacher of undergraduates. He always said that giving up lecturing in Economics 101, the large, introductory macroeconomics course the department had entrusted to him, was one of the costs of accepting the presidency. He insisted on teaching a class section in 101 throughout his tenure in the office. He relished the interaction with students and stayed in touch with many of them through their careers at Princeton and beyond. By showing that teaching undergraduates was an important part of the work of the Princeton president, Bowen created a model for his successors in the office. **This photo shows Bowen in the classroom in 101.**

Bowen played tennis as often as he could—until, that is, his elbow and knees told him that he had to give up the sport. During his years in the president's office, he spent as many lunch hours as possible playing with faculty colleagues. He was a fierce competitor; he hated to lose and expected to win, and win he usually did. With extraordinary powers of concentration, he had the capacity to leave his many official responsibilities back in the office and focus fully on the game at hand. **This photograph shows Bowen on the tennis court in a usual pose.**

Bowen worked all the time, usually at lightning speed, and he expected his colleagues to keep up with him. He was into everything; he knew everything that was going on, and he believed, possibly correctly, that he could do any job in the university at least as well as the incumbent. His drive and intensity, his commitment to excellence, inspired his colleagues to work harder, strive to do better, and reach for higher standards. The atmosphere in One Nassau Hall lightened up, literally as well as figuratively. The president's office was painted white, with modern furniture, modern art, and fabric sculptures made by Karen Bowen. **This photograph shows Bowen in the president's office.**

Bowen's two closest colleagues in the administration were the provost, Neil Rudenstine (*right*), and the dean of the faculty, Aaron Lemonick (*left*). Bowen and Rudenstine enjoyed extraordinary complementarity in style and skills. The two men struck up a strong working relationship when Bowen was provost and Rudenstine was dean of students. Bowen then promoted Rudenstine to dean of the college (1972) and provost (1977). He called Rudenstine "my closest steady colleague," "the ablest academic administrator I have ever known." Lemonick, dean of the graduate school while Bowen was provost, was appointed dean of the faculty in 1973. He was the other candidate taken seriously in the presidential search when Bowen was appointed.

Iconic roles, iconic places: By custom, the president of Princeton University presides at the university commencement exercises, held until the 2020s on the front lawn of Nassau Hall. In addition, the president—not an outside speaker—normally delivers the commencement address (the exception comes every half century, when the president of the United States fills that role). **Here Bowen presides at one of those commencements**, with the university motto—*Dei Sub Numine Viget* (she flourishes under the aegis of God)—on the banner behind him.

Here Bowen is pictured in the faculty room in Nassau Hall, the oldest building on the university campus. In the university's earliest years in Princeton, Nassau Hall housed the entire College of New Jersey, as it was then known, from the president's office to classrooms and student lodgings. Now it serves as the principal administration building, providing offices for the president, provost, and dean of the faculty, among others. The august, double-height, wood-paneled faculty room is the location for trustee meetings and faculty meetings. Portraits of generations of Princeton presidents line the walls.

Lighter duty: This photograph shows Bill and Mary Ellen, costumed for the occasion, reviewing the alumni P-Rade at reunions. Reunions brought thousands of alumni and their family members to Princeton. In the P-Rade, they paraded through the campus, the younger alumni in class costumes, the older in specially designed class blazers, waving banners and balloons, joined by marching bands, bagpipers, vehicles festooned in orange and black, bicyclists and unicyclists, animals caged or walking under their own steam, and other supporting characters. At its conclusion, the P-Rade passed a reviewing stand occupied by the president, his spouse, and alumni dignitaries, and ended in a gathering on a playing field.

Given the demands of the presidency, down time was hard to come by, whether for Bill and Mary Ellen alone or for the Bowens as a family. They particularly treasured trips to their house in Avalon on the Jersey shore. There was occasional travel with friends, whether to Europe or the Caribbean. And there were other iconic family occasions, like annual trips to watch tennis at the US Open in Forest Hills, NY. **This photograph shows a highly prized moment of near-off duty relaxation for Bill and Mary Ellen on a university trip to Greece.**

In January 1987, Bowen told the trustees that he would be stepping down as president of Princeton to take up the presidency of the Andrew W. Mellon Foundation. The provost, Neil Rudenstine, would also be departing to become executive vice president of the foundation. A short presidential search ensued, with Bowen's favored candidate, Harold T. Shapiro, named in April as Bowen's successor. Shapiro, a Princeton graduate alumnus in economics, was serving as president of the University of Michigan. Bowen would stay on until Shapiro could arrive in January 1988. **Here the newly appointed Shapiro (*center*) visits the campus,** with Bowen carrying his bags, and the director of public safety, Jerrold Witsil, looking on.

Princeton is legendary among major research universities for its long, unbroken stretch of outstanding presidential leadership, certainly from Robert F. Goheen forward. **This photograph, taken in the president's office in Nassau Hall during the Shapiro presidency, depicts three presidents (*left to right*)—Goheen, William G. Bowen, and Harold T. Shapiro—who together accounted for four and a half decades of that long run.**

A companion photograph depicts the presidents' wives (*right to left*)—Margaret Goheen, Mary Ellen Bowen, and Vivian Shapiro—on the front campus on an official occasion during the Shapiro presidency. By long tradition, presidents' wives supported their husbands in countless ways and provided hospitality of all kinds as well as leadership in campus organizations such as the university league and the infirmary. Vivian Shapiro, who earned a doctorate in social work during her husband's presidency, was the first presidential wife also to pursue her own professional career.

Like his predecessors and successors as president of Princeton, **Bill Bowen is depicted in a portrait** that hangs in the faculty room in Nassau Hall. Typically painted early in a new president's term in office, until the 2020s, the president's portrait first hung in the lobby of the Princeton Club in New York City and, after the president stepped down, was transferred to Nassau Hall.

Bowen took up the presidency of the Mellon Foundation in January 1988. He doubled down on Mellon's historical investments in graduate education, liberal arts colleges, libraries, museums, and performing arts institutions. As well, he inaugurated striking new initiatives, including JSTOR, the electronic journal storage project that transformed access to scholarly journals for faculty and students around the world, and the Mellon Mays (originally Mellon Minority) Undergraduate Fellowship Program to prepare students of color for the professoriate. He created a massive new database, College and Beyond, which supported his many books on key topics in higher education, including affirmative action, college athletics, and access and college completion for low-income and first-generation college students. **Here are two views of Bowen in his office at Mellon.**

Bowen retired from the presidency of the Mellon Foundation on July 1, 2006, when his successor, Don M. Randel, president of the University of Chicago, took office. Bowen then took up the chairmanship of the board of ITHAKA, a new nonprofit he founded with Mellon funding to explore ways of using information technology to accelerate college completion and control the rising costs of education in America's college and universities. **Here Bowen is pictured at his retirement celebration in the Mellon garden in the early summer of 2006.**

seven others teaching as lecturers, instructors, and assistants in instruction. In 1972–73 there were eight Black faculty in the professorial ranks and eleven others, six of whom were visiting the university.[35] Progress was slow; in 1975–76, there were eight Black faculty in the professorial ranks, along with four Black lecturers and instructors.[36] As for administrators, in 1964 Princeton had hired Carl A. Fields to take up a position in the Bureau of Student Aid, making him the first Black administrator in the Ivy League. In 1968, Fields became an assistant dean of the college. By 1972–73, there were twenty-eight Blacks employed at the university in various administrative ranks, ranging from an assistant provost and assistant deans to administrative assistants.[37]

From the outset, Bowen made clear to the university community where his administration stood on equal opportunity. He wrote to department and office heads in October 1974 about meeting the university's legal obligations by submitting an affirmative action plan "and making good faith efforts to achieve its goals," but he emphasized that legal requirements alone were not what was motivating the university's efforts. "I believe," he said, "that the University must make every effort to attract and retain the most outstanding individuals, whatever their sex or their racial or ethnic background. This is necessary in part simply because of the dictates of conscience and basic considerations of fairness. In addition, we have a clear interest in reaching out as widely as we can in the continuing effort to find the best possible people. Finally, I think all of us will agree that there are important educational benefits to be gained from cultural and ethnic diversity."[38] In other words, more diversity meant more effective learning.

35 "Black Faculty," in "Background Material for Trustee Student Life Committee Meeting," Jan. 19, 1973.

36 "Distribution of Faculty by Rank and Ethnic Status, for 1972–73 and 1975–76," in "Background Material for Trustee Student Life Committee Meeting," Oct. 21, 1976.

37 Carl A. Fields, "Black in Two Worlds: A Comparative Experience in Higher Education Administration," typescript, Jan. 12, 1974, Bowen president, box 171, folder 1; "Black Administrative Personnel," in "Background Material for Trustee Student Life Committee Meeting," Jan. 19, 1973.

38 Equal Opportunity within Princeton University, memorandum, William G. Bowen to All Heads of Departments and Offices, Oct. 15, 1974, Rees and Rudenstine provost, box 62, folder 2.

Bowen made his first foray into the public policy arena in September 1975 in testimony on affirmative action before the United States Department of Labor at the request of the American Council on Education and the Association of American Universities. With the Department of Health, Education, and Welfare poised to approve Princeton's affirmative action plan for hiring and promoting women and minority group members, Bowen was one of several university officials to testify at Labor Department hearings about the problems colleges and universities were having complying with the federal government's affirmative action requirements and procedures. The arguments were highly technical, having to do with the nature and amount of data required; the timeliness and effectiveness of the federal response; the shared understanding, or lack thereof, of such concepts as "availability" and "underutilization"; and the nature and definition of goals and timetables.

The analysis Bowen presented mattered greatly in terms of the hoops the government would or would not require institutions of higher education to jump through in order to meet criteria for the continued receipt of federal funding. What was important for purposes of the current discussion, however, were the overriding principles Bowen enunciated with respect to the "commitment to equal opportunity" felt so strongly by college and university presidents in the United States. "Historically," he said, "colleges and universities have failed to take full advantage of the contributions which women and members of minority groups could have made— could be making now—to higher education in this country. We should recognize explicitly these past deficiencies on our part. We should recognize also that more effective efforts to achieve equality of opportunity will strengthen the ability of our colleges and universities to achieve their educational purposes. Sensible programs of affirmative action can serve this educational purpose as well as the compelling goal of fairness to all concerned." He continued, ". . . the fundamental objective of the entire effort is to assure as well as we can that members of both sexes and of all races and ethnic groups have genuinely equal opportunities to be appointed, to be advanced, and to contribute to the fundamental educational purposes of colleges and universities. I believe that active, 'affirmative' efforts to deepen and broaden pools of candidates are needed to achieve genuine equality of opportunity; that a passive approach is not sufficient; that we need to work hard to overcome the subtle as well as overt forms that discrimination can take."[39]

Bowen's next foray into the public policy arena was much more consequential, both for Princeton and for federal policy on affirmative action. In 1977, a long paper that he wrote, "Admissions and the Relevance of Race," was published as the cover story in the September 26 *Princeton Alumni Weekly.*[40] Undergraduate admission was not affected by the affirmative action requirements imposed on the university by the Department of Health, Education, and Welfare as a condition of the receipt of federal funds for research—those requirements had to do exclusively with employment. But recruiting talented minority students who would thrive at Princeton and "contribute to the experience of the student body as a whole" was critically important to the university. "I am convinced . . . ," Bowen told a correspondent, "that the educational environment on the campus is far healthier and far more stimulating because of the presence of significant numbers of minority students."[41]

In "Admissions and the Relevance of Race," Bowen raised central questions: "What considerations should be taken into account in deciding which individuals to admit from among the large number who apply? Is it ever proper to consider the race of an applicant, among other attributes? If so, why, and in what ways? Are there significant distinctions to be drawn between the use of quotas and other approaches to the recruitment of minority students?"[42]

Bowen explained that race mattered in multiple ways. It mattered in terms of the life experiences of applicants and the circumstances

39 William G. Bowen, "Affirmative Action: Purposes, Concepts, Methodologies, Testimony before Department of Labor," Sept. 30, 1975, Bowen president, box 278, folder 4. See also "Affirmative Action: The Shortcomings of Statistics," *Princeton Alumni Weekly,* Oct. 13, 1975, 8–9.

40 William G. Bowen, "Admissions and the Relevance of Race," *Princeton Alumni Weekly,* Sept. 26, 1977, 7–13.

41 William G. Bowen to David W. Tibbott, Sept. 2, 1977, Bowen president, box 161, folder 4.

42 Bowen, "Admissions and the Relevance of Race," 7.

they had to contend with—"what a particular candidate has accomplished—and against what odds." It mattered in terms of the composition of the student body and the ways in which that composition affected opportunities for student learning. The task of the admission office, Bowen said, was "to assemble a total class of students, all of whom will possess the basic qualifications, but who will also represent, in their totality, an interesting and diverse amalgam of individuals who will contribute through their diversity to the quality and vitality of the overall educational environment." "If the University were unable to take into account the race of candidates," he argued, "it would be much more difficult to consider carefully and conscientiously the composition of an entering class that would offer a rich educational experience to all of its members."[43]

American society, indeed, the larger world, Bowen said, "is and will be multi-racial. We simply must learn to work more effectively and more sensitively with individuals of other races, and a diverse student body can contribute directly to the achievement of this end." A residential college or university provided "unusually good opportunities to learn about other people and their perspectives—better opportunities than many will ever know again."[44]

The final set of considerations in deciding how to compose a student body, Bowen explained, had to do with "potential contributions to society"—who among the institution's graduates had the long-range potential to make what kinds of contributions. Race was relevant in assessing an applicant's "drive and determination" in confronting challenges, obstacles, difficulties, even outright discrimination. It was also the case that the country needed "a far larger number of able people from minority groups in leadership positions of all kinds." "It seems to me indisputable," Bowen said, "that the welfare of the entire society will be advanced through the fuller development and application of the talents of minority members of our population and that this cannot be accomplished without over-

43 Ibid., 9.
44 Ibid., 10.

coming the substantial disparities which exist now between the races in professional opportunities and attainments."[45]

"If colleges and universities serve these large societal purposes through the individuals they have educated, as well as through scholarship and research," Bowen continued, "then it seems to me to follow directly that in making admission decisions educational institutions must take into account the needs of the society— including the need for minority persons who can contribute through the law, medicine, the ministry, business, and other professions; who can pursue scholarly careers in the arts and sciences; who can serve in positions of public trust; and who can, in fact, take a full part in every aspect of the life of the nation." Were educational institutions to be prohibited from taking race into account in admissions, "then it would be far more difficult—indeed impossible—to discharge responsibly the obligation to develop as fully as possible the 'social capital' of the country."[46]

The right course for Princeton, Bowen said, was "taking account of race with many other factors, but not through the mechanism of a separate admission procedure geared to filling an established number of places." That had the advantage of "encourag[ing], even forc[ing], comparisons of candidates who present different kinds of special attributes." And it made "clear to the minority students, as to all other students, that everyone who has been admitted has been part of a single admission process, carried out by a single admission staff." "Minority students, like all other students, should know that they have been admitted because they have earned admission—because they are expected to do well and to make important contributions to the University and to the society."[47]

Bowen's essay was very well received, and it proved to be broadly influential. A Princeton alumnus, who described himself as "a diehard conservative," "probably to the right of Ramses IV," said that Bowen had done "an excellent job of bringing this whole subject into focus. I can't say that I agree with all of your conclusions, but

45 Ibid., 10–11.
46 Ibid., 11.
47 Ibid., 13.

you certainly have made me pause and rethink my position relative to this very difficult problem."[48] Princeton professor of history Lawrence Stone, a notably tough critic, said that the paper was "really remarkable." "You have thought right through the problem, and certainly helped *me* to see my way through what I had previously thought was an impenetrable thicket."[49] The president of Johns Hopkins University, Steven Muller, wrote, "You have rendered all of us a great service by your sensitive and admirable consideration of the fundamental issues. It is an excellent statement. I agree with it, but I could never have put it so well."[50] The president of the Ford Foundation, McGeorge Bundy, called Bowen's paper "genuinely admirable"—"the best statement on the considerations surrounding admissions to a great college that I have ever seen."[51] The president of the Robert Wood Johnson Foundation, David E. Rogers, said that Bowen's statement was "thoughtful and nicely balanced"—"seems to me you take a sensible and considered middle position which is morally and philosophically appropriate." It was, Rogers said, "a real contribution to a troubled and sensitive area at this moment in our history. I like where you come out and I admire your guts in tackling it head on."[52]

The most consequential reaction to Bowen's statement came from Lewis F. Powell Jr., the Associate Justice of the United States Supreme Court who would, the following June, provide the crucial swing vote in *Regents of the University of California v. Bakke*, in which the court upheld the legality of affirmative action, outlawing specific racial quotas but allowing race to be used as one of several factors in college and university admissions.[53] While there were six separate opinions in *Bakke*, Powell provided the critical

48 Lawrence B. Morris Jr. to William G. Bowen, Sept. 29, 1977, Bowen president, box 125, folder 2.

49 Lawrence Stone to William G. Bowen, Sept. 15, 1977, Bowen president, box 125, folder 2.

50 Steven Muller to William G. Bowen, Sept. 13, 1977, Bowen president, box 125, folder 2.

51 McGeorge Bundy to William G. Bowen, Sept. 21, 1977, Bowen president, box 124, folder 8.

52 David E. Rogers to William G. Bowen, Oct. 3, 1977, Bowen president, box 125, folder 2.

53 *Regents of the University of California v. Bakke*, 438 U.S. 265 (1978).

fifth vote in the two most important judgments handed down in the case. On the one hand, he and four of the more conservative justices held that Allan Bakke, a white applicant, had been improperly denied admission to the medical school at the University of California at Davis, where sixteen places in the entering class were set aside for minority students, thus denying Bakke and other students like him the "equal protection" of the law. On the other hand, Powell and four more liberal justices held that race could be taken into account in admissions decisions in higher education.[54]

What did this have to do with Bowen? Princeton professor of politics Walter Murphy typically invited Supreme Court justices to come to Princeton to speak to his courses in constitutional interpretation and law and society. In October 1977, it was Powell who was Murphy's visitor from the court. The issue of the *Princeton Alumni Weekly* containing Bowen's statement on race and college admission had just been published, and when Powell returned to Washington, he brought a copy back to his chambers. He handed the magazine to his Princeton clerk, Robert Comfort, valedictorian of the class of 1973. Powell, Comfort later told Bowen, "had marked up your piece quite heavily and obviously was quite impressed by your views." Comfort was chagrined not to have read Bowen's essay himself; "in his genial manner," Comfort told Bowen, Powell "brushed aside my embarrassment at having failed to bring to his attention a relevant piece in my own alumni publication." What was important, Powell told Comfort, was to "work as many quotations . . . as possible [from the Bowen essay] into any forthcoming Powell opinion."[55]

And that was exactly what happened in *Bakke*, Comfort told Bowen, giving him "the 'inside' story" of how Princeton—and Bowen—"ended up playing so prominent a part in the Powell Opinion's footnotes."[56] Powell quoted Bowen at length in three footnotes. The first one accompanied this statement by Powell: "The

---

54 Thomas H. Wright Jr., "Princeton's Contribution to the Bakke Decision," *Princeton Alumni Weekly*, July 10, 1978, 16.

55 Robert Comfort to William G. Bowen, Aug. 22, 1978, Bowen president, box 124, folder 8.

56 Ibid.

atmosphere of 'speculation, experiment and creation'—so essential to the quality of higher education—is widely believed to be promoted by a diverse student body." The footnote read, in part: "The president of Princeton University has described some of the benefits derived from a diverse student body: '. . . [A] great deal of learning occurs informally. It occurs through interactions among students of both sexes; of different races, religions, and backgrounds; who come from cities and rural areas, from various states and countries; who have a wide variety of interests and perspectives; and who are able, directly or indirectly, to learn from their differences and to stimulate one another to reexamine even their most deeply held assumptions about themselves and their world. As a wise graduate of ours once observed in commenting on this aspect of the educational process, 'People do not learn very much when they are surrounded only by the likes of themselves.'" A second footnote described the admission program at Princeton, again quoting Bowen: "While race is not in and of itself a consideration in determining basic qualifications, and while there are obviously significant differences in background and experience among applicants of every race, in some situations race can be helpful information in enabling the admissions office to understand more fully what a particular candidate has accomplished—and against what odds. Similarly, such factors as family circumstances and previous educational opportunities may be relevant, either in conjunction with race or ethnic background (with which they may be associated) or on their own."[57]

Two decades later, Bowen's landmark study, *The Shape of the River: Long-Term Consequences of Considering Race in College and University Admissions*, coauthored with Derek Bok, would build directly on the insights in "Admissions and the Relevance of Race," making a powerful case for the importance of affirmative action in college and university admissions.

---

57 "Excerpts from Bowen's Article Quoted by Justice Powell," in Wright, "Princeton's Contribution to the Bakke Decision," 17. The third footnote quoting Bowen had to do with graduate admissions. See Thomas H. Wright Jr., response to letter to the editor, *Princeton Alumni Weekly*, Sept. 25, 1978, 3.

9

Inclusion—Religion and Residential Life

Helping Students "Feel More Included in the University"

Religion

Expanding the campus community to include women as well as men, Blacks and Hispanics as well as whites, was a common experience at American colleges and universities in the 1970s. Much less common was a key element of inclusion at Princeton: religion. From the time of its founding, Princeton had been formally nonsectarian, formally ecumenical, but in fact a very Protestant, especially very Presbyterian institution. In the 1950s, some three-quarters of Princeton students were Protestant Christians, mainly Presbyterians or Episcopalians. The university chapel, built in the latter years of the 1920s, a grand cruciform church reminiscent of an English Gothic cathedral, sat opposite Firestone Library, forming one side of the main academic quadrangle at the center of the campus. Attendance at chapel services, a requirement for generations of Princeton students, was relaxed gradually, with upperclass students relieved of the responsibility in 1935, sophomores in 1960, and freshmen in 1964. The fact that Princeton was so assertively Protestant often made Roman Catholic and especially Jewish students feel like outsiders (later, that would be true as well of Muslim and Hindu students).[1]

---

1 Frederick Houk Borsch, *Keeping Faith at Princeton: A Brief History of Religious Pluralism at Princeton and Other Universities* (Princeton, NJ: Princeton University Press,

The university's identification with Presbyterianism extended to the presidency; Princeton presidents were typically Presbyterian ministers or the sons of Presbyterian ministers or missionaries. That did not describe Bowen, of course. While he and Mary Ellen were at Denison, they had been drawn to Sunday services at the local Baptist church because of a charismatic minister. When they first came to Princeton, they had joined the First Presbyterian Church, again because of the minister, who took what Mary Ellen described as a "more intellectual approach to religion."[2] But this was not a major, enduring commitment. In the course of the presidential search, Bowen remarked later, he wanted to be sure that the trustees understood "that I was not really a religious person, and did not come out of the Presbyterian tradition that they were so used to—that Princeton was so used to—and that that just needed to be understood, and that if that was disqualifying, well, fine. I would understand that. But I didn't want there to be any misunderstandings." Bowen said that he "was assured, and indeed I remember very well, being assured by John Coburn, the Episcopal bishop of Massachusetts and a key trustee, that that was just not an issue here. That he thought this was a personal matter—that the president should do what the president believes in."[3]

That said, while the trustees had made plain in the course of the search that Bowen was free to do as he wished in terms of religious observance, the fact that Bowen did not attend the regular Sunday morning worship services in the university chapel was a significant departure from the practice of his predecessors, and it stood as one of the many irritants that fueled the displeasure of the breakaway conservative alumni group, Concerned Alumni of Princeton (CAP). In an interview in 1974, Shelby Cullom Davis '30, founder and co-chair of CAP, said, "I think the President should be a leader. I think when the students watch what he is doing, if he doesn't care enough to go [to services in the chapel] it has an influence." As a "public person," Davis said, Bowen effectively forfeited his right to free ex-

2012), introduction and chap. 1; "The University Chapel," in Alexander Leitch, *A Princeton Companion* (Princeton, NJ: Princeton University Press, 1978), 87.

2 Interview with Mary Ellen Bowen, July 20, 2018, Princeton, NJ.

3 Bowen oral history, June 25, 2009, 18.

ercise of religion; "I think if he is leading a university . . . he must do what the job entails regardless of his own feelings."[4]

Bowen came to the presidency determined to make Princeton more welcoming to a wider range of religious beliefs and practices. Religion was a significant part of what he meant when he spoke of greater inclusiveness, and Jewish students were the particular constituency he had foremost in his mind. Princeton had had a Jewish quota in undergraduate admission for many years. Under strong external pressure—political, legal, and intellectual—the university relaxed the quota as the 1940s drew to a close and, by 1950, deleted the question on religious affiliation that had been on the Princeton application since the 1920s. The university counted to some degree on the character of campus life to deter Jewish students from applying and matriculating. The eating clubs, the center of social life and dining for juniors and seniors, were a key element here; if Jewish students were seen by their peers as "unclubbable," they would be unhappy at Princeton, and, ideally, would choose not to come.

But as the number of Jewish students began to increase, pressure emerged from Princeton sophomores to guarantee that 100 percent of students who wanted to join an eating club would receive at least one bid. The campaign for 100 percent bicker was effective in the early 1950s, but it blew up in 1958 in what was known as "dirty bicker," with twenty-three students, fifteen of them Jewish, left without a bid from a single club.[5] When students leading the campaign turned to President Goheen for help, he responded that in the spirit of voluntary association, the eating clubs were free to select their own members. While he said that he would deplore the exclusion of students from membership on the sole ground of religion, he noted that each of the clubs had members drawn from among the three major faith groups, Protestants, Catholics, and Jews.[6]

<hr>

4 "Interview with Shelby Cullom Davis '30," *Princeton Alumni Weekly*, Nov. 5, 1974, 11.

5 Jerome Karabel, *The Chosen: The Hidden History of Admission and Exclusion at Harvard, Yale, and Princeton* (Boston: Houghton Mifflin, 2005), 236–44, 298–310.

6 Ibid., 309.

Bowen knew that Jewish students had not always had "an easy path" at Princeton. He understood the history, and he had firsthand testimony from the observant Jewish students, especially from the Ramaz School (a Jewish day school in New York City), who enrolled in the Economics 101 classes he was teaching. They told him that they did not feel "at home" or "comfortable" at Princeton—to the contrary, they felt isolated and unwelcome. Bowen believed that "the university would be a much richer, better learning environment if it had a variety of people from different backgrounds, different points of view, interacting easily and comfortably with each other."[7] "So one of my goals," he said, "was to help not only minority students and women, but also Jewish students, feel more included in the university."[8] "It was extremely important to me," he explained, "that the university not seem to belong to any particular group of people, and it was very important that any group, such as the Jewish students, not feel like second-class citizens."[9]

Bowen addressed the issue in two ways. The first involved rethinking the role of the chapel and the dean of the chapel in university life, making certain especially that important university gatherings typically held in the chapel, like opening exercises and baccalaureate, were refashioned in terms of timing and content to detach them from the traditional framework of Christian worship. The second involved planning for, and raising funds for, a university Center for Jewish Life.

The coming retirement in 1980–81 of the long-serving dean of the chapel, Ernest Gordon, a Scottish Presbyterian minister (his predecessors as dean had been a Congregationalist and an Episcopalian), opened the way for what the executive committee of the board of trustees called a thorough examination of "the ways in which the Chapel may best continue to serve the needs of the University com-

7 Bowen speaking in video, "Princeton Celebrates 100 Years of Jewish Life," Apr. 15, 2016, Office of Communications, Princeton University, princeton.edu/news/2016/04/15 /video-feature-princeton-celebrates-100-years-jewish-life.

8 Bowen oral history, July 21, 2009, not paginated.

9 Ibid., June 25, 2009, 18–19. See also William G. Bowen, *Lessons Learned: Reflections of a University President* (Princeton, NJ: Princeton University Press, 2011), 112–15.

munity." Bowen recommended, and the board concurred, that before beginning a search for Gordon's successor, it would be a good idea "to have a wide-ranging discussion of the role of the chapel and of the dean of the chapel." Toward that end, in October 1978, Bowen appointed a campus steering committee, cochaired by Near Eastern studies professor (and ordained Presbyterian clergyman) John H. Marks and university counsel Thomas H. Wright Jr. (son of the Episcopal bishop of the Diocese of East Carolina), and including also dean of the faculty Aaron Lemonick (Jewish), professor of English John V. Fleming (Episcopalian), professor of history Arthur S. Link (Presbyterian), professor of politics Paul Sigmund (Roman Catholic), and professor of classics Froma I. Zeitlin (Jewish). The trustees appointed their own committee, chaired by Bishop Coburn, to consult with the campus committee and make recommendations to the full board.[10]

After consulting widely about religious life on campus and the role of the chapel and its dean—consultation accomplished through meetings and correspondence with faculty, students, denominational chaplains, staff, alumni, and religious leaders at other institutions—the faculty committee submitted its report in May 1979.[11] In September, the trustee committee followed suit.[12] The two reports converged on several basic principles: The university should (in the words of the trustee report) continue to support religious activities as "an essential part of [Princeton's] educational purpose." The new dean of the chapel, possibly with a broader title (e.g., dean of religious life and dean of the chapel), should have responsibility for oversight (as the trustee report put it) "for the activities of all officially recognized religious bodies on the campus." There should be a broadly constituted advisory body to the dean, representing a wide variety of religious viewpoints and groups. The

---

10 Princeton University news release, Oct. 3, 1978, Bowen president, box 56, folder 8. On the issues at stake, see, e.g., Nicholas A. Ulanov, "Defining the Chapel's Mission," *Princeton Alumni Weekly*, Mar. 26, 1979, 15–18, 20.

11 "Report of the Faculty Committee on the Chapel," May 18, 1979, Bowen president, box 211, folder 3.

12 "Report of the Trustees' Advisory Committee on the Roles of the Chapel and the Dean of the Chapel," Sept. 28, 1979, Bowen president, box 56, folder 8.

Sunday morning worship service in the chapel should be overseen by a board drawn from the congregation, working in concert with the minister for the chapel. The denominational chaplains and the organizations they represented should be more formally organized as a functional group. The university should extend support from general funds to the dean, the dean's office, and university-wide religious activities, while the denominations should continue to be responsible for their own funding. And, perhaps most important symbolically, the official ceremonies of the university should be moved out of the eleven o'clock slot on Sunday mornings devoted to Christian worship and scheduled instead in midafternoon, with the ceremonies clearly organized as interfaith services.[13]

The reports naturally drew criticism from alumni convinced that Princeton was turning its back on its history as a Christian institution, on the chapel's history as a place of Christian worship, and, indeed, in fundamental ways, turning its back on God.[14] And after a new dean was in place, the efforts to create truly interfaith ceremonies sparked dismay when the cross in the center of the nave was covered by a screen, with interfaith religious symbols displayed in front of it. Despite protests from opponents of the move, who greatly overstated the implications of screening the cross during institutional ceremonies, the cross would not be removed from view at times other than when those ceremonies were scheduled.[15]

Bowen appointed John Marks to be acting dean during Ernest Gordon's sabbatical in 1980–81 and tasked Thomas Wright, assisted by the members of the faculty committee on the chapel, to

13 In addition to the aforementioned reports, see Princeton University news release, Oct. 20, 1979, Bowen president, box 211, folder 5. On how all of this worked in practice, see Borsch, *Keeping Faith at Princeton*, chap. 3.

14 See, e.g., Robert Connor to William G. Bowen, Oct. 5, 1979; James J. O'Donnell to J. B. Coburn, Oct. 1, 1979; Bowen to O'Donnell, Oct. 8, 1979; Thomas H. Wright to O'Donnell, Oct. 10, 1979; Lawrence N. Proctor to Bowen, Dec. 4, 1979; Bowen to Proctor, Dec. 12, 1979, all in Bowen president, box 211, folder 5; Philip F. Lawler, "Getting God out of Princeton," *National Review*, Oct. 3, 1980, 1192–93, 1196; Arthur S. Link to the Editor, *National Review*, Nov. 10, 1980, both in Bowen president, box 210, folder 2.

15 See, e.g., William H. Hudnut to Frederick H. Borsch, Mar. 16, 1982, and Borsch to Hudnut, Mar. 24, 1982, both in Bowen president, box 210, folder 3.

conduct a search for the new dean. That search resulted in the appointment as dean of the Reverend Dr. Frederick H. Borsch, president and dean of the Church Divinity School of the Pacific in Berkeley, California, an ordained Episcopal priest and a formidable scholar of the New Testament. Borsch, a member of the Princeton class of 1957, took up his position in 1981 and moved thoughtfully to implement the provisions regarding the chapel and the dean that had been agreed to by the trustees.[16] Even before Borsch's arrival, changes in university ceremonies created a palpable sense of belonging for Jews on campus. In September 1980, Edward Feld, the Hillel rabbi, wrote to Bowen, who was on leave in California, about "the wonderful way Opening Exercises came off": "The service managed to maintain a spiritual and religious character yet truly be inclusive of everyone. Jewish students who had not gone to Opening Exercises their own freshman year turned out for this one. They all report how deeply affected they were." And for the new freshmen, Feld said, "it was as if this had always been the Princeton tradition." "For myself," he added, "I walked proudly down the aisle, feeling at home here, in a way I never had before."[17]

That was part and parcel of Bowen's overriding plan. A related part was to change the baccalaureate service, not only by moving it out of "the Christian hour" but by changing the identity of the speakers. Instead of the Princeton president giving the address, as had been the case historically, Bowen looked to others, with a deliberate ordering of his choices. First came a Princeton professor, Gregory Vlastos, the preeminent scholar of ancient philosophy. Next came Father Theodore Hesburgh, the Roman Catholic priest who served for thirty-five years as president of Notre Dame. And then came Gerson Cohen, chancellor of the Jewish Theological Seminary of America from 1972 to 1986, who happened to be the

---

16 See, e.g., [Frederick H. Borsch,] "Report to the President on the University Chapel Ministry, 1981–82," and "Report to the President on the University Chapel Ministry, 1982–83" both in Bowen president, box 210, folder 3.

17 Edward Feld to William Bowen, Sept. 17, 1980, Bowen president, box 210, folder 2.

father of a graduating Princeton senior, and who gave what Bowen regarded as the best baccalaureate address he had heard.[18]

Making the university chapel more inclusive was the first step in realizing Bowen's aspirations to make Princeton more welcoming to Jewish students. The second was to engage in active recruitment of Jewish students, both to increase the size of the Jewish student community on campus and to take fuller advantage of the extraordinary talent available in Jewish day schools as well as public schools with a significant Jewish population. Aggressive recruitment was "critically important," Bowen said later; it was "blindingly obvious" that bringing more talented Jewish students to Princeton was an integral part of improving the quality of the university.[19]

The third step in Bowen's plan was to create a physical location for worship and fellowship for Jewish students and faculty, a counterpart to the chapel and Murray-Dodge Hall, the building that housed the dean and assistant deans of the chapel and provided space for gatherings of the various denominational groups on campus. Since 1971, one of the buildings in Stevenson Hall had served that purpose for Jewish students. Stevenson was a university-sponsored eating and social facility on Prospect Avenue, at the end of the row of eating clubs. It consisted of two buildings that had previously housed eating clubs that had since closed. Stevenson served, in the main, as an alternative for upperclass students who preferred not to join an eating club and who enjoyed a range of social, cultural, and intellectual activities organized by students, faculty fellows, and a faculty master and assistant master. One of the two Stevenson buildings—83 Prospect Avenue—housed a kosher dining facility, one of three university-sponsored kosher kitchens in the country (the others were at Jewish institutions, Yeshiva and

18 Bowen, video with Harold T. Shapiro and Janet M. Holmgren at the Celebration of 100 Years of Jewish Life at Princeton, Apr. 15, 2016, Media Central, Princeton University, https://mediacentral.princeton.edu/media/L'CHAIM!%20to%20Life%20-%20 Luncheon%3A%20A%20Discussion%20with%20Princeton%20University%20 Presidents%20Emeriti%20William%20Bowen%20and%20Harold%20Shapiro%20*64 /1_f3c2myqm.

19 Ibid.

Brandeis). Kosher Stevenson replaced Yavneh House, an off-campus kosher dining facility organized in 1961 by Orthodox students under the aegis of Princeton Hillel. Kosher Stevenson also served as the locus for religious, social, cultural, and intellectual activities organized by and for Jewish students on campus.[20]

In 1984 Princeton Hillel formed an ad hoc committee to study Jewish life on campus. The aspiration of Rabbi Feld and of Jewish students was for a larger, freestanding facility that would accommodate a more commodious kosher dining facility, multiple spaces for Jewish worship services, and spaces as well for social, cultural, and intellectual activities involving Jewish students at Princeton. It would provide much more physical space than was available at Kosher Stevenson; it would allow activities dispersed in multiple locations on campus to come together under one roof; and it would stand as an important symbol that Jewish students, like Christian students, had a home of their own at Princeton. Jewish students, Bowen thought, were too much on the periphery; they needed to be "at the core," "hosts" as well as "guests" in the university.[21] Borsch put it this way: Giving Jewish students a place of their own, "a place of hospitality," would allow them to "invite people to come to [them]" instead of "always coming to other people on their terms."[22] As Bowen described it, a new building for a Center for Jewish Life would also "fulfill a still larger purpose by providing a highly visible 'Jewish presence' at Princeton, at the very center of campus life, thus indicating to everyone that Princeton encourages and supports an active Jewish student life on its campus."[23]

Bowen took up the mission of establishing a Center for Jewish Life. After considerable discussion and exploration, the university settled on the location: 70 Washington Road, a university building next to Terrace Club at the corner of Ivy Lane and Washington

20 Marianne Sanua, "Stages in the Development of Jewish Life at Princeton University," *American Jewish History* 76 (June 1987): 391–93, Bowen president, box 159, folder 7.

21 Bowen, video with Shapiro and Holmgren.

22 Borsch oral history, 38.

23 William G. Bowen to Ivan Boesky, Aug. 19, 1985, Bowen president, box 409, folder 10.

Road, the main thoroughfare connecting the university with Route 1, the highway between Trenton to the south and New York City to the north. The building had been the home of Prospect Club, one of several eating clubs that had closed over the years for lack of interest on the part of students. Since then, it had been housing a variety of university offices that could be relocated; with the right investment, an architect could transform it into a commodious home for Jews on the Princeton campus. After a careful planning process, the fund-raising target was agreed on, and Bowen committed to find the money to proceed. He reached an agreement with the financial arbitrageur Ivan Boesky, the father of a student in the class of 1988, to contribute $1.5 million (half to the center and half to a new building for the Center of International Studies and the department of economics).[24]

When Boesky got caught up in an insider trading scandal, with a fine of $100 million to be paid to the federal government and an agreement to bar Boesky for life from the securities industry, the question arose about whether the university could still appropriately accept his gift. While that was under debate, Boesky took the institution off the hook by withdrawing his pledge.[25] Bowen set out once again to find a lead funder, and after some fits and starts, including another lead gift that came a cropper, he raised sufficient money to continue with the project.[26]

With additional funding finally in hand, the trustees approved the plan in 1988, and the university hired the architect Robert A. M. Stern to design the reconstruction of the building. The center opened

24 Memoranda, William G. Bowen to the files [re Ivan F. Boesky], Aug. 1, Oct. 11, Dec. 11, 1985; Bowen to Boesky, Aug. 19, 1985; Boesky to Bowen, Sept. 9, 1985, all in Bowen president, box 409, folder 10; Princeton University news release, Apr. 22, 1986, Bowen president, box 409, folder 11; memorandum, Bowen to the files [re Boesky], July 29, 1986, Bowen president, box 316, folder 3.

25 Ivan F. Boesky to William G. Bowen, Nov. 14, 1986; Bowen to Boesky, Nov. 17, 1986; statement by President William G. Bowen, Nov. 17, 1986; Craig A. Bloom, "University to Examine Boesky Gift Following Wall St. Scandal," *Daily Princetonian*, Nov. 17, 1986, and Bloom, "Boesky Withdraws $1.5 Million Pledge," Nov. 18, 1986, all in Bowen president, box 409, folder 11.

26 Memorandum, William G. Bowen to the files [re Michael J. Scharf], Nov. 26, 1986; Princeton University news release, Dec. 1, 1986; Bowen to Scharf, Dec. 2, 1986, all in Bowen president, box 316, folder 4.

in 1993, during the presidency of Harold T. Shapiro, Princeton's first Jewish president. But it was Bowen's impetus and drive that made it happen. For Bowen, it was all about inclusion: ". . . nothing has given me more satisfaction," he said, "than participating in what has been a broadly-based effort to enable students of all faiths, including importantly Jewish students, to feel 'at home' at Princeton."[27]

Eating Clubs

By the time Bowen became president of Princeton, the basic structure of campus social life had been in place for a century. Freshmen and sophomores ate in the university eating commons. Juniors and seniors ate and partied in private eating clubs located in often-grand stone, brick, or half-timbered buildings arrayed along Prospect Avenue, spilling over on the end of Prospect closest to the central campus onto Washington Road. Originally, all Princeton students ate in the college refectory, but the refectory closed after a fire in 1855, and upperclass students then took their meals in small, temporary eating clubs in boardinghouses in town. (A new eating commons for freshmen opened in 1906; sophomores were added two years later.) The more enduring of the temporary clubs in town, known originally as "select associations," became the basis for the modern eating clubs. The first eating club to build a separate, dedicated dining facility on Prospect Avenue was Ivy, in 1879; others followed in the next decades. By 1906 two-thirds of juniors and seniors were taking their meals on Prospect Avenue; after World War I, the proportion rose to three-quarters. The construction of most of the imposing clubhouses still in place today dates to the late nineteenth and early twentieth centuries.[28]

---

27 William G. Bowen to Henry Morgenthau, May 29, 1981, Bowen president, box 154, folder 4.

28 William K. Selden, *Club Life at Princeton: An Historical Account of the Eating Clubs at Princeton University* (Princeton, NJ: Princeton Prospect Foundation, 1994); "Eating Clubs," in Leitch, *A Princeton Companion*, 146–49; "A History of Princeton Clubs," memorandum, Carol P. Herring to William G. Bowen, July 27, 1978, Bowen president, box 360, folder 1.

Over the decades, the number of clubs waxed and waned; by the Bowen era, eleven of the original clubs were still in operation. By 1976, fewer than nine hundred upperclass students were club members. Six of the clubs were "sign-in" clubs, open to juniors and seniors who signed up for membership. Five were selective, as all clubs had been originally; the selective clubs depended on a sometimes genteel, sometimes brutal process known as "bicker" (resembling fraternity rush at other schools) to choose members from among the sophomores who presented themselves for consideration. The clubs were private—they owned their own buildings, were funded by dues from student members, and were run by undergraduate officers accountable to governing boards made up of alumni. But they were bound up inextricably with the university. Their membership was made up exclusively of Princeton students. They had fed the large majority of juniors and seniors at Princeton since the late nineteenth century. And the university provided the clubs with a variety of services, among them access to alumni records and mailing services, garbage collection and snow plowing, and, later, access to the university's computer network.[29]

The clubs symbolized the old Princeton—white, male, exclusive, a bastion of social prestige and gentility. That put them at odds with the Princeton of the highly political, highly egalitarian late 1960s and early 1970s. And they were clearly out of sync with the university Bowen was trying to build. Snobbery, gentility, exclusivity—that was not Bowen's inclusive Princeton. Inclusivity meant leavening the old Princeton with people of different races, ethnicities, religions, and economic backgrounds. And it meant women as well as men. The all-male clubs were a relic of Princeton's long single-sex history. With the coming of coeducation, that had to change. In the spring of 1970, a handful of women were accepted at three clubs, Campus, Charter, and Colonial. Now every club debated whether to admit women to their membership, and eight of them—Campus,

29 Herring, "A History of Princeton Clubs"; "Final Report of the Princeton University Trustee Subcommittee on Eating Clubs," Apr. 2, 1976, Bowen president, box 79, folder 7. Much of the following discussion of the eating clubs was previously published in Nancy Weiss Malkiel, *"Keep the Damned Women Out": The Struggle for Coeducation* (Princeton, NJ: Princeton University Press, 2016), 238–39, 299–302.

Cap and Gown, Charter, Cloister, Colonial, Dial Lodge, Quadrangle, and Tower—did so during bicker in 1971. Cannon Club remained all-male until it closed for lack of membership in 1975, leaving three of the more prestigious clubs—Cottage, Ivy, and Tiger Inn—as single-sex holdouts.[30]

Bowen disapproved of all-male clubs, but of necessity, he took a nuanced view of how to deal with them. On the one hand, he was absolutely clear about the university's "commitment to equal opportunity" for women and men students, and he declared repeatedly that he personally opposed selection "on the basis of sex" for any entity or activity associated with Princeton. "The University as an institution would be better off," he said, "if all the organizations that link themselves to it in any way were to elect members without regard to criteria that are irrelevant to the essential educational purposes of Princeton."[31] Sex was one of those criteria, but Bowen also made plain that the university could not "compel" the all-male clubs to change their selection processes. They were "independent of the University," and the university had to "respect the autonomy of those organizations over which we have no control."[32]

Those two imperatives required a balancing act. As Bowen wrote on another occasion, the trustees, having discussed the relationship of the university and the eating clubs at length, had "arrived . . . at a set of principles to govern this relationship: first, the University is opposed to discrimination on the basis of sex (or race, religion, or the like) in any program or activity that relates directly to the life of University students; second, the University affirms as a positive value the independence and autonomy of the eating clubs."[33]

30 Al Campi, "Five Clubs to Accept Women," *Daily Princetonian*, Dec. 4, 1970, 1; Al Campi, "Cap, Quad, Tower Vote to Allow Coeds in Bicker," *Daily Princetonian*, Dec. 11, 1970, 1, 3; Luther T. Munford '71, "On the Campus," *Princeton Alumni Weekly*, Jan. 26, 1971, 8; Robert Earle '72, "On the Campus," *Princeton Alumni Weekly*, Dec. 7, 1971, 5; Joel Achenbach, "Traditions Fall as Women Join the Clubs," *Daily Princetonian* supplement, "Women at Princeton: The First Ten Years," Nov. 1979, 5–6.

31 William G. Bowen to Francis M. Ellis, June 23, 1983, Bowen president, box 142, folder 16.

32 Ibid.

33 William G. Bowen to Oliver DeG. Vanderbilt, Sept. 29, 1986, Bowen president, box 162, folder 1.

With the university straddling two not-fully-compatible principles, the initiative for change had to come from students. Undergraduate women students began in the late 1970s to challenge
their exclusion from the three remaining all-male clubs. In
February 1977, two women in the class of 1979 tried but failed
to bicker there. In February 1978, five women, including Sally
Frank '80, tried to bicker at those clubs, but they encountered
many obstacles, including some clubs' refusal to grant them interviews. When Frank tried again to bicker at Cottage in the fall of
1978, the reaction was much stronger. Members poured beer over
her head, threw beer at her, and shouted, "Let's throw Sally Frank
into the fountain." Frank responded by filing a complaint with
the New Jersey Civil Rights Division against the university, Cottage, Ivy, and Tiger on the grounds that they discriminated against
women. As Frank went public with her charges of sex discrimination, she continued to be harassed, now verbally, "through anonymous phone calls, drunken screams of mockery, and insulting
comments."

The New Jersey Civil Rights Division ruled in June 1979 that
the clubs were "distinctly private" and that the division had no ju-
risdiction. Frank then filed a complaint with the US Department of
Health, Education, and Welfare, but HEW dismissed it on the
grounds that the clubs were private. Frank recognized that private
clubs had the right to discriminate against women. In her view,
however, the eating clubs did not meet that test; they were so closely
affiliated with the university as to be the equivalent of public accommodations, and excluding women from membership deprived
women of advantages and opportunities available to Princeton men.
But Frank's concerns were grounded in more than a legal argument;
they were "based on the moral conviction that the discrimination
[was] wrong." Discrimination in the clubs "create[d] an atmosphere
on campus in which sexism [was] more accepted"—an atmosphere at odds with the imperative that Princeton men should
learn "to accept women as equals."[34] That conviction led Frank to

34 The quotations in this paragraph and the one preceding are from "Sally Frank: The
Morality of Discrimination," *Princeton Forerunner*, May 1, 1979, clipping in Princeton

resubmit her complaint to the New Jersey Civil Rights Division in November 1979. Two years later, the division came to the same conclusion that it had earlier: The clubs were private, and state antidiscrimination laws did not pertain to them.

Bowen and Frank knew each other from her years as a student activist protesting various university policies, but they had not had a great deal of interaction. That changed after Frank appealed the decision of the Civil Rights Division to the Appellate Division of the New Jersey Superior Court. The university was still taking what amounted to a hands-off stance toward Frank's efforts. But at Princeton reunions in June 1983, Bowen asked Frank to wait for him after the P-Rade. The parade passed a reviewing stand occupied by the president, his spouse, and alumni dignitaries, and ended in a gathering on a playing field. Bowen wanted to walk with Frank on the way back to campus. Their route passed the eating clubs on Prospect Avenue. For Bowen to be seen walking Frank down Prospect Avenue was a major symbolic statement. Frank, usually sporting dozens of buttons signifying support for one political cause or another, had had a reputation as a rabble-rouser. Now Bowen wanted the clubs to see him in Frank's company; in her view, it marked a statement of real consequence that signified "a change in their relationship."[35]

In August 1983 the Appellate Division of the Superior Court sent Frank's complaint back to the New Jersey Civil Rights Division for reconsideration. In May 1985 the division reversed its earlier decision: The eating clubs were public accommodations; there was ample evidence of sex discrimination in their admission practices; and the university—inextricably linked as it was with the clubs—had aided and abetted that discrimination.

---

publications, series 3, box 35; and Colleen Baker, "Coeducation at Princeton: Sally Frank's Legal Battle against the Eating Clubs and the Social Reaction of Princeton's Campus," paper written for Freshman Seminar 149, Jan. 15, 2013, Princeton University, in possession of Nancy Weiss Malkiel. On the earlier attempt, see Bob Cooper and Seth Chandler, "1976–77: Year of Resignations, Labor Problems, Admissions Controversies," *Daily Princetonian*, July 25, 1977, 11.

35 Telephone interview with Sally B. Frank, Aug. 3, 2020.

Cottage Club decided in 1986 to admit women and reached a settlement with Frank. The university also settled with her.[36] As Bowen explained to the faculty, the trustees came to the view "that it was important for the University to sever itself from the suit." The agreement with Frank "include[d] a formal declaration by the University dissociating itself from the membership policies of the two remaining all-male clubs." The trustees also agreed to reimburse Frank for some of the expenses that she had incurred.[37]

Frank and Bowen had dinner together to mark the occasion. To Bowen's surprise, Frank gave him two checks from the settlement money: $1,200 to the Women's Center for a fund in her name and $1,300 to the university (separate from her contribution to annual giving). As Frank recalled, Bowen, impressed by her gesture, made sure the trustees understood that she was a supporter of the university, not a troublemaker. Frank tried symbolically to reinforce the point by showing up regularly at Alumni Day and reunions—conveying the message, she hoped, that she was not in opposition to the university; rather, her objective was to make it better.[38]

The actions on the part of Cottage left Ivy and Tiger as the targets of Frank's legal battle. In May 1987, the New Jersey Civil Rights Division issued a final decision ordering the two clubs to admit women in the next round of bicker and awarding Frank compensatory damages. The clubs responded with an appeal to the Appellate Division of the New Jersey Superior Court. In October 1988, the case was sent back to the Civil Rights Division on grounds of procedural errors in the previous investigation. Frank appealed again, this time to the New Jersey Supreme Court, which heard the case beginning in January 1990. While the case made its way through the courts, both clubs took their first votes to admit women—decisions that, by their rules, would need to be confirmed by second votes the following year. In July 1990 the New Jersey

36 News release, University Cottage Club, Jan. 8, 1986, Bowen president, box 363, folder 12; and, in *Princeton Alumni Weekly*, "Judge Rules Eating Clubs Subject to Anti-Bias Law," Jan. 15, 1986, 8; Andy Schneider, "Cottage Goes Coed," Jan. 29, 1986, 11; "University Settles with Sally Frank '80," Sept. 17, 1986, 10.
37 Faculty meeting minutes, Sept. 15, 1986, Dean of the Faculty, subseries 1A, vol. 34.
38 Frank interview.

Supreme Court ruled that Ivy and Tiger could no longer refuse to admit women to membership on grounds of gender. Efforts to appeal the court ruling came to naught, and Ivy and Tiger began extending bids to women in bicker in 1991 and settled with Frank in 1992.[39]

In 1990, at Bowen's urging, the university's alumni council gave Frank one of its awards for distinguished service to Princeton. The citation referred to her as a "loving critic" who had "committed herself to coeducation and an increased role for women in the life of the University. She campaigned for a Women's Studies program, for more tenured women faculty, and for the Women's Center." She had become, the citation said, "a symbol to student and alumni activists who look to her for inspiration and encouragement."[40] There was no mention of Frank's legal campaign against the all-male clubs, but everyone knew what she stood for. As Bowen recalled, the decision to honor Frank "enraged" some alumni leaders. But he knew it was the right move. "Honoring her in this way was an important statement of the University's values."[41]

Residential Colleges

For all that Bowen might prod or nudge or make symbolic gestures, he could not directly affect the fundamental organization of the eating clubs, which was up to their undergraduate members and their graduate boards. Where he could have a substantial effect, however, was in setting the terms for residential life on the campus. And here his overriding instinct to help students to feel at home at Princeton, to feel included, had an important influence on his actions.

39 In *Princeton Alumni Weekly*: "Ivy and Tiger Will Contest Frank Ruling," Mar. 12, 1986, 12; "A New Round in the Sally Frank '80 Case," Mar. 25, 1987, 8; "Ivy and Tiger Ordered to Admit Women," June 10, 1987, 16; "Ivy and Tiger Appeal Frank Decision," Sept. 30, 1987, 10; "Tiger Inn Motion Rejected," Dec. 9, 1987, 19–20.

40 "The Alumni Council Award for Service to Princeton: Sally B. Frank '80," text courtesy of Margaret Miller.

41 I am indebted to William G. Bowen for this story.

The Princeton for which Bowen was responsible in the 1970s was very different from what it had been in decades past, when the basic structures of residential life had been established. Previously, students had typically come to Princeton from a small number of feeder schools, such that freshmen would likely enter the university with a built-in group of friends from their prep schools or high schools. By the 1970s, however, the composition of the student body had changed significantly, with students coming from more schools, more varied backgrounds, and different parts of the country. That meant that a freshman could be the only student in the class from his or her secondary school, indeed, the only one from his or her hometown. As well, the size of the Princeton student body had grown, and it was all too easy for a new freshman to feel alone and anonymous in an unfamiliar institution. The physical arrangements for residential life contributed to the absence of a sense of community. Students typically lived in dormitories organized by entryways instead of hallways, with each staircase opening to two or three suites on each of four floors. The only true common spaces for encountering students beyond one's roommates were the gang bathrooms in the basement of each of the dormitories. Freshmen and sophomores ate in five large dining rooms in commons—not conducive to intimacy or community. While upperclass students enjoyed a robust set of associations through eating clubs, athletic teams, and extracurricular activities, many of which included sophomores, there were fewer opportunities for freshmen to build community through social, cultural, and recreational activities.

Bowen believed that the university needed to do better at building community, better at bridging academic and residential life, better at enriching the lives of underclass students outside the classroom, better at making the members of an increasingly diverse student body feel as though they belonged at Princeton. As he explained later to the board of trustees, "As a residential university, we have a powerful educational interest—educational obligation—to *encourage* as much constructive interaction as we can among the remarkable array of individuals and groups at Princeton. I believe—most sincerely—what all of us say so often about *poten-*

tial value of the diversity that we have here—for students while they study here and for the society later."[42] Or, as he put it in the prospectus for the capital campaign, which he distributed as his annual report for 1982, Princeton's *"strongly residential character,"* a defining element of the university, offered a wealth of possibilities for *"informal learning and personal growth"*; "our objective," he said, "is to encourage all enrolled at Princeton to take advantage of the opportunities for friendship and learning offered by a student body as rich in its diversity as in its talent."[43]

Pressed actively by students and young alumni to think about significant improvements in residential and social arrangements, in February 1978, Bowen appointed an eighteen-member Committee on Undergraduate Residential Life, made up of faculty, undergraduates, and administrators, to take stock of the effectiveness of the social and dining arrangements that had grown up over the years and to make recommendations for ways of revising and strengthening those arrangements to better support the quality of undergraduate life at Princeton.[44] There were different motives among the students and young alumni who were urging change. As Kenneth Offit '77, the newly elected young alumni trustee, noted, some of them were opposed to bicker on moral grounds. Others wanted more social options, such as a student center. The "most powerful argument," Offit said, "was the invoking of Princeton's educational mission," by which he meant "the goal of a leading university to foster the greatest social interactions amongst its students," a goal not easily achieved given what Offit called "the lack of cohesiveness and sanctioned exclusivity of the social system," with the

42 Concluding comments by WGB, attached to "Resolution for Consideration at the Meeting of the Board of Trustees of Princeton University," Oct. 19, 1979, Bowen president, box 360, folder 7.

43 William G. Bowen, *Report of the President, Princeton University, March 1982: A Campaign for Princeton*, 7–8, published in *Princeton Alumni Weekly*, Mar. 8, 1982.

44 On student and young alumni pressure, see, for example, Kenneth Offit to Nancy Weiss Malkiel, Oct. 1, 2021; Offit to William Bowen, July 27, 1977, [Dec. 1977]; Offit to Edmund N. Carpenter, Jan. 28, 1978; Offit to R. Manning Brown, Feb. 19, 1978; Nancy Van Meter, "Demonstrators Assail Bicker, Support More Social Options," *Daily Princetonian*, Feb. 3, 1978, all in Offit.

long-standing splintering of the upperclass student body along lines of class, race, and religion.[45] Over his term on the board, Offit, with other trustees, would work to devise a comprehensive residential plan for the university to expand its residential colleges to include upperclass students enrolled as members of nonexclusive eating clubs—a plan not realized then but implemented in part in a different context three decades later.

The CURL committee, as it came to be known, issued its final report in June 1979. There were two transformative proposals. The first, focused on freshmen and sophomores, addressed Bowen's concerns about maximizing the educational value of diversity. The report called for the creation of a residential college system, with five colleges that would house all freshmen and sophomores and a limited number of juniors and seniors. Students would be assigned to their colleges at random and would live in the same college in their freshman and sophomore years. The plan would encourage more interaction among the highly diverse students entering the university. The necessity of rubbing up against, of sharing meals and activities with, of rooming with, students from the widest variety of backgrounds would greatly enhance the educational experience of undergraduates at Princeton. Creating smaller units within the larger university would give students a home base from which to engage the larger institution. And the colleges would enable the establishment of a wide range of intellectual, cultural, social, and recreational activities that would enrich the experience of their members.

A second part of the report, focused on juniors and seniors, responded to the worrisome pressures on eating clubs—the numbers of clubs fluctuated as student interest waxed and waned, and the numbers of students interested in the individual clubs varied considerably, even from year to year, making it difficult to plan reliably for current and future operations. Financial stability was hard to achieve, and a number of clubs had serious challenges in terms of deferred maintenance. The CURL proposal invited the individual eating clubs to enter into contractual agreements with the

45 Ken Offit's chronology, n.d.; Offit to Malkiel, Oct. 1, 2021.

university, where the university would guarantee financial stability, assistance with major maintenance, and consistent membership in return for the club admitting women as well as men and renouncing selectivity.[46]

The CURL proposals had gone through multiple iterations as a result of extensive consultation with constituencies on and beyond the campus. As well, a parallel trustee committee had been deeply engaged in the deliberative process. In October 1979, as the trustees were preparing to act on the proposals, Bowen made his own position clear. He "felt compelled," he told the board, "on a matter of such fundamental importance to the University to express his personal views. He was persuaded that the CURL Report expressed 'the right direction' for the University to pursue at this time. He reached this conclusion particularly for educational reasons, because in his view the proposed developments would encourage an appropriate 'balance' between educational objectives and individual choices." By a vote of thirty-seven to one, the board endorsed "the objectives and the general directions" outlined in the final report of the Committee on Undergraduate Residential Life.[47]

The proposal for a residential college system succeeded. The proposal with respect to the eating clubs failed. Rather than having the university impose its will on the clubs—an action akin to what happened with respect to fraternities at Amherst, Williams, Middlebury, and, later, Bowen's alma mater, Denison (albeit, in each case, under circumstances different from Princeton's), where Greek life was banned and the facilities absorbed into a unified, college-sponsored system—the matter was left to a vote of the clubs. The final vote was close—four clubs in favor, three opposed, one abstention. The university had judged that seven clubs was the minimum threshold for the new system to work (eight would have been more desirable). Despite the intense negotiating efforts of the

---

46 "Report of the Committee on Undergraduate Residential Life," May 28, 1979, Bowen president, box 362, folder 1.

47 Minutes of a stated meeting of the Board of Trustees of Princeton University, Oct. 19, 1979, 5, Princeton trustees.

provost, it was impossible to persuade a sufficient number of clubs to sign on.[48]

While Bowen would have preferred that the upperclass part of the CURL proposal succeed, it was the creation of residential colleges where he had the greatest chance of achieving the educational objectives he had outlined to the trustees. The idea of residential colleges had a long history at Princeton. It was first articulated by President Woodrow Wilson of the class of 1879, who presented to the board of trustees in 1907 a plan for the division of the university into colleges (Wilson's term was "quadrangles") in order to bring faculty and students together in a "truly organic way which will ensure vital intellectual and academic contacts, the comradeships of a common life with common ends." The faculty and trustees rejected the quadrangle plan, handing Wilson the first of the important political defeats that would mark his final years at Princeton.[49]

The first evidence of a revival of the Wilsonian ideal came a half century later with the creation of the Woodrow Wilson Lodge, which grew, in turn, into the Woodrow Wilson Society and, ultimately, Woodrow Wilson College. Woodrow Wilson Lodge was founded in 1957 by a small group of students in the class of 1959 as an alternative to the eating clubs. From the outset, it sought to combine intellectual and social activities, and it incorporated a group of faculty fellows, who took meals with the undergraduates. Initially, the Lodge organized its dining and social activities in spaces created in an existing university dining facility, Madison Hall. With

48 On the direction and fate of the CURL proposals, see "From the University: Questions & Answers on CURL," *Princeton Alumni Weekly*, Feb. 12, 1979, 7–9; Steven Bernstein, "Board of Trustees Endorses CURL Proposals," *Daily Princetonian*, Oct. 22, 1979, Bowen president, box 403, folder 1; E. N. Carpenter II, "The Case for CURL," *Princeton Alumni Weekly*, Nov. 5, 1979, 6–7, attached to memorandum, Robert K. Durkee to Members of the Board of Trustees, Nov. 12, 1979, Bowen president, box 360, folder 7; and in Rees and Rudenstine provost, R. Manning Brown Jr. to Dear Princetonian, Nov. 14, 1979, with attached questions and answers about CURL, box 127, folder 4; and in box 128, folder 2, Neil L. Rudenstine to Garrett Heher, Dec. 4, 1980; Carpenter to Rudenstine, Dec. 8, 1980; memorandum, Rudenstine to Club Representatives, Nov. 6, 1981. I owe much of the formulation in the text to Kenneth Offit.

49 Wilson quoted in Arthur S. Link, *Wilson: The Road to the White House* (Princeton, NJ: Princeton University Press, 1947), 46.

the construction of a new dormitory quadrangle down campus (the "New Quad") and the opening of an adjacent dining and social facility, Wilcox Hall, the Lodge relocated in 1961, changing its name to the Woodrow Wilson Society and broadening its membership to include sophomores. The Society sought, in the words of President Goheen, to realize the Wilsonian vision "of closely interweaving the intellectual and social life on campus." Led by a faculty master, with a corps of affiliated faculty fellows, the Society offered a wide variety of intellectual, cultural, social, and recreational activities framed in response to the interests of its members. In 1968 the Society became a four-year residential college.[50] Two years later, the former Princeton Inn, renovated as a student residential facility to accommodate the increased undergraduate enrollment that came with coeducation, opened as the university's second four-year residential college.

The college system proposed by the CURL committee was designed to provide entering students with a ready-made community within the larger university. It would give freshmen and sophomores the opportunity to get to know each other more easily and effectively than was the case under existing arrangements, where underclass students were scattered in dormitories across the campus. As well, the colleges would give all freshmen and sophomores the benefit of the kinds of programs and facilities already in place at Wilson and Princeton Inn Colleges, with an expanded emphasis on cultural and recreational activities in such areas as music, drama, and intramural athletics. There were three key differences between the existing colleges and the proposed system: the new system would be universal and mandatory instead of voluntary; it would involve two-year rather than four-year colleges; and—with the decentralization of decanal functions into the colleges—it would incorporate a formal academic component.

The ability to develop the new residential college system depended critically on raising funds to create three new colleges: to

---

50 Quoted in Charles Creesy, "Goheen Says Society Fulfills Wilson Ideal," *Daily Princetonian*, Apr. 16, 1963, 1. I am indebted to Amanda Ferrara, public services archivist at Seeley Mudd Manuscript Library at Princeton University, for this reference.

build a new dining and social facility that, in conjunction with the modern dormitories of the "New New Quad," would form a new college down-campus; and to renovate the five dining rooms of commons to become the dining, library, and social spaces for two up-campus colleges, which would incorporate a number of the most desirable collegiate Gothic dormitories on the campus. The project advanced more quickly than anticipated owing to strong support from key donors. Lee D. Butler '22, a former alumni trustee, and his wife, Margaret, gave a gift of land that, once sold, enabled the creation of Butler College down-campus; and Gordon Y. S. Wu '58 made a contribution that enabled the construction of Gordon Wu Hall, the new dining and social facility for Butler. As for the two colleges up-campus, Laurance S. Rockefeller '32, the John D. Rockefeller 3rd Foundation, and other members of the Rockefeller family funded the imposing John D. Rockefeller 3rd College in memory of John D. Rockefeller 3rd '29. The Bunbury Company made the major contribution to enable the creation of Dean Mathey College, named for Dean Mathey '12, the longtime trustee and legendary manager of the university's endowment. The three new colleges—Lee D. Butler College, Dean Mathey College, and John D. Rockefeller 3rd College—opened in 1982, joining with Woodrow Wilson College and Princeton Inn College to form a coherent college system for freshmen and sophomores. A subsequent gift from Malcolm S. Forbes '41 made possible the renovation of Princeton Inn College, which was rededicated in 1984 as Malcolm S. Forbes Jr. '70 College.

In each case Bowen took the lead in soliciting the gift. The first commitment came from Butler, an automobile dealer for half a century in Washington, DC. Butler owned a farm in Essex County, Virginia, where he bred prize-winning Black Angus cattle. The gift to Princeton came in the form of a parcel of Virginia land that, when sold by the university, yielded roughly $3 million. Butler was deeply committed to Princeton; he had been an alumni trustee (1952–56), a director of the alumni association, and president of the Princeton Club of Washington. Bowen told the trustees of his "great personal pleasure" in talking at length with Lee and Margaret Butler, whom he described as "so fully dedicated to the best interests of the University."[51] Their meeting, and the Butler gift, came two years before Butler's death on Christmas Day in 1981. Butler College opened eight months later.[52]

Wu had already given $1 million at Bowen's behest to fund a professorship—the Gordon Wu '58 Professor of Chinese Studies—to support the appointment in 1980 of Denis Twitchett, whom Bowen was recruiting from the University of Cambridge to the department of East Asian studies. Now Bowen stopped in Hong Kong to see Wu again, this time to talk about his aspirations for the college system. After ten minutes or so, as Wu recalled, he cut Bowen short—"the question," he told Bowen, "is not whether I should give, but when and how much." The two men together "worked out the numbers." Wu would give 25 million Hong Kong dollars (US $4.3 million) in honor of his twenty-fifth reunion in 1983; Wu Hall would be built and ready to dedicate at the reunion. Wu wrote Bowen to confirm their understanding and explain his interest in supporting the university. "As a foreign student at Princeton from 1954 to 1958," he said, "I felt that my presence was due entirely to the hospitality and generosity of the American people in general and to Princeton in particular. The tuition fees I paid no way represented the true cost of providing such an excellent education. It was only through the generosity and efforts of thousands of alumni and friends of the University who throughout the ages donated their valuable time and resources to make Princeton as it is today. . . . It is with this in mind that I feel very strongly that I should do my share in joining the many others who continue the honourable tradition of contributing toward a stronger Princeton."[53]

---

51 Minutes of a stated meeting of the Board of Trustees of Princeton University, Jan. 26, 1980, 8, Princeton trustees.

52 For Butler's obituary, see "Lee D. Butler, 84," *Washington Post* archive, https://www.washingtonpost.com/archive/local/1982/01/01/lee-d-butler-84/aca3b090-8f09-43c9-9b74-25d34c922ab5, accessed Aug. 20, 2020.

53 Telephone interview with Gordon Y. S. Wu, Aug. 20, 2020; Wu to William G. Bowen, Nov. 27, 1981, Bowen president, box 164, folder 4. For Bowen's account of his interactions with Wu, see Bowen, *Lessons Learned*, 121. On the genesis and execution of the Wu gift, see also William McCleery, *The Story of A Campaign for Princeton, 1981–1986* (Princeton, NJ: Princeton University, 1987), 40, courtesy of Van Zandt Williams Jr.

Laurance S. Rockefeller was a long-serving Princeton trustee (1967–80) whom Bowen knew well. In addition to their connection through Princeton, Bowen chaired the Rockefeller Trust Committee, about which more will be said later, and the two men served together on the board of *Reader's Digest*. An exchange of correspondence when Rockefeller retired from that board made plain the strength of the relationship. Bowen wrote him: "[Y]ou know not only how much I respect your contributions, but how much I value our *friendship*, which is, I trust, immune from any 'retirement.'" Rockefeller replied: "I just wanted to tell you what an honor and privilege it has been to work with you over the years on so many varied projects. You have instilled a great sense of purpose and direction for so many of us, and your wisdom and encouragement have meant a great deal to me, personally. I am grateful for our years of working together and am particularly proud to have shared your friendship."[54]

John D. Rockefeller 3rd had also served on the Princeton board (1937–67), and Bowen crafted his proposal to Laurance (so Laurance thought) to take particular account of "John's commitment to Princeton, his interest in bringing young people of every kind together, and his belief in the restoration of beautiful buildings and open spaces." Laurance responded enthusiastically to Bowen's overture, agreeing to use the same mechanism—a gift of land in Wyoming, this time valued at $5 million—that he had employed to fund the construction of Spelman Halls (named for his grandmother, Laura Spelman Rockefeller), dormitories to accommodate the expansion of the student body with the coming of coeducation. Now the $5 million gift would cover half the costs of the two new colleges; John D. Rockefeller's family, Laurance told Bowen in making his own commitment, was considering a pledge of $1.5 million, and the university had committed to raising $3.5 million from other sources. The proposal Bowen had made to him, Rockefeller said, was "clearly responsive to the needs of today's students and will improve significantly the quality of undergraduate life at Prince-

54 William G. Bowen to Laurance [S. Rockefeller], Jan. 12, 1993; Rockefeller to Bowen, Jan. 27, 1993, Rockefeller, RG43 (FA1325), box 64, folder 4.

ton." It was "a project of the greatest importance" to the university, and he was delighted to have the opportunity to work with Bowen in "addressing pressing contemporary needs and preserving Princeton's priceless heritage." While there was additional fundraising still to be done, the Rockefeller gift in 1980, the trustee minutes recorded, "enabled the University to move ahead with the establishment of five residential colleges."[55]

Later, Malcolm Forbes, serving on the board, took Bowen aside after a trustee dinner and told him that—after he had already made a commitment to the campaign for professorships—he intended to make an additional gift of $3 million to support the renovation of Princeton Inn College, which he wanted named for his son, Steve (Malcom S. Forbes Jr. '70), president, chief operating officer, and deputy editor in chief of Forbes, Inc. In announcing the gift, Forbes said, "I asked myself, 'why should everyone be dead before they're honored?' What I was interested in was a living relationship, not a salute to the departed, and Steve's very much alive. . . . He'll be around for a while and so he can be held to account for what he writes or for what they don't have down there. You've got somebody alive you can go to instead of cussing this dead immortalized person." "The combination of things," he added, "—our own Princeton connections, the nostalgia, the fact that this was aimed at undergraduate life—was irresistible."[56]

In addition to accomplishing the fund-raising for the new colleges, Bowen personally recruited prominent faculty members to lead them. For Rockefeller, he signed up Stanley N. Katz, Class of 1921 Professor of the History of American Law and Liberty, one of his major faculty hires in the late 1970s, who taught courses in American legal history. For Butler, he chose Emory B. Elliott, professor of English and director of the program in American studies,

55 Minutes of a stated meeting of the Board of Trustees of Princeton University, Apr. 19, 1980, 5, Princeton trustees. Laurance Rockefeller's letter to Bowen, dated Apr. 16, 1980, appears in the minutes as appendix D-2.

56 Forbes quoted in "Forbes Family Sets Campaign Record," *Princeton Alumni Weekly*, Feb. 8, 1984, 22. Bowen spoke about the conversation with Forbes as one of the memorable vignettes from the campaign in the remarks he delivered at the celebration of the conclusion of the campaign—"A Campaign for Princeton: Reflections," Oct. 24, 1986, Bowen president, box 252, folder 4.

who taught popular courses in American literature. For Mathey, he selected Nancy J. Weiss, professor of history, who co-taught large courses in twentieth-century American history with her senior colleague Richard D. Challener, and who had been the first woman faculty member to come up through the ranks as an assistant professor and be promoted to tenure at Princeton.

The residential colleges quickly became the center of residential life and an important locus of academic activities for freshmen and sophomores at Princeton. The colleges gave new students an immediate sense of identity and community within the larger university. They provided academic advising for freshmen and sophomores, hosted freshman seminars (once those were established in 1986–87) and other formal class meetings, and offered opportunities to get to know faculty members in informal settings. As well, the colleges served as the vehicle for a rich and varied intellectual, cultural, social, and recreational life for freshmen and sophomores. At the heart of the residential college concept was the close nexus between academic and residential life, the conviction that the residential setting offered important opportunities for enhancing undergraduate learning, both within and beyond the formal curriculum. It was the model Bowen had in mind for realizing the educational potential of an increasingly diverse undergraduate student body.

The residential college system Bowen put in place remained in force until 2007, when the expansion of the undergraduate student body enabled construction of a sixth college, the collegiate Gothic Whitman College; major renovation of Butler College; and the conversion from a two-year to a four-year college system. Now three of the colleges—Mathey, Butler, and Whitman—became four-year colleges, with significant numbers of juniors and seniors in residence, and all juniors and seniors not in residence in a four-year college remained affiliated with their freshman-sophomore colleges for purposes of nondepartmental academic advising and decanal support. With yet another move to further expand the size of the student body, the university built two more colleges, opening in 2022, with space for still more juniors and seniors in residence. While eating clubs remained a significant element of upperclass life, the basic contours of residential arrangements at Princeton were quite different from what they had been, thanks in large part to Bowen's initiative.

All told, in terms of race, gender, and religion, the Princeton that Bowen left when he retired from the presidency in 1988 looked very different from the Princeton whose leadership he had assumed in 1972. Thanks to his vision and leadership, the preppy, southern-inflected, overwhelmingly white Protestant boys' school was on its way to becoming a fully diverse, inclusive, coeducational university.

10

Board of Trustees

"There Was Never Any Broken Glass on the Floor"

A Campaign for Princeton

A Campaign for Princeton ended triumphantly, with a total of $410.5 million, compared with the original goal of $275 million, with Laurance Rockefeller's $10 million for Lewis Thomas Laboratory as the single largest gift.[1] Scores of engaged, energetic alumni volunteers contributed to the success, as did a development office operating at the top of its game. But the critical element was the impressive leadership of William G. Bowen. James A. Henderson '56, president of Cummins Engine Company, who chaired the campaign, wrote to Bowen:

> While you characteristically have given credit to many other people, I know full well that it is your handiwork and inspiration that has made the difference. Your vision enabled you to select thoughtfully and logically from among the University's needs and to gain the support of the Trustees, Faculty, Administration and finally the constituency for those priorities. The care you put in at the outset—in, for example, writing the Case Statement and explaining it at luncheon and dinner meetings—through to completing the solicitation of all the

---

1 William G. Bowen, "Notes for Sept. '86 Faculty Meeting," Bowen president, box 284, folder 2.

key prospects and pushing us all as we approached the Campaign close was the work of a true leader.[2]

Another trustee, lawyer Michael Kelly '59, wrote to Bowen "to say how much you are to be credited with a spectacular managerial achievement of the Campaign for Princeton. I hope you know that so many people associated with the University understand that your leadership is one of the greatest resources and assets of Princeton."[3] And a third, John L. Weinberg '47, chair of Goldman Sachs, who funded a professorship in economics, told Bowen, "I . . . was just absolutely thrilled to be in a position to help Princeton. The main reason I got so much fun out of it was because you were involved providing such outstanding leadership. . . . I am sure that . . . it never would have happened if you hadn't been the guy running the University and giving of yourself so generously to the drive [the campaign]."[4]

Of what did that leadership consist? The first element was foresight. In 1977, at the conclusion of Bowen's first development initiative, the successful $125 million program, he tasked the new provost, Neil Rudenstine, with figuring out what resources Princeton would need over the next ten to fifteen years, and for what specific purposes, "to maintain its eminence."[5] The financial climate had not yet improved enough to support a campaign. The stock market ended the 1970s at the same level at which it began the decade, and inflation accelerated through the period. The casual observer might have said that the budgetary austerity of the 1970s was wholly incompatible with raising money for major new initiatives. But Bowen knew that the climate would change eventually, and he wanted the university to be ready to seize the opportunity when that happened.

2 James A. Henderson to William G. Bowen, July 1, 1986, Bowen president, box 252, folder 4.

3 Michael Kelly to William G. Bowen, Aug. 5, 1986, Bowen president, box 252, folder 5.

4 John L. Weinberg to William G. Bowen, Oct. 30, 1986, Bowen president, box 252, folder 4.

5 William McCleery, "The Birth of A Campaign for Princeton," *Princeton Alumni Weekly*, Mar. 8, 1982, 17.

The second part of Bowen's leadership was preparation of a different kind. He spent two months drafting the prospectus for the campaign and many weeks testing it in luncheon and dinner conversations with alumni leaders, most of them prospective major donors, listening carefully to their reactions and fine-tuning the prospectus accordingly.[6] As well, he vetted it thoroughly with leading faculty members and administrators.

The third portion comprised Bowen's unusual combination of personal qualities: comprehensive knowledge of the university, high intelligence and extraordinary analytic skill, unusual intensity, unwavering confidence, clear vision, outsize capacity for hard work, and striking ability to size people up and forge personal connections with them.[7] Gordon Wu was one of the donors with whom he established such a connection. Over time, Wu would respond to Bowen's entreaties by funding a professorship, the eating and social facility for one of the new residential colleges, and a new building for materials science that he insisted be named for Bowen. Wu described Bowen's approach this way: He was "a really genuine person," direct and straightforward, someone who did not "sweet-talk" the donor but was "matter-of-fact" in presenting what he was trying to accomplish—"This is where we're headed; this is how you can help."[8]

The fourth piece of Bowen's leadership was simpler—the feat of showing up, all the time, everywhere, to carry forward the process of solicitation. Bowen was a master at making the ask, and he relished the task. His president's office speechwriting colleague Carol Herring, who became director of leadership gifts at Princeton, said that Bowen "could take an ask and turn it into something elevated, illuminated—he could make the donor feel that his gift was the most important gift Princeton was going to get in the next five years."[9] He met with countless prospects to impress on them the

6 Ibid., 20.

7 Telephone interview with James A. Henderson, Oct. 18, 2018.

8 Telephone interview with Gordon Y. S. Wu, Aug. 20, 2020. Wu's largest gift to Princeton—$100 million for the School of Engineering and Applied Science—would come later, during the presidency of Harold T. Shapiro.

9 Interview with Carol P. Herring, Oct. 23, 2018, Princeton, NJ.

seriousness of the need, the excitement of the possibilities, and the ways in which they would be rewarded by becoming major donors. As Weinberg suggested, Bowen knew how to draw in prospective donors in a way that made the whole process rewarding, even fun for them. And he approached the work with an energy, a zest, a commitment that was positively infectious.[10] He loved persuading people that they would enjoy making the gift he was asking for. Mary Ellen Bowen recalled a dinner with Doris and Don Fisher, chief executive officer of the Gap, whom Bowen approached about funding a new building for the department of economics. Don Fisher said later that he was initially "aghast" at the ask, but he and Doris agreed to make the gift to support what became Fisher Hall. "This is the most fun I've had in a long time," Don Fisher said.[11]

One of Bowen's friends, sociology professor Marvin Bressler, called Bowen's efforts "disciplined energy mobilized in the service of a vision." Bowen was a study in perpetual motion; Bressler told the faculty, tongue in cheek, of a "near collision" of "two commuter jets flying over Fargo, North Dakota," where it was discovered that "President Bowen was a passenger on both planes." Bowen could not, Bressler added, "have been the architect of an effort in which so many parted with so much except for the contagion of his own reverence for universities as houses of intellect and imagination, and his passionate commitment . . . to Princeton as it is and as it is in the process of becoming."[12]

Fifth was his competitive nature. It was a challenge for Bowen, as it would have been for any president, to persuade people to donate large sums, knowing full well that there were many other ways that they could use these funds. But he believed that people could and should do worthwhile things with their money and that he

10 William McCleery, *The Story of A Campaign for Princeton, 1981–1986* (Princeton, NJ: Princeton University, 1987), 16–18, courtesy of Van Zandt Williams Jr. On Bowen's ability to draw people in, get them to trust him, and believe that he would do the right thing, also see interview with Leigh B. Bienen, Nov. 5, 2018, Chicago.

11 Interview with Mary Ellen Bowen, June 25, 2018, Princeton, NJ.

12 Marvin Bressler, "The President and the Campaign: A Statement to the Faculty," in McCleery, *The Story of A Campaign for Princeton*, 81–82.

could help them accomplish objectives they often did not know they had.[13]

The final component of Bowen's leadership was a sense of humor, combined with a tolerance for absurdity. One example: arriving in Los Angeles with vice president for development Van Zandt Williams Jr., properly attired in jackets and ties, to meet with Lloyd Cotsen '50, CEO of Neutrogena, about his involvement in the campaign, only to have Cotsen take them to the beach near the airport for a picnic, with socks and shoes shed, pants legs rolled up, and carpeting from the trunk of the car substituting for picnic blankets.[14] A second example: showing up for a President's Program dinner with campaign prospects at the Argyle Club in San Antonio even when, as it turned out, Bowen was really sick. As Bowen was being introduced by James H. Clement '39, president of the King Ranch, he blacked out and slid to the floor in full respiratory arrest. He had been under the weather for days and had taken antihistamines to fight the flu but was still pushing himself to carry on with his punishing speaking schedule. When Bowen came to, he was whisked off to the hospital for overnight observation and rehydration, his protests to the contrary notwithstanding.[15]

Working with the Board

Bowen's leadership went well beyond the campaign, and to begin to understand it, I turn next to his working relationship with the board of trustees.

The Princeton board was large—thirty-nine men and women in addition to the president. It met frequently—full board meetings five times a year in Princeton, with committee meetings in addition to the plenary session, and additional committee meetings (executive committee, finance committee, others as necessary) at other times, in Princeton or in New York. The president chaired the board; the chief independent trustee was designated chair of

13 Interview with Marcia H. Snowden, June 25, 2018, Lawrenceville, NJ.
14 Interview with Van Zandt Williams Jr., July 12, 2018, Princeton, NJ.
15 Ibid.; telephone interview with Philip Cannon, Jan. 14, 2019; e-mail, Cannon to Nancy Weiss Malkiel, Jan. 15, 2019.

the executive committee. The chair of the executive committee from 1970 to 1985, R. Manning Brown '36, chair and chief executive officer of the New York Life Insurance Company, was a Princeton resident who was constantly available to Bowen; the two men struck up the closest of personal as well as working relationships.[16] When Brown fell ill with the cancer that ultimately claimed his life, he was succeeded for the year 1985–86 by the vice-chair of the executive committee, John C. Kenefick '43, chair and chief executive officer of the Union Pacific Railroad. At the conclusion of the campaign, Jim Henderson then took up the leadership of the board.

Bowen communicated constantly with the board as a whole, with its high-powered leadership, and with individuals who had something on their minds or needed to be reoriented, gently, in their behavior as trustees. His typical modus operandi was to reach out personally to welcome new trustees to the board and set up informal opportunities to get to know them. To Franklin P. "Bill" Agnew '56, just elected as an alumni trustee from Pittsburgh, he said, "Mary Ellen and I would love to meet you and Penny [Agnew's wife]. Do you get to New York or Philadelphia regularly?" The Bowens and Agnews had dinner at Lutèce, the upscale restaurant in New York City, an effort on Bowen's part, Agnew thought, to establish a personal relationship at the outset of his board service.[17]

For trustees who lacked previous experience with boards and might profit from some additional orientation, Bowen spent time tutoring them, one on one, so that they would understand what was going on and be in the best position to contribute. Juanita James '74, then at the very early stage of what would become a significant career in the private and public sectors, was initially awed by the high-profile group she was joining; she felt "nervous about being among such heavy hitters" and worried that her voice might not carry much weight. Bowen put her concerns to rest immediately and "made [her] feel like an equal partner at the table." He had a

16 On Bowen and Brown, see especially "William G. Bowen Tribute, Memorial Service for R. Manning Brown, Jr.," Oct. 25, 1985, Bowen president, box 165, folder 3.
17 Telephone interview with Franklin P. Agnew, June 29, 2018. On Bowen's efforts to establish a personal relationship with new trustees, see also e-mail, James C. Parham Jr. to Nancy Weiss Malkiel, June 14, 2018.

way, she said, "of engaging and embracing everyone, making them feel valued, and treating everyone with tremendous respect."[18] The architect Elizabeth Plater-Zyberk '72 recalled her first board committee meeting. Bowen motioned to her to sit beside him and proceeded to draw the table, naming all the trustees, so that she would know who was who. He was "trying to make me feel comfortable and knowledgeable," she said.[19]

As for cases where trustees needed to be corrected about their behavior, some examples illustrate the point. To one outspoken colleague who, in a meeting with students, had represented his own personal views on a complicated subject, Bowen sent a firm but respectful reminder that trustees were to represent the stated views of the board.[20] To the occasional young alumni trustee tempted to participate in campus protests, announce dissent from institutional policy, or press the board to act on matters generally outside its purview, he conveyed his own guidance about the proper role of trustees and engaged a more experienced trustee to counsel the younger colleague.[21]

On issues small and large, the Bowen playbook for trustees followed well-established procedures. Describe the issue in detail; analyze it carefully; present relevant data and history; evaluate alternative paths; make a clear case for a compelling choice. Materials came to the board in carefully compiled board books, at least an inch or two thick, distributed in advance of board meetings. Proposals that came to the board for action would have been vetted thoroughly in the cognizant board committee. Ordinarily, the board would be ready to act, but in cases where significant questions were raised in the board discussion, proposals might be sent back to committee for further consideration.

18 Telephone interview with Juanita James, Feb. 20, 2019.

19 Telephone interview with Elizabeth Plater-Zyberk, Jan. 11, 2019.

20 William G. Bowen to Robert K. Hudnut, Nov. 20, 1973, Bowen president, box 82, folder 3.

21 Theodore W. Foot to Aaron P. Harber, Apr. 22, 1977; William G. Bowen to Harber, Sept. 22, 1978, both in Bowen president, box 82, folder 1; Bowen to Oppit Webster, Oct. 12, 1979, June 16, 1980, Mar. 16, 1981; Stephen Ailes to Bowen, June 19, 1980, all in Bowen president, box 83, folder 6; telephone interview with Harber, Jan. 10, 2019; telephone interview with Armistead J. ("Oppit") Webster, Mar. 19, 2019.

The Manhattan mergers and acquisitions lawyer James C. Freund '56 wrote to Bowen about how impressed he was with the administration's preparation for board meetings. "You and your administration do a masterly job of building a consensus for action, through solid preparation, excellent exposition, and a strong sense of the process by which things get done. From my window into the corporate world, I see how a lot of institutions work; and I've encountered no company which functions any better than Princeton or which has a more effective chief executive officer."[22] Bowen offered, Freund said, "a master class in how to run a board."[23]

Bowen's unusually skillful leadership of board meetings grew out of his deep experience as a teacher. He used the Socratic method to extraordinarily good effect, asking questions in such a way as to elicit the response he wanted, framing the issues and discussion so that the members themselves would come up with the right answers and would get to his desired endpoint. It was the same approach he used in handling the faculty and in teaching students, and it was a masterful performance.

Bowen managed the board with clear intentionality and great care. Nothing was left to chance. He read individual trustees extremely well, and he interacted with them with a potent mix of toughness and charm. The amount of advance planning that went into a meeting was very unusual for a board. He listened closely to what each trustee had to say; he had "great patience in the way he listened," Susan Savage Speers, a teacher at a secondary school in Connecticut, said. It was a delicate balancing act: encouraging open discussion, making sure that everyone had a chance to have his or her views heard and considered, changing course just enough where necessary to respond to people's views, but making certain also that the board's decision in the end would be the one he wanted.[24] W. Michael Blumenthal *53, *56, successively corporate executive,

---

22 James C. Freund to William G. Bowen, May 29, 1984, Bowen president, box 143, folder 9.

23 Telephone interview with James C. Freund, Jan. 11, 2019.

24 Telephone interview with Susan Savage Speers, June 16, 2018. On the same themes, see also James interview. With respect to getting the board to come to the conclusion Bowen wanted them to reach, also see Freund interview.

public official, and, again, corporate executive, said that in a university, "the trick is for the president—and Bill Bowen was very good at that—behind the scenes—to make sure that it comes out the way he wants it to come out."[25] As the Cleveland lawyer Robert H. Rawson '66 put it, Bowen was "famous among the trustees because there would be a course of action proposed and he always knew where he wanted to get."[26]

Elizabeth E. Bailey *72, an economist then on the economic research staff at Bell Labs, observed that Bowen was always in control—firmly but quietly. He knew where people stood, knew what issues might be raised; he was never taken by surprise. It took great skill and endless attention to detail. Individuals needed to be heard in conversation before meetings; they needed the chance to have their say in meetings. It was important to decide who should be called on and in what order (it usually worked best to hear the objector first and follow with a respected person to respond to the objection). He got people to make the argument the way he wanted it made. Other trustees might be mobilized to talk issues through with someone in advance of a meeting or to respond in the meeting to particular points of concern. He "did his homework," Speers said, "in terms of talking to people to win them over—to arrive at the port he was seeking." He would deliberately reach out to people to make sure they were on board. Where trustees made dissenting arguments, he was extremely skilled at paraphrasing what they said and pointing out, very diplomatically, the flaws in their position and why a different course of action made more sense. In the end, even in the case of strong disagreement, both Bowen and the board understood that they needed to come to a mutual understanding. No one left meetings feeling angry or disrespected. As the physician Michael Iseman '61 put it, Bowen had a "singular ability to reconcile differences, to make everybody feel good at the end of the day." He "patiently listed to advocates with seemingly irreconcilable differences," Iseman said, "then almost magically synthesized solutions." And he "used his sense of humor to soothe ruffled feelings

---

25 Blumenthal oral history, 24.
26 Rawson oral history, 19.

and leave all parties feeling respected." The musical instruments company executive Arnold Berlin '46 phrased it this way: "There was never any broken glass on the floor."[27]

Part of the careful management had to do with who was asked to take on specific responsibilities. Bowen painstakingly identified the people he wanted involved, people he thought could work most effectively to advance an issue, people who could make the best contribution and who could best bring reluctant board members along. He knew clearly who could help him and who would likely frustrate him, and he was very good at using the likely helpers to his advantage. Assembling the right group of trustees and providing appropriate support from university staff was key to addressing specific matters that had to be attended to or resolved. Bowen conveyed his own views, but often through other people. His hand was in the process throughout, but he was typically working behind the scenes, working thoughtfully, not manipulatively, putting groups of trustees together who were best suited to deal with the issue under consideration and matching them with the cognizant university administrators who could work with them to get the job done. As Jim Henderson put it, Bowen was strikingly gifted at "telling the board gently what to think." Bowen was "not managing the trustees like marionettes," Bill Agnew observed, but he was "a subtle force behind everything." He put "the right people in the right jobs" and gave them the running room "to make their own contributions."[28]

The carefully calibrated working relationship between president and board meant that Bowen's Princeton could take on and contend with highly complicated issues. Two examples illustrate the

27 Telephone interview with Elizabeth E. Bailey, Jan. 14, 2019; Henderson interview; Speers interview; Harber interview; telephone interview with Michael Iseman, Jan. 11, 2019; e-mail, Iseman to Nancy Weiss Malkiel, Jan. 8, 2019; telephone interview with Arnold Berlin, Sept. 5, 2018. Also see e-mail, James C. Parham Jr. to Malkiel, June 14, 2018; interview with Robert J. Rivers, Aug. 29, 2018, Princeton, NJ; telephone interview with Thomas A. Barron, Aug. 27, 2019; Freund interview; Cannon interview; telephone interview with Gerald W. Parsky, Jan. 22, 2019; telephone interview with Michael J. Kelly, Feb. 7, 2019; telephone interview with Eric S. Lander, Mar. 19, 2019.

28 Henderson interview; Agnew interview. See also interview with W. Michael Blumenthal, July 17, 2018, Princeton, NJ; telephone interview with Hodding Carter, July 24, 2018.

point: One, an initiative that came from Bowen, had to do with the modernization of the management of the Princeton endowment. The other, institutional policy with respect to investments in companies doing business in South Africa, an issue that bedeviled colleges and universities in the 1970s and 1980s, was forced upon him.

Modernizing Systems: Endowment Management, Endowment Spending

For generations the Princeton endowment had been managed by highly experienced trustees in the field of investment management—first Dean Mathey, class of 1912, then Harvey Molé, class of 1929. Technically, the arrangement was that a committee of three trustees made the decisions, operating with advice from an outside investment counsel. But there was no doubt that Mathey, and then Molé, were the men in charge. With Molé less than five years from completing his service as a trustee, the board in the fall of 1973 began a review of the way the university handled its investments, with attention to possible alternatives.[29] Some trustees were pushing for professional management: The endowment was growing too large for such personalized management, the legal environment was changing, and the probability of having another highly qualified trustee available and willing to dedicate so much of his or her own time was increasingly unlikely.[30] Still, departing from long-standing practice was a sensitive matter, and there was considerable delicacy in not offending some of the trustees. After some years of careful study and deliberation, the board moved first, in December 1977, to delegate responsibility for endowment management to four outside investment managers and moved next, in October 1986, to establish a separate corporate entity, a dedicated investment company, the Princeton University Investment Company,

29 "Report of the Investment Committee," in minutes of a stated meeting of the Committee on Finance, Nov. 9, 1973, Bowen president, box 65, folder 8.

30 "Consideration of Investment Structure and Procedures," minutes of the meeting of the Committee on Finance, Dec. 10, 1976, Bowen president, box 65, folder 9. Mike Blumenthal was one of those pushing for professional management; see Blumenthal oral history, 27.

or PRINCO, to take on the job. PRINCO would be run by a highly capable investment professional, and it would have its own professional staff. Its board, appointed by the university trustees and made up primarily of alumni with investment expertise, would be chaired by an alumnus or alumna who would serve at the same time on the board of trustees. PRINCO began operations in July 1987.[31]

At the same time that the Princeton board changed the way the endowment was managed, it also approved a change in the formula for endowment expenditure, moving from the old approach of spending all dividends and interest to a more modern, more sustainable formula where the university spent each year a specific share of the endowment's value over the previous three years, increased annually by a percentage established by the board. The change was voted by the board in January 1979. Spending according to a predetermined rule, as Bowen explained, served to "smooth the spending of endowment returns," and it also kept as part of the endowment some portion of the dividends and interest earned. The spending rate was determined by estimating how much needed to be retained so that the real (inflation-adjusted) value of the endowment did not decrease. By reviewing the percentage regularly, the board kept full control of the process. When the market did so well that the formula yielded too little spending, the board was able to adjust the percentage upward, a step first taken in 1982 and repeated a number of times since then.[32]

Being able to engineer institutional change without alienating trustees wedded to old ways was a remarkable accomplishment,

31 "Endowment Income Spending at Princeton University," n.d. [1978–79], Rees and Rudenstine provost, box 68, folder 2; "University to Establish Investment Company," *Princeton Alumni Weekly*, Nov. 12, 1986, 18.

32 In Rees and Rudenstine provost, box 68, folder 1: Princeton University news release, Jan. 20, 1979; "Endowment Income Spending Policy," Mar. 29, 1982, attached to memorandum, Bowen to the Finance Committee of the Board of Trustees, Apr. 2, 1982; in box 68, folder 2: "Endowment Income Spending at Princeton University," n.d. [1978–79]; Carl W. Schafer, "Report of the Special Committee on the Endowment Income Spending Rule," Oct. 8, 1982; "Report on Proposed Changes to the Spending Rule and Associated Accounting and Budgeting Adjustments," n.d. [Sept. 1986]. The quote comes from William G. Bowen to N. Beverley Tucker Jr., May 18, 1979, Bowen president, box 161, folder 4. Also see Schafer to Harold T. Shapiro, June 24, 1987, Bowen president, box 213, folder 4.

a testament to the care and skill with which Bowen went about his work.

Navigating Challenges: South Africa

The second example of Bowen's ability to mobilize the board to navigate through highly contentious territory has to do with university policy toward investments in companies doing business in South Africa. Along with the war in Vietnam, apartheid in South Africa was the pressing moral cause of the era. The evils of apartheid made it highly problematic for colleges and universities to implicate themselves in any way in the deeply offensive racial practices of the South African regime. Where the issue was joined was with the question of how the endowment was invested. No one favored direct investment in banks and businesses domiciled in South Africa. Much more complicated were the many multinational companies that did some fraction of their business there. Was investment in those companies a way of supporting a regime whose values and practices were antithetical to everything educational institutions stood for? Or was the presence of multinational corporations in South Africa a force that could exercise some influence from the inside to encourage change in those practices? Was divestment an appropriate way of claiming moral high ground? Of exerting economic influence in the interest of change? Or was it an exercise in moral futility, unlikely to produce change but likely to be costly to institutional endowments?

These questions had roiled colleges and universities since the 1960s. In some instances, explosive student protests over investment in South Africa shut down entire institutions. In others faculty and students took a principled stand for divestment, approving resolutions calling for institutional action, sometimes involving disruption of normal university functions, as in takeovers of buildings, to dramatize the urgency of their cause. Even trustees held a range of views on the right way for institutions to proceed.

What Bowen had to do was to lead Princeton in grappling with the challenges of moving forward in this complicated, controversial domain. He needed to hold the board together, and he needed to listen carefully to faculty and students to avoid an explosion that could tear the institution apart. Whether he claimed the right moral ground can be debated; that he held the trustees and the larger university together is a testament to his strategic judgment and political skill.

Questions about the university's investments in South Africa were first raised in the late 1960s. Students had proposed that the university divest itself of investments in companies domiciled in southern Africa, as well as in multinational companies that did business there ($127 million in thirty-nine companies), and, further, that the university refuse to accept any funds that might come to it primarily from profits made there. In response, President Goheen in September 1968 established a faculty-student-administration committee, chaired by economics professor Burton G. Malkiel, to provide counsel about these proposals and, further, to recommend ways in which "Princeton can most effectively contribute to the abolition of apartheid and racism."[33]

The committee report, issued in January 1969, recommended against divestment. The moral question was unambiguous: "It is difficult to exaggerate the horrors of apartheid and the inhumane and tyrannical practices that accompany it. . . . No one who highly values freedom and human dignity can fail to abhor the evils of apartheid, and this Committee expresses its unequivocal opposition to these racial policies."[34]

The report questioned the appropriateness of selling shares of companies that were exerting significant leadership in providing job training for disadvantaged workers and in investing in ghetto businesses in the United States. It argued, too, that disengaging from such companies would have no practical effect on the South African economy or on the abolition of apartheid and racism in southern Africa.[35]

33 Quoted in Princeton University news release, Jan. 6, 1969, Bowen provost, box 23, folder 4.

34 "Report of the Ad Hoc Committee on Princeton's Investments in Companies Operating in Southern Africa," [Jan. 6, 1969], 2–3, Bowen president, box 267, folder 7.

35 Ibid., 8–9.

Divestment could, however, have a significant financial impact on Princeton. Selling Princeton's shares in the companies specified by the students would likely incur onetime transactions costs of $5 million and could then cost the university as much as $3.5 million a year—about 10 percent of Princeton's educational budget—because of the need going forward to eschew the kinds of "aggressive, innovative, and growth-minded multinational companies" operating in all parts of the world, including southern Africa.[36] Moreover, the effect of a decision to divest would establish, de facto, a moral test for university investments, a situation that would hamstring the institution in making prudent investment decisions in the future.[37]

All of these considerations led the committee to recommend against selling the designated shares.[38] It did recommend, however, that the university find appropriate ways to express its views about racial injustice, and specifically about apartheid, to the corporations whose stock it held, and that it urge those corporations to improve their labor practices in southern Africa. The likely effect of these steps would be modest; probably more effective would be educational initiatives to aid Blacks in southern Africa and promote long-run improvement in race relations.[39]

The university faculty endorsed the committee report, with the amendment "that Princeton not hold any securities in companies that do a primary amount of their economic activity in South Africa."[40] The undergraduate student government concurred. In March the trustees had their say; the university "will not hold securities in companies which do a *primary* amount of their economic activity in South Africa"; divestment from companies designated by the students "cannot be accepted," for the reasons stated in the Malkiel report. What the university would do was "to convey to

36 Ibid., 11–13. The quote is on 11.
37 Ibid., 15–17.
38 Ibid., 17.
39 Ibid., 18–25.
40 "Abstract and Summary of Actions Taken, Special University Faculty Meeting," Jan. 20, 1969, Office of the Dean of the Faculty Records, subseries 1B, Abstract of Minutes of Faculty Meetings, box 1, folder 1; statement from Norman Mather, Clerk of the Faculty, n.d. [re Jan. 20, 1969 faculty meeting], Bowen provost, box 23, folder 4.

the managements of companies doing business in South Africa the deep concerns felt" at Princeton "over the whole question of *apartheid* in Southern Africa"; to help students and faculty members gain opportunities to make presentations to corporate management in the interest of influencing their business activities in South Africa; and to support educational initiatives involving the free movement of scholars in and out of South Africa, as well as to promote the education of South Africans in Africa and in the United States.[41]

As clear as the policy was, and as strong as the campus consensus was in support of it, the issue was still very much alive when Bowen became president. Through the Bowen presidency there was increasing pressure from students and faculty for stronger action against the backdrop of increasing repression and violence in South Africa. Student restiveness evolved over time. There were three notable outbursts. The first was an overnight sit-in of 210 students in Nassau Hall on April 14–15, 1978, engineered by the People's Front for the Liberation of South Africa, demanding full divestment from companies with operations in South Africa.[42] Next came the overnight occupation on March 14–15, 1980, of the Pliny Fisk Library of Economics and Finance in Firestone Library, "an act of civil disobedience," again by the People's Front, with the students asserting that they would spend the night doing research on corporate involvement in southern Africa.[43] On May 23, 1985, came a blockade of Nassau Hall, organized by the Princeton Coalition for Divestment, where proctors seeking to clear the building arrested the protesters and took them to Borough Hall to be charged.[44]

41 Memorandum, "The President to the University Community, Statement on the Issue of the University's Investments in Companies doing Business in South Africa," Mar. 4, 1969, Bowen president, box 267, folder 7.

42 "Acting on South Africa," *Princeton Alumni Weekly*, Apr. 24, 1978, 11; David Michaelis, "The Nassau Hall Sit-In," ibid., 12–15; "Report on the Events in Nassau Hall on April 14 and 15, 1978," memorandum, J. Anderson Brown to Robert Hollander, Apr. 27, 1978, Bowen president, box 271, folder 4.

43 Untitled statement, People's Front for the Liberation of South Africa, Mar. 16, 1980 (source of the quote), Bowen president, box 352, folder 10; Evlin Attia, "Protesters Leave Library Room, May Face Disciplinary Action," *Daily Princetonian*, Mar. 18, 1980, clipping in Bowen president, box 403, folder 2.

44 "90 Protesters Arrested for Blockading Nassau Hall," *Princeton Alumni Weekly*, May 22, 1985, 22; Princeton University news release, May 23, 1985, Bowen president,

As student pressure grew, so did concern from members of the faculty. At first the faculty focused on what the university could do as an educational institution. In May 1979, they voted to establish an Ad Hoc Working Group on South Africa, chaired by history professor Robert L. Tignor, to consider ways in which the university could act positively in its educational capacity. The university agreed to the working group's recommendations of an increase in library holdings, additional lectures and colloquia, and efforts to enroll disadvantaged South Africans at Princeton.[45] Over time, however, members of the faculty grew more impatient. By May 1985 a faculty petition for divestiture drew 250 signatures. In September Bowen and Rudenstine convened an ad hoc faculty group to give advice. That group came down against divestiture, which aggravated the distributors of the May petition, who called for a special faculty meeting so that there would be a recorded faculty vote. The vote was closely divided—114 to 96 in favor of divestiture. Speakers against: senior faculty. Speakers for: junior faculty, instructors. Supporters of divestiture were overrepresented among those who turned out for the meeting. Two large departments opposed to divestiture were not represented at all because of conflicting commitments. (Had Bowen expected the vote to go the way it did, he would undoubtedly have seen to different scheduling to enable those opponents of divestiture to be present.) The vote for divestiture, Bowen told Derek Bok at Harvard, showed "erosion of support" since the petition. What he might have added was that his vaunted control of the faculty was showing some slippage.[46]

---

box 353, folder 7; memorandum, William G. Bowen to Thomas H. Wright, June 4, 1985, attached to memorandum, Bowen to Members of the Board of Trustees, June 4, 1985, Bowen president, box 48, folder 6.

45 Memorandum, N. L. Rudenstine to Members of the Faculty, Apr. 23, 1980, Bowen president, box 283, folder 7.

46 William G. Bowen to Derek C. Bok, Dec. 20, 1985, Bowen president, box 458, folder "South Africa: WGB Correspondence"; "Abstract of Minutes of Special Faculty Meeting," Nov. 18, 1985, Office of the Dean of the Faculty Records, series 1, Faculty Meetings and Minutes, subseries 1A, Complete and Final Minutes of Faculty Meetings; memorandum, Bowen to Members of the Board of Trustees, Nov. 19, 1985, Bowen president, box 284, folder 2; "Faculty Votes for Total Divestment," *Princeton Alumni Weekly*, Dec. 4, 1985,

Bowen's most important role with respect to South Africa was to work carefully and patiently to move the trustees toward a more assertive institutional policy while at the same time stopping short of a step—divestiture—that neither he nor the board could embrace. The trustees were the actors; Bowen was working hand in hand with them at every turn. At one important board meeting, when a young alumni trustee changed her mind overnight and said she could no longer support the wording of the trustee resolution up for a vote, Bowen left his chair, went to kneel beside her, and worked out new wording on the spot that she would be able to support.[47]

And the policy evolved in significant ways. In May 1978 the trustees asserted once again the importance of companies doing business in South Africa acting "to ensure equal employment opportunity and improved standards of living for black workers," and they embraced adherence to the Sullivan Principles as a measure of the effectiveness of company policies. Those principles called for "non-segregation of the races in all eating, comfort and work facilities"; "equal and fair employment practices"; "equal pay for . . . equal or comparable work"; training programs to prepare Blacks and other nonwhites for supervisory, administrative, clerical, and technical jobs; increasing the number of Blacks and nonwhites in management and supervisory positions; and improving housing, transportation, schooling, recreation, and health facilities for employees. The trustees now urged banks "not to loan money directly to the government of South Africa and government-owned corporations," and they made an explicit decision to press Eastman Kodak over the company's actions in selling photographic equipment to the South African government to use in applying the repressive pass laws.[48]

14; John C. Kenefick to Ernest F. Johnson, Dec. 16, 1985, Bowen president, box 60, folder 5.

47 Telephone interviews with John W. McCarter, Jan. 11, 2019, Aug. 17, 2020.

48 "University Investments and South Africa: Statement by the Board of Trustees of Princeton University," May 16, 1978, 2–3, 5, and appendix A, attached to William G. Bowen to Members of the Princeton University Community, May 16, 1978, Bowen president, box 271, folder 8. The Sullivan Principles were named for the Philadelphia civil

As for general disinvestment, the trustees continued to believe that it was not the right thing to do. If Princeton divested, it would have "no direct effect on apartheid in South Africa." It was unlikely to have any significant impact on the companies and their behavior. Someone else would buy the stock, possibly someone less concerned than Princeton with racial policies in South Africa. Divestment would deprive Princeton of the opportunity to argue for what it believed to be right. The trustees needed to consider the financial implications of any action; the effects of disinvestment on Princeton would be "dramatic and clearly negative."[49]

In October 1985 the board moved to embrace benchmarks for considering selective divestiture, where a company's behavior "has been found to represent, to a substantial degree, a clear and serious conflict with central values of the University."[50] The benchmarks included: "unwillingness to sign [or comply with] the Sullivan Principles"; "failure to adhere to certain prohibitions . . . concerning direct bank loans to the South African government and sales of certain kinds of equipment to the South African military and police"; and "persistent failure" to communicate responsibly with representatives of the university.[51] Review of these benchmarks would be carried out by the policy and budget subcommittee of the finance committee, and the full board would act on its recommendations. If disassociation resulted, the university would also decline to solicit gifts from the company.[52] Accordingly, meetings were held with the Ferro Corporation and the Interpublic Group of Companies, and the trustee executive committee voted in May 1986 to disassociate from

rights leader and preacher, the Reverend Dr. Leon H. Sullivan, who first enunciated them in 1977.

49 Ibid., 6–11. The quotes are on 7 and 10.

50 "Report of the Policy and Budget Subcommittee to the Board of Trustees," Oct. 19, 1985, 12 (source of the quote); Princeton University news release, Oct. 19, 1985, both in Bowen president, box 54, folder 5; "Trustees Amend South Africa Policy," *Princeton Alumni Weekly*, Nov. 6, 1985, 16.

51 "Report of the Policy and Budget Subcommittee," 13–14.

52 Ibid., 14–15.

Ferro.[53] In January 1987, the board voted to disassociate from Raytheon and Schlumberger.[54]

Bowen's role with respect to South Africa was to communicate with faculty members, students, alumni, and trustees; join board members in visits to management of companies at risk for disassociation; encourage the United States government to impose sanctions; and work with other university presidents and foundations on educational initiatives.[55]

On and off the campus, he was the explainer in chief. The issues were complicated, and he was as clear and eloquent as he could be. As he wrote to US Senator Paul S. Sarbanes '54 (D-MD) in April 1985:

> I continue to believe that many of those dissatisfied with the University's policies give insufficient attention to the particular characteristics of the university as an institution in considering various actions. In particular, our Trustees have been very committed to protecting the independence of the University and its openness to all points of view. Among other things, this has implied to us that it is unwise to attempt to use economic leverage to persuade companies or others to behave as we would like them to behave. The sure consequence would be efforts directed *at* the University, pressuring us to take one position or another vis-à-vis the teaching of economics, abortion, etc., etc. Also, we have thought that our role as

53 Memorandum, William G. Bowen and Robert Rawson to the file, May 7, 1986 (re Ferro); memorandum, John C. Kenefick, John Beck, Nancy Peretsman to the Executive Committee of the Board of Trustees, May 12, 1986 (Ferro, Interpublic), both in Bowen president, box 270, folder 3; Princeton University news release, May 16, 1986, Bowen president, box 60, folder 7; "Trustees Order First South African Divestment," *Princeton Alumni Weekly*, May 21, 1986, 7; memorandum, Kenefick to Members of the Board of Trustees, May 29, 1986, Bowen president, box 269, folder 1.

54 William G. Bowen to Howard R. Swearer, Jan. 27, 1987, Bowen president, box 271, folder 1.

55 William G. Bowen to Stanley N. Katz, July 14, 1980, Bowen president, box 270, folder 7; Bowen to Oppit Webster, Mar. 16, 1981, Bowen president, box 271, folder 5. On sanctions, see, e.g., Bowen's effort in 1985, together with nineteen other university presidents (all writing as individuals) in calling for the US Senate to pass legislation imposing sanctions on the South African government. "Bowen Joins Call for South Africa Sanctions," *Princeton Alumni Weekly*, Sept. 11, 1985, 12.

fiduciary is important. . . . [I]t is much more sensible for people opposed to U.S. policies in South Africa to direct their attention to the actors with clear responsibility—namely, those of you in Washington.[56]

In May 1985, at a campus forum on South Africa, Bowen started with the assurance that everyone in board and campus discussions was "unanimous" in condemning apartheid: "For me personally, apartheid is a violation of every principle of decency and of right relationships among people." He explained again the many reasons why the trustees thought divestiture was not the right course of action. Trustees were concerned to maintain the university's independence and openness to different viewpoints—they believed that the United States government should focus on policy, and that Princeton should stay out of policy debates not in the province of the university.[57]

"As best we can," he explained on another occasion, we should "avoid aligning the University *as an institution* with political positions, with particular ideologies, or with specific strategies, outside the educational arena. In short, it is important for Princeton to decide in which areas it is most important to be prepared to be cantankerous, to decide through what mechanisms inescapably cantankerous views are to be expressed, and to base such decisions on a reasonably clear sense that this is a university, and not a state, a church, a social club, or a political organization."[58]

Throughout the long years of debate over Princeton's stance on South Africa, Bowen and the board marched in lockstep, always coming to clear agreement over the right next steps for the univer-

56 William G. Bowen to Paul S. Sarbanes, Apr. 25, 1985, Bowen president, box 271, folder 1.

57 Remarks by William G. Bowen at Forum on University Investments in Companies Doing Any Part of Their Business in South Africa, May 7, 1985, Bowen president, box 269, folder 6 (source of the quotes); memorandum, Bowen to Members of the Board of Trustees, May 8, 1985, Bowen president, box 118, folder 4.

58 William G. Bowen to Anthony W. Marx, July 31, 1985, Bowen president, box 458, folder "South Africa: WGB Correspondence." For an elaboration on this theme, see Bowen's address at opening exercises in Sept. 1985, "At a Slight Angle to the World," in *Ever the Teacher: William G. Bowen's Writings as President of Princeton* (Princeton, NJ: Princeton University Press, 1987), 5–12.

sity to take. Sometimes trustees took the lead in pushing for further consideration; sometimes the impetus came from the president and the campus. But there was no question that the president and the trustees were the closest of partners. Bowen was not fully successful; he did not satisfy students, and he lost some significant support from the faculty. While he did not completely defuse the issue, he succeeded in keeping the lid on, at holding the institution together at a time when South Africa caused so many colleges and universities to blow up.

11

Students

"Cheerleader," "Talent Scout," and a Complex Legacy

Working with Students

Students were at the center of Bowen's wheelhouse. As we have seen, he was an unusually accomplished teacher, and he continued to teach during his presidency. He had close working relationships with student leaders—student government officers, editors of the student newspaper, heads of student organizations, members of the CPUC and its committees. Some of them became lifelong friends. He spent a lot of time with these students, helping them think through responsibilities they were struggling to carry out, listening as they talked about academic and personal challenges, tutoring them in university policy decisions, and providing a sounding board when they needed one. That put Bowen at one end of the spectrum among presidents of major universities—contenders for the other end exemplified by Nathan Pusey of Harvard, who famously said of students during the troubles of the late 1960s, "I don't have any time to see students. I have a whole university to run."[1]

Bowen spoke eloquently about the importance to him of the undergraduates with whom he had the closest connections. As he wrote to Jerome Davis '71, who had written to congratulate him on his election as president, "'Stern economist' that I have been reputed to be, associations and friendships with students and col-

---

1 Pusey quoted in Geoffrey Kabaservice, *The Guardians: Kingman Brewster, His Circle, and the Rise of the Liberal Establishment* (New York: Henry Holt, 2004), 380.

leagues have meant more to me than anything else, and I put you right at the top of the list of students whom I respect and admire. Your friendship has meant more to me, and to my family, than you can possibly know."[2]

At the same time, students testified repeatedly to the importance of their connections to Bowen. Eva Lerner-Lam '76, who was elected sophomore class president, chaired the Honor Committee, and would later be appointed to the board of trustees, was one of the early Chinese American students on campus. She first met Bowen after opening exercises in her freshman year, when she thanked him for enabling her to come to Princeton, a dream she had held since elementary school. Bowen, she told him, had "made her dream come true." After that, whenever Bowen saw her on campus, he "would always ask her what she was doing"; that he would even remember who she was "made her feel special." He mentored Lerner-Lam and encouraged her in ways that still stood out for her decades later. There was so much to do on campus beyond her studies, he told her. She should get to know faculty and administrators and participate in extracurricular activities—advice, she said, that encouraged her to take advantage of all the opportunities available to her at the university.[3]

Bowen had instincts about students that usually served him very well. One was to encourage them to seize opportunities. In multiple instances he pushed students to apply for Rhodes Scholarships, and he wrote letters to support them. Joel Goldstein '75, chair of the *Daily Princetonian*, was one of the students Bowen urged to apply for the Rhodes. Goldstein insisted that *Prince* reporters could not ask for letters of recommendation from administrators they covered, and he told Bowen that while he would apply, he could not accept a recommendation. Undeterred, Bowen submitted a letter anyway, and Goldstein won the Rhodes. Writing to Bowen later about his decision to stay at Oxford for a third year to pursue a doctorate, Goldstein said, "When I reflect back upon my reticence to apply for a Rhodes and my doubts about coming to Oxford at

2 William G. Bowen to Jerome Davis, Dec. 12, 1971, courtesy of Jerome Davis.
3 Telephone interview with Eva Lerner-Lam, Feb. 8, 2019.

the time you and Dean Rudenstine first broached the idea, I can't help but see the humor in my decision to stay a third year. . . . Getting me to apply for the Rhodes must have taxed your and Dean Rudenstine's powers of persuasion as they are rarely taxed. But I am very glad that you made the effort and that it was successful."[4] Goldstein's Oxford dissertation, a study of the American vice presidency, would be published later by Princeton University Press.[5]

A second Bowen instinct was to try to be helpful to students in situations where the help would truly matter. Randall Kennedy '77, who was also headed to Oxford as a Rhodes Scholar, had one more tuition payment due for the final semester of his senior year. Kennedy's father, a postal worker in Washington, DC, called him to say that money was unusually tight at home and that it would be very helpful if he could find some additional resources. Kennedy wrote to Bowen—whom he did not really know well—to describe his situation and to say that if there was anything the university could do to help, he would appreciate it. Bowen provided the money that enabled Kennedy to complete the school year, likely from a presidential discretionary fund. "As far as I view this," Bowen told him, "it's a good investment. I feel very confident Princeton will be paid back." Kennedy later wrote to Bowen from Oxford:

> I am finally doing what I've wanted to do for a long while: write you a proper letter. Actually I've been wanting to write you since before my graduation. For one thing, I never formally thanked you for the thousand dollars you gave me during my final semester at Princeton when financial hardship really pinched my family's resources. But now I'd like to thank you for more than that, for that one episode of kindness was simply the last in a series. I was, and am, touched by how you interested yourself in my well-being and provided help: the letter of introduction to [the Columbia University sociologist]

4 Joel Goldstein to William G. Bowen, June 22, 1977, Bowen president, box 144, folder 14. Also see interview with Nicholas W. Allard, Sept. 11, 2019, Princeton, NJ.

5 Joel Goldstein to William G. Bowen, Sept. 6, 1982, Bowen president, box 144, folder 14. For more Bowen-Goldstein correspondence, see Bowen to Goldstein, Sept. 16, 1982, Apr. 10, 1984, Jan. 2, 1988, Bowen president, box 144, folder 14.

Robert Merton, dinner at your home, your willingness to write letters of recommendation, having me over to meet [the University of Chicago historian] John Hope Franklin, etc. Although I'm tardy, please accept my deepest thanks.[6]

Later, when Kennedy, clerking for United States Supreme Court Justice Thurgood Marshall, accepted an offer to join the faculty at Harvard Law School, he wrote to Bowen: "As you may recall, when I was at Princeton you suggested that I pursue a career in academia. I was flattered by the suggestion but thought that you were way off base. Well, as it turns out I followed your suggestion despite myself."[7] Kennedy reflected that he thought of Bowen "as a cheerleader" for him and for other people, especially young people of color, whom he helped, usually behind the scenes, in various ways. Bowen viewed himself, Kennedy said, "as something of a talent scout" who could make things happen to advance the fortunes of people he considered to have potential for future leadership.[8]

Bowen was on the lookout for ways of supporting students who might not fit into the traditional Princeton mold. Nancy Newman told the story of his interaction with her family when she shared the Pyne Prize, the highest general distinction awarded to an undergraduate, in 1978. The prize was awarded at Alumni Day, a gathering of more than a thousand Princetonians that skewed older, white, Protestant, and conservative. Newman's parents—Long Island Jews—were there with her at the head table, feeling like "fish out of water." Her mother had gone to Brooklyn College; her father had become a dentist on the GI bill. Bowen spoke to them throughout the meal; he went out of his way, she recalled, not just to make them comfortable, but to make them "feel they were royalty, the most important people in the world."[9]

---

6 Interview with Randall L. Kennedy, July 26, 2018, Cambridge, MA; Kennedy to William G. Bowen, Nov. 14, 1978, Bowen president, box 148, folder 14.

7 Randy Kennedy to William Bowen, received Dec. 6, 1983, Bowen president, box 148, folder 14. Merton was an important source for Kennedy's senior thesis on the Columbia historian Richard Hofstadter.

8 Kennedy interview.

9 Telephone interview with Nancy J. Newman, Nov. 11, 2018.

Another of Bowen's instincts was to take advantage of unscripted opportunities to get to know students. The Bowens often invited students whom they knew could not get home for Thanksgiving to join their family for the holiday dinner.[10] At the same time, Bowen responded affirmatively when students invited him for informal socializing. Jean McClung Halleran '75 led an Outdoor Action trip for a group of freshmen in the week before orientation began. Later in the fall, she invited Bowen to have pizza with the group. To the amazement of the freshmen, he came, and there they were, sitting cross-legged on the floor of a dormitory room with the president of the university, who was clearly delighted to be with them.[11] Joel Achenbach '82 recalled inviting Bowen for a chili supper in the kitchen in the basement of his dormitory. A group of seniors sat around the table with Bowen—eating, drinking wine, talking about Princeton, talking about ideas, having a relaxed, enjoyable time.[12] Jocelyn Russell '85 invited Bowen to lunch at a local restaurant after she was elected sophomore class president and was "shocked" when he accepted. It seemed to her, she said, that he was "so happy to be there"; he made her feel that "she was his only priority that day."[13]

Sometimes students came to dinner at Lowrie House, which gave Bowen a chance to exercise what his son called his "personal style of humor." David Bowen recalled many instances of "sitting at the dinner table with some unsuspecting Princeton student." "In the middle of telling one story or another," he said, "Dad would make some completely outlandish statement, just to test the reaction of the student. At that point my sister and I would roll our eyes and exclaim 'Oh, Daaaad.'"[14]

Bowen especially liked spending time with the students who tended bar and served meals at Lowrie House. He came to know

10 See, e.g., telephone interview with Luther T. Munford, Aug. 30, 2019; interview with Legrome Davis, Sept. 17, 2019, Princeton, NJ; telephone interview with Chuck Howard, Aug. 26, 2020.

11 Telephone interview with Jean McClung Halleran, Sept. 30, 2019.

12 Telephone interview with Joel Achenbach, Jan. 9, 2019.

13 Telephone interview with Jocelyn Russell, Jan. 21, 2019.

14 David Bowen remarks, memorial service for William G. Bowen, Princeton University Chapel, Dec. 11, 2016, courtesy of David Bowen.

them well, laughed off their gaffes (the bartender who had no idea how to make mixed drinks; the student worker who accidentally turned off the lights in the library, seeming to signal that it was time for the guests to leave; the server who dropped ice cream in the lap of the secretary of state, George Shultz '42), and chose to spend time talking with them, even at the expense of time he was supposed to be spending with official guests. Often Mary Ellen would come into the kitchen and remind him that he needed to leave the students and go out and talk with his distinguished visitors.[15]

From the time David and Karen Bowen were young, the Bowens often had a Princeton student living with them. In part it was an instinct for hospitality. Taylor Reveley '65, headed for law school, signed on to work for Bowen in the summer following his graduation, helping Bowen prepare the book he was writing with William Baumol on the economics of the performing arts. Reveley first imagined that he would be living in a rooming house in Princeton; when Bowen heard that, he invited Reveley to live with the Bowen family in their house on Maclean Circle. The two would work during the day at Bowen's office on campus, come home for dinner with the family, play a few rounds of croquet with Mary Ellen and David after supper, go back to work at the office, and come home again for dessert. On weekends they would work on the book, "though at a somewhat reduced pace," play with David (Karen was still in her crib), and work on building a rock wall in the backyard using rocks carried up from a nearby stream.[16]

Once the Bowens moved to Lowrie House, they invited a woman undergraduate to live with them each year to provide company and care for Karen, since they were often out of the house or out of town. The student had a separate apartment upstairs. She had dinner with the family on a regular basis and was welcome to bring friends from the campus to visit. Karen Rosenberg '73 was the first of these students. She was a serious scholar of Russian literature

15 Allard interview; e-mail, Jonathan Smolowe to Nancy Weiss Malkiel, Oct. 27, 2018; telephone interview with Smolowe, Feb. 6, 2019.

16 Taylor Reveley, "William Gordon Bowen," remarks at Bowen memorial service, Princeton University Chapel, Dec. 11, 2016, courtesy of Taylor Reveley. The quote is from e-mail, Reveley to Nancy Weiss Malkiel, Dec. 29, 2021.

who would go on to graduate school and a teaching position. David Bowen, then a young teenager and a huge sports fan, had a poster of the New York Knicks great Willis Reed on the wall in his room. "Who's that?" Rosenberg asked him. David found it difficult to believe that anyone would not know such an important basketball star. His father, in Rosenberg's defense, asked if David knew who Chekhov was (Chekhov was the subject of Rosenberg's senior thesis). David's retort: "No, who does he play for?"[17]

Susanna Badgley Place '75 lived with the Bowens from the spring of her sophomore year through her junior year. She recalled late afternoon teas with Mary Ellen, an invitation to add her favorite foods to the grocery list, homework sessions with Karen, Ping-Pong games after dinner, watching sports together on television, and five-mile runs with Bowen through the woods at the Institute for Advanced Study. Bowen, she said, would often say, "How was your day, what happened today?" And then he would add, "What did you *think* about what happened today?" She found him to be endlessly curious about how students experienced their Princeton education and what they thought about it.[18]

Living in Lowrie House was an "amazing opportunity," Jane Kenney Austin '76 said. She was made to feel like part of the family. The Bowens were down-to-earth, friendly, and warm, always interested in what she was doing. Bowen kept track of her academic progress; the night before her senior thesis was due, she was in his office making a copy so that she could get it to the binder on time. She was a member of the field hockey team, and the Bowens invited the team to Lowrie House to celebrate the end of their season. When she was job hunting, he wrote letters of introduction for her. At graduation, her family stayed at Lowrie House, and the Bowens had a special dinner for her, her boyfriend (whom she later married), and both of their families.[19]

17 Interview with David Bowen, Sept. 29, 2018, Princeton, NJ; interview with Karen Rosenberg, Sept. 27, 2019, Princeton, NJ.

18 Telephone interview with Susanna Badgley Place, Sept. 6, 2019.

19 Telephone interview with Jane Kenney Austin, Aug. 29, 2019. Also see Phil Witte, "Senior Kenney Lives at the Bowens'," *Daily Princetonian*, May 17, 1976, 5–6.

Amie Knox '77 said that mealtimes at Lowrie House were "about as normal as you could imagine"—a lot of fun, with "a lot of laughter," just a "regular family dinner." Bowen would ask Mary Ellen and Karen about their days, and he would ask Knox questions about what was happening on campus and what she was doing. Bowen, she said, "loved to laugh, loved a good joke, loved to make other people laugh." Knox was a member of the women's squash and tennis teams, and sometimes she and Bowen played together. He was "crafty," she recalled, "a little unorthodox," "always with a sly grin on his face," all told, "an excellent player, an incredible competitor." By the end of her senior year, she had earned twelve varsity letters (she also played field hockey); Bowen, introducing her at an awards event, remarked that she had won twelve letters while the most accomplished male player had won only nine. (That made her the second athlete in Princeton history to win four letters in each of three varsity sports. The first, a year earlier, was Emily Goodfellow '76.) "Wow, nine letters, that's really good for a boy," Knox interjected. Bowen, she said, "thought that was the funniest thing" and repeated the story often.[20]

Cynthia Nitta '80, a Japanese American from Palo Alto, California, felt like "a fish out of water at Princeton"; before coming east for college, she said, she had never talked to, no less hung out with, people who had gone to private school. Living with the Bowens offered a wealth of unique experiences. She met the famous visitors who came to Lowrie House, had the chance to participate in interesting conversations, and interacted comfortably with Bill and Mary Ellen. She was invited to join in family outings, including a trip to Saratoga Springs, and she went to Princeton basketball games with them. She had been raised in a very strict family with exceedingly high expectations for her, so living in a relaxed, supportive family environment was "very refreshing." There was "lots of joking," lots of "good-natured family teasing" among the Bowens, she remarked; she recalled the rest of the family making

20 Telephone interview with Amie Knox, Sept. 9, 2019. On Knox's athletic accomplishments, see *Greenwich Time*, Mar. 8, 1977, clipping in Bowen president, box 153, folder 7.

fun of Bowen for his lack of knowledge of popular culture. When she was applying to graduate school, she later learned, he wrote a recommendation for her to go to MIT in nuclear engineering physics—she hadn't asked; he just did it for her.[21]

Bowen followed the professional and personal lives of a remarkable number of the students with whom he had the strongest connections. Each year at commencement, he wrote congratulatory notes to students he had taught in Economics 101 who had achieved distinguished academic records. To Ira Davis '82 he wrote, in a typical message: "Just a brief note, following Commencement, to say how pleased I was to see from the program that you received High Honors in Biology. I am delighted, though certainly not surprised. I remember so well your participation in my section of Economics 101, and I want to take this opportunity to thank you again for your friendship."[22]

He did the same for students who had held leadership positions or who had won major awards. To Elena Kagan '81, headed for Oxford with a Sachs Scholarship, he wrote: "Just a brief note, now that Commencement is over, to congratulate you on having received highest honors in History and having been elected to Phi Beta Kappa. These fine recognitions are all the more noteworthy in light of the enormous amount of time you devoted to *The Daily Princetonian* [where she served as editorial chair]. I also want to say how much I have enjoyed knowing you. While we have not always agreed (and you must even regard that as an understatement, though I hope not), I have always respected your point of view and admired the intelligence and concern that you have brought to bear on issues."[23]

21 Telephone interview with Cynthia Nitta, Aug. 31, 2019. For more such testimony, see Rosenberg interview; interview with Alysa Christmas Rollock, Oct. 3, 2019, Princeton, NJ; telephone interview with Beatrijs Stikkers-Muller, Dec. 12, 2019.

22 William G. Bowen to Ira C. Davis, June 11, 1982, Bowen president, box 140, folder 17. In Bowen president also see Bowen to Christine Downs, June 18, 1980, box 141, folder 2; Bowen to Margaret L. Frisbie, June 16, 1987, box 143, folder 9; Bowen to Stephen K. Koo, June 15, 1983, box 149, folder 4; Bowen to Susan Mariscal, June 21, 1985, box 151, folder 7; Bowen to Jennifer L. Thiessen, June 19, 1986, box 161, folder 2; Bowen to David H. Mehnert, June 16, 1987, box 152, folder 4.

23 William G. Bowen to Elena Kagan, June 12, 1981, Bowen president, box 148, folder 12. In Bowen president, also see Bowen to Susan J. Craighead, June 19, 1986, box

For the students Bowen knew best, there were years of correspondence and visits: letters of recommendation to graduate and professional schools, recommendations for jobs, advice about academic and professional directions, invitations to visit at Lowrie House or in Avalon, congratulations on professional achievements, commiseration over personal difficulties, connections to influential people who might help them, ruminations about university issues and national events, and general encouragement and openness to providing a listening ear.[24]

The relationship with Bowen had a shaping effect on the lives of so many of these young people. Two examples illustrate the point. Jon Barfield '74, who turned to him for advice on numerous occasions, said that Bowen "always provided a new perspective on what I might be missing in my calculus." Barfield's relationship with his father and the family business was a case in point. His father, who had finished tenth grade, had enlisted in the army, worked as a janitor at the University of Michigan, and started a cleaning business, which he sold to ITT in 1969. He then built a second business, this one global, with $4 million in annual revenues. Jon, taking issue with his father over company management and offered a significant position at General Electric, wanted to leave the business, and he went to talk it over with Bowen. Bowen offered a perspective that Barfield had not thought of on why it might be important to stay with the company, what it meant to build a successful Black business, and why he should find a way to manage the disagreement with his father. Barfield said that Bowen gave him reason "to pause and think deeply" about what he was doing. Staying with

140, folder 2; Bowen to Jacqueline A. Jackson, June 15, 1978, box 148, folder 6; Bowen to Nancy A. Jeffrey, June 16, 1987, box 148, folder 6; Bowen to Yvonne Gonzalez, June 17, 1987, box 144, folder 14.

24 In Bowen president, see, e.g., William G. Bowen to Jerome Davis, July 9, Oct. 19, 1973, Mar. 6, 1974; Davis to Bowen, Oct. 11, 1973, Feb. 20, Apr. 10, 1974, Mar. 11, 1975, box 141, folder 7; Bowen to Edson M. Chick, Jan. 7, 1980 (re Karen Rosenberg), box 157, folder 1; Bowen to Office of Admissions, Graduate School of Journalism, Columbia University, Jan. 30, 1981 (re Amie Knox), box 149, folder 4; Bowen to Nancy S. Goodman, Jan. 31, 1984, box 144, folder 14; Bowen to MBA Admissions Board, Harvard Business School, Apr. 2, 1986 (re Michele Warman), box 163, folder 6; memorandum, Bowen to Whom It May Concern, Aug. 27, 1986 (re Kevin Guthrie and Sara Chang), box 145, folder 1.

the family business, he said, was "one of the best decisions he ever made," a decision attributable directly to Bowen's influence.[25]

Kevin Guthrie '84, a football star at Princeton whose father, General John R. Guthrie '42, was serving on the Princeton board, was one of the many students to receive a note from Bowen congratulating him on his graduation and wishing him well. Some months later, Guthrie moved to Princeton and "needed an inexpensive place to live." As he told the story, "I saw President Bowen leaving a football game, and on a whim I approached him and asked if he knew someone local for whom I could house-sit." Within a couple of days, the Bowens invited him to live with them at Lowrie House, which he did for the next fifteen months. There ensued the closest of family friendships and, eventually, a succession of career opportunities for Guthrie, encouraged and provided by Bowen, which culminated in Guthrie's presidency both of JSTOR and of ITHAKA.[26]

A Student Affair

While Bowen was known for his investment in student relationships, he instigated one known relationship with a student that went far beyond acceptable norms. The student was one of the women who lived in Lowrie House, Wendy Zaharko '75. Zaharko was a star squash player, and she and Bowen often played squash and tennis together. Partway through her year in Lowrie House, he initiated an intimate personal relationship with her that continued, off and on, for at least the next half dozen years. The affair was widely known, or rumored, on and off the campus.

Upon learning that I was writing this book, Zaharko herself, now a medical doctor, requested a long, on-the-record, in-person conversation with me about her relationship with Bowen. She admitted freely to the relationship, described it as entirely consensual, and said that it was extremely important to her, then as well as subsequently. My understanding of the circumstances is informed directly

---

25 Telephone interview with Jon Barfield, Jan. 14, 2019.
26 Kevin M. Guthrie, remarks for Bill Bowen memorial service, Princeton University Chapel, Dec. 11, 2016, courtesy of Kevin M. Guthrie.

by her perspective on her own story. As well, many of the people I interviewed for the book offered their own perspectives on the relationship, and their views contributed importantly to my framing of the account presented here.

There was never any public reporting of the relationship. No newspaper or magazine wrote about it; the *Daily Princetonian* thought it had the story on at least one occasion but was unable to confirm it with university officials, and the student newspaper declined to publish under those circumstances. And yet administrators knew. Faculty knew. Students knew. Alumni knew. Even townspeople knew.

Make no mistake: This situation was impossibly difficult at the time for Mary Ellen Bowen. It was hugely complicated for Bowen's closest friends and colleagues, who needed to manage the daily work of the administration and feared that the affair could become public at any moment and blow up the Bowen presidency. It was difficult for people who worried about Wendy Zaharko's well-being—her close friends and the faculty members and administrators in whom she, and her friends, confided, all of whom wrestled with the likely consequences for Zaharko of an inevitably unbalanced power relationship. And it was difficult, of course, for Zaharko, who was living a college and post-college experience so out of normal bounds that the emotional and practical risks were ever-present, even to a willing participant.

And the affair remains highly problematic today. My writing about it in this book will be difficult for Mary Ellen Bowen and her family; for Bowen's closest friends and professional colleagues, many of whom wish the book could focus exclusively on his professional contributions; for Princeton women graduates, some of whom are deeply conflicted about what to make of this facet of the record of a major leader of their university; and for Zaharko herself, who, despite a subsequent marriage, two children, and a divorce, still regards this relationship as a very significant part of her life.

Beyond the obvious inappropriateness of what Bowen was doing, the affair raised three overriding questions. First was how he could have carried on the affair and kept his job. Second was how he could have carried on the affair and maintained his marriage. And the third was what impact the affair may have had on Wendy Zaharko and how we should read Bowen's behavior in light of the inherent power dynamics at play in the relationship.

For all of Zaharko's unqualified enthusiasm about the importance of the affair to her life then and subsequently, we need to acknowledge the complexities of a consensual affair that occurred within a strikingly uneven and inappropriate power dynamic. We need, too, to recognize the impact of the affair on the many people who witnessed or heard about it at the time, an impact so significant that it was addressed in a large percentage of the interviews I conducted. In the main, my interviewees took the initiative to raise the subject when we talked. Often, they insisted on discussing the issue off the record. All of this speaks both to the broad impact of the affair and to the complexity of deciding how to remember a greatly admired figure who made a choice that can easily be identified as unacceptable and damaging.

From Bowen's side of the affair, it is difficult to square how he could carry on a relationship with a student while maintaining a marriage that was deeply important to him. He and Mary Ellen were a couple for almost seventy years. "You see," he told Derek Bok, "Mary Ellen and I brought each other up."[27] Together they invented themselves in a world completely unlike what they had known growing up. Together they learned how to navigate that world and how to fashion their respective roles in it—she, more patient, more graceful socially, complementing and completing him. Their friend Lois Shepetin said that they "fit each other hand and glove."[28] Together they raised a family; built a life in Avalon, on the Jersey Shore, alongside their life in Princeton; and traveled with and without their children. They enjoyed going to dinner with friends, taking vacations with friends, watching Princeton teams compete in basketball and football, making an annual visit with children and friends to watch professional tennis at the US Open in Forest Hills. He valued her judgment, talked over with her the thorny issues he

27 Interview with Derek C. Bok, June 20, 2018, Cambridge, MA.
28 Interview with Lois Shepetin, Feb. 8, 2022, West Palm Beach, FL.

was contending with, and often quoted her views in discussions with colleagues. They clearly enjoyed each other's company, and they had a strong and enduring partnership.

The affair provided something Bowen craved at that point in addition to that partnership: the sexual and emotional companionship of a young woman whose company he enjoyed. This companionship was compelling enough that he put at risk his presidency of Princeton; his credibility with the board of trustees; his credibility with the faculty, alumni, students, and parents; and his reputation as an educational leader. And, of course, most important, he put at risk the survival and stability of his marriage. Friends tried to talk to him about the inadvisability of what he was doing, but he insisted that it was part of his private life, unrelated to his public life and not discussable. He believed, for whatever reason, that his private life could be separated from his presidential life and that responsible norms did not apply to him. His actions suggested that he believed, inexplicably, that he was entitled to have an affair with an undergraduate student.

We do not know why Bowen thought he could have the relationship, keep his job, and sustain what had been a sterling reputation. No one would have condoned the choices he made. No one could have made a case that cheating on one's wife was fine to do. Nor could anyone have made a case that there was nothing wrong with sexual relationships between students and much older men (usually men) in positions of power, or between students and their professors, or between students and university administrators.

In universities—indeed, in many institutions—in this period, there were not yet any stated rules against such relationships, nor any institutionalized rules concerning sexual harassment. At Princeton, it was not until the late 1980s that institutional policy began to be developed.[29] Until then, when Princeton faculty members engaged in inappropriate relationships with students, there were only the most rudimentary procedures for addressing the problem: deans would call the faculty member in and tell him (almost invari-

29 See, e.g., faculty meeting minutes, May 4, 1987, Dean of the Faculty, series 1, Faculty Meetings and Minutes, subseries 1A, vol. 34.

ably him) to put a halt to the behavior. The infamous case at Princeton where a senior male professor in the English department sexually assaulted a male graduate student came only in 1988 and caused an uproar among the department faculty, who felt that their colleague, who was put on leave for a year and allowed then to retire early, had not been given anything close to adequate punishment.[30] Clear rules governing intimate personal relationships between faculty and students would not be instated at colleges and universities for decades to come—and, even still, there are too many examples of these rules being overstepped or ignored altogether. This is in no way meant as a defense of Bowen's behavior; it simply sketches the larger context in which it occurred.[31]

We know very little about how the Princeton board handled Bowen's affair. There is no documentation, and the many surviving trustees of the era say that the issue never came to the full board, not even formally to the executive committee. The assumption—perhaps the knowledge, but certainly the general assumption—is that Manning Brown handled the matter, possibly alone, possibly in consultation with one or more trusted colleagues. It is believed that Brown told Bowen to end the affair, a message that may have been given more than once. It is further believed that Bowen's sabbatical at the Center for Advanced Study in the Behavioral Sciences in Palo Alto in the fall of 1980, ostensibly to write the case statement for the capital campaign, was intended also to get him out of Princeton and put some distance between him and Zaharko.

Today, Bowen would have been required to step down. But the perceived needs of the institution apparently superseded a meaningful accounting for his behavior—a pattern still so often seen today. The Princeton trustees had a big investment in Bowen. The board could not risk a failed presidency. There was so much riding

---

30 "Accused Princeton Professor to Retire Early," *New York Times*, May 27, 1989, https://www.nytimes.com/1989/05/27/nyregion/accused-princeton-professor-to-retire-early .html, accessed May 6, 2021.

31 Princeton policy as of 2022 is clear and specific in prohibiting such relationships. From Rules and Procedures of the Faculty: "1. Prohibition of Consensual Relations with Students. Faculty members shall not initiate or engage in romantic or sexual behavior with undergraduate or graduate students." https://dof.princeton.edu/policies-procedure /policies/consensual-relations-students.

on his success. Ending his presidency so early would have reflected badly on the board's judgment in appointing him. It would have presented the board with problems almost as vexing as allowing him to continue in office. Dismissing Bowen, or asking him to resign, would have rocked the university profoundly. And it would have put an abrupt end to a career that proved important to Princeton and, later, to higher education. So we are left with the complex legacy of a man whose choices place him in the middle of pressing conversations around sexual intimacy and institutional power dynamics despite the incomparable value he contributed to the learning of his students, the growth of his institution, and to higher education more broadly.

Entr'acte: Leaving Princeton
for the Mellon Foundation

The Princeton trustees' faith in Bowen was amply justified. By all measures, he had an extremely successful presidency. A Campaign for Princeton concluded in 1986, raising over $410 million, a total that greatly exceeded not only the initial goal of $250 million set in 1981, but also the increased goal of $330 million announced in 1984.[1] Bowen saw to the creation of a first-class department of molecular biology, with a major new building, Lewis Thomas Laboratory, completed in 1986. He raised money for a new building for the department of economics, Fisher Hall, along with new facilities for international studies in the adjacent Bendheim Hall, both of which would be completed in 1990. He launched a system of residential colleges for freshmen and sophomores, with Mathey, Rockefeller, and Butler Colleges opened and Forbes renovated on his watch. At his direction, there was a significant increase in the diversity of the undergraduate student body. He measurably strengthened the faculty with a large number of outstanding appointments. In addition to molecular biology, he could claim new, freestanding departments of comparative literature and computer science and new interdisciplinary programs in fields as varied as materials science and women's studies. He put in motion the modernization of important administrative functions, from budgeting

---

1 Minutes of meeting of the Board of Trustees of Princeton University, Jan. 21, 1984, 8; minutes of meeting of the Committee on Plans and Resources, Sept. 26, 1986, in minutes of meeting of the Board of Trustees of Princeton University, Oct. 24, 1986, appendix E, both in Princeton trustees.

240

to management of the university's endowment. The dramatic increase in the size of the endowment in the Bowen years—$658.7 million in 1979 to $2.5 billion in 1989—gave Princeton the largest endowment per student of any college or university for decades to come.[2] It was a good time for Bowen to think about declaring victory and moving on.

The academic year 1986–87 marked Bowen's fifteenth year as president, the same length as Robert F. Goheen's tenure. In January 1987, Bowen told the trustees that he intended to resign to become president of the Andrew W. Mellon Foundation in New York City. His closest Princeton colleague, provost Neil Rudenstine, would depart as well to take up a new post as executive vice president at Mellon.[3] That was the surprise. Many people had expected that Rudenstine would succeed Bowen as president of Princeton. But Rudenstine declined to be a candidate. As he said, he had been "an administrator at Princeton for 20 years," and he thought "that it was time to take on something else." (Another thing that he said—"I had long before decided that I did not want to be [a] university president"—went by the wayside when Rudenstine was named president of Harvard University in 1991.)[4]

A short presidential search ensued at Princeton, and in April 1987, the trustees announced the appointment of Harold T. Shapiro, a Princeton PhD in economics (1964) then in his eighth year as president of the University of Michigan, as the eighteenth president of Princeton. Bowen, though technically abiding by the widely accepted principle that incumbents should have no role in choosing their successors, had made plain to the trustee search committee his great enthusiasm for the Shapiro appointment, and he had communicated discreetly with Shapiro to encourage both his interest and

2 June 30 closing market value, attached to e-mail, Andrew K. Golden (PRINCO) to Nancy Weiss Malkiel, May 4, 2022; e-mails, Jennifer M. Birmingham (PRINCO) to Nancy Weiss Malkiel, May 20, June 6, 2022, presenting data from 1990 through 2021 from the National Association of College and University Business Officers (NACUBO) and the National Center for Education Statistics (NCES).
3 Minutes of meeting of the Board of Trustees of Princeton University, Jan. 24, 1987, 10, Princeton trustees.
4 Rudenstine oral history, 35.

his positive response once the offer was made.[5] "[T]he appointment of Harold Shapiro is an absolute ten-strike for Princeton," he
told a young alumna whom he knew well. "To use a baseball
idiom, it is a bit like having recruited Joe DiMaggio to play center
field."[6] Because Shapiro said that he could not leave Ann Arbor
until the end of the calendar year, Bowen agreed to stay on as
president until Shapiro could be installed in early January 1988.
Rudenstine, it was agreed, would remain at Princeton for several
months beyond that until Shapiro had his own provost in place.

5 Telephone interview with James A. Henderson, Oct. 18, 2018; interview with Nancy
Peretsman, Aug. 13, 2018, New York City; interview with Thomas H. Wright Jr., June 29,
2018, Princeton, NJ; interview with Harold T. Shapiro, June 19, 2018, Princeton, NJ.
    6 William G. Bowen to Nancy David, May 5, 1987, Bowen president, box 162, folder 1.

Part III

Mellon

12

Mellon

"The Pace of Things, the Excitement of Things"

Taking up the Presidency of the Mellon Foundation

Bowen's discussions with Mellon had gone on for some time, conducted by the chair of the foundation's board, William O. Baker, a Princeton graduate alumnus who had earned his PhD in chemistry in 1939. Baker was well known to Bowen. He had served as vice president for research at Bell Laboratories from 1955 to 1973 and as president there from 1973 to 1979. In 1975 he was awarded Princeton's James Madison Medal, the highest distinction conferred on a graduate alumnus of the university. Baker had served on the Mellon board from the time of the incorporation of the foundation in 1969, and he chaired the board from 1975 to 1990. With the retirement looming of Mellon's president, John E. Sawyer, previously president of Williams College, who had led the foundation since 1975, Baker set out to find a worthy successor.[1]

It had been rumored before that Bowen was a candidate for the presidencies of the Rockefeller and Ford Foundations, both of which he had denied.[2] He was happy at Princeton; he had major

1 John E. Sawyer, "President's Report: The Decade 1969–1979," *Report of the Andrew W. Mellon Foundation, 1979*, 26; William G. Bowen, "President's Report," *Report of the Andrew W. Mellon Foundation, 1990*, 7–9. The Mellon annual reports are available on the Mellon Foundation website, https://www.mellon.org, in the section labeled "About."

2 Lesley Oelsner, "Ford Foundation Seeks a Skipper for Future Course," *New York Times*, Jan. 3, 1979, B1; Kathleen Teltsch, "Rockefeller Foundation Screening 5 for President," *New York Times*, Jan. 1, 1980, 22; Kitty Teltsch, "Rockefeller Group Selects a New Head,"

work still to accomplish; and Rockefeller and Ford were both too large, with overly expansive portfolios, to appeal. Mellon was a different matter. It was very well endowed but smaller and nimbler than its principal peers. It had traditionally focused on higher education, arts, and culture, all central concerns of Bowen's. It had a small staff and a small board, both susceptible to almost-immediate revitalization. It was the sort of place where Bowen could make a major impact programmatically through his chosen grant-making. As well, it offered an opportunity for Bowen to go back to work as a scholar and to pursue studies of higher education that could make a difference not only to the academy but to public policy.

The Mellon Foundation grew out of the consolidation in 1969 of two foundations established previously by the children of the banker and businessman Andrew W. Mellon: the Avalon Foundation, founded in 1940 by Mellon's daughter, Ailsa Mellon Bruce, and the Old Dominion Foundation, established in 1941 by Mellon's son, Paul. The new foundation was named for their father, who, in addition to his career as a banker and industrialist, served as secretary of the treasury in the Harding, Coolidge, and Hoover administrations, and later as United States Ambassador to the Court of St. James's. The broadly stated purpose of the foundation was to "aid and promote such religious, charitable, scientific, literary, and educational purposes as may be in the furtherance of the public welfare or tend to promote the well-doing or well-being of mankind"—a rubric capacious enough to accommodate the desires and objectives of the foundation's successive presidents and boards.[3] Bowen's predecessors as president, John E. Sawyer (1975–87) and Nathan M. Pusey (1971–75, after his presidency of Harvard University), had established a "strong foundation" for Mellon, which, "unlike so many other foundations was very clear about what it was interested in supporting and then stuck to it."[4]

New York Times, Jan. 27, 1980, 17. Franklin A. Thomas, former head of the Bedford-Stuyvesant Restoration Corporation in New York City, was named president of the Ford Foundation in 1979; Richard W. Lyman, president of Stanford University, was named president of the Rockefeller Foundation in 1980.

  3 Sawyer, "President's Report: The Decade 1969–1979," 5.
  4 E-mail, Mary Patterson McPherson to Nancy Weiss Malkiel, Oct. 17, 2021.

At the end of 1970, the first full year of the new foundation's operations, Mellon's assets had a market value of $698 million. By the end of 1979, they had grown to $827 million, and by the time Sawyer stepped down as president in December 1987, the market value totaled $1.478 billion. Annual grants grew from $34 million in 1975 to almost $51 million in 1979, and then increased even further, with half a billion dollars expended in the eight years 1980 through 1987. Higher education accounted for almost 53 percent of the grants in both the periods 1969–79 and 1980–87. The next-largest categories of expenditure in 1980–87 were cultural programs (17 percent) and medicine, public health, and population (also 17 percent). Beyond that, conservation and the environment accounted for 8 percent of the foundation's grant activity, and public affairs 5 percent.[5]

What that meant, in practice, was that Bowen had a lot of money to spend and a lot of leeway in how to spend it.[6] By the beginning of 2006, Bowen's final (but partial) year as president, the market value of the endowment was $4.863 billion, more than three times what it had been when he took office in January 1988. As table 12.1 shows, at the beginning of Bowen's tenure, Mellon was

5 Sawyer, "President's Report: The Decade 1969–1979," 6; William G. Bowen, "President's Report" and "Financial Appendix," *Report of the Andrew W. Mellon Foundation, 1987*, 7, 8, 29.

6 Writing about Bowen and Mellon presents unusual challenges. The Mellon Foundation maintains a thirty-year rule for access to its records, so most if not all of the Bowen papers were unavailable to me (indeed, they had not yet been processed when I was doing my research). I therefore have two main sources: the published annual reports of the foundation, and oral history interviews. Where there are specific details to be documented, I will cite the relevant annual reports. As for interviews, the reader should assume that the account that follows has been constructed as a composite of a significant number of interviews with Mellon board members and staff, and that I will not ordinarily be footnoting individual interviews unless I am quoting directly. The board members with whom I have spoken are Danielle Allen, Lewis W. Bernard, Hanna Holborn Gray, Sir Colin Lucas, Walter E. Massey, and W. Taylor Reveley III. The staff members are Rachel N. Bellow, Stacy Dale Berg, Matthew Chingos, Elizabeth A. Duffy, Richard H. Ekman, Alice F. Emerson, Jacqueline Ewenstein, Ulrica Fredsvik-Konvalin, Ira H. Fuchs, Joan Gilbert, Kevin M. Guthrie, Martin Kurzweil, Kelly A. Lack, Deborah Longino, Carolyn Makinson, Mary Patterson McPherson, Thomas Nygren, Susanne Pichler, Richard E. Quandt, Don M. Randel, William Robertson IV, Neil L. Rudenstine, James L. Shulman, Julie Ann Sosa, T. Dennis Sullivan, Sarah Levin Taubman, Eugene M. Tobin, Michele Warman, Donald J. Waters, Patricia T. Woodford, and Harriet Zuckerman.

TABLE 12.1. MELLON, ROCKEFELLER, AND FORD FOUNDATIONS

	Mellon	Rockefeller	Ford
Endowment 1987	$1.478 billion	$1.639 billion	$5.263 billion
Endowment 2005	$4.863 billion	$3.356 billion	$11.424 billion
Grants 1987	$69.8 million	$70.9 million	$228.6 million
Grants 2005	$201.8 million	$150.2 million	$571.9 million

Sources: For Mellon, see note 8. For Rockefeller, see Rockefeller Foundation Annual Report, 1987, https://rockefellerfoundation.org/wp-content/uploads/Annual-Report-1987-2.pdf; and Rockefeller Foundation Annual Report, 2005, https://rockefeller foundation.org/wp-content/uploads/Annual-Report-2005-1.pdf, accessed May 3, 2022. For Ford, see Ford Foundation Annual Report, 1987, https://www.ford foundation.org/about/library/annual-reports/1987-annual-report; and Ford Foundation Annual Report, 2005, https://www.fordfoundation.org/about/library/annual-reports/2005-annual-report, accessed May 3, 2022.

slightly smaller in asset size than the Rockefeller Foundation and significantly smaller than Ford. By the end of his tenure, Mellon was larger in asset size than Rockefeller; while it was still smaller than Ford, the gap had narrowed.[7] Mellon's annual grants in 1987, just before Bowen took over, were $69.8 million. They were $201.8 million in 2005, his last full year as president. The relationship among the three was similar in grant-making: Mellon was roughly comparable to Rockefeller but significantly smaller than Ford in 1987. In 2005, Mellon grants outdistanced Rockefeller's but still fell well short of Ford's, now by a slightly smaller margin than had been the case before.[8]

By the early years of the twenty-first century, Mellon's programmatic emphases were even more concentrated than they had been when Bowen took office. Higher education and the humanities— "defined broadly to include research libraries, centers for advanced

7 Bowen commented in his 2004 president's report that Mellon was "appreciably larger" in asset size than the Carnegie, Rockefeller, and Sloan Foundations, about the same size as the MacArthur Foundation, but smaller than the Ford Foundation. William G. Bowen, "President's Report," *Report of the Andrew W. Mellon Foundation, 2004*, 8–9 (the quote is from 9).

8 "The Andrew W. Mellon Foundation: Statements of Activities for the years ended Dec. 31, 2006 and 2005," *Report of the Andrew W. Mellon Foundation, 2006*, 99.

study, art museums and art conservation, and the performing arts"—accounted for 60 percent of the foundation's outlays in the period before 1988, compared with nearly 80 percent ("of a far larger appropriations total") by 2004 and more than 90 percent in 2005.[9]

With the Shapiros' impending arrival in Princeton, the Bowens had moved from Lowrie House to 87 College Road West, a gracious house near the Graduate College that had been built in 1957 for Harold and Margaret Dodds at the conclusion of the Dodds presidency. In New York, there was an apartment provided by Mellon for the president of the foundation. Bowen typically went to New York on Monday afternoon or Tuesday morning and returned to Princeton on Friday. Weekends were spent in Princeton or, in the warmer weather, at the Bowens' home in Avalon on the Jersey Shore, where they also spent at least a month in the summer. Mary Ellen went to New York a couple of days a week. From time to time she attended meetings of the Foreign Policy Association or met friends during the day for visits to museums, and she joined Bowen in the evenings for Mellon functions or dinner with friends. As well, she accompanied Mellon staff members on some of their trips abroad, and she traveled on occasion with her friend Lois Shepetin on trips sponsored by such institutions as the Smithsonian and the Metropolitan Museum. In Princeton the foundation bought and renovated a house at the corner of Alexander Street and Faculty Road, within walking distance, across the golf course, of College Road West, to provide Bowen with an office for the days when he stayed in New Jersey.

Working with Staff

Bowen brought to the foundation qualities that had infused his presidency of Princeton: outsize energy, clear vision, boldness, commitment to hard work, disposition to collaborate with colleagues,

9 Bowen, "President's Report," *2004*, 9 (source of the quotes); "The Andrew W. Mellon Foundation: Notes to Financial Statements," *Report of the Andrew W. Mellon Foundation, 2006*, 106.

willingness to make big bets, desire for long-term impact, and pre-dilection for action, knowing that the right path might not always be clear, and that subsequent data and experience might require some adjustment in course.

When Bowen came to Mellon, he found a lean staff: a vice pres-ident/secretary, a treasurer/assistant secretary, and four program di-rectors. He asked members of the staff for memos describing their roles and responsibilities and their vision for the future, and within the year, two of the program directors had left the foundation and the vice president/secretary had retired and been named a senior fellow.[10] William Robertson IV, who had been in charge of the foundation's programming in conservation and the environment since 1979, offered to resign, knowing that the environment—which had been one of Sawyer's particular interests—was not one of Bow-en's. Bowen said no—he was happy for the program to continue (and Robertson said that he had a lot more freedom to act under Bowen's aegis, so that the environmental program not only contin-ued, but developed in innovative ways during the Bowen presi-dency), and he also had other things he wanted Robertson to do. "I want you to help run the place," he told Robertson, "while Neil and I change it."[11]

And change it they did, in terms of personnel, programming, and facilities, such that Bowen's Mellon came to look quite different from Sawyer's Mellon. The personnel began to change almost im-mediately, and by the time Bowen left Mellon, only Robertson re-mained from the staff Bowen had inherited from Sawyer. In terms of facilities, as we shall see, Bowen renovated the foundation's of-fices and made major changes in its overall footprint. When it came to programming, Bowen and Rudenstine divided up the turf, so that Bowen concentrated on higher education and Rudenstine on the humanities and the arts. While they worked together on some proj-ects and "remain[ed] very collaborative," Rudenstine said later, they "simultaneously [had their own] special spheres."[12]

---

10 *Report of the Andrew W. Mellon Foundation, 1987, 1988.*
11 Telephone interview with William Robertson IV, Sept. 2, 2020.
12 Rudenstine oral history, 36–37.

What was most different for the two men, of course, was the opportunity to give money away. Bowen's approach to grant-making was built on several pillars. The first was to double down in areas of traditional Mellon strength, like graduate fellowships in the humanities. The second was to innovate within traditional program areas, such that Mellon's support for museums and libraries, to take two examples, came to look quite different from how it had before. The third pillar—completely new—was to ground programming in research, so that thorough collection of data would inform decisions about where to invest resources. The fourth was to depend on the advice of experts, sometimes convening college and university presidents and deans to discuss big issues, sometimes gathering individuals on an ad hoc basis for assistance with a particular question or challenge, but also by appointing senior scholars of great prestige as senior advisers to the foundation. The point of all of this activity was to inform the thinking of Bowen and his colleagues about the next Mellon initiative. The fifth pillar was to wind down programs that had accomplished their goals or outlived their usefulness—for example, after Bowen took over, the foundation quickly stopped making grants in medicine, public health, and population. And the final pillar—again, a Bowen innovation—was to harness technology to change the face of the foundation's activities in traditional program areas.

Undergirding all of these pillars was a commitment to hire strategically. In higher education, Bowen appointed highly experienced senior administrators and scholars from colleges and universities to lead important programmatic initiatives, including Harriet Zuckerman, professor of sociology at Columbia; Alice F. Emerson, stepping down as president of Wheaton College; Mary Patterson McPherson, completing a long run as president of Bryn Mawr College; and later Eugene N. Tobin, coming off a complicated ending of his presidency at Hamilton College. "What was distinctive about Bill's leadership from that of so many of the other leading foundations," Pat McPherson said, "was that he appointed as program officers only people who had actually worked in, and/or given leadership to the sorts of institutions, whether educational or cultural that the foundation focused on. They were not career foundation people. Bill expected staff to give real leadership in their individual areas and this made for a very interesting, often quite exciting atmosphere in which one was learning all the time from one's colleagues."[13]

Bowen backstopped the senior people by bringing on staff really bright young people, just out of college or graduate school, novices in their fields but ready to work very hard, to support and collaborate with the senior leaders. So Julie Ann Sosa, just graduated from Princeton in 1988, signed on to work with Bowen on a book, *Prospects for Faculty in the Arts and Sciences*. Elizabeth Duffy, another Princeton alumna in the class of 1988 who was finishing up at Stanford Business School, came to write a book with Bowen, published as *The Charitable Nonprofits*, and to work with Tish Emerson on the liberal arts college program. Sarah Turner, a Princeton graduate in the class of 1989, another coauthor of *The Charitable Nonprofits*, became an important collaborator on Bowen's social science research projects. Bowen also took on Matthew Chingos, a Harvard graduate, who was hired as a research associate but ended up as a coauthor of *Higher Education in the Digital Age*; Martin Kurzweil, another Harvard graduate, also hired as a research associate, who became one of the coauthors of *Equity and Excellence*; and Sarah Levin Taubman, another Harvard graduate, with an undergraduate degree in mathematics, who came to work with Bowen as a research associate on his studies of college athletics and became the coauthor of *Reclaiming the Game*.

Two of the young hires had long runs at the foundation, stretches of real consequence. Kevin Guthrie, Princeton '84, who had lived with the Bowens for a couple of years after graduation, came to the foundation to write a book on the history of the New-York Historical Society as part of Mellon's interest in understanding the functioning of nonprofit cultural institutions in the city; eventually, he would run JSTOR and ITHAKA, two of the signature affiliated organizations that Bowen created during his tenure at Mellon. James Shulman, a Yale alumnus, came to the foundation as a member of the research staff after completing his PhD in Renaissance

---

13 E-mail, Mary Patterson McPherson to Nancy Weiss Malkiel, Oct. 17, 2021.

studies. His portfolio expanded widely: He oversaw the building of the College and Beyond database, about which more will be said shortly; he collaborated with Bowen and Derek Bok on their book on affirmative action, *The Shape of the River*, and coauthored, with Bowen, the first Mellon book on athletics, *The Game of Life*; he assisted in the management of the foundation's endowment and in the development of internal budgeting practices; from 2001 to 2016, he served as the founding president of Artstor.

That young people should be taken so seriously at Mellon was remarkable. Julie Ann Sosa had gotten to know Bowen when she wrote about him and his administration—vigorously, combatively, with no holds barred—as editor in chief (then called chairman) of the *Daily Princetonian*. Amidst the intensity of the relationship between student journalist and university president, the two built an understanding of trust and respect. After Bowen's intended departure from Princeton for Mellon was announced, he began talking to Sosa about her future plans. She had studied public policy at Princeton and had won the university's Sachs Scholarship, which would take her to Oxford for a year to pursue a course of study in human sciences, an interdisciplinary degree program illuminating the interconnections among biological, social, and cultural phenomena as they influenced the problems of human societies. After Oxford, she was headed for medical school at Johns Hopkins. Sosa told Bowen she was not yet sure how to bring together her interests in medicine and public policy. He proposed a pathway: work with him on data collection and analysis for his book on prospects for faculty in the arts and sciences, which would teach her something about doing data-based science. She would do some of the work during term-time at Oxford; she would work full-time at the foundation in the summers of 1988 and 1989 and during Oxford vacations, and the foundation would fly her back from Oxford from time to time so that the two could meet to review her progress.

Once Sosa arrived at Oxford, she encountered a practical challenge: How was she to communicate with Bowen? It was long before the days of routine use of cell phones and e-mail. Sosa was living in the attic of a centuries-old dormitory at Worcester

College; the closest telephone was two entryways away, with no door to protect from the rain and cold. While she was worrying about getting heat and hot water, Bowen was worrying about where to find a jack for a telephone and a fax machine. In classic Bowen fashion, he managed to get her room changed to a more modern dormitory and to have a fax machine with a telephone installed. "He was on a mission," she said, to create the conditions under which she could do her work. The two would talk several times a week, sometimes a couple of times a day, about the data Sosa was collecting and the analysis she was undertaking. When she was back in New York, Bowen would frequently come up to her office or call her to come down to his to review what she was accomplishing. She did the analysis; he guided the work, always pointing out—gently— how it could be stronger. She drafted chapters based on her data; he edited liberally and rewrote, and he personally wrote the chapter on the implications of their findings. He was the model mentor, she said, empowering and enabling—guiding, driving strategy and interpretation, but all the while giving her the confidence that she was doing the work herself. And he included her at every turn, inviting her to board meetings, drafting press releases together for the book, making sure she joined in interviews about the book at major newspapers. He was fully prepared to "share the limelight," she said—he was "so generous, so eager for [her] to succeed."[14]

Liz Duffy, too, illuminated Bowen's engagement as a mentor. He "never gave up" being what he had been for so much of his earlier career—"a teacher and mentor." He would have lunch with young staff members individually and as a group—deliberately "building relationships, building community." She noted that he had "no obsession with hierarchy, position, or age"—he was interested in good ideas, and he would "listen to anyone." Duffy, who worked at Mellon for five years, said that Bowen had "blinders on" when it came to his protégés; he was not always objective about their strengths and weaknesses, and he gave them "opportunities way above what we should have had at that age." Bowen, she said, "convinced you that you could do things you didn't know you

14 Zoom interview with Julie Ann Sosa, June 15, 2021.

could do" and opened doors for opportunities that changed young people's lives and careers. Early on in Duffy's time at the foundation, for example, he sent her to a College Board roundtable that he was supposed to have attended himself. Around the table were college presidents—and Duffy. That sort of experience was intimidating but also invigorating, she said—"you felt validated, supported, and challenged."[15]

Higher education was Bowen's wheelhouse. He was very much interested in arts and culture, but he lacked the direct personal experience to know whose judgment to trust and where investments would be most likely to pay off. To carry forward the foundation's programming, he again looked for staff with deep experience in one or more of the relevant fields. Rachel N. Bellow, the first program director for arts and culture hired by Bowen and Rudenstine, had been the founding executive director of Poets House in New York City, and before that, director of national arts policy at the American Council for the Arts. Her successor, Catherine Wichterman, president of Meet the Composer, a national organization dedicated to contemporary music, had previously been the executive director of three symphony orchestras. Angelica Zander Rudenstine, for many years in charge of Mellon's museum program, was a well-respected museum curator and art historian.

Bowen made Mellon a fast-paced, challenging, exhilarating environment in which to work—one with few established boundaries, where good ideas claimed pride of place and where even the most junior person could be heard and taken seriously. His "energy, imagination and creativity engaged everyone such that we all felt part of an important and useful enterprise," Pat McPherson said.[16]

Bowen's office door was always open. He would call out to his assistants, Ulrica Fredsvik-Konvalin and Pat Woodford, whenever he needed something—help with a balky computer, help finding a missing piece of correspondence, help locating his BlackBerry— Blackie, as he called it—which so often went missing. Bowen frequently roamed the halls and looked in on colleagues: What were

---

15 Interview with Elizabeth A. Duffy, Aug. 30, 2018, Princeton, NJ.

16 E-mail, Mary Patterson McPherson to Nancy Weiss Malkiel, Oct. 17, 2021.

they doing? Could he be of help? What did they think about this new idea? Bowen's Mellon was a world in which work—hard work, intense work—bled over into breakfasts and dinners, seminar-style debate and conversation. It was an intense atmosphere, an atmosphere almost *en famille*, where staff members were in thrall to the president of the foundation, around whom so much of their lives revolved.

To a large extent, Bowen's work was coterminous with his personal life, and his staff was the functional equivalent of his family. The upside of the family atmosphere was that Bowen knew everyone's personal issues, and he used his time and connections to help them where he could. As had been true at Princeton, if a staff member or one of their family members needed medical help, he was on the case. Pat Woodford had health problems that had persisted, undiagnosed, for a year. Bowen sent her to see a doctor he knew, and the Bowens were waiting at the doctor's office to introduce her when she arrived. The doctor said that she needed a total hip replacement. She said that she could not have the surgery on the proposed date, which conflicted with a Mellon board meeting. From the other side of the room came Bowen's pronouncement to the contrary: That date was just fine. When Bill Robertson's daughter had trouble sorting out a necessary medical procedure, Bowen saw to it that she would be seen promptly by the appropriate specialist. When Robertson's wife had to be hospitalized at New York Presbyterian / Weill Cornell Medical Center, Bowen made sure that she had a private room on the top floor of the hospital. When the Mellon receptionist, Deborah Longino, asked Bowen if there might be any emergency funds to help her make a small down payment for a house for her mother, he took care of it right away—though whether the money came from a Mellon emergency fund or from his own pocket, she never knew.

The downside of the family atmosphere was that it was intense— too intense, with Bowen in the middle of people's personal lives in ways that could be unsettling. It was especially true for the young women, where the working relationships Bowen forged sometimes spilled over into territory that was too sensitive, too personal. Working on a research project with Bowen meant seeing him all the time and having his undivided attention, a powerful emotional as well as intellectual experience. His mentorship, intended as a generous gesture, could easily be confusing—was this Bowen seeking to be helpful, or Bowen coming too close? For a young woman strong enough to set boundaries, the intensity could be kept at a reasonable remove. For a young woman who was more vulnerable, the emotional element of the relationship sometimes became more overwhelming than could easily be managed.

But that was Bowen, that was his modus operandi. The older women staff members knew it, and so did some of the men. They protected the younger women by seeing to it that they left the foundation at reasonable hours, or that they sat at some remove from Bowen when the staff gathered for dinner at restaurants. The playbook was relatively innocent—the hand on the knee, the arm around the shoulder, the intense absorption in the conversation at hand—any of which could be rebuffed without fear of consequences. But it was confusing, and it could be unsettling, and the distortion in the power relationship was undeniable.

The familylike atmosphere of the foundation went along with the absence of boundaries. That was true in terms of the running room given to senior staff members—trusted, experienced, wise— to propose the programming they thought best, always, of course, checking their instincts with the president and needing to argue persuasively to the board. Junior staff members, as we have seen, were given huge opportunities to learn and grow—encouraged, if they were able, to show that they could take on responsibility well beyond their years and experience. Bowen intentionally kept the staff very small—no more than fifty positions, no matter how the endowment grew or the number of additional areas the foundation investigated. "The strict control of staff size," Pat McPherson observed, together with Bowen's "constant refrain that this money was to go out the door and must never be thought of as our own, set us apart from most other foundations."[17]

There was little that Bowen asked of others that he was unwilling to do himself—even, for example, joining a younger colleague

17 Ibid.

in moving a couch from one floor to the next. More typical evidence of the absence of boundaries was that Bowen commonly phoned colleagues at home at seven o'clock in the morning or eleven o'clock at night, unless Mary Ellen was at hand to restrain him. Staff members were on call all the time. Joan Gilbert, who ran the Princeton office for a period in the 1990s, came to expect phone calls from Bowen through the day and evening, including at dinner parties where she and her husband, the philosopher Harry Frankfurt, were guests. Often Bowen would ask her to retrieve things from the Princeton house that he had forgotten, to the point where she became fully familiar with the arrangement of his bookshelves and the items in his closet and dresser drawers. And once e-mail was the order of the day, Bowen would be there, in the lives of his staff, at every hour of the night as well as the day. In normal working hours, and well into the evening, he expected virtually instant responses, and he returned messages accordingly. Members of the senior staff took to checking their e-mail routinely if they awoke in the middle of the night, certain that they would have messages waiting from the president.

Bowen's expectations for his staff were sky-high: work done quickly, work done competently, operating at double speed, double intensity, no corners cut, the boss's standards always met. Bowen "worked around the clock," Stacy Berg Dale, the data analyst in the Princeton office, said; "nothing was beneath him"—he would willingly "get his hands dirty" if that was what it took to move the effort along. She recalled Bowen wanting to get something done at a moment when the data entry person was not in the office. "We're going to do this right now," he told her; "you read me the numbers, I'll type them in."[18] "You would do more," Rachel Bellow reflected, not because Bowen imposed his extraordinary work ethic on others, "but because of watching him." His demands were inspiring and motivating, not onerous; the foundation was invigorating, the most exciting place so many members of the staff had ever worked. He "never asked anyone to do more than he was will-

---

18 Telephone interview with Stacy Berg Dale, June 15, 2021.

ing to do" himself, Bellow said. "He would do it with you"; it made you "feel pushed in a great way."[19]

While Bowen made Mellon exhilarating by the intensity of his demands and the range of his imagination, he also made it a hugely appealing place to work. Michele Warman, whom he recruited from the law firm Davis Polk as Mellon's general counsel and secretary, described his recruiting philosophy as seeking to surround himself with talent and expertise that would supplement his own strengths. One way of implementing that philosophy was to take on as senior colleagues college presidents who were long accustomed to wielding their own authority. That was a tricky business to manage, but Bowen made it work to the great benefit of the foundation. Tish Emerson, stepping down after sixteen years as president at Wheaton, spent eight years at Mellon, taking up the portfolio for liberal arts colleges. Bowen, she said, was wonderfully encouraging; "if he didn't know something, he'd let you try it, then take the project on in a full way" when it proved successful. "One idea sparked another and another." He left Emerson "to do what [she] wanted to do"; "he was very open to having you come and discuss" ideas—"you'd initiate it, and he'd help you build it." "He was perfectly prepared," she reflected, "to take on really bold things and spend the money to pursue them." He understood that he had "a responsibility to make some difference in the world," and he "brought others along" with him in making that happen.[20]

Pat McPherson, finishing up a nineteen-year run as president of Bryn Mawr, first came to the foundation to work on the liberal arts college program. She overlapped with Emerson for a couple of years, took over the program, and stayed at Mellon for a decade, with increasing responsibility as a vice president for overseeing staff and programming. It was, she said, "the most interesting group of people" she had ever worked with. They "worked very hard and supported each other," and Bowen gave them their heads, with the attention, support, and running room they needed to do their jobs. Mellon, she said, was "a very collegial place" where staff were

19 Interview with Rachel N. Bellow, Sept. 11, 2018, New York City.
20 Interview with Alice F. Emerson, Oct. 31, 2018, Bryn Mawr, PA.

motivated to "work at their best capacity, as hard as they could," inspired by the fact that such an effort was what Bowen asked of himself. It was, she said, "a very heady experience." "The pace of things, the excitement of things, the way he made things happen. It was the golden period for all of us—a marvelous high point in people's professional lives."[21]

For Harriet Zuckerman, the challenge in coming to Mellon was not adjusting after a long run as a college president but rather dealing with the possibility of giving up tenure to take an administrative role at the foundation. She spoke about Bowen's efforts to recruit her from a professorship in the sociology department at Columbia to a senior position at Mellon. She had first come to the foundation for a year on a quarter-time basis as a senior adviser, working at Bill Baker's behest on what Mellon might do in the history of science. But giving up tenure at a major research university to join Mellon on a permanent basis was something else again. With Rudenstine departing for Harvard, Bowen kept asking; she kept saying no. Zuckerman told her husband, the Columbia sociologist Robert K. Merton, about Bowen's inquiries. "Have you noticed," he said, "that when you leave early to go to Mellon, you're smiling, and when you return home late, you're smiling? Why not try it for a year?" She went to Mellon for a year, took on a lot of the work that Rudenstine had been doing, and found herself deeply immersed in Bowen's efforts. When Bowen asked her to stay, she decided to join the foundation on a full-time basis. "What was really important to me," she said later, "was that Bill was wonderful to work with and for. I was never bored. He wanted to know what I thought about [everything from] what he was writing to potential new staff members to the Foundation's interior décor. He was glad to turn some things over to me and I found watching him do his job really instructive. I learned a lot."[22]

Bowen made Mellon fun. He had a quirky, whimsical sense of humor; he enjoyed pranks and practical jokes. He had a collection

21 Interview with Mary Patterson McPherson, Aug. 8, 2018, Rosemont, PA.

22 Interview with Harriet Zuckerman, Sept. 11, 2018, New York City; e-mail, Zuckerman to Nancy Weiss Malkiel, Dec. 2, 2021 (source of the quotes).

of cows—ceramic, fabric, and other—on a table in his office, which he and the staff referred to routinely as the cow table. He kept stuffed animals given to him by people who were important to him—on his desk, on his bookshelf; sometimes one of them accompanied him to meetings or informal meals. There were turtles in a pond in the garden behind the Mellon offices; after they came out of hibernation each year, Bowen wanted to be updated regularly about their well-being. When the garden was encumbered because of Mellon renovations, he cared for some of the turtles in a terrarium in his office. He loved dogs; an enormous Newfoundland who lived down the street would stop in sometimes for a visit. Richard Ekman, secretary of the foundation in the 1990s, had his office on the third floor, where he could grow vegetables in flower boxes on the terrace outside. One of his cucumber vines dangled down outside Bowen's office window, and Bowen would bring visitors upstairs to see Ekman's tomatoes.

Relaxed, even irreverent as he could sometimes be, Bowen was fully comfortable exercising power. Princeton had given him ample experience, and he had no reluctance to wield the authority given to him or to expand it where that seemed useful. But he disliked the trappings of power. He carried a beat-up canvas briefcase that he had been given at the University of Pittsburgh, and when it wore out, his staff replaced it with a similarly unpretentious bag. He favored khakis and open shirts or, if he had to dress more appropriately to his position, rumpled suits (a better way to put it is that his suits invariably looked rumpled). Hanna Gray described his self-presentation this way: "As the day wore on, Bill's nice suits began to look as though tailored by Goodwill Industries. His shirt hems seemed reluctant to make contact with his waistband. So far as I could tell, he owned two neckties for regular wear and perhaps a third for special occasions."[23]

Bowen was uncomfortable in settings where he had to engage in small talk, and he resisted backslapping. He did not want to waste

23 Hanna Holborn Gray, "Afterword: William G. Bowen," in Kevin M. Guthrie, ed., *Ever the Leader: Selected Writings, 1995–2016, William G. Bowen* (Princeton, NJ: Princeton University Press, 2018), 319.

time talking to people he did not know, did not like, and would not learn anything from. Whenever he could (which was most of the time), he eschewed the cocktail party and benefit circuits in New York, and he hated putting on a tuxedo. Ulrica Fredsvik-Konvalin recalled one occasion where Bowen had to dress formally, when he practically had to be bribed to wear a white tie. He also hated stretch limousines; after one occasion where a stretch limo picked up Bowen and Mary Ellen, his staff had strict orders never to let that happen again.

Bowen was irritated by pomp, and he steered clear of ceremony whenever he could. Sometimes, though, he made questionable decisions about avoiding ceremonial occasions. When Paul Mellon, an honorary trustee of the foundation for decades, died in February 1999, there was a memorial service at the National Gallery in Washington. The Mellon board was in attendance, minus Bowen, who had a competing commitment to give a talk about affirmative action at the University of Michigan and chose not to try to reschedule it.

As had been the case in Princeton, Bowen strongly preferred low-key socializing, centered around dinners at family-run restaurants with good food where he was well-known to the owners. An informal Greek restaurant, Periyali, on West Twentieth Street, was a particular favorite; for a slightly more upscale meal, he favored Jubilee, a French restaurant on First Avenue near Fiftieth Street. As at the Homestead Inn in Hamilton Township and 410 Bank Street in Cape May, he forged relationships with the owners; he knew about their families, asked for updates on how their children were doing, and was embraced warmly as a special, regular guest. He might have dinner with members of the Mellon staff, or members of the board, or, if Mary Ellen was in town, with friends. Bowen loved to talk, loved to tell stories, but he also had a gift for listening and drawing out the interests of those with whom he was dining. Dinner would usually end around nine o'clock; more likely than not, he would then go back to the office to do more work. If he had had a lot to drink, he would go straight home, sometimes aided in getting there safely by younger members of his staff. Breakfast meetings—normally beginning at seven o'clock in the morning—

usually found him at a diner near the foundation, where he would spend hours doing foundation business. Richard Ekman recalled one two-and-a-half-hour coffee with Bowen, where the bill was $10 and the tip $20. "I tip based on the time I've occupied the table, not the price of the food," Bowen told him.[24]

Working with the Board

With his board, Bowen could be more formal. It was a very different board from the one he had worked with at Princeton. There he had needed to manage a large group, nearly all of them alumni, representing many different constituencies deeply invested in the life of the university. The Mellon board was very small—at the outset, just nine members, including the president; the number increased to eleven before Bowen left office. They knew each other well, enjoyed each other, and were well prepared to discuss vigorously and speak up to express their views. With one exception, Timothy Mellon, Paul's son, none of them had a preexisting intimate relationship with the foundation. Tim Mellon left the board in 2002 (he had served for twenty-one years) because of some disagreements about direction and board leadership. Otherwise, the departures came when trustees reached the Mellon retirement age of seventy. Bowen had the strongest hand in choosing their successors—academics, heads of educational and cultural institutions, and business leaders chief among them. The appointments were made, of course, in consultation with his board chairs, but the trustees were his people, and he was uniquely able to manage a board and get it to do his bidding, a gift he demonstrated as much at Mellon as he had at Princeton. As Taylor Reveley, dean of the law school and later president of the College of William and Mary, who served as a Mellon trustee and chair of the Mellon board, put it, Bowen was "highly effective at letting other people have his way."[25] There were board retreats each fall where the trustees discussed longer-

24 Telephone interview with Richard H. Ekman, Sept. 17, 2020.
25 Taylor Reveley, "William Gordon Bowen," remarks at Bowen memorial service, Princeton University Chapel, Dec. 11, 2016, courtesy of Taylor Reveley. Also see e-mail, Reveley to Nancy Weiss Malkiel, Dec. 29, 2021.

term strategic directions. Dockets for regular board meetings were carefully constructed—dense, well documented, clearly argued. If the board raised questions, answers were given; if trustees pushed back, which they sometimes did, a proposal might be withdrawn, reworked, and brought back at a subsequent meeting, the new version clearly reflecting the board discussion. Rarely would a proposal simply be shelved.

Bowen worked with four board chairs during his presidency: William O. Baker, who chaired the board from June 1975 to September 1990; the investment banker John C. Whitehead, who had been chair of Goldman Sachs as well as deputy secretary of state in the Reagan administration, from September 1990 to March 1997; Hanna Holborn Gray, president of the University of Chicago from 1978 to 1993, from March 1997 to March 2003; and Anne M. Tatlock, chair and chief executive officer of the Fiduciary Trust Company, who took over the Mellon chairmanship in March 2003. Among those chairs, Bowen's closest working relationship was with Gray, a longtime friend whom he respected deeply. If Bowen was a formidable figure, so was Gray. It was widely understood that Gray was the one board member who could really stand up to him. He was always in a hurry to get things done. Sometimes Gray needed to slow him down, to tell him that he needed to wait, to learn more, to do more extensive preparation. "Now, Bill," she might say. The two would argue over some point, sometimes intensely; Bowen could be visibly irritated, but he listened, took in her views, and thought about them. By the next morning, he would usually acknowledge that she was probably right.[26]

As well as Bowen and Gray knew each other, as much as each one could count on the other's respect, Bowen still needed Gray to know that he was working all the time to advance the foundation's purposes. As Gray said, "Bill rather assumed that everyone was, or should be, as productively workaholic as himself. He also wanted to be sure that you knew he was not slacking off. Each year, before leaving with Mary Ellen for their winter visit to St. Croix, he would call to reassure me that he would be working hard, for this would

26 Interview with Hanna Holborn Gray, Sept. 18, 2018, New York City.

be no vacation, except for an hour a day on the tennis court, and that he would begin drafting his annual report as soon as they had boarded the plane."[27] And that was no hyperbole; for years, staff members who worked with Bowen at Mellon and afterward would arrange with the hotel in St. Croix, the Buccaneer, to set up a room for him to use as an office, equipped properly with the necessary technology as well as relevant documents shipped down from New York to allow him to work and to communicate back and forth so that the weeks in St. Croix produced not only the Mellon annual report but any scholarly writing currently on Bowen's agenda. After his death, the conference/meeting room where he worked at the Buccaneer was named in his honor.

Gray's successor as Mellon board chair, Anne Tatlock, told a similar story, this one about a Merck board trip to Paris, where Bowen was the only board member to decline the planned flight on the Concorde for a commercial flight because "the Concorde would arrive too quickly" and Bowen "would not have enough time to finish [his] work!"[28] The man worked all the time (or almost all the time). He could not help it; it was how he was wired, how he found purpose in life, how he defined himself. And the products of that work, as we have seen and will still see, were formidable.

27 Gray, "Afterword: William G. Bowen," 318.

28 E-mail, "Note for Bill Bowen," Anne Tatlock to J[ohanna] B[rownell], Sept. 14, 2016, Bowen Ithaka.

13

Shaping the Mellon Agenda

"Perfectly Prepared to Take on Really Bold Things"

Higher Education

Mellon gave Bowen the opportunity to marshal formidable resources in the interest of supporting institutions, enhancing processes, and advancing the careers of groups of individuals that he
cared deeply about. There was no need to raise money, no need to
sell alumni on his vision. As long as he and his staff did the serious
work of research and analysis to frame a plan and convince the
board of its importance, he could proceed as he wished. Higher education was his first priority. Mellon's investments in higher education in the Bowen era were richer, deeper, and more varied than
had been the case previously. So much happened during the Bowen
presidency that turned out to be of enduring value: the Mellon
Mays (originally Mellon Minority) Undergraduate Fellowship
Program;[1] the electronic journal project JSTOR; the establishment
for varied purposes of consortia of small liberal arts colleges to provide the requisite scale for certain activities and to encourage
shared information and problem solving; institutional collabora-
tions among liberal arts colleges in areas including faculty career
enhancement and staffing, health care for emeriti, study abroad
programs, uses of information technology, and administrative sup-

---

1 The name was changed and the program's mission broadened slightly in 2003 in
the wake of the Supreme Court's decision in *Grutter v. Bollinger*, when the foundation
adjusted its race-exclusive programs to allow the participation of non-minority students
with a demonstrated commitment to diversity.

port. There were special investments in colleges in Appalachia to strengthen the faculty, the creation of networks to connect students and faculty, and the development of libraries. There were awards to senior scholars of special achievement and distinction in the humanities; support for emeriti to encourage faculty to transition to retirement; support for postdoctoral fellowships at major humanities centers and libraries; postdoctoral fellowships at leading liberal arts colleges; fellowship support for graduate students, initially given at the outset of their studies, but later, instead, involving financial assistance for dissertation writing; support for departments that overhauled their training of PhD students; and the establishment at selected universities with special strengths in the humanities, social sciences, and foreign cultures of the Sawyer seminars in comparative historical and cultural studies. The foundation funded major research libraries as well as prominent academic centers in the humanities, including the New York Public Library, the New-York Historical Society, the American Academy in Rome, the American School of Classical Studies in Athens, the American Philosophical Society, the American Academy of Arts and Sciences, and the American Council of Learned Societies.

One of the distinctive aspects of the foundation's initiatives in the Bowen era was the close link between research and programming. Bowen deliberately built an in-house research capacity that had not previously existed at Mellon. His intention was to produce careful studies of aspects of higher education and culture that he considered important—studies based on intensive data-gathering, high-level statistical analysis, and, where appropriate, old-fashioned archival research. Usually the studies resulted in scholarly books; usually they informed and shaped the foundation's programming.

As Bowen himself acknowledged, it was unusual for a foundation to proceed in this fashion. Normally grants would be made to outsiders—colleges, universities, other organizations—so that scholars could conduct research in fields of interest to the foundation. And Mellon did handle some of its grants in that manner. What was unique about Mellon was that its staff members also undertook scholarly research. The "rationale for the Foundation's own research activities," Bowen explained, had "four elements": first, staff members had research projects they wanted to pursue, the findings of which could provide value to grantees as well as "a broader audience of scholars and policymakers"; second, research in areas where the foundation already had programmatic commitments might allow it to be more effective in its grant-making; third, research projects might yield insights that would point to new programming; and fourth, undertaking research made the foundation a more stimulating place to work. What Bowen might have added was that doing research played directly to his own personal interests, and that Mellon devoted significant resources to supporting his research agenda.[2]

Bowen focused his first investigation on prospects for faculty staffing in the arts and sciences. As we have seen, he enlisted Julie Ann Sosa, the Princeton alumna in the class of 1988 who was headed for Oxford and then medical school, to gather the data and join him in undertaking the analysis. The resulting book, William G. Bowen and Julie Ann Sosa, *Prospects for Faculty in the Arts and Sciences* (Princeton University Press, 1989), argued that with student enrollments increasing markedly, there would be a serious shortage of faculty in the arts and sciences, especially in the humanities and social sciences, in the period 1997–2002. There would likely be acute competition for faculty members. The remedy for the excess demand? Increase the size of the pool by producing more doctorates.[3] In fact, however, there was no such explosion of demand; rather, there was a significant contraction in demand, with limited availability of positions for new faculty and a worrisome trend toward the appointment of adjunct faculty to provide teaching that would otherwise have been done by faculty on a tenure track.

In other words, Bowen and Sosa simply got it wrong. Why were their projections so far from the mark? They were counting on the impending retirement of the large numbers of professors who had joined college and university faculties in the 1950s and 1960s. They

2 William G. Bowen, "President's Report," *Report of the Andrew W. Mellon Foundation, 1997*, 19–20.
3 Ibid., *1989*, 7–15.

had not imagined that with the abolition of mandatory retirement, legislated by the United States Congress to take effect for universities on January 1, 1994, significant numbers of faculty members would simply choose to remain in place, thus actually reducing the availability of faculty positions in the arts and sciences. Nor had Bowen and Sosa foreseen the dramatic public disinvestment in higher education and the concomitant replacement of tenure-track jobs with cheaper non-tenure-track faculty. And they had not predicted the increasing financial pressures on all colleges and universities—technology costs, federal mandates such as Title VII and Title IX compliance, for example—that would further point toward getting by in the classroom with adjuncts rather than expanding the tenure-track faculty.[4]

Before all of that would become clear, however, the foundation doubled down on the research in this area to understand in more fine-grained detail the causes of attrition from excellent PhD programs. For example, what were the impediments to timely degree completion for those graduate students who persisted? How successful were the various types of national fellowship programs in producing PhDs? What could be learned from their impact? What could be understood about the effectiveness of different kinds of financial support in facilitating progress toward the degree?[5] The next Mellon book, William G. Bowen and Neil L. Rudenstine, *In Pursuit of the Ph.D.* (Princeton University Press, 1992), sustained the flawed argument for an impending shortage in faculty staffing but made important contributions in pointing to what had been an inexorable increase in time to degree, especially in disciplines in the humanities and social sciences. In response, Mellon devised targeted programming to reduce time to degree through a Graduate Education Initiative led by senior vice president Harriet Zuckerman, where forty-seven graduate programs at ten universities were awarded a total of $80 million over ten years to support experiments to improve the quality of graduate training and facilitate

4 Vimal Patel, "How a Famous Academic Job-Market Study Got It All Wrong—and Why It Still Matters," *Chronicle of Higher Education*, Sept. 9, 2018, https://www.chronicle .com/article/How-a-Famous-Academic/244458, accessed Sept. 19, 2018.

5 Bowen, "President's Report," *1989*, 12–13.

more effective completion of the doctorate. These included rethinking graduate programs; reorganizing financial aid; trying out new approaches, like summer support for students who had completed their general examinations and were ready to embark on dissertations; and other measures. After the ten years, there were two more years of tie-off grants so that institutions would not face a cliff in funding.

The outcomes of the initiative were complicated to assess. Data collection was very slow, from the institutions as well as the students, and it was hard to get a clear fix on which departments had done well and which had not. There had been no full longitudinal data before the initiative began, so it was difficult to assess change over time. Reports from participating institutions were slow to come in and not easy to compare. In some cases, the Mellon investment accelerated degree completion, in others not. Mellon support sometimes resulted in delaying dropouts that would otherwise have occurred earlier. Graduate students in the humanities and humanistic social sciences were not necessarily motivated to respond to economic incentives. Faculty members were ready—probably too ready—to give students leeway instead of holding them to account. They believed that it took time to master fields in the humanities, and they cared more about their students becoming excellent scholars than about speed of degree completion. Accelerating time to degree—a priority of the foundation—was not necessarily a priority of the faculty.[6]

A second strand of the foundation's research in the 1990s had to do with nonprofit organizations: the 1992 study by Anthony M. Cummings and others, *University Libraries and Scholarly Communication*; the 1994 book by Bowen and others, *The Charitable Nonprofits: An Analysis of Institutional Dynamics and Characteristics*; the 1995 book by Jed Bergman on independent research

6 Ibid., pp. 14–15; *1992*, 10–11; Harriet Zuckerman and Joseph S. Meisel, "The Foundation's Programs for Research Universities and Humanistic Scholarship," *Report of the Andrew W. Mellon Foundation*, 2001, 37–39; William G. Bowen, "President's Report," *Report of the Andrew W. Mellon Foundation*, 2004, 10–11; Rudenstine oral history, 39; e-mail, Zuckerman to Nancy Weiss Malkiel, Dec. 2, 2021.

libraries, *Managing Change in the Nonprofit Sector*; and the 1996 study by Kevin M. Guthrie, *The New-York Historical Society: Lessons from One Nonprofit's Long Struggle for Survival*. All of these studies helped to shape the foundation's thinking about nonprofit organizations and ways to advance their fortunes through targeted grant-making.[7]

The most provocative of the Mellon studies of higher education grew out of College and Beyond, a massive database created at Mellon in the mid-1990s at Bowen's behest, wherein thirty-two (initially, later thirty-four) academically selective public and private colleges and universities contributed a raft of data on students who entered college in 1951, 1976, and 1989. In announcing the establishment of the database, Bowen said it would allow for scholarly analyses of a wide range of issues, "including admission policies, affirmative action, changing expectations and experiences of women students, the state of intercollegiate athletics, the evolving contributions of academically selective institutions as 'engines' of upward mobility, and, finally, 'returns' to private and public investments in this set of colleges and universities."[8] One outgrowth of the analyses enabled by the database was a series of important books on such topics as the consequences of affirmative action, the costs and benefits of varsity athletics, and the relationship of socioeconomic status to college enrollment and college completion. Those books are explored in detail in the next chapter.

Other Mellon investments in higher education proved to have a lasting impact. One was the Mellon Mays Undergraduate Fellowship Program, an effort to bring underrepresented minority students into doctoral programs in the arts and sciences in the near term, with the longer-term goal of diversifying the professoriate in American colleges and universities. The idea grew out of a series of discussions with college and university presidents, who, "when asked

7 "The Foundation's 'In-House' Research Capacity," Andrew W. Mellon Foundation, https://web.archive.org/web/20101129065225/http://www.mellon.org:80/grant_programs /research, accessed June 18, 2021.

8 William G. Bowen, "President's Report," *Report of the Andrew W. Mellon Foundation, 1995*, 9. Also see *1997*, 28–30.

to identify the most serious problems facing higher education," frequently cited "the lack of minority faculty members."[9]

Bowen saw diversifying the professoriate as "akin to a moral imperative," which he approached in a "tactical, practical, and entrepreneurial" fashion.[10] First he needed good leadership. The program was directed in its first five years by Henry N. Drewry, whom Bowen brought to the foundation from Princeton, where he had taught African American history and directed the university's Program in Teacher Preparation. When Drewry retired, he was succeeded as director of MMUF first by Jacqueline Looney, assistant dean for graduate recruitment at Duke, and then by Lydia English, an associate dean of the college at Brown.

Beyond leadership, a plan was required to make the program work. Each institution appointed a faculty coordinator for the program, selected its own fellows, typically in the sophomore year, paired each student with a faculty mentor, and organized enrichment activities for the group as a whole. Students were encouraged to apply to graduate school in fields where minority students were underrepresented—humanities disciplines, but also anthropology, mathematics, and physics. MMUF students received modest term-time stipends for academic assignments that replaced work requirements for financial aid; they had the opportunity to participate in compensated summer research activities; and MMUF alumni who enrolled in PhD programs were eligible to receive up to $10,000 from Mellon to repay a portion of their undergraduate student loans.[11]

The first eight Mellon grants to colleges and universities to establish MMUF programs were made in December 1988. A year

9 Ibid., *1988*, 9. Bowen wrote in *Lessons Learned: Reflections of a University President* (Princeton, NJ: Princeton University Press, 2011), 96, that his "frustration in dealing with this problem at Princeton"—by which he meant the problem of "increas[ing] the number of well-qualified minority graduates of PhD programs" as a step toward "achieving greater faculty diversity"—led him to create the MMUF program as his first initiative at Mellon.

10 Telephone interview with Michele Warman, Mar. 18, 2022.

11 Henry N. Drewry, "The Mellon Minority Undergraduate Fellowship Program," *Report of the Andrew W. Mellon Foundation, 1993*, 22–27.

later, grants had been made to nineteen colleges and universities.[12] By 1993, when Drewry retired from the foundation, the number had increased to twenty-four. By the time Bowen left Mellon, there were thirty-four participating colleges and universities, and by the end of 2005, Bowen's last full year in office, 164 MMUF fellows had earned doctorates and 500 additional fellows were in graduate school.[13] By 2021, more than 6,000 fellowships had been awarded, more than 1,000 fellows had earned PhDs, and more than 190 MMUF fellows held positions as tenured faculty members— by any measure, a significant infusion of underrepresented minority students into the academy.[14]

MMUF was just one of the initiatives undertaken by Bowen and his colleagues that had a significant effect on American higher education. But if one had to rank all of the Bowen-initiated, Bowen-funded projects in higher education that were incubated at Mellon during Bowen's presidency, doubtless the most consequential, in terms of impact and reach, had to be the electronic journal storage project JSTOR. The idea for JSTOR grew out of a weekend Bowen spent at a trustee meeting at Denison University late in 1993. The college librarian made a presentation to the board about the pressing need for more space; scholarly journals were overrunning existing shelf space, and the only way she could see to ameliorate the crunch was to spend $5 million "to relieve the crowding and permit new acquisitions to be shelved." Bowen learned that "journals published prior to 1990, combined with government publications, occupied more than a quarter of all shelf space." He imagined that this was not a problem specific to Denison, and that "electronic technologies ought to be helpful in finding new solutions."[15]

Bowen came home from Denison and called Ira Fuchs, whom he had hired as vice president for information technology at Princeton, to begin a conversation about another way to proceed. Wouldn't it

---

12 Bowen, "President's Report," *1988*, 9; *1989*, 18.
13 Ibid., *2005*, 13.
14 Warman interview.
15 William G. Bowen, "The Foundation's Journal Storage Project (JSTOR)," *Report of the Andrew W. Mellon Foundation, 1994*, 26. Also see telephone interview with the then-president of Denison, Michele Tolela Myers, June 26, 2020.

be possible to digitize back issues of scholarly journals, make them available to libraries, and thereby free up large amounts of library shelf space at colleges and universities across the country—indeed, around the world? The upshot could be powerfully important: Not only would libraries be freed of the obligation to continue to expand shelf space to accommodate back issues of journals, but students and scholars would gain the capacity through powerful search engines to access runs of journals from their own computers and print out articles of interest—thus dramatically simplifying the process of research.[16] The effect on scholarly research would be striking: Research could be done more quickly, saving students and scholars huge amounts of time; the researcher's reach would be much more sweeping, with easy ways of identifying the full range of published articles on the subject at hand.

The plan was to focus on journals published before 1990 so as not to interfere with the income stream publishers derived from selling subscriptions to current issues. There were many challenges to address, among them getting copyright permission from publishers; developing imaging sophisticated enough to create picture-perfect electronic replicas of each page, including maps, graphs, figures, and equations; and figuring out the business model to sell the product to college and university libraries in order to cover the costs of the work. In 1994 Mellon made two grants to the University of Michigan to develop software and purchase computer hardware; found a vendor who could produce images of the requisite sophistication and accuracy; and launched a pilot project to digitize back copies of five core journals in economics and five in history. Once that process had been completed, the foundation in 1995 set up five test sites at colleges and universities to try out the pilot version of JSTOR.[17] The success of the pilot project led to the decision "to include more fields and more journals," to make the

16 Bowen, "The Foundation's Journal Storage Project (JSTOR)," 26–32; interview with Mary Ellen Bowen, June 13, 2018, Princeton, NJ; interview with Ira H. Fuchs, July 20, 2018, Princeton, NJ. The definitive scholarly study of the creation of JSTOR is Roger C. Schonfeld, *JSTOR: A History* (Princeton, NJ: Princeton University Press, 2003).

17 Bowen, "The Foundation's Journal Storage Project (JSTOR)," 26–32; Bowen and Kevin M. Guthrie, "JSTOR Update," *Report of the Andrew W. Mellon Foundation, 1995,* 19–29.

database available at an unlimited number of sites, and "to explore linking current issues to backfiles."[18]

The Mellon trustees decided in June 1995 to spin JSTOR off into a separate not-for-profit entity, effective July 31, and fund its start-up costs. Kevin Guthrie was brought on as executive director, Ira Fuchs was named chief scientist, and Bowen became chair of the JSTOR board.[19] In the Mellon annual report for 1995, Guthrie and Bowen made the case for the powerful potential of JSTOR: "By reconciling the sometimes competing interests of scholarly associations, other publishers of scholarly journals, libraries, and individual users of journal literature, JSTOR offers the exciting prospect of dramatically improved access to scholarly materials for faculty and students, reductions in capital and operating costs for libraries, and greater long-term financial stability for publishers."[20] Those expectations were amply borne out in subsequent years as JSTOR expanded and became a fixture of the academic landscape. Bowen reported in 2004 that JSTOR's collection of journal literature was "now used by more than 2,300 libraries in 85 countries."[21]

Arts and Culture

While higher education claimed the lion's share of Mellon's grants during the Bowen presidency, there were also important investments in the arts and culture: grants given to early-music and contemporary-music ensembles, to chamber orchestras and symphony orchestras and opera companies, to nonprofit regional theaters, to ballet schools and dance companies, and to museums for curatorial, conservation, and scholarly activities. A significant grant supported the digitization of the architecture and design collection of the Museum of Modern Art. Leading artistic institutions received major endowment grants: for example, the Jacob's Pillow Dance Festival, the Brooklyn Academy of Music, the American Symphony Orchestra

18 Bowen and Guthrie, "JSTOR Update," 22.

19 Bowen, "President's Report," *1995*, 17–18; Bowen and Guthrie, "JSTOR Update," 22–24.

20 Bowen and Guthrie, "JSTOR Update," 19.

21 William G. Bowen, "President's Report," *Report of the Andrew W. Mellon Foundation, 1996*, 16–19; *1999*, 10–18; *2004*, 18.

League, and the Alvin Ailey Dance Foundation.[22] To honor Paul Mellon, the foundation made a $15 million grant to the National Gallery of Art, the largest single appropriation it had made to that point.[23]

Mellon's most audacious investment in the arts and culture involved two projects centered on the application of digital technology to art. One of those projects involved digitization of some of the cave paintings in Dunhuang, China; the other, the establishment of an electronic database of digital images of artworks to parallel JSTOR.

The Dunhuang project began when Sarah Fraser, a professor of art history at Northwestern University, came to Mellon to request modest funding for high-resolution photography of a small number of ninth-century wall paintings made by Buddhist monks in caves in Dunhuang, China. Bowen, visiting Northwestern in 1998, saw a demonstration of the work Fraser had done thus far and "was entranced by the power of the high-resolution photography [and] the international scope of the work." Convinced "that China was going to be the central node of global growth in the coming years," he created a major project centered on digitization of a significant number of the cave paintings.[24]

Dunhuang, located in northwestern China in the Gobi Desert, had been "a major stopping point for the caravan trade between China and the West." As Bowen explained in accounting for Mellon's new endeavor,

> Between approximately the 5th and 10th centuries, Buddhist art was introduced to Dunhuang, a great many cave shrines

---

22 Bowen, "President's Report,"*1989*, 16; *1998*, 11–13; *1999*, 21–22; *2003*, 54–56; Rachel Newton Bellow, "The Foundation's Program in the Arts and Culture," *Report of the Andrew W. Mellon Foundation, 1991*, 17–29; Catherine Wichterman and Harriet Zuckerman, "The Foundation's Program in the Arts," *Report of the Andrew W. Mellon Foundation, 1996*, 29–38; Wichterman, "The Orchestra Forum: A Discussion of Symphony Orchestras in the US," *Report of the Andrew W. Mellon Foundation, 1998*, 29–49; Rudenstine oral history, 40.

23 William G. Bowen, "President's Report," *Report of the Andrew W. Mellon Foundation, 1994*, 9–10.

24 James L. Shulman, "The Synthetic College: Shared Solutions to Save Institutions from Disruption and from Themselves," unpublished draft, Jan. 9, 2022, 72, courtesy of James L. Shulman (source of the quotes); Warman interview.

were built there, and extraordinary collections of manuscripts were amassed in what was called the "hidden library" (because it was walled off in 1002 to protect it from invaders). These treasures were undiscovered, and protected by the dry air of the desert, for almost a millennium. The "hidden library" was reopened by a Chinese monk in 1900. In the following 25 years, various European adventurers and archaeologists came upon the caves and transported a considerable number of their finds back to sponsors in Britain, France, Germany, India, Russia, and other countries. The Chinese stopped this unauthorized export of their art in the mid-1920s, moved some objects to Beijing, and have since attempted . . . to protect the very considerable amount of cave art that remains.

"Dunhuang," Bowen said,

is arguably the most important site of Buddhist art and culture in Asia. Wall paintings and sculptures chart the transmission of Buddhism—from India to China—through the crucial transportation routes of Central Asia. Moreover, the thousands of documents originally stored in Dunhuang's library cave provide one of the most extensive records available of the exchange of goods, people, ideas, and languages across the world's largest land mass. The creation of an online Dunhuang Archive that re-connects the remaining cave art with the most important manuscripts and objects now dispersed all over the world would produce an invaluable scholarly resource for the study of the history, art history, archaeology, religion, and culture of medieval China.

The archive Mellon intended to create, Bowen summed up, "has the potential to transform the way that Chinese art is viewed and discussed and to serve as a model for reuniting materials now physically dispersed in many libraries and museums around the world."[25]

25 Bowen, "President's Report," *1999*, 23–24.

Beginning in 1999, the foundation committed more than $10 million over a five-year period to create and process high-quality digital images of the art in forty of more than two hundred caves in Dunhuang, to catalog that art, and to undertake digitization and cataloging of manuscripts and other works of art in museums outside China that could now be studied in relation to the relevant cave art. The forty caves illustrated different periods in the history of Buddhist cave art. The Mellon International Dunhuang Archive stands alongside other efforts to digitize the cave art as an important resource for scholars around the world.[26]

More than that, the Mellon initiative made a notable contribution to the conservation and preservation of cave art, and it changed the way the Chinese presented Dunhuang to the world. Dunhuang was a national heritage site whose potential was only modestly developed before Mellon's intervention. As a result of Bowen's personal negotiations with local Chinese authorities and the ensuing evolution of the Dunhuang initiative, the Chinese came to appreciate the potential of digital technology not only for scholarly but for touristic purposes. The construction of a visitors center at Dunhuang followed, where a documentary film is shown that introduces the caves and provides high-resolution images of cave paintings that would previously have been unavailable for viewing. Visitors then proceed into the caves, in much larger numbers than had previously been the case, but for much shorter visits, thus allowing considerably more tourist traffic—an important source of income for Dunhuang—while preserving the physical integrity of the caves and the paintings. The Mellon initiative gave great impetus to the creation of a major project, Digital Dunhuang, and Dunhuang has now been designated by Chinese cultural authorities as the leader in digitization of Chinese murals.[27]

---

26 Ibid., 23–25. On Dunhuang the principal study is Dora C. Y. Ching, ed., *Visualizing Dunhuang: Seeing, Studying, and Conserving the Caves* (Princeton, NJ: P. Y. and Kinmay W. Tang Center for East Asian Art and Princeton University Press, 2021).

27 Telephone interview with June Mei, June 30, 2022. Mei served as Bowen's translator and as his point of connection with authorities in Dunhuang and at the provincial and national levels. I am indebted to her for much of my understanding of Dunhuang.

The second major Mellon initiative involving art and digital technology was Artstor, which was imagined as the digital image counterpart to JSTOR. The idea was to create and distribute electronic archives of art images and related scholarly materials that could be used by students and scholars in art history and other fields.[28] Artstor would manage and distribute the Dunhuang and Museum of Modern Art archives, and it would develop and make widely available an array of other collections of digital images of art objects, along with the software tools to search and use those collections. Such collections would provide important support to museums, colleges, universities, and other educational institutions for research and teaching in art history. The foundation began thinking about Artstor in 1999 and decided to proceed with the project in 2001.[29] By 2004, Artstor had been spun off as an independent entity under the leadership of James Shulman, with Neil Rudenstine, back at Mellon after his presidency of Harvard University, as chair of the board.[30] At the outset, Artstor offered a suite of six "charter" collections: in addition to Dunhuang and MOMA, there were four other major collections with more than 250,000 digitized images, including a major slide library to be used for undergraduate art history courses, as well as collections ranging in subject area from Asian to Old European to American art. The expectation was that more collections would follow.[31]

As Shulman has written, "The key goal of Artstor was to build one shared reservoir of content, and in doing so to help U.S. colleges and universities avoid the enormous costs of building and indexing their own library of 50,000 to 100,000 (or more) digitized images."[32] In theory, Artstor would short-circuit this process by providing high-quality images that colleges and universities could access through subscriptions sold to their main libraries. But faculty members had their own views about which images were of

28 Bowen, "President's Report," *1999*, 11, 20–22. The fullest account of the history of Artstor is Shulman, "The Synthetic College," chaps. 2, 5.

29 Bowen, "President's Report," *1999*, 25–30; *2002*, 25–26.

30 Ibid., *2003*, 12–23.

31 Ibid., *2001*, 19–21; *2003*, 14–15.

32 Shulman, "The Synthetic College," 43–44.

appropriate quality, indeed, of which views of individual objects needed to be provided. Moreover, Artstor could easily be understood to compete with the hand-tailored services of departmental slide libraries, with staff whose jobs depended on the existing system. And college and university libraries had not, to that point, been in the business of buying images, and any savings realized through Artstor were unlikely to benefit libraries, so the advantage to them in signing up for a subscription to the digital archive was not immediately clear. That made Artstor expensive and complicated to sell.

There are different perspectives on Artstor's successes and challenges. In his annual reports as president of the Mellon Foundation, Bowen told a story—mainly prospective—that emphasized the challenges. The costs of Artstor were large—much greater than those of JSTOR. Digitizing art objects at a very high level of quality was much more complex than digitizing text. The wide variety of art objects to be digitized meant that economies of scale were hard to realize. The objects were held by a wide variety of institutions and individuals—again, quite different from scholarly journals. The intellectual property issues were different as well. And there was a risk that other entities and individuals would try smaller digitization projects of their own.[33] Mellon funded the start-up costs for Artstor and was committed to providing a more modest level of funding for recurring costs, but Artstor would need to attract subscriptions from educational and cultural institutions to make a go of it as an independent entity.[34]

With the advantage of a longer view, Shulman told a different story. By 2009 Artstor's library of images was in use at 1,400 institutions; it contained 1.4 million images from over 500 contributors. (By comparison, in 2004, JSTOR was already being used in more than 2,300 libraries.) A decade later, 2,000 institutions had signed on. Artstor gave museums and artists the ability to "reach educational audiences who weren't likely to come to their institutional website." Artstor was bringing in $6 million in annual rev-

33 Bowen, "President's Report," *1999*, 27–30; *2003*, 17–23.
34 Ibid., *2002*, 29–30.

enue. And participating colleges and universities were realizing real savings even after the cost of subscriptions by using the resource for instruction in art history.[35]

Where Artstor struggled, Shulman said, was in its ambition to offer a new product, Shared Shelf, "cloud-based software that would allow campuses to catalogue, manage, and use their own image and video collections according to the constraints associated with each campus collection and users' needs." Finding the money for Shared Shelf proved beyond Artstor's grasp. The recession of 2008–9 made it a bad time to try to launch a new product that colleges and universities would need to pay for, no matter that Shared Shelf might enable them to eliminate inefficiencies and thus save money.[36] And with Bowen's retirement from Mellon in 2006, Artstor no longer had a champion who could persuade the Mellon board to provide millions of dollars in grant funds to get Shared Shelf under way. In 2014, with Bowen's immediate successor, Don Randel, already succeeded by Earl Lewis, Mellon ended its funding of the independent Artstor and required that it be merged into ITHAKA, about which more will be said later.

Public Affairs

Turning finally to public affairs, Mellon first pursued a set of initiatives in eastern Europe, largely at the behest of the board chair, John C. Whitehead. The impetus was the political upheavals of 1989, with the opportunity for the first time in decades to improve "the economic, political, and cultural environments in the countries of the region" as Communist control gave way to democratic rule. Richard E. Quandt, the Hungarian-born Princeton economist, came on staff on a part-time basis as a senior adviser to superintend the initiative. Mellon chose to focus on Czechoslovakia, Hungary, and Poland, with grants in two principal areas: one, "assisting the restructuring of the East European economies by funding training

35 Shulman, "The Synthetic College," 60; Zoom interview with James L. Shulman, Dec. 9. 2021.

36 Shulman, "The Synthetic College," 63–64; Shulman interview. See also interview with Peter C. Wendell, Sept. 28, 2019, Princeton, NJ.

efforts in economics, management, and business, and by promoting the development of market-oriented institutions"; the other, "strengthening the infrastructure of universities and other institutions of higher learning, primarily by assisting research libraries and by providing higher educational institutions with computing and computer networking capabilities."[37] By the mid-1990s, Mellon's grant-making in eastern Europe had begun to wind down—the annual funding in 1993 and 1994 had been $8 million; it was $5 million in 1995 and $3 million in 1996, the latter grants focused not on "new starts" but on "sustaining and institutionalizing the most promising of the initiatives funded in prior years."[38] In all, from 1988 to 1996, the foundation invested $45 million in eastern Europe.[39]

Thereafter, the focus for Mellon's engagement in public affairs shifted to South Africa. Bowen, of course, had struggled with divestment during his presidency of Princeton, a bruising fight that was especially difficult because it produced so little of consequence to help Blacks in South Africa.[40] Now he had the resources to make some difference. With the change of government in South Africa in 1994 and the transition from apartheid to majority rule, it was a propitious time to make significant investments. Mellon developed a robust array of activities "to sustain and strengthen the capacity of South Africa's system of higher education to prepare a broad range of students for leadership roles in Africa." Significant grants began in 1995, with $2.9 million for the University of Cape Town and the University of Witwatersrand in the areas of graduate education, faculty development, and library support.[41] By 1998 grants had increased to $13 million, still with a focus on graduate educa-

---

37 Richard E. Quandt, "The Foundation's Program in Eastern Europe," in *Report of the Andrew W. Mellon Foundation, 1992*, 17, 20; interview with Richard E. Quandt, July 18, 2018, Princeton, NJ.

38 Bowen, "President's Report," *1995*, 14.

39 Ibid., *1996*, 23.

40 Morton O. Schapiro speculates on the relationship between the divestment struggle at Princeton and Mellon's grant-making in South Africa in e-mail to Nancy Weiss Malkiel, Dec. 27, 2021.

41 Bowen, "President's Report," *1995*, p. 15. On the rationale for the shift to South Africa, also see *1996*, 23–25.

tion and faculty development, and with a new emphasis on regional library automation and collaboration. The range of universities supported grew to include Pretoria, Natal, and Rhodes in addition to Cape Town and Witwatersrand. The foundation made investments in the development of new teaching tools, utilizing technology to enhance instruction and improve learning in basic subjects as well as more advanced disciplines. Mellon also made grants for demographic research and training, a field highly politicized to the point of ineffectiveness in the apartheid era.[42] Bowen reported in 2001 that, since 1988, Mellon's grants in South Africa had totaled more than $50 million; the board had agreed that grants in the range of $5 to $8 million would continue for the next five years, with Mellon's new senior adviser, Stuart Saunders, former vice chancellor of the University of Cape Town, playing a significant role in shaping the grant-making. South Africa, Bowen said, was "an important example of how one of the most repressive regimes in the world could be—and has been—transformed peacefully," and Mellon was determined to do what it could, especially in higher education, to contribute further to that transformation.[43] Mamphela Ramphele, Saunders's successor as vice chancellor at Cape Town, said that Bowen "left a huge footprint globally," and that Mellon's "commitment to helping South African universities transform themselves into serious academic entities"—in other words, "transforming South African higher education"—was his legacy.[44]

Letting Go

Bowen's presidency ended on July 1, 2006, three months short of his seventy-third birthday. The original plan had been to end his tenure in March 2006, but his successor, Don Randel, president of the University of Chicago, though named president of Mellon in July 2005, was committed to remaining at Chicago through the 2005–6 academic year. Retiring at the age of seventy-two was a

42 Ibid., *1998*, 17–22.
43 Ibid., *2001*, 32–33.
44 Telephone interview with Mamphela Ramphele, Feb. 4, 2022.

stretch—the usual Mellon retirement age for staff as well as trustees was seventy, but Bowen insisted that Bill Baker had promised him that he could stay until he reached seventy-two, and the board agreed to honor the presumed (though undocumented) commitment. Robust programming continued to the end of the Bowen presidency, subject to Bowen's insistence that the foundation reduce its recurring grants to give Randel room to take on new initiatives without waiting for existing grants to wind down.[45]

Bowen's last years as president were complicated. He had launched three expensive affiliated nonprofit organizations, all funded by Mellon—the highly successful JSTOR, the more problematic Artstor, and a third not-for-profit entity, ITHAKA Harbors. ITHAKA, named after the poem "Ithaka" by the Greek poet Constantine P. Cavafy, which Bowen loved and quoted frequently, was designed to "accelerate the adoption of productive and efficient uses of information technology for the benefit of the worldwide scholarly community." Bowen began talking about ITHAKA in 2002, when Mellon provided a year-end $5 million start-up grant (an additional $5 million would come from the Hewlett and Niarchos Foundations). He said that it would have "four interconnected functions": "incubat[ing] promising new projects and entities"; "work[ing] with a 'family' of affiliated organizations, linked to JSTOR, in order to facilitate a mutually beneficial sharing of resources, experiences, and strategies"; "conduct[ing] comprehensive research on the impact of digital technologies on the scholarly community, mapping what has been done ... and identifying new opportunities"; and "offering a specialized advising service to selected organizations," from which ITHAKA would derive revenue. ITHAKA would be led by Kevin Guthrie as president, with Bowen chairing the board, thus defining what would become his most important affiliation after his retirement from the foundation. Like Artstor, ITHAKA was launched as an independent nonprofit in Jan-

45 William G. Bowen, "President's Report," *Report of the Andrew W. Mellon Foundation*, 2005, 9.

uary 2004.[46] In 2008, JSTOR and ITHAKA merged, with JSTOR now providing a continuing funding stream for the combined entity.[47] In 2015, in a more complicated move, Artstor was brought into the fold.[48] I will have more to say about ITHAKA in the last chapter.

Bowen wanted ITHAKA, JSTOR, and Artstor held close. He also knew that Mellon needed more space and that the townhouses on Sixty-Second Street would need major renovation. He had the foundation buy three townhouses on Sixty-First Street, across the garden from and essentially mirroring the current footprint, and he had them renovated in 2004 to provide offices for the three new entities (and space for staff providing IT and other services to them as well as Mellon). He would also have an office there, as board chair of ITHAKA, after his retirement from Mellon. Once the spaces on Sixty-First Street were ready to be occupied, Bowen set in motion the necessary renovation of the original townhouses, completed by the end of 2005. Trustees who had been on the board when the decisions were taken to establish ITHAKA, JSTOR, and Artstor recognized the importance of "a close, continuing relationship with Mellon." Newer trustees were readier to have Mellon "cut, or at least materially reduce, its ties" to the three, and some of them thought that what Bowen was really doing was less building in the interests of the foundation than investing in arrangements for his retirement.[49]

There was a disagreement over whether Bowen was still entitled by virtue of his role at ITHAKA to the New York apartment provided for him by the foundation. The trustees thought that he was not, a difficult judgment for him to accept. Eventually, he found his own apartment nearby.[50] As Bowen told the story to his friend

---

46 Ibid., *2002*, 30–31 (source of the quotes), 35. Bowen elaborates on each of these functions on 31–36. On ITHAKA, also see *2003*, 9–13, 23–34.

47 Ithaka trustees, July 25, 2008; "Resolutions Adopted by the Board of Trustees of Ithaka Harbors, Inc.," July 25, 2008.

48 Ithaka trustees, Oct. 21, 2015, I-B-1 to I-B-2.

49 Bowen, "President's Report," *2004*, 16–17; *2005*, 14, 25. The quotes are from e-mail, Taylor Reveley to Nancy Weiss Malkiel, Dec. 29, 2021.

50 E-mail, Taylor Reveley to Nancy Weiss Malkiel, Dec. 29, 2021.

Morton Schapiro, president of Williams College and later North-western University, the negotiations for the new apartment were challenging. In the course of his interview with the condominium board, a woman member "asked him why so many of his references were from Jews." Bowen, enraged, responded, "'I have lots of Black friends too and I can get them to write as well.'"[51]

The apartment was not the only bone of contention between Bowen and the board. Bowen imagined that Mellon would continue to support his research, but the board took the view that his presidency was over. Letting go was hard; as Taylor Reveley put it, Bowen "never said it, but it was perfectly normal for someone in charge for so long to wonder if he really wanted to take his hand off the wheel." And it was difficult for Bowen to absent himself from Mellon once Randel took over; he followed the practice of coming to his new office every day by entering the Mellon offices on Sixty-Second Street, walking through the building, greeting anyone he saw, and traversing the courtyard between the two sets of buildings.[52]

While in the short run Randel asked Bowen "to continue to oversee the Foundation's in-house research associated with the use of the College & Beyond database," especially the more recent studies "on ways in which opportunity in higher education can be extended to larger numbers of students from modest circumstances and from racial and ethnic minorities," he later closed down the social science research activities so central to the Bowen presidency.[53] Randel was "not inclined" to have Mellon "be an operating foundation," and he reduced support for the "incubated entities," ITHAKA, JSTOR, and Artstor, which had achieved legal independence of the foundation.[54] Eventually, they moved to other office

51 E-mail, Morton O. Schapiro to Nancy Weiss Malkiel, Dec. 28, 2021.
52 Interview with T. Dennis Sullivan, Nov. 8, 2018, Princeton, NJ; interview with Taylor Reveley, Sept. 4, 2018, Princeton, NJ.
53 Bowen, "President's Report," *2005*, 25 (source of the quotes); Don M. Randel, "President's Report," *Report of the Andrew W. Mellon Foundation, 2006*, 10–11; telephone interview with Don M. Randel, Aug. 5, 2020.
54 Randel interview.

space and, in two cases, became self-supporting. With Bowen's departure, Randel closed down the Princeton office. In short, Randel, with the support of the board, wound down the costly infrastructure that had supported Bowen's personal projects. The foundation under Randel's leadership would return to a much lower-key, more traditional Mellon emphasis on higher education, arts, and culture.

14

Books That Helped Define the Agenda
of American Higher Education

William G. Bowen is widely regarded as the most thoughtful and provocative scholarly commentator on American higher education in the modern era. From the 1990s through the second decade of the twenty-first century, Bowen did more than any other scholar to shape the agenda of American higher education. In such books as *The Shape of the River, The Game of Life, Reclaiming the Game, Equity and Excellence in American Higher Education, Crossing the Finish Line, Lessons Learned, Higher Education in the Digital Age, Locus of Authority*, and *Lesson Plan*, Bowen, with his various co-authors, had a profound impact on the way colleges and universities operate, on the values they hold, and on the challenges they seek to address in strengthening American higher education.

In October 2016, when Bowen died, that was the thrust of the many tributes to him in the popular and the educational press. Of course, note was taken of his presidency of Princeton University and his presidency of the Andrew W. Mellon Foundation, of his creation of JSTOR and Artstor to transform access to scholarly journals and visual images, of the establishment of ITHAKA to promote productive uses of information technology in higher education. But Bowen's scholarship was a central focus. The *New York Times* said that the Bowen books "helped define the nation's academic agenda."[1] *Inside Higher Ed* said that Bowen was one of

---

1 Sam Roberts, "William G. Bowen, Princeton Educator Who Championed Poor and Minority Students, Dies at 83," *New York Times*, Oct. 22, 2016, A21.

Derek Bok & William Bowen, by David Levine, 1998.

"relatively few major university presidents [who] influence higher education more after they leave office than while they are in it," noting, "Bowen may be best known of all . . . for his writings and commentary on higher education."[2] The *Chronicle of Higher Education* put it this way: "It was as an author that Mr. Bowen fully made his mark as one of academe's consciences—and, often, as one of its most influential [critics]. . . . [He] assayed higher education from a strikingly wide range of vantage points, often predicting, if not activating, tectonic shifts in the industry."[3]

2 Doug Lederman, "William G. Bowen, Former Princeton and Mellon President, Dies," *Inside Higher Ed*, Oct. 24, 2016, https://www.insidehighered.com/news/2016/10/24 /william-g-bowen-former-president-princeton-and-mellon-foundation-dies, accessed Aug. 25, 2020.

3 Brock Read, "William Bowen, Influential Higher-Ed Thinker and President of Princeton and Mellon, Dies at 83," *Chronicle of Higher Education*, Oct. 21, 2016, https://www .chronicle.com/article/william-bowen-influential-higher-ed-thinker-and-president-of -princeton-and-mellon-dies-at-83, accessed Aug. 25, 2020.

While Bowen wrote frequent commentaries on current educational issues in educational publications and the popular press, his métier was the scholarly book. In most cases he wrote his books with one or more collaborators, some of whom were very senior, very seasoned educational leaders. He partnered with Neil Rudenstine on *In Pursuit of the Ph.D.*; with Derek Bok, president of Harvard University, on *The Shape of the River*; with Michael McPherson, president of Macalester College and later of the Spencer Foundation, on both *Crossing the Finish Line* and *Lesson Plan*; and with Eugene Tobin, president of Hamilton College and later a program officer at the Mellon Foundation, on both *Equity and Excellence* and *Locus of Authority*. Usually he enlisted one or more young research associates to join in the work; in many cases, he also gave the young people authorial credit. With the exception of *The Shape of the River*, Bowen was the progenitor of each of the many studies.

Bowen's books addressed a wide range of timely, often controversial topics: affirmative action, athletics, college access, college completion, digital learning, and university governance. Ever the reformer, he wanted to transform key aspects of higher education. His modus operandi, if you will, was straightforward: assemble— which meant build from scratch—a voluminous trove of relevant data, mobilize able young colleagues to analyze those data using every tool available to the sophisticated social scientist, and present the findings of the research in clear, compelling, persuasive prose.

College and Beyond

Mellon gave Bowen every opportunity to do this work. He had the wherewithal to support a robust research operation. He had the influence to persuade college and university presidents to give him the data he wanted. And he had the connections in the academic world to recruit highly talented students of economics and statistics, just out of college, to work with him, as well as to recruit other academic leaders to collaborate with him. For a labor economist skilled at asking big questions about higher education, there could have been no better setting to pursue policy-related scholarly projects. The work took place at the Mellon Foundation, and it was subsidized by the Mellon Foundation. This represented a considerable departure for a foundation accustomed to funding research done by individuals at other institutions. Now Mellon had its own research arm, over which its president presided. People referred to the research projects as "Bill Bowen's sandbox."[4]

Bowen started the research work by creating a database unlike anything that had previously existed for higher education. He asked the presidents of thirty-four academically selective colleges and universities to release to Mellon highly sensitive data on nearly one hundred thousand students who entered these institutions in 1951, 1976, and 1989. The database was assembled between 1994 and 1997. Although the colleges and universities were linked by their academic selectivity, they were a varied group—private universities, public universities, coeducational liberal arts colleges, and women's colleges. Stated formally, the purpose of collecting the data was to enable the study of "the long-term consequences of attending academically selective colleges and universities in the United States."[5]

The data included high school grades, test scores, family background, undergraduate grades, major field of study, participation in varsity athletics or other time-intensive extracurricular activity, whether the student graduated from college, and if so, in how many years. A follow-up survey, conducted for Mellon by Mathematica Policy Research, gathered information about students' "subsequent education, occupations, life satisfaction, civic involvement, and retrospective views of college."[6]

4 Interview with Hanna Holborn Gray, Sept. 18, 2018, New York City; telephone interview with Matthew M. Chingos, June 1, 2021 (source of the quote).

5 William G. Bowen and Derek Bok, *The Shape of the River: Long-Term Consequences of Considering Race in College and University Admissions* (Princeton, NJ: Princeton University Press, 1998), 291, 293; the quote is on 291. *The Shape of the River* used data from twenty-eight of those schools, representing eighty thousand students.

6 James Shulman, "College and Beyond II: The 21st Century: Measuring the Impact of Liberal Arts Education," Mellon Research Forum, 2019, https://www.mellon.org/research/college-and-beyond-ii, accessed June 8, 2021 (source of the quote); Bowen and Bok, *The Shape of the River*, xxvii–xxx.

Not every college and university president—nor every registrar—was comfortable releasing data ordinarily thought to be highly private. But the request for data came from the Andrew W. Mellon Foundation, which had the capacity to be of significant financial assistance to the institutions in question. Moreover, Bowen was an extraordinarily persuasive man; in the event that a registrar balked, all Bowen had to do was to call the president to ask for help in making the data available. The president, sensitive to Bowen's ability to be helpful down the road, told the registrar to cooperate.[7]

The College and Beyond database that Bowen built was a unique resource, extraordinarily rich in terms of what the data it held could reveal about American higher education. To mine it effectively, Bowen hired a series of young research associates—students of economics most often, but also of mathematics and statistics—to come to Mellon for a year or more to help him with data analysis and writing. Some of the hires were people he knew, most often from Princeton. Bowen found people, too, by surveying labor economists he trusted to ask for their recommendations—who were their most talented students (usually graduating seniors) who might be appropriate for the work? Caroline Hoxby, then at Harvard, was a prime source.[8] While candidates were invited to Mellon for a day of interviews before a formal offer was made, the purpose was mainly to have them meet Bowen and other members of the staff—what might normally have been the evaluative function of such a visit was superseded by the trust Bowen had in the recommender. Martin Kurzweil, a Hoxby student in the class of 2002 at Harvard, recalled his interview with Bowen this way: Bowen "burst into the room, proceeded to talk for twenty minutes about work going on at the foundation, and then left," giving Kurzweil the opportunity to say "only a couple of words"; the next day, Bowen's colleague Pat Woodford called Kurzweil to offer him the job—Bowen, she said, had been "very impressed" with him.[9]

Bowen threw the young research associates into the deep end as soon as they arrived at the foundation. He assumed that they had

7 Chingos interview; telephone interview with Thomas I. Nygren, May 27, 2021; telephone interview with Michael S. McPherson, Aug. 20, 2020.

8 Telephone interview with Caroline Hoxby, Oct. 26, 2021.

9 Telephone interview with Martin A. Kurzweil, June 4, 2021.

highly developed technical and analytical skills and could handle challenging assignments. If they demurred—Kurzweil told Bowen he was not familiar with the complicated regression analysis Bowen asked him to undertake and would need some time to figure it out—Bowen sent them to other, more experienced research associates to familiarize them with the statistical packages being used and learn the steps necessary to do the requisite analysis.[10]

When the research associates presented the results of their work, Bowen talked them through what they had found, asked pointed questions to push the analysis further, and engaged them in intensive conversation about what the findings meant. Bowen was "just a natural teacher," Sarah Levin Taubman said. Taubman, too, came to work for him right out of Harvard, but she was a mathematician, not an economist, and she had been brought to Bowen's attention by her father, Richard C. Levin, the president of Yale. Bowen would ask a teacher's questions, Taubman said: How are we going to explain this? What hypotheses can we come up with? Do we need more data? When a book project was under way, the research associates might be expected to draft some or most of the chapters—certainly those based most directly on the data. Bowen would return their drafts promptly, making detailed comments, raising questions for further exploration, and rewriting—sometimes rewriting extensively—what they had given him. But along with all the commentary came effusive praise for the wonderful work they had done, praise that made the implicit, if not obvious, criticism much easier to handle. As Matt Chingos, another Hoxby student whom Bowen hired in 2005, observed, Bowen had the ability to be tough on the research associates, criticize their work, push them to do better, *and* make them feel good at the same time. Tom Nygren, who first went to work for Bowen in 1991 and stayed for a dozen years, put it this way: "If Bill said you were good at something and could do it, you could do it."[11]

While Bowen drafted many chapters on his own, his style of engaging the research associates was to write together, in real time,

10 Ibid.
11 Telephone interview with Sarah Levin Taubman, June 1, 2021; Chingos interview; Nygren interview.

at his computer. Bowen's office was not commodious enough for two people to work easily, so the collaborator would pull up a small, three-legged wooden stool, sit beside Bowen, and the two would pass the keyboard back and forth as they drafted. What do you think of this? Bowen might ask, trying out a sentence or paragraph. You take a stab at this next section, he might suggest, passing the keyboard over to his colleague. The work was intense, highly collaborative, and often exhausting, but it was also rewarding, and sitting together at Bowen's computer turned out to be a good way to generate new ideas. For young people just out of college, it was heady stuff—to have Bowen show such interest in their ideas, to be taken so seriously, to be respected as a collaborator, even as a peer, by a person of Bowen's experience and stature.[12] It was, they reported, "a profoundly influential experience."[13]

At the same time, Bowen enlisted senior, experienced labor economists to oversee the College and Beyond database. Alan Krueger, the economics professor who directed the Survey Research Center at Princeton, was one of them. He described it as an example of Bowen "reaching out for expertise"—Bowen knew his own limits as a labor economist who had been out of the business, in effect, for some decades, and he was "not embarrassed to ask for advice when he needed it." It was a "tribute to Bowen," Krueger said, that he was comfortable bringing in leading scholars to give him advice.[14]

Once Bowen pulled young people into his circle, he elevated them, pushed them into the spotlight, and gave them unexpected opportunities. With *Grutter v. Bollinger* on the docket for the United States Supreme Court, Bowen brought Martin Kurzweil into a high-level strategy session on affirmative action, with Lee Bollinger, then president of the University of Michigan; Martin Krislov, then Michigan's general counsel; and Harvard Law School professor Christopher Edley. Bowen sent Sarah Levin Taubman, collaborating with him on *Reclaiming the Game*, to interview deans of

12 Kurzweil interview; Taubman interview.
13 Hoxby interview.
14 Interview with Alan B. Krueger, Sept. 14, 2018, Princeton, NJ.

admission and directors of athletics, as well as to attend seminars of the working group on education at the National Bureau of Educational Research. Once the book was published, he had her handle a share of the publicity—interviews, for example, at NPR and Fox News. When *Equity and Excellence* won the outstanding book award from the American Educational Research Association, neither Bowen nor Eugene Tobin, his more senior collaborator, could go to the meeting, so Bowen sent Kurzweil to give a speech at the plenary session, where the award was being conferred.[15]

Bowen elevated the young research associates beyond anything they expected. In many cases he named them as coauthors. He treated them as equals, even though they knew they were not; as Tom Nygren observed, that "had an incredible impact in giving confidence, in encouraging us to work hard." They felt that they were part of the team, doing important things, working with interesting people. Bowen's confidence in them inspired extra effort, intense loyalty, and, in some cases, set young people on a career path that they may not have anticipated. "He loved finding these bright young people," Nygren said, "launching them" and watching them grow.[16]

The upshot of Bowen's policy-related scholarly efforts can be illustrated in three areas: affirmative action, college athletics, and college access and completion.

Affirmative Action

If Bowen had a soapbox—and he did, through his books—his overarching message was that higher education needed to embrace populations previously excluded from its benefits, especially minority students and students from modest socioeconomic backgrounds. As we have already seen in his stated priorities as president of Princeton, inclusion was his highest priority. It was a matter of fundamental fairness, but it was also key to the effective functioning of America's democratic society. As a labor economist, Bowen

---

15 Kurzweil interview; Taubman interview.
16 Nygren interview.

had documented the extraordinary economic returns from higher education; failing to include these groups was a huge waste of human capital. In a nation where the minority school-age population was rapidly becoming a majority, a nation where higher education could unlock opportunity for students from low-income backgrounds (as it had for Bowen himself), it was essential that top-tier private colleges and universities and flagship public universities participate fully in educating individuals from those groups, who would not only advance their own well-being but would come to provide leadership in the public and private sectors in the United States. "Society at large," Bowen wrote later, "needs all the trained talent it can marshal."[17]

In *The Shape of the River*, published in 1998, Bowen and his coauthor, Derek Bok, made a compelling case for affirmative action in college and university admissions. For Bowen, writing about affirmative action followed logically from his long essay as president of Princeton, "Admissions and the Relevance of Race." Bok told the story of how their collaboration came about. "The idea of writing *The Shape of the River*," he said, "began in 1996 when two gentlemen with lengthy careers in higher education appeared in my office and asked me to write an op-ed piece defending the use of race-conscious admissions policies by selective colleges like Harvard and the University of Michigan." Bok dismissed the suggestion—there were many such arguments already in print. What was needed was not another opinion piece but a study grounded in "hard evidence about the actual effects" of affirmative action. "What happened to the minority students admitted to college in part because of their race? Did they graduate? Were they pleased with the education they received? Have they prospered since leaving college? What kind of relationships did they have with their white classmates?"[18] Bok remembered that Bowen was as-

17 William G. Bowen, Martin A. Kurzweil, and Eugene M. Tobin, *Equity and Excellence in American Higher Education* (Charlottesville: University of Virginia Press, 2005), 161–62.

18 Derek Bok, "Afterword," in William G. Bowen and Derek Bok, *The Shape of the River: Long-Term Consequences of Considering Race in College and University Admissions*, Twentieth Anniversary ed. (Princeton, NJ: Princeton University Press, 2019), 291.

sembling a wealth of empirical evidence about the experience of students admitted to academically selective colleges and universities, and he suggested that those data might yield the insights he was looking for with respect to students admitted under race-sensitive admission policies. He sent his interlocutors to talk to Bowen.[19]

At a meeting at Mellon, a team of high-powered visitors tried to persuade Bowen to use the College and Beyond database to provide that empirical evidence.[20] One of the visitors was Martin Michaelson, a lawyer who had been in the general counsel's office at Harvard in the 1980s but was then practicing at the firm of Hogan Lovells in Washington, where he represented national higher education organizations as well as individual colleges and universities in regulatory, litigation, and transactional matters. He knew Bok well, and he was one of the two men who had visited him in his office at Harvard.[21] A second participant in the meeting was John Payton, for twenty years a partner at WilmerHale, the law firm that represented the University of Michigan in *Gratz v. Bollinger* and *Grutter v. Bollinger* as the two cases made their way through the trial courts and the court of appeals. Payton was the lead counsel for Michigan in the lower courts, and he argued *Gratz* before the United States Supreme Court. In 2008 Payton became the sixth president and director-counsel of the NAACP Legal Defense Fund, a position he held until his death in 2012.[22] The third visitor was Joel Fleishman, professor of law and public policy at Duke University and founding director of Duke's Sanford School of Public Policy, who was also serving on a part-time basis as president of the Atlantic Philanthropic Service Company, the American programming arm of Atlantic Philanthropies.[23]

19 Interview with Derek C. Bok, June 20, 2018, Cambridge, MA.

20 This account comes from telephone interview with James L. Shulman, June 25, 2021.

21 Telephone interview with Martin Michaelson, July 1, 2021; Michaelson biography at Hogan Lovells, https://www.hoganlovells.com/en/martin-michaelson.

22 "LDF Director-Counsels: John Payton, 2008–2012," NAACP Legal Defense Fund, https://www.naacpldf.org/about/history/john-payton.

23 "Joel L. Fleishman," American Academy of Arts & Sciences, https://www.amacad.org/person/joel-l-fleishman.

The visitors tried to persuade Bowen, first, that he and Bok needed to speak out about the importance of affirmative action. There was nothing new to be said beyond what was already in print, Bowen said. But we need you, the visitors responded; *Gratz* and *Grutter* were going to be *the* cases on affirmative action. Bowen said that he was building a database, but it was not going to be ready for some time, and it had been designed for a different purpose. (College and Beyond was originally intended to support the work on college sports that came to fruition later in Bowen's two books on the subject.) The mention of the database caught the visitors' attention. Fleishman asked whether Atlantic Philanthropies—interested in higher education, interested in minority issues, impressed with Bowen—might do something to accelerate the work to make the database useful for the purposes of the Michigan cases. Bowen said he would think it over.[24]

Several days later, Bowen changed his mind and called Bok—he "would agree to undertake the project if [Bok] joined him."[25] After that, Bok traveled to New York to meet with Bowen to plan out the study.[26] At the same time, Atlantic Philanthropies contributed almost $660,000 to expand the database through a Mathematica survey documenting the postcollege experiences of the entering cohort of 1989, with a particular emphasis on "early career accomplishments and educational attainment" of the underrepresented minority students and "attitudes toward diversity and interactions with people of different races" on the part of white students.[27] Given Bowen's reputation and the issues at stake, Atlantic Philanthropies was well prepared to make the investment, Fleishman said later. Bowen, he added, was "venerated" in the foundation world

24 This account comes from Shulman interview (Shulman attended the meeting), and Zoom interview with Joel Fleishman, July 16, 2021. On the original purpose of College and Beyond, also see telephone interview with Stacy Berg Dale, June 15, 2021.

25 Bok, "Afterword," in Bowen and Bok, *The Shape of the River*, Twentieth Anniversary ed., 291. Bok told the same story in Bok interview.

26 E-mail, Derek Bok to Nancy Weiss Malkiel, Aug. 12, 2021.

27 Grant proposal to Atlantic Philanthropic Services, as described in Herbert Abelson, director of the Survey Research Center at Princeton University, to Joel L. Fleishman, Feb. 11, 1997, courtesy of Joel Fleishman.

as someone "in whose judgment" one ought to have confidence, "someone who knew how to tell the difference between something that would make a difference and something that wouldn't."[28]

Bowen and Bok were wading into the midst of one of American society's most controversial public policy issues. Ever since the passage of the civil rights legislation of the 1960s, there had been a hot debate over what the struggle for civil rights had accomplished for Black Americans. Was it sufficient to remove legal obstacles to full participation so that Blacks and whites started from the same point in seeking access to education, employment, public accommodations, housing, voting rights, and so many other fundamental elements of American citizenship? Or was it important to take affirmative action to ensure that Blacks, hobbled by the legacy of centuries of segregation and discrimination, could avail themselves of the opportunities now available to them?

As Bowen and Bok took up their work together, courts, legislatures, and voters were chipping away at the legality of affirmative action in admissions and hiring. In 1978, as we have seen, the United States Supreme Court in *Regents of the University of California v. Bakke* upheld the constitutionality of affirmative action, but in the 1990s it came under ferocious assault. In 1996 California voters overwhelmingly approved Proposition 209, a state ballot initiative banning "race-conscious admissions and hiring by the state government, including the university system." Also in 1996 the Supreme Court let stand a lower-court decision in *Hopwood v. Texas* that banned race-conscious admissions at the University of Texas Law School. In 1998 voters in Washington State approved an anti–affirmative action ballot initiative modeled on California's. Two lawsuits making their way through the courts challenged the legality of race-based affirmative action in admissions decisions in the undergraduate college and the law school at the University of Michigan. The stakes for the work that Bowen and Bok set out to

28 Fleishman interview.

accomplish—literally rescuing affirmative action in selective college and university admissions—could not have been higher.[29]

Drawing extensively on the College and Beyond database, combining sophisticated quantitative analysis with qualitative personal testimony from the Mathematica survey, Bowen and Bok demonstrated conclusively that race-sensitive admissions policies brought tangible benefits to individuals admitted to highly selective colleges and universities and, through them, to the larger society. Measured in many different ways, minority students "had strong academic credentials when they entered college," "graduated in large numbers," and did "very well after leaving college," taking positions of consequence in law, business, medicine, and other professions, and playing significant roles in the civic life of their communities.[30] The more selective the college or university the student attended, the better the student's record of achievement and the higher the level of satisfaction with the college experience. Black students at selective colleges and universities graduated at far higher rates than Black students graduating from all colleges and universities (and at significantly higher rates than white students at all NCAA Division I schools). They were much more likely than other Black college graduates to earn graduate or professional degrees. They enjoyed significant economic success, with salaries much higher than all Blacks with BA degrees—and higher also than the top tier of all students graduating from college in their cohorts. They were "as likely as their white classmates to become doctors, lawyers, and business executives." And they were "extensively involved in a wide range of civic and community activities."[31]

In other words, Bowen and Bok demonstrated that affirmative action worked. It worked in creating college and university student bodies where everyone—whites as well as minority students— would learn and thrive; it worked in building a robust Black middle class; it worked in contributing to the establishment of a more just society. In *The Shape of the River*, as Harvard law pro-

29 Nicholas Lemann, "Foreword," in Bowen and Bok, *The Shape of the River*, Twentieth Anniversary ed., xxi–xxii.
30 Bowen and Bok, *The Shape of the River*, 256.
31 Ibid., 256–57, 261.

fessor Randall Kennedy put it, the two presidents moved from "aspirational" essays about affirmative action—"here is what we should be doing to contribute to the betterment of society"—to providing empirical social scientific analysis of affirmative action—here is what we have done, and here are the results.[32]

The data Bowen and Bok assembled had not existed before—as one reviewer put it, "facts have been sorely missing in accounts of the role played by race in admissions to institutions of higher education"—and they proved to be powerfully important.[33] Because of the detailed documentation and analysis presented in *The Shape of the River*, the book played a significant role in the evolution of public policy with respect to affirmative action. It became required reading in domestic policy circles in Washington. Rebecca M. Blank, the labor economist who joined the Council of Economic Advisers in the fall of 1997, had a call one Saturday morning from the chair of the council, Janet Yellen. President Bill Clinton had heard about the book and wanted to know more about it. Could she get a copy and produce a short summary by Sunday evening?[34]

For Lee Bollinger, dean of the law school (1987–94) and president (1996–2002) of the University of Michigan, Bowen and *The Shape of the River* provided key support as the Michigan affirmative action cases made their way through the courts. The more important case, *Grutter v. Bollinger*, had to do with admissions policies at the University of Michigan Law School, where race was one of many factors taken into consideration in a holistic review of an applicant's credentials. The companion case, *Gratz v. Bollinger*, addressed undergraduate admission to the University of Michigan, a trickier proposition in that the admissions office used a point system to rate applicants, wherein Blacks were automatically

32 Interview with Randall L. Kennedy, July 26, 2018, Cambridge, MA.
33 Alan Wolfe, "Affirmative Action: The Fact Gap," *New York Times*, Oct. 25, 1998, https://www.nytimes.com/1998/10/25/books/affirmative-action-the-fact-gap.html, accessed June 11, 2021. The most thorough, thoughtful review is Ronald Dworkin, "Affirming Affirmative Action," *New York Review of Books*, Oct. 22, 1998, https://www.nybooks.com/articles/1998/10/22/affirming-affirmative-action/?lp_txn_id=1255745, accessed June 11, 2021.
34 Telephone interview with Rebecca M. Blank, Aug. 29, 2019.

assigned a set number of additional points because of their race.[35] What Michigan needed in the two cases was "empirical evidence to support the view that student body diversity enhances the educational experience," with no "tradeoff with respect to quality."[36] They found that evidence in *The Shape of the River*.

As well, Bollinger found in Bowen "an ally of major significance" in making the case for affirmative action. Public sentiment, as we have seen, had shifted against such policies; it was a great boon to Michigan for someone of Bowen's "prominence and intelligence" to make the case that affirmative action was consistent with the academic mission of educational institutions and to provide the empirical evidence to sustain that argument.[37] Bowen was so willing to be "out there" with the book, echoed Nancy Cantor, dean of the graduate school and subsequently provost of the university. Having "esteemed leaders" like Bowen speaking out was so crucial.[38] Other leaders of the day, in various sectors, were distancing themselves from Michigan; it was "a brave move" on Bowen's part to stand "out there alone" beside the university, Bollinger said. "I'm there with you," Bowen would tell Bollinger repeatedly, support that made a critical substantive as well as symbolic difference.[39]

The Shape of the River had a notable impact on the public sector in American higher education. Public universities rallied to stand beside Michigan, and Bowen and Bok provided the ammunition for the *amicus* briefs they drafted in support of Michigan's efforts to defend affirmative action. William E. "Brit" Kirwan, at that time president of Ohio State, which took the lead in submitting an *amicus* brief, said that he "drew heavily on [Bowen's] work," as did his counterpart presidents. "Publics not only face the moral argu-

---

35 *Grutter v. Bollinger*, 539 U.S. 306 (2003); *Gratz v. Bollinger*, 539 U.S. 244 (2003).

36 Telephone interview with Marvin Krislov, June 28, 2021. Krislov became vice president and general counsel at Michigan in 1998. Also see telephone interview with Nancy Cantor, Oct. 1, 2021. The authoritative account of Michigan's efforts to defend affirmative action is Patricia Gurin, Jeffrey S. Lehman, Earl Lewis, et al., *Defending Diversity: Affirmative Action at the University of Michigan* (Ann Arbor: University of Michigan Press, 2004).

37 Telephone interview with Lee C. Bollinger, Sept. 21, 2021.

38 Cantor interview.

39 Bollinger interview.

ment for affirmative action but, in states with large African American populations, a political imperative as well," Kirwan said. "As leaders of state institutions, we are expected as we should be, to ensure our institutions serve all the citizens of the state." Thus Bowen's "work in this area was, if anything, even more important to the publics than the privates."

Furthermore, Kirwan was on the board of the American Council on Education, "which had taken a strong stand in support of Michigan." As the "voice of higher education, in Washington and to the nation," ACE represented "all higher education, public and private." "In making our case to the public," Kirwan said, "we drew heavily on Bill's research and conclusions. In fact, his language became standard phrases in speeches by presidents across the country whenever we spoke on this topic. It got to the point that many presidents didn't even realize they were using Bill's words as their own." But the impact of Bowen's work went well beyond language. "With this rhetoric, more and more presidents had to 'walk the walk' and beef up their efforts to recruit and retain more minority students," Kirwan reflected. "I think it's fair to say that the research done for *The Shape of the River* and the eloquent and persuasive prose in the book did more to increase the commitment to diversity at America's public colleges and universities than anything else during this era."[40]

By far the strongest impact of *The Shape of the River* came at the United States Supreme Court. Just as Justice Lewis Powell had cited Bowen's early writings on the educational value of diversity in upholding the constitutionality of affirmative action in university admissions in the *Bakke* case in 1978, so the court in *Grutter v. Bollinger* (2003) "reaffirmed the constitutionality of using race as a factor in admissions decisions" and cited *The Shape of the River* "in support of the proposition that admitting a racially diverse class served a compelling public interest."[41]

40 William E. "Brit" Kirwan, reader's report for Princeton University Press, June 2022.

41 Bok, "Afterword," in Bowen and Bok, *The Shape of the River*, Twentieth Anniversary ed., 292–93.

The book influenced the flood of *amicus* briefs submitted to the Supreme Court in support of the law school. Bowen worked closely with Kenneth Frazier, then general counsel of Merck, to get other corporate general counsels to sign onto the corporate brief.[42] Bowen's "advocacy and scholarship," Kenneth Chenault, an executive at American Express, echoed, had a clear impact on the decision of major corporations to join in a brief that proved to be especially significant in the eyes of the court.[43] Having corporate and military leaders speaking out in behalf of affirmative action "made it a broad argument, not just a Michigan argument," Nancy Cantor said.[44] Student body diversity, they all argued, better prepared students for the increasingly diverse workforce they would be entering, for the society in which they would be living, and for the many professional roles they would be inhabiting.[45]

The Shape of the River directly informed the brief of the lawyers at Latham & Watkins who were representing the University of Michigan Law School before the Supreme Court.[46] Their challenge was to show that there were no race-neutral alternatives to affirmative action. Opponents of race-based affirmative action had been grasping for other ways of achieving what they considered to be diversity. The Bush administration filed a brief in support of Barbara Grutter arguing for the 10 percent plan adopted by the State of Texas in the wake of *Hopwood*. The plan called for the admission to the University of Texas of students in the top 10 percent of all high schools in the state, a move that obviated the need for a holistic review of candidates. In addition to the Texas plan, arguments were made that one could substitute socioeconomic characteristics for race and achieve the same objectives in composing a diverse class. Bowen and Bok provided empirical data proving that abandoning affirmative action would have a very small effect on

42 Telephone interview with Kenneth C. Frazier, Sept. 9, 2020.
43 Telephone interview with Kenneth I. Chenault, Jan. 8, 2020.
44 Cantor interview.
45 Gurin, Lehman, Lewis, et al., *Defending Diversity*, 90.
46 Maureen E. Mahoney et al., "Brief for Respondents: Grutter v. Bollinger, 539 US 306 (2003)(No 02-241)," (Feb. 2003), 9, 36, 46, in *Appellate Briefs*, 1, University of Michigan Law School Scholarship Repository, https://repository.law.umich.edu/briefs/1.

the fortunes of white applicants, the vast majority of whom would still be rejected. They demonstrated, too, that relying only on grades and test scores would still yield a large disparity between whites and underrepresented minorities. As for socioeconomic status as a substitute for race, they showed that there were so many more poor white students in the United States than poor Blacks that any race-blind method of admission was bound to fail to achieve any significant diversity in the admitted class.[47]

The Shape of the River also provided important ammunition with respect to outcomes for underrepresented minority students benefiting from affirmative action. Opponents of affirmative action propounded a mismatch theory, arguing that affirmative action harmed underrepresented minorities by placing them at the wrong schools. With grades less strong than those of their white classmates, they bore a practical and psychological burden that could have been avoided by having them enroll at lower-tier schools. *The Shape of the River* demolished the mismatch theory. The book was "extraordinarily powerful," Scott Ballenger, one of the lawyers on the team, reflected, "in demonstrating that underrepresented minority students do really well in college and in later life." Their outcomes were more like those of their white counterparts than those of minority students with similar credentials who attended much less selective institutions. Measured in terms of graduation rates, earnings, and professions, minority students benefiting from affirmative action at top-tier institutions did very well in absolute as well as relative terms in later life. And they continued by wide margins to support race-sensitive affirmative action, as did their white classmates, who clearly appreciated the value of having a diverse group of classmates.[48]

In her majority opinion in *Grutter*, Justice Sandra Day O'Connor declared, "today we endorse Justice Powell's view [in *Bakke*] that student body diversity is a compelling state interest that can justify the use of race in university admissions." The question before the

---

47 Telephone interview with J. Scott Ballenger, June 21, 2021. Ballenger, one of the junior lawyers on the team, was tasked with reading *Shape of the River* and figuring out how best to use it.

48 Ibid.

court, then, was whether Michigan's use of race met the test of "a compelling state interest." O'Connor said that it did; "today, we hold that the Law School has a compelling interest in attaining a diverse student body." She cited *The Shape of the River* as one of the authorities demonstrating "the educational benefits that flow from student body diversity," among them positive learning outcomes and better preparation to function as citizens and professionals in "an increasingly diverse workforce and society."[49]

O'Connor noted the importance of the *amicus* briefs that Bowen had helped to generate. "The Law School's claim of a compelling interest," she said, "is further bolstered by its *amici*, who point to the educational benefits that flow from student body diversity." Numerous studies and reports showed that such diversity "promotes learning outcomes and better prepares students for an increasingly diverse workforce and society." "Major American businesses," she said, "have made clear that the skills needed in today's increasingly global marketplace can only be developed through exposure to widely diverse peoples, cultures, ideas, and viewpoints." And "high-ranking retired officers and civilian leaders" have asserted that "a highly qualified, racially diverse officer corps" is essential to the military's ability "to provide national security."[50] Because "universities, and in particular, law schools represent the training ground for a large number of our Nation's leaders," O'Connor observed, "the path to leadership [must] be visibly open to talented and qualified individuals of every race and ethnicity."[51]

As we have seen over the quarter century since the publication of *The Shape of the River*, colleges and universities that have continued to practice affirmative action in admissions have continued to see positive results in the composition of their student bodies, the effectiveness of the on-campus interactions among students of different racial groups, and the impressive contributions of graduates from minority populations both to leadership in business and

49 *Grutter v. Bollinger*, 539 U.S. 306 (2003) at 325–30. For a detailed account of *Gratz* and *Grutter*, see Barbara A. Perry, *The Michigan Affirmative Action Cases* (Lawrence: University Press of Kansas, 2007).

50 *Grutter v. Bollinger*, 539 U.S. 306 (2003) at 330–31.

51 Ibid., at 332.

the professions and to civic leadership in the nation and their local communities. And the economist of higher education Caroline Hoxby asserts that *The Shape of the River* remains "the best book" available in terms of evidence to support the importance of diversity in American colleges and universities.[52]

Athletics

The question of impact becomes less clear when we turn to Bowen's work on athletics. Concerns about what had become of college athletics had been the initial impetus for the collection of data in the College and Beyond database. Bowen was worried that college sports "had become an arms race." Schools were devoting more and more admissions slots to athletes, to the detriment of spaces for all-around talented students. Bowen wanted to collect data to demonstrate the huge admissions advantage that had come to accrue to varsity athletes and the effects on academic and nonacademic life of an increasingly disproportionate number of athletes in the student body.[53] College and Beyond had been created to support the work on intercollegiate athletics, but it was expanded, as we have seen, to support the analysis of affirmative action. Bowen thought for a time that Mellon might be able to carry both projects forward simultaneously, with James Shulman taking the lead on athletics and Bowen on affirmative action. He soon came to realize, though, that it would be better to work on one project at a time, so he and Shulman set the sports project aside to focus on affirmative action and returned to it only after the completion of *The Shape of the River*.[54]

There is considerable irony in Bowen emerging as a prominent critic of college athletics. People who had known him at Princeton were frankly surprised. Bill Carmody, the basketball coach at Northwestern who had previously coached at Princeton, doubtless spoke for many of them when he said, "I thought Bill was on our

52 Hoxby interview.
53 Dale interview.
54 Shulman interview.

side."[55] As we have seen, Bowen himself was a highly successful college athlete, and he continued playing tennis as long as his elbow and knees permitted. He believed in the value of college sports. As he told a Denison interviewer, "[Athletics] has always seemed to me an avenue, an activity which really does permit kinds of personal development, self-discipline, learning to work with other people, learning to lose more or less gracefully. Things of that kind are very important to the individual."[56]

As president of Princeton, Bowen was a big fan of Princeton teams and a fierce defender of varsity athletics as a fundamental element in the fabric of student life. On Jim Wickenden's first day on the job as Princeton's new dean of admission, Bowen told him, "I have two directives for you: one is to help the football team, the other is to help the hockey team." While Bowen professed publicly that he had nothing to do with admissions, he, like other presidents, had a list of applicants whose admission he considered to be important to the university—alumni children, athletes, faculty children, children of development prospects, children of parents who were important to him personally. While he respected the independent authority of the dean of admission, he was prepared to lean in when he thought the stakes were high for the university. Sometimes Bowen won the case, sometimes he lost, but he made plain what he believed to be important to the institution.

Bowen's most controversial defense of the admission of a varsity athlete came at the end of his presidency, long after Wickenden had left the admission office. The candidate, Lyle Menendez, a student at Princeton Day School, was known to be an excellent tennis player, but the rest of his application raised a number of red flags, and the admission office initially turned him down. With Lyle of great interest to the tennis coach and Bowen's own interest known, the admission office agreed to an unusual meeting with Lyle's father, José, to discuss the case. Under intense pressure from

55 Carmody made this comment to Eugene Y. Lowe Jr., assistant to the president at Northwestern, who had been dean of students at Princeton. Lowe interview, Nov. 6, 2018, Evanston, IL.

56 Bowen quoted in Thomas B. Martin, "A Light in Pataskala: Interview with Dr. Bowen," *Denison Alumnus* 63 (February 1972): 7, Denison.

José, they reached an agreement to allow Lyle to matriculate a year after his graduation from PDS if he took some courses at Rutgers and achieved satisfactory grades. Lyle enrolled at Princeton in the fall of 1987 but was suspended for a year (the standard punishment) because of a finding of plagiarism in coursework in his first semester. He came back in the spring of 1989 as a second-term freshman, on probation because of the disciplinary infraction, which blocked him from playing on the tennis team. That summer, in a case that would transfix viewers of Court TV for years to come, Lyle and his brother Erik murdered their parents at their home in Beverly Hills, California. After a highly publicized trial, both sons were sentenced to life in prison.[57]

Among Ivy League presidents, Bowen operated as a responsible defender of both athletic admissions and academic standards. He had devised an academic index to provide a reliable comparative measure of the academic credentials of athletes seeking admission to Ivy institutions. It was a "method," he said later, "of measuring qualifications of students to be sure that the Ivy League in general did not keep dipping too low in terms of the athletes that were recruited." What he "failed to understand entirely—I just didn't get it—," he said, "was that what really matters is not what students look like when you take them in, but what they look like when they leave. . . . And what I didn't understand was that recruited athletes especially . . . systematically under-perform, by which I mean that they do less well academically than their qualifications tell you that they should do."[58]

The Ivy president during Bowen's tenure who best understood that the league had a problem with varsity athletics was A. Bartlett Giamatti, president of Yale University. In the spring of 1980, Giamatti made a public statement arguing that Ivy athletics was growing out of control, far out of proportion to its proper role in Ivy institutions. Had anyone among his counterparts in the Council of

57 Interview with James Wickenden, June 22, 2018, Princeton, NJ; telephone interview with Timothy C. Callard, June 18, 2018; interview with Anthony M. Cummings, March 22, 2019, Princeton, NJ; interview with David A. Benjamin, Sept. 10, 2019, Skillman, NJ.
58 Bowen oral history, July 21, 2009, unpaginated.

Ivy Group Presidents shared his reservations, it would have been a moment to rethink, even rein in, the way athletics operated on their campuses. Giamatti had some ideas about what to do about the problem. He proposed a ban on off-campus recruiting by coaches, a deemphasis on postseason national competition in favor of Ivy competition, the shortening of practice seasons and competitive schedules, and a reduction in the number of coaches, with multi-seasonal coaching assignments.[59] Far from wanting to seize the opportunity to consider reforms, Bowen was among those expressing "serious reservations" about Giamatti's proposals.[60]

Years later, Bowen had a different take on the matter: "I kick myself in retrospect—again, you learn from your mistakes—for not having paid more attention" to Giamatti, he told an interviewer. "He was even more convinced then than I became later that the whole system was on the wrong path and that we needed to go back and we needed to do less recruiting, college sports needed to be less professional, there needed to be more emphasis on ordinary students playing sports because they were fun to play and they had real educational value if done the right way. And I, along with my colleagues, basically rejected Giamatti's plea that we band together and do something." Giamatti's "great speech," Bowen said, "just fell by the wayside. It was a big, big missed opportunity."[61]

Given Bowen's history, then, it seems surprising that he should have taken up the role of critic of college and university athletics. Two prompts for his engagement are worth noting. The first was the struggle over wrestling at Princeton, when, as part of the budget cuts undertaken during the presidency of Harold Shapiro, and in the context of the decline of wrestling as a varsity sport at peer institutions, the decision was taken in 1993 to reduce the status of wrestling to a club sport, without institutional support for coaching, and without support for enrolling wrestlers through the admis-

59 Jon Healey, "Bowen, Myslik Discount Need for Giamatti Plan," *Daily Princetonian,* May 1, 1980, Bowen president, box 403, folder 2; "Giamatti's Challenge," *Princeton Alumni Weekly,* Jan. 26, 1981, 19.

60 The quote is from William G. Bowen to William D. Snyder, Apr. 21, 1980, Bowen president, box 159, folder 1.

61 Bowen oral history, July 21, 2009, unpaginated.

sion process. The ensuing furor, stoked by two-time Secretary of Defense Donald Rumsfeld '54, a varsity wrestler at Princeton, had the effect over time of restoring wrestling as a university-sponsored intercollegiate sport. While Bowen himself was not engaged in the dispute, he watched it unfold, and it reinforced his growing sense that things were out of balance in intercollegiate athletics.

The second catalyst for Bowen's engagement came from an encounter he had while he was president of Princeton. Morton Schapiro once asked him "why as an accomplished jock he was so angry about special standards for college athletes." Bowen told him that he "once met a first year Princeton student who, when he asked her why she came to Princeton, replied that she was a catcher and that the coach picked her," an encounter that stayed with him and helped to inspire his investigation.[62]

Bowen embarked on a careful, data-driven analysis of the effects of varsity athletics in selective colleges and universities. By now the College and Beyond database had expanded to include more than 275,000 student records over four decades—an ample source for the scholarly investigation Bowen set out to accomplish.[63] In *The Game of Life* (2000) and *Reclaiming the Game* (2003), Bowen and his coauthors documented a widening divide between athletics and the academic mission of institutions of higher education. They argued bluntly that "college sports in their current form represent a distinct threat to academic values and educational excellence."[64] Athletes "enter college less academically prepared and with different goals and values than their classmates."[65] With the preferences given to athletes in admission, there was a stark opportunity cost when academically strong applicants were turned away in favor of

62 E-mail, Morton O. Schapiro to Nancy Weiss Malkiel, Dec. 27, 2021. For a different version of this story, but with the same moral, see Louis Menand, "Sporting Chances," *New Yorker*, Jan. 22, 2001, 85, https://archives.newyorker.com/newyorker/2001-01-22/flipbook/084.

63 William G. Bowen, "President's Report," *Report of the Andrew W. Mellon Foundation, 2004*, 22.

64 Bowen, Kurzweil, and Tobin, *Equity and Excellence in American Higher Education*, 171.

65 James L. Shulman and William G. Bowen, *The Game of Life: College Sports and Educational Values* (Princeton, NJ: Princeton University Press, 2001), dust jacket.

less qualified students who were coming to school to play sports. Recruited athletes underperformed academically "not just relative to other students, but relative to how they themselves might have been expected to perform"—evidence that in emphasizing athletic admission to the extent that they did, "colleges and universities are failing to put their most valuable resources—their faculty and their academic offerings—to their highest and best use."[66] Moreover, recruited athletes were more likely than nonathletes to engage in behavioral and academic misconduct. Bowen had believed that athletic admission, as it was being practiced, could be compatible with "the overall educational mission" of selective colleges and universities, but as he looked carefully across a range of institutions, he became persuaded "that the academic compromises were more than he wanted initially to believe."[67]

The challenges were most pressing at the most selective institutions—Ivy League colleges and universities and top coeducational liberal arts colleges. These institutions had no athletic scholarships, which served at other schools to limit significantly the population of students who came to college for intercollegiate athletics. There was vastly more pressure on admission slots at nonscholarship schools, and the proportion of the student body composed of individuals admitted to play sports was much higher. That was true partly because of the smaller size of the institutions and the concomitant commitment to support a very large number of sports. It was also true because these institutions needed to over-admit prospective athletes since they had no mechanism for ensuring that those students would follow through and compete for the period of their enrollment. The result of these pressures was "major opportunity costs" where the most academically selective institutions had to forgo the admission of too many of the talented applicants who were coming to college for other, arguably more compelling, purposes.[68] The issue, Shulman and Bowen wrote, was not "that the athletes who are admitted are bad people, that they will

---

66 Ibid., 271.
67 Lowe interview.
68 Shulman and Bowen, *The Game of Life*, 269.

not benefit from attending these schools, or that attending one of these institutions will fail to help them achieve their personal goals. The more difficult, and more relevant, question is whether admitting other students in their place might not have done even more to fulfill the educational mission of the school."[69]

Assessing the impact of *The Game of Life* and *Reclaiming the Game* inevitably devolves into an "on the one hand–on the other hand" appraisal. The books on athletics attracted positive attention in the popular press. In a long review in the *New Yorker*, for instance, Louis Menand assessed *The Game of Life* as "one of the most important books on higher education published in the last twenty years."[70] A reviewer in the *Education Digest* called the findings in *Reclaiming the Game* "striking and sobering."[71] The economist of higher education Caroline Hoxby points out that *The Game of Life* put forward "a great insight"—that the resources of great colleges and universities were being absorbed disproportionately by athletics and that college sports were distorting the makeup of college classes in terms of the academic preparation and socioeconomic status of admitted students. "No one had wrapped his head around the insight," she said, before Bowen.[72]

That said, private colleges and universities generally wanted to "sweep [the Bowen books] under the rug" and avoid talking about the findings.[73] Some presidents conceded that the problems were real but insisted that they occurred on other campuses, not on their own.[74] The reactions in the top-tier athletic establishment ranged from defensive to ferocious. One prominent university athletic director, for example, was certain that Bowen was wrong and that his analysis did not apply locally, and he carried the books around and made his disagreement plain in every possible setting. But he

69 Ibid., 270.

70 Menand, "Sporting Chances," 84.

71 *Education Digest*, Dec. 2005, 78. For a more critical appraisal, see *Review of Higher Education*, Fall 2006, 88–89.

72 Hoxby interview.

73 Shulman interview.

74 Karen W. Arenson, "Study of Elite Colleges Finds Athletes Are Isolated from Classmates," *New York Times*, Sept. 15, 2003, A12.

read the books, and he had to reckon with the themes Bowen addressed.

Bowen's work had an impact on conversations about athletics in the public sector. William E. "Brit" Kirwan, president of Ohio State University (1999–2002) and chancellor of the University System of Maryland (2002–15), chaired the Knight Commission on Intercollegiate Athletics (2007–16), which had been created "to serve as a watchdog and moral compass for intercollegiate athletics." "Many of us on the Commission and across higher education were increasingly concerned by the distortion of values that 'big time' athletics was causing our leading public universities," Kirwan recalled. "Costs were rising at an exponential rate in athletics, with outsized salaries for coaches, at the very time public universities were facing state budget cuts." According to Kirwan's account, Bowen's work helped to galvanize the commission to take action:

> Based in part on reading the book, as well as the enormous respect for Bill, the Knight Commission began a serious study of revenues and expenditures in Division I intercollegiate athletics. We collected massive amounts of data on sources of revenues and objects of expenditures at Division I institutions. . . . The Commission began publishing this data around 2011 or 2012, with updates every few years. Reporters at major newspapers regularly used and continue to use this data to write articles on the enormous discrepancies in rates of expenditures in athletics and academics by our major public universities. Of special note was the extraordinary growth in coaches' salaries and the stagnant nature of student athlete financial support. This discrepancy subsequently led to court challenges by student athletes, which they won, giving players rights to NIL (name, image, and likeness) revenue. . . . These court decisions are causing an upheaval in Division I athletics, the outcome of which is uncertain at this moment. However, it has forced universities across the country to come to grips with the fairness of how athletes are treated and will in time, I believe, force universities to develop an intercollegiate model more in keeping with the traditional values of academe.

"This was Bill's goal," Kirwan noted. "There is little doubt in my mind that *The Game of Life* played a catalytic role in forcing universities and the larger society to face and, hopefully, someday come to grips with the insanity of the expenditures on modern day intercollegiate athletics."[75]

As for private colleges and universities, Bowen raised people's consciousness and made them pay attention to issues they had previously ignored. The work may have been polarizing, but it opened up a conversation about what it meant to be a student athlete at a selective liberal arts institution. In other words, Bowen succeeded in using data to make people think about what they were doing. But it was hard going. Richard C. Levin, president of Yale when the Bowen books were published, said that Bowen's findings put him on a lengthy crusade to try to get the Ivies to reduce the number of recruited athletes and the number of sports supported through the admission process, as well as to raise the academic bar for admitted athletes. The pursuit was essentially fruitless; Levin found no appetite among his fellow presidents for such moves.[76]

That said, Bowen prompted a number of private colleges and universities to focus on what they were achieving for athletes, not just what athletes were accomplishing on the playing field. And, a related point, he prompted athletic departments to find new ways of connecting the academic enterprise with the athletic experience, and to take initiatives that have resulted in some positive changes in campus culture. Beyond that, though, it would be hard to claim much tangible effect from Bowen's work.[77] Levin said that with

75 Kirwan, reader's report.

76 Interview with Richard C. Levin, Sept. 20, 2019, New Haven, CT.

77 Mellon itself took some steps with the creation in 2003 of the College Sports Project, a collaborative effort among NCAA Division III colleges and universities "that seek[s] to achieve two critical objectives: (1) greater 'representativeness'—athletes should be representative of their classmates in academic outcomes and should be actively engaged in multiple facets of campus life; and (2) greater 'integration'—coaches and athletic staff should be more fully integrated into campus life and given greater opportunities to enhance the educational experiences of a wide range of students." One upshot of the project was the preparation in the fall of 2004 of a report, "Athletics and the Academy," which was circulated to Division III schools. Another was the creation of a data-gathering center, located at Northwestern University, to "measure students' academic outcomes over their college careers and report the results to participating institutions." A third was a summer institute in 2005 addressing the fuller integration of coaches and athletic staff, as well as athletes, into campus life. Bowen, "President's Report," *2004*, 20, 21n15. Also see

his insightful scholarship, Bowen pointed clearly to the need for reform but had less practical impact than one might have hoped.[78] While that was true in the Ivies, the impact on liberal arts colleges was more significant. Morton Schapiro, president then of Williams College, said that the school's review of the data Bowen and Shulman presented led it to revise the system used by the New England Small College Athletic Conference colleges for giving preference to athletes in admission, deliberately using fewer slots than was permitted under NESCAC rules and "raising the admissions standards of varsity athletes to a considerable degree."[79]

James Shulman, coauthor of *The Game of Life*, acknowledged that the book "did not have a huge influence." Part of the impetus for *Reclaiming the Game*, he said, was Bowen's frustration that their empirical findings were not being taken more seriously.[80] It was probably not surprising. As the economist of higher education Catharine Bond Hill, who served as provost of Williams College and president of Vassar College and now directs Ithaka S & R, pointed out, athletics is "the third rail" of higher education; "even evidence" is unlikely to change anything.[81]

Access and Completion

Turning finally to college access and completion, it is worth noting that the theme of access coincided most closely with Bowen's own personal history. Bowen came, as we have seen, from a family of very modest means, with no tradition of higher education. His college education at Denison and his graduate study at Princeton opened opportunities to him that would otherwise have been unimaginable, and those opportunities, together with his personal qualities, allowed him literally to invent himself as a major leader

Robert Malekoff, "The College Sports Project and the Reform of Division III Athletics," Forum for the Future of Higher Education, Massachusetts Institute of Technology, 2005, http://forum.mit.edu/articles/the-college-sports-project-and-the-reform-of-division-iii-athletics, accessed June 19, 2021.

78 Levin interview.

79 E-mail, Morton O. Schapiro to Nancy Weiss Malkiel, Dec. 27, 2021.

80 Shulman interview.

81 Telephone interview with Catharine Bond Hill, Feb. 1, 2022.

in American higher education. It made perfect sense that Bowen should care as a matter of policy about access to higher education for students from backgrounds like, or even more modest than, his own.

In *Equity and Excellence*, published in 2005, drawing on the expanded College and Beyond database, Bowen and his coauthors focused on the near-absence of the poorest students in selective colleges and universities in the United States, a reality at odds with the rhetoric of inclusiveness that infuses American higher education. They presented the stark statistics that "the odds of getting into the pool of credible candidates for admission to a selective college or university are *six* times higher for a child from a high-income family than for a child from a poor family; they are more than *seven* times higher for a child from a college-educated family than they are for a child who would be a first-generation college-goer."[82] Equally striking, once a student made it into that pool, he or she got *"essentially no break in the admissions process"*—that is, there was no positive weight given to the fact that the student had come from a poor family and had "overcome all of the attendant barriers in order to compete with a candidate from a very different background for a place in the class." Fixing the problem by improving the educational preparedness of low-income students would be the long-term solution, but in the short run, Bowen and his colleagues argued for class-based admission preferences as a complement to, not a substitute for, race-based preferences. Selective colleges, they said, ought to put a modest "thumb on the scale" in the admission process when considering "candidates with outstanding credentials who come from poor families"—a thumb on the scale comparable to what they were already doing for children of alumni.[83]

82 Bowen, Kurzweil, and Tobin, *Equity and Excellence in American Higher Education*, 248.

83 Ibid., 166, 171, 178–83, 254–56. *Equity and Excellence* was widely reported and reviewed. See, e.g., Garry Boulard, "College Access Still Tied to Income, Report Says," *Black Issues in Higher Education*, May 20, 2004, 6; Ben Gose, "The Chorus Grows Louder for Class-Based Affirmative Action," *Chronicle of Higher Education*, Feb. 25, 2005, 85–86; Karen Arenson, "Access Denied: Economics and the Elite," *New York Times*, Apr. 24, 2005, https://www.nytimes.com/2005/04/24/education/edlife/access-denied

In *Crossing the Finish Line*, published in 2009, Bowen and his coauthors addressed the success of America's leading public universities in graduating their students. Initially the book was to be coauthored by Bowen and Michael S. McPherson, the economist of higher education who had been president of Macalester College and was at that point president of the Spencer Foundation. Bowen had recruited Matt Chingos from Harvard to be their research assistant; it turned out, McPherson said, that Chingos was "the spark plug behind the data collection" for the book, someone who was so "astonishingly able" that they made him a coauthor.[84] They approached their study from a basic presumption: Educational attainment was too low in the United States, and public universities had a central role to play in changing that reality. The fundamental issue was college completion: As important as it was for students not otherwise well represented in higher education to gain access to college, the key was finishing college, which contributed to the creation of an educated citizenry and hence to the effective functioning of American democracy. To test the success of leading public universities in promoting college completion, Mellon assembled a new data set from twenty-one flagship public institutions, as well as four statewide systems of higher education. The data showed convincingly that public universities were falling short in graduating students, especially in graduating lower-income and minority students. Graduation rates were especially low for students who enrolled in institutions less selective than the schools they were qualified to attend. The moral according to Bowen: Instead of undermatching by enrolling in less selective, less competitive institutions, students should enroll in the best colleges or universities they were eligible to attend. And the institutions should give them the financial resources and academic support necessary to succeed in completing their degrees.[85]

-economics-and-the-elite.html, accessed Apr. 20, 2022; Elisabeth Lasch-Quinn, "A Thumb on the Scale: The Case for Greater Equity in College Admissions," *Journal of Blacks in Higher Education*, Summer 2005, 122–25; *History of Education Quarterly*, Fall 2006, 426–29.

84 Telephone interview with Michael S. McPherson, Aug. 20, 2020.

85 William G. Bowen, Matthew M. Chingos, and Michael S. McPherson, *Crossing the Finish Line: Completing College at America's Public Universities* (Princeton, NJ: Princeton University Press, 2009).

As always, the process of creating the book was classic Bowen: intense, each author fully engaged, sharing drafts back and forth, "writing pieces of the book while rethinking the outline of the whole," improving each other's work until they were satisfied that they had a finished manuscript. Were the chapters in the right order? What had they left out? Had they marshaled the requisite data and explained clearly what those data meant? Had they made the case they wanted to make in a fashion that would be compelling to readers? If one coauthor or another failed to do what he said he would do, Bowen simply stepped in and did it himself, which served, McPherson said, as an "enormously effective motivational force." McPherson likened the process of writing a book with Bowen to "being tied to the outside of a space shuttle."[86]

In terms of the practical impact of Bowen's work on access and completion, one should note the extent to which access and support for low-income and first-generation college students has become a major theme in selective colleges and universities. Doubtless other voices and advocates have played roles in this new focus. But it is surely the case that Bowen and his coauthors provided data and analysis that raised the consciousness of leaders of selective colleges and universities and helped to shape their priorities. In other words, they provided scholarly underpinnings for a shift in societal emphasis. Christopher L. Eisgruber, president of Princeton University, said that reading *Equity and Excellence* had a big influence on the way he framed his priorities as he took up his presidency, making access and support for low-income and first-generation students a key part of his agenda. And later, well into his presidency, he "regularly invoke[d]" the book whenever people asked him why he was "so committed to getting more low-income students to-and-through college."[87] Daniel Greenstein, then director of the Postsecondary Success division at the Bill & Melinda Gates Foundation, told Bowen when he wrote to him in the last weeks of Bowen's life that *Crossing the Finish Line* was "required reading" for new staff at the foundation. "It accelerated the completion

---

86 McPherson interview.

87 Interview with Christopher L. Eisgruber, Dec. 6, 2019, Princeton, NJ; e-mail, Eisgruber to Nancy Weiss Malkiel, Sept. 28, 2021 (source of the quote).

movement," he said, "which appears to have sustaining momentum at this point."[88] One needs to be cautious, however, about assuming lasting impact. As Catharine Bond Hill has observed, it has proven very difficult to make real headway in this sphere, especially in recent years as income inequality has risen and antagonism has grown between haves and have nots in American society—both phenomena that postdate Bowen.[89]

The importance of scholarship so often lies in asking the right questions. Bowen's books opened the way for younger generations of labor economists to take up the problems he identified and do the empirical and analytical work to push toward sharper understanding of the issues at hand. Caroline Hoxby, one of the preeminent economists of higher education of her generation, said that *The Shape of the River* has sparked hundreds of scholarly articles, and that College and Beyond has been used by at least forty different authors.[90] Rebecca M. Blank, a noted labor economist who went on to become chancellor of the University of Wisconsin–Madison, said that through his publications, Bowen stimulated younger labor economists to amass data to understand social phenomena not previously examined through rigorous empirical analysis. It was not that his work was the last word, the most sophisticated technically, the most definitive analytically. Rather, Bowen put issues in a new, more coherent framework, and he helped other people understand how to think about issues, how to understand what was at stake. Bowen "got a lot of people thinking and talking," he helped define conversations, he "gave shape to further conversations," so that other scholars could push beyond what he had done to more fully analyze and understand compelling societal challenges.[91]

Crossing the Finish Line was a notable example. Bowen coined the term "undermatching" and presented his data using relatively simple tabulations. Virtually every chapter has sparked further research by scholars in the field. Hoxby's work on undermatching,

88 E-mail, Daniel Greenstein to William G. Bowen, Sept. 19, 2016, Bowen Ithaka.
89 Hill interview.
90 Hoxby interview.
91 Blank interview.

for example, followed on Bowen's work and is now regarded as "the foundational paper in the field." The new insights in *Crossing the Finish Line* and its broad influence in stimulating further scholarship, Blank said, make it "one of the best books in higher education."[92]

Hoxby put it this way: Bowen's books on higher education have "a brilliant streak of insight run[ning] through them." While many people write about higher education, "no one else has written books as good." Bowen's forte, she said, was "rich, descriptive analysis," not causal analysis. To accomplish that kind of evaluation required "a deep understanding of institutions" in order to be able to "see patterns in data." Bowen set out a hypothesis to be tested and gathered data to test it. He "cut through the noise, focused on the issue, and did the hard analysis" to explicate it. The result was "brilliant insight supported by data"—in her judgment, the most influential works in the field.[93]

Bowen's Values Shine Through

It is worth noting, finally, how Bowen harnessed his scholarship in the interest of values he held dear. The last example—college access and completion—directly reflected the ways in which Denison University opened a new world to him that profoundly shaped the whole trajectory of his life and career. Bowen got to Denison because his high school principal saw to it, in the wake of his father's death, that he could be admitted with substantial financial aid, supplemented by funds from the Gardner Board and Carton Company. When he embarked on data-driven investigations of college access and completion, Bowen was looking for ways to ensure that able students from backgrounds like his might be able to take advantage of opportunities like the ones that had meant so much to him.

One sees Bowen's values clearly in the contrast between *The Shape of the River* and his books on college athletics. The sociologist and Columbia University provost Jonathan Cole, who served

92 Ibid.
93 Hoxby interview.

as an informal adviser to Bowen on *The Game of Life*, called Bowen on what he saw as an obvious difference between the two. "I pointed out" to Bowen, Cole recalled, "that the 'advantage' given athletes in terms of SAT scores was somewhat over 100 points for the major sports—roughly the same as that found between the African American applicants and others in the applicant pool" in *The Shape of the River*. But while Bowen backed affirmative action for Black students because of the educational and societal payoffs, he lamented the opportunity costs and other drawbacks of admitting too many athletes. He had "no problem" justifying the difference in his views: Affirmative action, he told Cole, "was far more important than having more athletes at the Ivy League schools."[94]

94 Jonathan Cole, Princeton University Press reader's report, May 2022.

Part IV

The Full Measure of the Man

15

Director and Trustee

"Graced with a Seemingly Endless Supply
of Practical Wisdom"

Bowen joined his first corporate board in 1975 while he was serving as president of Princeton. It was an unusual move—a long-established rule barred Princeton presidents from serving on corporate boards. But this invitation was irresistible: The board was NCR, the company for which Bowen's father had worked for so many years selling cash registers out of the back of his car. The chair of NCR, William S. Anderson, had a daughter in the Princeton class of 1974. When Anderson and his wife came for graduation, they met Bowen, who told them of his father's long association with the company. By Anderson's account, Bowen said "that he had been brought up living and breathing the NCR culture. His father would practice his sales approaches on him at home." Anderson wanted to add an academic to the NCR board, and Bowen seemed to be the perfect choice. Bowen told him about Princeton's rule, and the two men agreed that if Anderson could convince the chair of the Princeton trustee executive committee, R. Manning Brown, he would be happy to join the board. Anderson made the case to Brown: "I pointed out that companies like mine wanted to know how to recruit the best graduates. Also, I suggested that university presidents needed to know what corporations wanted from the graduates they interviewed. In other words, both parties needed to understand each other better." Brown agreed, and Bowen became a director of NCR. Bowen later told the *Daily Princetonian* that his father's history with the company provided a "'sentimental' reason for his desire to be a director." Bowen served on the board until NCR was acquired by AT&T in a hostile takeover in 1991.[1]

To a faculty member who suggested that Bowen might want to reconsider serving on boards to support his insistence on keeping the university out of external political controversies, Bowen wrote at some length about the logic of his involvement. The consensus of university presidents whom he knew, Bowen said, was that "if we are serious ourselves about encouraging more effective dialogue between the academic and business communities, then it is not enough for those of us on the academic side of the fence to refuse to participate in the corporate world—especially now that as a matter of public policy more and more effort is being made to persuade people other than businessmen to serve as 'outside directors.'" He continued, "One of the reasons why a number of us have thought it advisable to serve on well-chosen corporate boards is precisely to negate [the] presumption" that universities are anti-business—"and also to suggest that on occasion we may even learn something from the business community, as we would like them to learn from us."[2]

Other boards, corporate and not-for-profit, followed on NCR.[3] So did membership on the committee overseeing the private family trusts of the Rockefellers. Two of the boards, of Fortune 500 companies, involved complicated situations that were especially challenging to navigate. In the case of one of the companies, American Express, Bowen was caught up in a fight within the board over leadership of the company, a fight that he did not initiate; while he

1 E-mail, William Anderson to Nancy Weiss Malkiel, Jan. 14, 2019; J. Todd Weber, "Bowen Says Post at NCR Creates No Role Conflict," *Daily Princetonian*, Jan. 13, 1978, Bowen president, box 402, folder 10. On Bowen's role as a board member during the AT&T takeover, see telephone interview with R. Elton White (then executive vice president of NCR), Oct. 31, 2019.

2 William G. Bowen to Rufus E. Miles Jr., Mar. 27, 1978, Bowen president, box 130, folder 11.

3 The list includes the Reader's Digest Association (1985–97); the DeWitt and Lila Wallace-Reader's Digest Funds (1986–97); Merck (1986–2007); American Express (1988–2006); Denison University (1966–75, 1992–2000); the Center for Advanced Study in the Behavioral Sciences (1978–84, 1989–92); the Smithsonian Institution (1980–92); Teachers Insurance and Annuity Association and College Retirement Equities Fund Boards of Overseers (1995–2009); and the Rockefeller Trust Committee (1976–2016).

took sides, he was mainly an observer. At the other company, Merck, there were transitions in leadership and a rocky stretch having to do with general underperformance and the forced recall of a leading drug; here Bowen was much more of an involved actor. It was at the family company, the Rockefeller Trust Committee, that Bowen had the clearest responsibility for leadership.

The Rockefeller Trust Committee

For three decades Bowen led the high-powered, five-member trust committee that was charged with legal responsibility to oversee two trusts set up by John D. Rockefeller Jr.—one in 1934, one in 1952—for the benefit of his six children and their descendants. The trust committee approved strategic investment directions and ruled on requests for distributions from trust assets. John D. Jr.'s two surviving sons, Laurance and David, and other family members could offer suggestions and make requests, but they were barred from making decisions by the terms of the trusts. Bowen joined the committee in 1976, doubtless at the initiative of its chair, Manning Brown. Bowen's formidable friends Hanna Holborn Gray and Paul Volcker were among the committee members. With Brown's illness and death in 1985, Bowen took over as chair, and as committee members rotated off, the committee began to appoint new members in whom Bowen had high confidence. "Whenever a vacancy arose," Volcker said, Bowen "had a list of university people to propose." These included Lawrence Bacow, president of Tufts University and later president of Harvard; Taylor Reveley, Princeton '65, dean of the law school and later president of the College of William and Mary; and Peter Wendell, Princeton '72, founder and managing director of Sierra Ventures, a Silicon Valley technology-oriented venture capital firm, and board chair at the Princeton University Investment Company.[4]

While the trust committee had traditionally been deferential to the family, Bowen "took charge," in Volcker's words, and was well

4 "Bowen Tied to Rockefeller Empire," *Forerunner*, Apr. 22, 1978, Bowen president, box 402, folder 10; interview with Paul A. Volcker, July 13, 2018, New York City.

prepared to make judgment calls at odds with the family's prefer-ences.[5] That caused continuing tension with David Rockefeller, the former chair and chief executive officer of Chase Manhattan Bank, who thought that he was the senior person in the room.

The trust committee's most controversial decision was to sell Rockefeller Center, the crown jewel of the Rockefeller real estate empire, to the Japanese firm Mitsubishi in 1989. It was just the right move financially—the Rockefeller holdings were overweighted in real estate, and the benefit of the sale to the family's resources was inarguable. The Rockefeller Trust Committee put a very high price on the building, one that could only be justified in the con-text of the extraordinary bubble in real estate prices in Japan. Japa-nese investors were willing to meet it, which meant, in effect, to overpay significantly for the property. But the sale infuriated David Rockefeller. David was chair of Rockefeller Center, Inc., which operated the complex as well as other properties. He regarded Rockefeller Center as an important physical symbol of the family's historic prominence in New York City, and he saw the sale as a major symbolic loss. As chair of the trust committee, Bowen be-came the target of David Rockefeller's anger. The two men tussled over the decision; both of them were accustomed to being in charge, and in this case, Bowen, with the backing of the other members of the trust committee, had the upper hand.[6]

The decisions were the trust committee's; as chair, Bowen was the one to interact most directly with bankers and lawyers. He not only steered the high-level strategy, he immersed himself in the smallest details of the sale. Griffith Sexton, the Morgan Stanley banker who executed the deal for the trust committee, said that he met with Bowen regularly, sometimes multiple times a day. Bowen grilled Sexton: Why was he recommending what he was recom-

---

5 Volcker interview; telephone interview with Lawrence S. Bacow, Sept. 3, 2020.

6 Joan Lebow, "Japanese to Buy a Rockefeller Group Stake," *Wall Street Journal*, Oct. 31, 1989, A4; David Rockefeller, *Memoirs* (New York: Random House Trade Paperbacks, 2003), chap. 30; Volcker interview (source of the quote); Bacow interview; interview with Hanna Holborn Gray, Sept. 18, 2018, New York City; interview with Taylor Reveley, Sept. 4, 2018, Princeton, NJ; interview with Griffith Sexton, Oct. 8, 2019, Princeton, NJ.

mending? What alternatives were there? He would lecture Sexton about something Sexton knew more about than he did, intent on making sure that Sexton understood what he was saying; then he would catch himself, look up, and say, as if in apology, "Griff, I'm always the teacher."[7]

The trust committee took decisions as a group; they met in person on a regular schedule, and where necessary, they held telephone meetings in between. Bowen was the convener, but each of the high-powered members had his and her own say. Bowen's leadership of the group resembled his leadership of the Princeton board: collegial, gracious, low-key, listening respectfully, making sure that everyone had the chance to participate. Bowen aimed to achieve consensus; as Barbara Paul Robinson, the committee's counsel, observed, he "would reinforce what he heard" and, in the way he presented what he heard, signal "where he wanted [the committee to go]." He managed the process so that his fellow committee members got what they wanted, even as they "always [came] out the way [Bowen] want[ed]."[8]

Bowen remained chair of the trust committee through February 2016. The last meeting he attended was in June, four months before he died. Bowen's voice was weak, Taylor Reveley said, and he was in terrible shape physically (indeed, he left halfway through for a medical appointment), but he was there, committed still to the importance of the enterprise. "Seeing him make his way haltingly out of the room, bent with disease, affected us all deeply," Reveley said. Shaking his head at the fact that Bowen showed up, sick as he was, Paul Volcker remarked on his "amazing dedication" to the committee. Reveley summed up Bowen's influence as the leader of the committee: "He could wrap his mind around complex facts quickly, was graced with a seemingly endless supply of practical wisdom, and did not shrink from making the tough calls."[9]

---

7 Sexton interview.

8 Telephone interview with Barbara Paul Robinson, Oct. 8, 2021.

9 Reveley interview; e-mail, Taylor Reveley to Nancy Weiss Malkiel, Dec. 29, 2021; Volcker interview; Reveley, "William Gordon Bowen," remarks at Bowen memorial service, Princeton University Chapel, Dec. 11, 2016, courtesy of Taylor Reveley.

Merck

Those same qualities, Reveley argued, applied to Bowen's director-ship at Merck, as they did to his roles on the boards of other for-profit and not-for-profit companies. But Merck presents a more complicated case than the trust committee. David Rockefeller was a formidable opponent, but he could be managed. At a public com-pany like Merck, there were different kinds of constraints and challenges, and Bowen had more limited running room to make the tough calls. The record shows clearly the complexities of the situ-ation but gives fewer clues about Bowen's basic instincts.

Under the leadership of chair and chief executive officer Roy Vagelos, the pharmaceutical giant had flourished in the late 1980s and early 1990s. But when Vagelos reached retirement age in 1994, the board decided to appoint as his successor Raymond Gilmartin, chair and chief executive officer of the medical device manufacturer Becton, Dickinson and Company. Bowen was part of a five-man search committee, chaired by H. Brewster Atwater, chair and chief executive officer of General Mills. There had been a wealth of pre-sumed inside candidates, some of whom left Merck during the search, some of whom were set aside in favor of Gilmartin. Gilmar-tin was the first outsider appointed to lead Merck, and while he had done very well at Becton, Dickinson, he had no experience in pharmaceutical companies. Why the board chose him is not known; it is clear, however, that the choice came as a surprise. Reacting to the appointment, an analyst at Merrill Lynch told the *New York Times*, "It's unbelievable. He's a total outsider."[10]

During Gilmartin's tenure, Merck's product pipeline dried up, its most important drugs went off patent, its stock had a subpar per-formance relative to its industry and the market as a whole, it fre-quently missed expected earnings, some important drug trials failed,

10 The quote is from Milt Freudenheim, "Merck Gets Outsider as New Chief," *New York Times*, June 10, 1994, https://www.nytimes.com/1994/06/10/business/merck-gets-outsider-as-new-chief.html, accessed July 17, 2021. The members of the search commit-tee are listed in "Merck Names Gilmartin New CEO," United Press International, June 9, 1994, https://www.upi.com/Archives/1994/06/09/Merck-names-Gilmartin-new-CEO/8897771134400, accessed July 17, 2021.

and the company ran into huge trouble with a blockbuster nonsteroidal anti-inflammatory drug, Vioxx.[11] It had been developed during the tenure of the highly successful head of research (1985–2002) at Merck Research Laboratories, Edward M. Scolnick. The drug, first launched in May 1999, was taken off the market in September 2004 because of its association with heart attacks, strokes, and deaths in individuals taking the medication for a long period of time. Vioxx was part of a class of drugs known as COX-2 inhibitors; what made it so attractive was that it reduced the pain and inflammation of arthritis without the side effects associated with other competing drugs, like ulcers and gastrointestinal bleeding. By 2003, it had annual sales of $2.5 billion. But there were clear cardiovascular risks, which Merck seemed to have known about and discounted. As well, Merck scientists had ghostwritten articles in medical journals touting the drug, and Merck was accused of skewing the results of clinical trials in the drug's favor.[12] The board asked the new president of Merck Research Laboratories, Peter S. Kim (2003–13), how he wanted to handle the Vioxx problem; he said that the drug should be withdrawn.[13]

Not everyone thought that the company should have taken the drug off the market. As the business columnist Joe Nocera wrote, "If Merck's first mistake was overselling the drug, its last mistake was withdrawing it entirely. The company says it did so because it was putting patient safety first, but from a litigation standpoint, it was like walking into a bullring dressed in red. . . . In its naiveté, Merck thought that its move would win it plaudits for 'doing the

11 Reed Abelson, "Out of the Merger Rush, Merck's on a Limb," *New York Times*, Aug. 4, 2002, B1.

12 "Merck Manipulated the Science about the Drug Vioxx," Oct. 12, 2017, Union of Concerned Scientists, https://ucsusa.org/resources/merck-manipulated-science-about-drug-vioxx, accessed July 14, 2021. Also see Harlan M. Krumholz et al., "What Have We Learnt from Vioxx?" *BMJ*, Jan. 20, 2007, available at National Center for Biotechnology Information, https://www.ncbi.nlm.nih.gov/pmc/articles/PMC1779871, accessed July 14, 2021; Joan Elias, Spencer Hutchins, and Andrea Nagy, "Merck & Co.," Yale School of Management, Case 06-013, Sept. 25, 2006, available for purchase at https://shopcases.som.yale.edu; Mitchell A. Petersen and Rashmi Singhai, "Vioxx: Too Risky for Merck?," Kellogg School of Management, Case KEL289, Jan. 1, 2007, available for purchase at https://www.kellogg.northwestern.edu/faculty/casestudies.aspx.

13 Telephone interview with Samuel O. Thier, July 30, 2021.

right thing.' Instead, its decision was viewed by the plaintiffs' bar as an admission of guilt—and the perfect club with which to beat the company into submission."[14]

In December 2004, the Merck board constituted a seven-member committee of outside directors, chaired by Bowen, to determine whether the company had acted properly in its handling of Vioxx. The committee engaged the law firm Deveboise & Plimpton to conduct the investigation. Bowen said, "The board concluded that its responsibilities to Merck shareholders made it important to conduct an independent review in order to assure that the company acted in an appropriate and ethical manner."[15] Twenty months later, the judgment was that it had.[16]

Eventually, Merck had to contend with tens of thousands of lawsuits from individuals who had taken Vioxx. The board took the view initially that the cases should be consolidated and the complainants paid off; analysts estimated the probable cost to the company in the tens of billions of dollars. Kenneth Frazier, then Merck's general counsel, argued instead that Merck should not settle; the cases should be defended, one at a time, which would make it possible to disaggregate the effects of the drug from other indices of poor health. The company identified a core group of board members to be Frazier's liaison with the board. Bowen and Lawrence A. Bossidy, who had been chair and chief executive officer of both AlliedSignal and Honeywell, worked with Frazier to figure out how to defend the company's reputation while Frazier was defending individual cases in court. By 2007 sixteen cases had been decided, with Merck winning eleven of those judgments. The other five were under appeal. Merck had not yet paid a dollar in judgments, and appeals of the negative judgments had already resulted in major reductions in awards. But the company had already incurred more

14 Joe Nocera, "Forget Fair; It's Litigation as Usual," *New York Times*, Nov. 17, 2007, C1, quoted in Joan Elias, Spencer Hutchins, Andrea Nagy, Constance E. Bagley, and Douglas W. Rae, "Merck and Vioxx (A)," Yale School of Management, Case 08-016, Jan. 21, 2008, available for purchase at https://shopcases.som.yale.edu.

15 Alex Berenson, "Merck's Board Appoints Panel to Investigate Handling of Vioxx," *New York Times*, Dec. 8, 2004, 6.

16 Alex Berenson, "Merck Inquiry Backs Conduct over Vioxx," *New York Times*, Sept. 7, 2006, C1.

than a billion dollars in legal fees, and the courts were clogged with a major backlog in cases. Judges began putting pressure on Merck to settle. In 2007, in a shift in strategy, the company settled twenty-seven thousand remaining claims at a total cost of $4.85 billion.[17] In 2011, in a controversial move, Merck agreed to pay $950 million to the United States government in connection with illegal marketing of the drug.[18]

As far as leadership of the company was concerned, one cannot help recalling the opening dictum in Bowen's book, *Inside the Boardroom: Governance by Directors and Trustees*: The first function of a board of directors is *"to select, encourage, advise, evaluate and, if need be, replace the CEO."*[19] The first question on the minds of many observers was why the Merck board held the spectacularly successful Roy Vagelos to mandatory retirement at the age of sixty-five. The second was why the board appointed an outsider without pharmaceutical experience to run a pharmaceutical giant. And the third was why they kept him on for as long as they did. Gilmartin finally stepped down in May 2005, nearly a year before the planned end of his contract.[20]

As the *New York Times* put it in December 2004, "Finding people who like Raymond V. Gilmartin is easy. Finding people who like the way he has run Merck . . . is much harder." When Gilmartin took over, Merck "was one of the most respected companies in the

17 Interview with P. Roy Vagelos, Oct. 1, 2018, Bedminster, NJ; telephone interview with Kenneth C. Frazier, Sept. 9, 2020; Lewis Krauskopf, "Merck Agrees to Pay $4.85 Billion in Vioxx Settlement," Reuters, Nov. 9, 2007, https://www.reuters.com/article/us-merck-vioxx-settlement/merck-agrees-to-pay-4-85-billion-in-vioxx-settlement-idUSL0929726620071109, accessed July 14, 2021; Elias, Hutchins, Nagy, Bagley, and Rae, "Merck and Vioxx (A)"; Joan Elias and Constance E. Bagley, "Merck and Vioxx (B)," Yale School of Management, Case 08-017, Jan. 27, 2008, available for purchase at https://shopcases.som.yale.edu; "Merck: Managing Vioxx (G)," Harvard Business School case 9-109-086, Apr. 20, 2009, available for purchase at https://store.hbr.org/case-studies.

18 Duff Wilson, "Merck to Pay $950 Million over Vioxx," *New York Times*, Nov. 22, 2011, https://www.nytimes.com/2011/11/23/business/merck-agrees-to-pay-950-million-in-vioxx-case.html, accessed July 14, 2021; "Merck: Vioxx Case Study," Future of Healthcare, Mar. 9, 2020, https://thefutureofhealth.care/free/09/03/2020/merck-vioxx-case-study, accessed July 14, 2021.

19 (New York: John Wiley & Sons, 1994), 18.

20 Joanne Silberner, "Merck CEO Gilmartin Steps Down," National Public Radio, May 6, 2005, https://www.npr.org/templates/story/story.php?story Id=4632943, accessed July 17, 2021.

United States." "Now, after a decade of Mr. Gilmartin's leadership, Merck is in crisis." The company had "only one new drug anywhere near federal approval." It "faces a criminal investigation, a raft of plaintiff suits and severe damage to its reputation over . . . Vioxx." In a cost-cutting measure, the company said it would eliminate more than five thousand jobs by year's end, 8.5 percent of its workforce. It had underperformed expectations in three of the past four years, and its stock price had "fallen almost 70 percent since 2000."[21]

Given Merck's problems, attracting a star to succeed Gilmartin would not have been easy. Instead, the board appointed an insider, Richard T. Clark, president of the Merck manufacturing division and previously CEO of Medco Health Solutions, as chief executive officer. Instead of also naming Clark chair, however, the board left the chairmanship vacant and created a committee of three board members to oversee, or partner with, Clark. Bossidy chaired the committee. The other members were Bowen and Samuel O. Thier, president of Massachusetts General Hospital and of Partners HealthCare and a professor of medicine at Harvard. While the three would work as a team, Bossidy would take the lead on business strategy, Bowen on Vioxx litigation, and Thier on public policy.[22]

Sharing the responsibilities of the chair among three independent directors was unorthodox. Bowen said, "Where is it written in stone that it has to be one person?"[23] The arrangement worked, Thier said, because the three directors "talked and met regularly," "trusted each other," "heard each other out," and "agreed on pretty much everything." When Bowen and Bossidy retired from the board

21 Alex Berenson, "Not Everybody Loves Raymond: Some Trace Merck's Problems to Its Chairman," *New York Times*, Dec. 15, 2004, https://www.nytimes.com/2004/12/15/business/health/not-everybody-loves-raymond-some-trace-mercks-problems-to.html, accessed July 17, 2021.

22 Christopher Bowe, "Merck Chief Steps Down amid Vioxx Fallout," *Financial Times*, May 5, 2005, https://www.ft.com/content/1901dc64-bd66-11d9-87aa-00000 e2511c8, accessed July 14, 2021; John Simons, "A New CEO's R$_x$ for What Ails Merck," *Fortune*, May 30, 2005, https://money.cnn.com/magazines/fortune/fortune_archive/2005/05/30/8261222/index.htm, accessed July 14, 2021.

23 Bowen quoted in Patrick McGeehan, "A Friar Speaks, and Lightning Strikes," *New York Times*, May 8, 2005, https://www.nytimes.com/2005/05/08/business/yourmoney/a-friar-speaks-and-lightning-strikes.html, accessed July 14, 2021.

in 2007, the board named Clark to be chair as well as chief executive officer, with Thier as lead director.[24]

In the Vagelos era, according to a *Fortune* magazine survey, Merck had topped the list of the most admired companies in the United States for seven straight years.[25] What had happened? And what responsibility did Bowen and his fellow board members bear?

It is difficult to find critics who will attribute responsibility on the record. Instead, one hears praise for Bowen—and, by association, for his fellow board members as well. Peter Wendell, who overlapped with Bowen on the board, characterized him as "thorough," "thoughtful," and "action-oriented," more consultative than his natural instincts might have suggested, willing to listen and let a discussion unfold, with a preternatural sense of where the discussion was headed, well before other participants knew. He provided a "steady hand" and "good judgment"; his impact came through "force of will" and "sheer intellect." Thomas Shenk, who also served on the board with Bowen, said that he was "regarded as a man of wisdom who would listen and always say the right thing"—"a generalist with broad knowledge of how things should work."[26]

Samuel Thier said that Bowen was "*the* key person at Merck." When questions arose of what to do next, "people would automatically look to Bill." "He was seen as the wise man" at the table, and "he was willing to make clear what he thought should happen." It wasn't that Bowen leaned heavily on the board; what counted was that "he had a great track record," and "he was so well respected" that people were inclined to follow his lead. His analytic and communication skills were superb. "The fact that he was attended to as he was reflected the fact that people had a very strong sense that when he looked at a problem, there was nobody better at that than he was."[27] But whatever Bowen's contributions may have been, no one would dispute that the years of Bowen's involvement with

24 Thier interview.

25 Elias, Hutchins, Nagy, Bagley, and Rae, "Merck and Vioxx (A)."

26 Interview with Peter C. Wendell, Sept. 28, 2019, Princeton, NJ; interview with Thomas E. Shenk, July 31, 2018, Princeton, NJ.

27 Thier interview.

Merck in the Gilmartin and Clark eras were one of the less successful periods in the company's history.

Bowen was influential in developing a consensus in the board that Frazier should succeed Clark as chief executive officer. He worked patiently over a number of years to make sure that the board appreciated Frazier's contributions. He encouraged Frazier to take broader responsibility in the company to equip himself to run it; in 2006, Frazier became executive vice president in addition to his role as general counsel, and in 2007, he took the leadership of human health, the company's largest division. He became chair and chief executive officer in January 2011, one of the tiny cohort of African Americans running Fortune 500 companies. With Bowen's encouragement to continue to take on broader responsibility in order to prove his capability, Frazier said, he "made my career possible."[28]

Frazier came to regard Bowen as "*the* central member of the board." He had the capacity, Frazier said, to "think very big picture"—to locate business issues in a larger societal context. Bowen was "supernaturally intelligent" with "great curiosity across traditional boundaries." When he listened to presentations from Merck scientists, he questioned them carefully to make sure he understood the key issues. "Watching how he influenced people, how he carefully stated and reframed issues, helped me understand," Frazier said, "what it meant to be a leader." With Bowen, as well as Roy Vagelos, as mentors, Frazier reflected, "I hit the jackpot."[29]

American Express

American Express provided Bowen's most frustrating board experience. It is worth recounting not so much because of Bowen's importance in guiding the board or in determining the final outcome of a difficult leadership transition, neither of which he did, but because the irrationality of what Bowen saw at American Express

---

28 Frazier interview.
29 Ibid.

prompted him to write a book on board governance, about which I will say more shortly.

Bowen joined the Amex board as an outside director in 1988. James D. Robinson III had been chief executive officer since 1977. Determined to turn American Express into a major financial services company, Robinson went on a buying spree: first the securities firm Shearson Loeb Rhoades, next Lehman Brothers Kuhn Loeb, after that Investors Diversified Services, followed by E. F. Hutton & Co. At every turn, there was a new name: Shearson/American Express, then Shearson Lehman/American Express, then Shearson Lehman Hutton. None of the acquisitions was especially smooth; by 1992 the brokerage subsidiary was far from an industry leader and was losing more than $100 million for the year while other Wall Street firms were earning record profits. While the company as a whole was still profitable, its income had fallen precipitously from a year before. There had been a string of other bad purchases. There were real questions about whether Robinson had overreached, whether American Express worked as an integrated financial services company, or whether it was expanding far beyond its core competencies. As well, the iconic American Express card was losing market share to competitors like Visa and MasterCard, and the travel-related services division, previously the heart of the company, was having major difficulties.[30]

Amex had a big, sprawling board, made up of outside directors as well as company-affiliated directors, some of whom were personally close to Robinson, approved of his stewardship of the company, and supported his continuation in office, others of whom

---

30 On the difficulties at Amex and the turmoil over succession, see a number of sources in the popular press, including Bill Saporito, "The Toppling of King James III," *Fortune*, Jan. 11, 1993, https://archive.fortune.com/magazines/fortune/fortune_archive /1993/01/11/77369/index.htm, accessed July 10, 2021; Stefan Fatsis, "Amex Board Picks Golub as Chief Executive, Robinson to Remain as Chairman," AP News, Jan. 25, 1993, https://apnews.com/article/5c3392ce0d190fee09ddb1bca2ba3d61, accessed July 10, 2021; James B. Stewart, "Wild Card," *New Yorker*, Jan. 25, 1993, 38–45, https://archives .newyorker.com/newyorker/1993-01-25/flipbook/038, accessed July 10, 2021; Brent D. Fromson, "American Express: Anatomy of a Coup," *Washington Post*, Feb. 11, 1993, https://www.washingtonpost.com/archive/politics/1993/02/11/american-express-anatomy -of-a-coup/caff8987-495c-4a79-bf0a-24ae454023a2, accessed July 10, 2021. Also see "American Express (A)," Harvard Business School, case 9-494-093, rev. Aug 1, 1996.

believed Robinson needed to be replaced. One of Amex's longest-serving outside directors, Rawleigh Warner Jr., former chair and chief executive officer of Mobil, led the charge in taking Robinson on. Bowen agreed with Warner that the company was not in good hands, but he was more of a supportive observer in the Amex saga than he was a critical actor. In other words, he was smart enough to see the problems but not in a position to be a key actor to right the ship.

In late 1991 the outside directors gained Robinson's agreement to meet privately a few times a year, a normal practice at other companies, but not previously at American Express. A meeting in February 1992 was uneventful. That was not the case in September. Robinson had promised in February that he would lay out a plan for succession. He told the board that Harvey Golub, who had joined American Express in 1983 as president and chief executive officer of IDS Financial Services and had become vice chair of Amex in 1990, was "developing well but still need[ed] seasoning." Robinson planned to stay for perhaps two more years, and then "(if all goes as anticipated) to pass the mantle on to Harvey." Following his presentation, Robinson left the meeting.[31]

Rawleigh Warner spoke about Robinson's "failures of leadership over a long time," notably "a whole series of very bad business judgments"—Shearson, Hutton, problems with the credit card business, a steep drop in the stock price; and with all of that, the departure of many executives, and Robinson's failure to develop "new talent." Warner said that the board "had a responsibility to say 'enough' and to move at once to recruit new leadership"; the board "could not continue to overlook poor performance." Other directors spoke in support of Warner's position. Bowen noted that employee surveys, presented to the public responsibility committee of the board, which he chaired, "showed lack of employee confidence in the leadership and integrity of top management." The question was not whether to keep Robinson, but how quickly to move to

31 Bowen was so exercised by what he saw that he recorded twenty pages of typewritten notes on the "American Express Saga," Feb. 6, 1993. This document, in Bowen personal, is the source for these quotes.

replace him. Warner would have done so immediately and had a committee of outside directors supervise the company while they searched for a new chief executive officer, but the board demurred, and Robinson not only continued in office but took a role in the search for his successor.[32]

Robinson described himself as cochair of the search and did what he could to sabotage the fortunes of a strong outside candidate. He pushed for an arrangement where Golub (whom no one had thought was ready for the job, Robinson included) would be elected chief executive officer and he himself would become chair. After untold difficulties with the search and persistent tensions in the board, Golub was made CEO on January 25, 1993; Robinson (following a revolt of shareholders, a drop in the price of the stock, and the resignation of three board members, including Warner) resigned from the company on January 29; and the senior outside director, Richard Furlaud, former president of Bristol Myers Squibb, was made nonexecutive chair by vote of the board on February 1.[33]

From the point of view of process, everything was wrong with the way the board handled the question of succession and the execution of the search. The directors themselves were deeply divided; each "camp" regarded the other with suspicion, if not disdain. Some directors thought clearly about leadership issues and presented candid assessments to their fellow board members; others, closely allied with the incumbent chief executive officer, told him offline who said what about him, coached him about how to respond, and advised him about what he should anticipate in terms of board action. Some directors mistrusted their fellow board members and accused them of malfeasance of various kinds—deliberately leaving some of them out of the loop, convening meetings without

32 Ibid.

33 Allen R. Myerson, "American Express Chairman Quits after Days of Corporate Turmoil," *New York Times*, Jan. 31, 1993, https://www.nytimes.com/1993/01/31/us/american-express-chairman-quits-after-days-of-corporate-turmoil.html, accessed July 10, 2021; Thomas McCarroll, "Board Games," *Time*, Feb. 8, 1993, http://content.time.com/time/magazine/article/0,9171,977649,00.html, accessed July 10, 2021; "American Express (B)," Harvard Business School, case 9-494-094, Apr. 25, 1994.

providing adequate notice, and leaking information to the financial press (an article in the *Wall Street Journal* where some directors were accused by name of bad behavior was a particular irritant).

The upside in terms of process, however, is that the company established a six-person executive committee, five of them outside directors, including Bowen, which gave outside directors more control over senior management than had previously been the case.[34]

The messiness of the search process notwithstanding, Harvey Golub served until 2001, when he was succeeded as chair and chief executive officer by Kenneth Chenault, another of the very small number of African American CEOs of a Fortune 500 company in the United States. Chenault had joined American Express in its strategic planning group in 1981, and Golub had made him president and chief operating officer of the company in 1997. Chenault came to know Bowen in the early 1990s when he was a division president; Bowen told him early on that "he had the capabilities to become CEO" of American Express, and Chenault came to lean on him for advice. Bowen had a "unique ability," Chenault said, to "translate insights from his academic experiences to the business world"; he was "very strategic" from a business standpoint and a "great judge of people." Bowen was "passionate about leadership and the development of leadership skills," and he emphasized the importance of understanding and working to promote the "core values of the institution." Chenault thought that Bowen possessed both "broad-gauged intellectual curiosity" and the ability to think ahead and "anticipate where the puck was going." At the same time, he had "insight into the character and abilities of people"—the personal attributes that were "important to focus on from a leadership standpoint." Bowen combined a "thorough understanding of issues" with a unique mix of "intellect, experience, judgment, and intuition" that made him an unusually effective and far-sighted board member.[35] And he was an enthusiastic supporter of Chenault.

---

34 Brett D. Fromson, "Former American Express Chairman Gets $10 Million Package," *Washington Post*, Feb. 28, 1993, https://www.washingtonpost.com/archive/politics/1993/02/28/former-american-express-chairman-gets-10-million-package/425b81c0-b5ac-472d-9767-a65fc1a887f2, accessed July 10, 2021.

35 Telephone interview with Kenneth I. Chenault, Jan. 8, 2020.

Prompted by his dismay at what he had seen at American Express in the Robinson-Golub handoff, informed by the strengths and experiences as a board member that Chenault remarked on, Bowen produced a book, *Inside the Boardroom: Governance by Directors and Trustees*, first published in 1994, and later revised, expanded, and reissued in 2008 as *The Board Book: An Insider's Guide for Directors and Trustees*. Bowen discussed the functions of boards and the way boards are organized, including, notably, two issues clearly dictated by his experience at American Express—the question of whether the CEO should chair the board (Bowen thought so, though he understood the potential benefits of separating the CEO and board chair functions), and the role of a retiring CEO in the selection of his or her successor (advice and counsel only). He laid out twenty "presumptive norms" about the way boards are constituted, including size (ten to fifteen members for corporate boards), membership, composition, inside versus outside directors ("outside directors should predominate"), specific attributes of individual directors, diversity of backgrounds, independence of directors (again, informed by the experience at American Express, with particular attention to "subtle issues of conflict" and "excessively close relationships with the CEO"), term limits for directors (Bowen said yes), and whether a retired CEO should remain on the board (Bowen said no).[36]

"The overarching issue" facing for-profit boards, Bowen said, "is how to achieve a sensible balance between mechanisms that encourage crisp executive decision-making and mechanisms that encourage the right kinds of oversight by governing boards." CEOs, he said, "need to be strong leaders. They should be expected to come to clear conclusions, to advocate decisive steps, and to act." At the same time, boards needed *"to be less supine."* "Boards," he explained, "should be reliable sources of constructive skepticism, and board members should be good critics as well as compatriots." Strong CEOs and strong boards needed to work in partnership, and directors needed "the will to act"—needed, in other words, to be

36 Bowen, *Inside the Boardroom*, xviii.

prepared to *"exercise courage"* in making decisions in the best interests of the company.[37]

And CEOs and board members read and learned from the books. John H. Biggs, chair and CEO of Teachers Insurance and Annuity Association–College Retirement Equities Fund (TIAA-CREF) during Bowen's tenure as an overseer of the financial services company, later told Bowen that he had taught *Inside the Boardroom* in a course he offered for many years as an adjunct at the Stern School of Business at Yeshiva University. He added, "Conversations with you and your book were powerful influences in all my work on corporate boards."[38] A reviewer of *The Board Book* said, "Bowen's facts and straightforward narrative make a compelling and critical read for wannabe directors—and for every student of corporate affairs."[39]

37 Ibid., 145–46.
38 E-mail, John H. Biggs to William G. Bowen, Sept. 25, 2016, Bowen Ithaka.
39 Barbara Jacobs in *Booklist*, Apr. 1, 2008, 12.

16

"President-Whisperer"

"A Kind of Switchboard for Higher Education"

Because of his leadership and influence, William G. Bowen stands out, arguably, as the preeminent figure in American higher education in the late twentieth and early twenty-first centuries. He was the person others consulted, the person whose writings had the greatest impact, the person best able to speak for higher education in his era. Bowen, according to the legal historian Stanley N. Katz, former president of the American Council of Learned Societies, made his mark in part as a "thoughtful, research-oriented student of higher education." No one, Katz said, "has written more or better about higher education." Bowen's reach was unusually broad: widely read speeches, articles, annual reports, and books on every important topic in higher education, from "admissions and inclusiveness to athletics."[1] As well, Bowen was responsible for educational innovations promoted through the Mellon Foundation and ITHAKA, and for leaders nurtured at his initiative and leadership positions filled at his recommendation.

Gerhard Casper, former president of Stanford University, called Bowen "a gigantic figure" in American higher education—distinctive for the combination of his shaping effect on Princeton, the significance of his work at Mellon, and the broad influence of his books.

---

1 Katz oral history, 33. Katz said that Bowen, together with Derek Bok, was unique in undertaking "engaged, serious scholarship on the problems of the university"—in trying to think systematically about what higher education was, what the problems were, and what a responsible institution should do about them. Katz interview, July 18, 2018, Princeton, NJ.

In terms of "sheer effectiveness" beyond the borders of his university, he stood out among other presidents—he was "the outstanding example of someone who had influence well beyond the institution he led." For "overall impact on American higher education," Casper said, "it was Bill Bowen whom I'd think of first."[2] Lee Bollinger, president of the University of Michigan and then of Columbia University, said that Bowen was "a singular figure" in higher education: a "fearless" president who "spoke with intellectual authority" and used social science techniques to analyze important issues facing American colleges and universities.[3] Paul LeClerc, former president of the New York Public Library, characterized Bowen as "staggeringly capable, intelligent, [and] game-changing."[4] Lawrence Bacow, president of Tufts and later of Harvard University, said that Bowen "thought deeply about who we educate [and] how we educate"; it was "hard," Bacow said, "to find any slice of higher education that did not benefit from Bill's penetrating analysis."[5] Vartan Gregorian, president of the Carnegie Corporation, called Bowen a respected, highly regarded, influential standard-bearer for higher education. "Wherever Bill sat," he said, "was the head of the table."[6] Michael Schill, president of the University of Oregon and later of Northwestern University, described Bowen as "the voice of higher education."[7] Richard C. Levin, former president of Yale University, called him "the most important thought leader" in American higher education."[8]

2 Telephone interview with Gerhard Casper, Feb. 19, 2020.

3 Telephone interview with Lee C. Bollinger, Sept. 21, 2021.

4 Telephone interview with Paul LeClerc, July 1, 2021.

5 Telephone interview with Lawrence S. Bacow, Sept. 3, 2020.

6 Telephone interview with Vartan Gregorian, Aug. 11, 2020.

7 Telephone interview with Michael H. Schill, Feb. 7, 2020. Also see e-mail, Ronald D. Liebowitz, president of Brandeis University, to William G. Bowen, Sept. 15, 2016, Bowen Ithaka: "I cannot think of another individual who has had such an impact on higher education leaders as you have."

8 Interview with Richard C. Levin, Sept. 20, 2019, New Haven, CT. In writing to Bowen, Levin elaborated: "Your contributions to higher education are unparalleled in our generation. The wisdom conveyed in your many books, and the insights drawn from your rigorous scholarship, have lighted the way for so many of us. . . . Your achievements at Princeton, Mellon, J-STOR, and Ithaka have been monumental." E-mail, Levin to Bowen, Sept. 15, 2016, Bowen Ithaka.

It is worth noting that Bowen's work as a kingmaker reinforced the central themes of his books—and picked up important threads both from his presidency of Princeton and from his boards. This was a man committed to access, to inclusivity, to affirmative action, to broadening the population of people equipped to lead important institutions in American society. In his work at Princeton and at Mellon, he wrote about access to opportunity, and he encouraged access. By promoting two Black men to become CEOs of Fortune 500 companies, by supporting an unprecedented number of Jewish academics to become presidents of major colleges and universities, he helped in practical ways to realize the goals that he espoused so strongly. To understand these claims, we need to look to Bowen's promotion of and support for individuals who would become presidents of leading colleges and universities and of major cultural institutions.

The organizing themes in Bowen's book on boards—identifying the elements of good leadership, choosing good leaders, bolstering or replacing ineffective leaders—applied also to his informal role in recommending, placing, and supporting leaders in major institutions in the United States. We have already seen his influence in encouraging and preparing Kenneth Frazier and Kenneth Chenault for the top leadership positions in two Fortune 500 companies. The same influence applied, even more powerfully, in major institutions in American higher education and American culture. Bowen had a Rolodex like no one else. He knew everyone, and he thought he knew who was best suited for every important vacancy. He had a strong hand in both sides of the process: his encouragement made a difference, sometimes the critical difference, in motivating people to become candidates for major positions, and his recommendation carried unusual weight in the deliberations of individuals conducting searches. Trustees looking for new presidents called him all the time, and he gave them specific recommendations and candid judgments about individuals. In turn, he assigned himself the delicate job of brokering conversations between those trustees and people he believed to be top candidates—often people who held presidencies elsewhere and could not easily present themselves as available for new positions. While Bowen sometimes claimed more influence than he actually had, there is no doubt that he was a unique force to reckon with. Hanna Holborn Gray, former president of the University of Chicago, described him as "a kind of switchboard for higher education." He "made a kind of specialty in knowing presidents," and he "always had candidates" to offer when search committees called.[9]

Nannerl O. Keohane, then a member of the Harvard Corporation, consulted Bowen about potential candidates during the presidential search in 2006–7 that resulted in the appointment of Drew Gilpin Faust. Keohane was "struck," she said, "by how much he knew about people, how concise and elegant his formulas" were for describing and assessing them. Bowen "had people slotted for particular institutions." He was "very frank," willing to "criticize as well as give praise"; he had "very strong opinions," and in his positive assessments, Keohane said, he was "right on target."[10]

Kenneth Chenault, who succeeded Harvey Golub as CEO of American Express, said that Bowen was a "college president–whisperer."[11] Morton Schapiro, president successively of Williams College and Northwestern University, called Bowen "a kingmaker"— dozens and dozens of leaders, he said, took particular college and university presidencies "because of Bill."[12] No one else in American higher education played, or even contemplated playing, a comparable role.[13]

---

9 Interview with Hanna Holborn Gray, Sept. 18, 2018, New York City. On trustee search committees consulting Bowen, also see telephone interview with John W. McCarter re Chicago search, Jan. 11, 2019.

10 Interview with Nannerl O. Keohane, Apr. 29, 2019, Princeton, NJ.

11 Telephone interview with Kenneth I. Chenault, Jan. 8, 2020.

12 Telephone interview with Morton O. Schapiro, Aug. 19, 2020. Michael H. Schill, president of the University of Oregon and later of Northwestern University, told Bowen, "Your scholarship and your example provided the intellectual and leadership framework for me as I contemplated making the move from law school dean to president. . . . Your advice, your encouragement and your advocacy were extraordinarily important in enabling me to obtain the presidency of the University of Oregon." E-mail, Schill to William G. Bowen, Oct. 18, 2016, Bowen Ithaka.

13 In addition to the presidents cited below, others making this point include Gerhard Casper, president of Stanford University (telephone interview, Feb. 19, 2020), Lee C. Bollinger, president of Columbia University (telephone interview, Sept. 21, 2021), and Vartan Gregorian, president of Brown University and of the Carnegie Corporation (telephone interview, Aug. 11, 2020).

Bowen "prided himself," Henry Bienen, former president of Northwestern University, said, "on building up a stable of people whose careers he pushed forward." He quickly came to judgments about people—sometimes too quickly; sometimes the judgments were accurate, sometimes not. Bowen admired intelligence and hard work, not status or class; he was "without ascriptive biases," "as merit-oriented a person" as Bienen ever knew. What was at issue for Bowen: not who you were but "how well you could do the job"—whether you "had the skills" to do the job at hand.[14]

Building up a stable of people meant, in part, focusing on young people. Bowen found jobs for young people he knew whom he considered to be well suited to university administration in positions other than presidencies, placing them in increasingly responsible administrative roles that defined their careers. He did that for Robert Kasdin, Princeton class of 1980, who had gone to law school and was a third-year associate at a Wall Street firm when he told Bowen he was not expecting to practice corporate law for the long run. Bowen arranged for Kasdin to become general counsel of PRINCO, and he was directly responsible for making the connections that led to Kasdin's next two positions: treasurer and chief investment officer at the Metropolitan Museum in New York, and executive vice president and chief financial officer at the University of Michigan.[15] Just as Lee Bollinger appointed Kasdin to the Michigan post on Bowen's recommendation, so, too, when Bollinger became president of Columbia University, he brought Kasdin to New York as senior executive vice president, and he took Bowen's counsel and made Jerome Davis, Princeton class of 1971, secretary of the university.[16] Eugene Y. Lowe Jr., also Princeton '71, who had been a trustee and dean of students at the university, took up a new post as assistant to the president at Northwestern in the administrations of Henry Bienen and Morton Schapiro. Kevin Guthrie, Princeton '84, got his start running institutions in the nonprofit world—JSTOR, then ITHAKA Harbors—because Bowen placed him in those roles.

14 Interview with Henry S. Bienen, Nov. 5, 2018, Chicago.
15 Telephone interview with Robert A. Kasdin, Aug. 25, 2020.
16 Bollinger interview; telephone interview with Jerome Davis, Nov. 19, 2021.

("In taking me under your wing and then teaching me to fly," Guthrie reflected later, "you have enabled me to live a life of service to education and knowledge.")[17] At the same time that he launched administrative careers, Bowen made a point of introducing young people new to senior administrative responsibility to other people among his contacts, senior administrators at other institutions from whom they could learn.[18] The venture capitalist Peter Wendell called him a "connector of people to opportunities."[19]

But launching and supporting presidencies was where Bowen focused the lion's share of his attention and efforts. He had a gift for picking people he thought would be winners, adopting them, helping them to succeed, and taking some of the credit—sometimes more credit than he deserved—for their accomplishments. A case in point: Richard Levin had become chair of the economics department at Yale shortly before Bowen left Princeton for Mellon. Bowen kept track of such things. When he began thinking about JSTOR, he called Levin for help; once JSTOR was up and running, he asked Levin to join the board. Bowen told Levin that he was pushing for him in the Yale presidential search in 1993, to the point that he later claimed credit for finding Levin and putting him forward. There was doubtless exaggeration in the claim. Levin had been named dean of the graduate school of arts and sciences at Yale some months before the presidential search began, and he was championed by one of Yale's most important faculty members, the Nobel laureate James Tobin, and was well known to the members of the Yale Corporation. But it was typical of Bowen, who enjoyed telling the people he liked that he had been instrumental in their success. Once Bowen adopted Levin, he showed unusual generosity in supporting him. Early in Levin's presidency, Bowen, noting

17 E-mail, Kevin Guthrie to William G. Bowen, Sept. 13, 2016, Bowen Ithaka.

18 On introducing younger people new to administration to more senior people in his circle, see, for example, telephone interview with Rebecca M. Blank, Aug. 29, 2019; Schill interview.

19 Interview with Peter C. Wendell, Sept. 28, 2019, Princeton, NJ. He also made life-changing connections for people he cared about who were outside the academy. When he saw an opportunity for an individual he wanted to help, he was "on fire till he got it done." In Wendell's case, Bowen introduced him to Louis Marx, who provided the initial capital that launched Wendell's venture capital firm, Sierra Ventures, in 1982–83.

the persistence of a lot of disaffected Yale alumni, a legacy of the presidency of Kingman Brewster, volunteered to host a dinner party where Levin could work to bring some of those men back into the fold. The Bowen dinner, Levin said, proved to be "unbelievably fruitful"; a number of influential men in attendance became important Yale supporters over time. It was, Levin said, "a wonderful gift" that Bowen "gave to Yale."[20]

Another case in point: Henry Bienen, a good friend and tennis and squash partner of Bowen's at Princeton, got his first administrative appointments during Bowen's presidency: first director of the Center for International Studies, then dean of the Woodrow Wilson School of Public and International Affairs. Bienen described Bowen as "very instrumental" in his appointment in 1995 as president of Northwestern University; Bowen's recommendation, Bienen was later told by his board chair, who spoke with Bowen, was "very important" in the position being offered.[21]

Lawrence Bacow's first substantive interaction with Bowen came early in his presidency of Tufts University, when Bowen, who had just published *Reclaiming the Game*, invited Bacow to meet with the NESCAC presidents to discuss the book's findings. Bacow, accustomed to the approach to athletics at MIT, where he had been chancellor (no recruited athletes, no preferences for athletes in the admission process), bonded with Bowen over the book and struck up a relationship. Bacow visited Bowen at Mellon, discussed his plans for Tufts, and got Bowen's advice on a number of key concerns. As for admissions, in addition to trying to scale back the influence of athletics, Bacow was resisting pressure from the Tufts board to award merit aid. In 2004, the third year of Bacow's presidency, he invited Bowen to come to a trustee meeting to talk about admissions. It turned out that Bacow had to miss the meeting because of the death of his father-in-law, so Bowen had a conversation with the Tufts board in his absence. Afterward, Bacow called his board chair and asked how the session went. "How much did you pay him to tell us what he did?" the chair responded. Bowen

---

20 Levin interview.
21 Bienen interview.

had told the board that they had better treat Bacow well, because if they did not, another institution would swoop in and take him away.[22] Bowen later told the president of MIT, Chuck Vest, "Larry Bacow may be the best president out there at this time."[23]

Michael McPherson, an economist of higher education and later dean of the faculty at Williams College, first came to know Bowen at the outset of his tenure at Mellon. Bowen wanted to support research "that would matter in a practical way" to higher education, and he invited McPherson to come to Mellon to talk. "You and your friends at Williams should think about work you would like to do and send me a proposal," Bowen told him. The upshot: the Williams Project on the Economics of Higher Education. Williams became an early test site for JSTOR, where the economics journals were removed from the library and electronic copies made available in their place. Williams, too, became "a guinea pig for the survey research" portion of the College and Beyond database, helping to develop surveys that would be sent to the alumni whose records were collected at Mellon. McPherson frequently attended meetings at Mellon as adviser, commentator, and working participant.

McPherson went on from Williams to become president of Macalester College (1996–2003) and president of the Spencer Foundation (2003–17). He described Bowen's influence on the evolution of his career this way: It was Bowen's role "to help him have the opportunity," but Bowen, "not into arm-twisting," left it to him "to decide if he wanted it." As for the Macalester presidency, Bowen was on the board of *Reader's Digest*, whose founders, DeWitt and Lila Wallace, were major benefactors of the college. DeWitt Wallace, the son of Macalester president James Wallace, was a Macalester alumnus, class of 1911. Thanks to the Wallaces' generosity over the years, especially a large gift in 1990, *Reader's Digest* stock made up the lion's share of the Macalester endowment. When the company went public in 1990, Macalester's endowment more than quintupled, making it one of the best-endowed liberal arts colleges

22 Bacow interview.
23 E-mail, Charles M. Vest to Lawrence S. Bacow, June 15, 2006, courtesy of Lawrence S. Bacow.

in the United States. Bowen pointed out to McPherson that the stock would be a crucial strategic asset for the college. But over-concentration in a single asset was generally unwise, and by the early 2000s, the college had sold most of its *Reader's Digest* stock and invested the proceeds in a diversified portfolio of stocks, bonds, and alternative investments.[24]

Once McPherson took the job at Macalester, Bowen was "enormously supportive and helpful." "I'll do anything for you that you want," he told McPherson. McPherson asked him to meet with his board and advise them on how to be effective. He told Bowen that his main concern was to help the trustees understand the difference between the role of the president and the role of the board. Key people on the board, with a lot of time on their hands, were eager to do a lot of things at the college, well beyond their proper sphere. McPherson needed them to understand what was and was not their responsibility. Later, on a number of occasions, McPherson found that he could refer back to the discussions with Bowen as he charted a path forward with the trustees.[25]

Another Williams economist of higher education, Morton Schapiro, became president of Williams (2000–2009) and then Henry Bienen's successor as president of Northwestern (2009–22). Bowen, Schapiro said, was "my most trusted academic adviser and mentor"; he had great confidence in Bowen's judgment and talked with him at length before making any major decisions. Schapiro described Bowen as "a supportive, interested friend," always trying to build him up; "my life would have been very different" without him. "He picked me up," Schapiro said, "and took a tremendous interest in my career." Schapiro called Bowen a "matchmaker of the first order" and counted him responsible for both of his

24 Telephone interview with Michael S. McPherson, Aug. 20, 2020; "Frequently Asked Questions (FAQ)—Macalester College," https://www.macalester.edu/investmentoffice/faq, accessed July 14, 2021; Matt Day, "Reader's Digest Files for Bankruptcy," *Mac Weekly*, Sept. 11, 2009, https://themacweekly.com/63701/archive/readers-digest-files-for-bankruptcy, accessed July 14, 2021; Kathleen Teltsch, "EDUCATION; Macalester's Endowment Rises to $320 Million," *New York Times*, Oct. 17, 1990, https://www.nytimes.com/1990/10/17/us/education-macalester-s-endowment-rises-to-320-million.html, accessed July 14, 2021.
25 McPherson interview.

presidencies. When the Northwestern position became available, Bowen told Schapiro that it was "the great job" for him. Bowen knew it, Schapiro said, before he did.[26]

Once Bowen's protégés assumed leadership positions, his advice and example influenced the way they conducted themselves, the actions they took, and the decisions they made. The advice was both substantive—how to be a good president, how to work with a board, how to handle particular issues—and personal. After Schapiro accepted the Williams presidency, he and his wife, Mimi, had a "memorable dinner" with Bill and Mary Ellen, where Mary Ellen talked about the challenges of family life during a presidency and gave Mimi Schapiro specific advice about how to handle young children in the president's house. Later, when the Schapiros were in London for an alumni event, the Bowens were also in town, staying at the same hotel. The four had a dinner reservation for 9:30 p.m. The Bowens, whose daughter, Karen, had graduated from Williams in 1986, came to the event, which was scheduled from 7:00 to 9:00 p.m. At 9:01, Bowen walked up, took Schapiro's elbow, and said, "Time for the president to leave." For years thereafter, at the stated conclusion of alumni events, Mimi Schapiro walked up to Morty, took his elbow, and said, "Bill Bowen."[27]

Daniel H. Weiss came to know Bowen early in his tenure as dean of arts and sciences at Johns Hopkins University. A colleague asked him, "If you could have lunch with anyone in the world," who would it be? Weiss said he'd love to meet Bowen. Some months later, Bowen invited him to lunch at Mellon. He "welcomed me as though I was the most important person in his life," Weiss said; "I walked out feeling like the luckiest person in the world." Weiss took to going to New York every few months to see Bowen; Bowen, he said, "asked a lot of questions," was "always responsive," and "took a deep interest in my work." Bowen told Weiss that he thought he should be a college president and put his name in for consideration at Lafayette. The school, he told him, was "a good place that could

26 Schapiro interview.
27 Ibid.

be a lot better with the right leadership." It was Bowen's idea and Bowen's support "that put me there," Weiss said.

Weiss served as president of Lafayette from 2005 to 2013. He and Bowen talked at least every few weeks and usually saw each other once a month. When Weiss had done what he thought he could do at Lafayette and the Haverford presidency came up, Bowen was the person he turned to for advice. And when, early in Weiss's tenure at Haverford (he served only from 2013 to 2015), he was approached about the presidency of the Metropolitan Museum of Art, a job he ended up taking, he turned once again to Bowen for counsel. "Every time I needed his help, he was there," Weiss said. "He believed in me in ways that elevated my own ambitions."[28]

Even when Bowen had not had a hand in placing someone in a leadership position, he reached out where he saw talent that he thought should be encouraged and supported. When Rebecca M. Blank became chancellor of the University of Wisconsin, Bowen called, "out of the blue," to congratulate her and offer her any help he could provide. Blank joined the board of ITHAKA as Bowen was stepping down; later, Bowen and McPherson sent her a draft of *Lesson Plan* for review. She sent back extensive comments; when the book was published, Bowen sent her flowers, with the message that the book would not have been as good as it was without her observations. To the end of his life, Blank said, Bowen "engaged with [her] very personally and closely" and "made a point of reaching out and being in touch."[29]

Bowen also made his mark beyond colleges and universities in identifying and supporting potential leaders. He started at Mellon the same year that Paul LeClerc became president of Hunter College. The two men came to know each other as they pursued complementary efforts to encourage high-achieving minority students to earn doctorates and become college professors. When the presidency of the New York Public Library became available unexpectedly after the sudden death in 1992 of the Reverend Timothy S. Healy,

28 Telephone interview with Daniel H. Weiss, Sept. 17, 2020.
29 Blank interview.

LeClerc was invited to interview for the position. The chair of the library board told him, "You are on everybody's list, but the one that counted was Bill Bowen's."[30]

It would be wrong to assume from these accounts that Bowen was always right or that he always had his way. He could be wrong in his assessment of people and their fit for important leadership positions. He had blind spots both ways: He was sometimes a big fan of people who flamed out, and he was sometimes adamantly opposed to people who succeeded spectacularly. Search committees and appointing officers did not always heed his judgment. And sometimes, when they did, they quickly found that they had made a mistake and had a problem they needed to remedy. That said, Bowen's track record was very, very good—he had many more wins than losses, and he spotted, nurtured, and supported some of the leading talent in American higher education in his era. He played a distinctive role, which none of his peers emulated or even tried to emulate, and he launched or helped to launch the administrative careers of some of the most important educational leaders of his day.

He also provided a model for how to be a college or university president, a model as important to presidents early in their careers as to seasoned veterans. Brian Rosenberg, who succeeded Michael McPherson as president of Macalester College, told Bowen, "You have for many years been a model, mentor, and inspiration to me."[31] Richard Levin, former president of Yale, told him, "You stand among my heroes and role models."[32] Derek Bok, the highly experienced former president of Harvard University, reinforced the point: "Your example has always helped me understand more clearly how to be a college president."[33]

30 LeClerc interview.

31 E-mail, Brian Rosenberg to William G. Bowen, Sept. 15, 2016, Bowen Ithaka.

32 E-mail, Levin to Bowen, Sept. 15, 2016. Also see e-mail, William "Brit" Kirwan, chancellor of the University System of Maryland, to William G. Bowen, Sept. 13, 2016, Bowen Ithaka: "You are my academic hero and role model."

33 Derek Bok to William G. Bowen, Sept. 16, 2016, Bowen Ithaka.

17

The Last Decade

"As Many Good Days as Can Be Managed"

After nearly four decades in charge at major institutions (including the five years as provost at Princeton), Bowen faced a stark life change. He was accustomed to running things, accustomed to doing truly important work with great success—and to being seen as doing really important work. Now there was no institution to run, and it was more difficult to figure out how to have an impact comparable to what he was accustomed to. He had wielded an immense amount of power for such a long time, so he had never had to confront these issues before. But now he no longer had the platform, the infrastructure, that he was used to, and it was challenging, sometimes frustrating, to figure out how to situate himself, to decide what projects to embrace to make the kind of difference he had made for so many years.

Bowen came to structure his last decade around several pursuits: chairing the board at ITHAKA and trying as he could to influence its development and impact; publishing more books; writing long essays in popular educational publications; and making his voice heard in public settings. These were useful pursuits, though none of them rose to the level of accomplishment of his years at Princeton and Mellon. They were powered, though, by the same intense drive to accomplish, the same commitment to working hard for causes he believed in, that had animated Bowen's many efforts in previous decades. Moreover, they spoke to his deep need, as we have seen before, not only to work, but to have others know that he was working, fully immersed in the project at hand. To take one example, Bowen called his Princeton labor economist colleague Alan Krueger every year on Christmas Day with a work-related question. Krueger thought that Bowen did it because he wanted Krueger to know that he was working. There was "a little insecurity" in the overture, Krueger said; it was as if Bowen feared "being viewed as slacking off."[1] It was the same instinct that prompted Bowen to end long food- and wine-laden dinners with friends with the assertion that he was going home to go back to work. He did not always do that, Mary Ellen said, but he wanted people to think that he was going to do it.[2]

ITHAKA

ITHAKA afforded Bowen his one remaining formal role.[3] He had set it up that way when he was still at Mellon. With Kevin Guthrie in charge of the new organization as founding president, Bowen served as founding board chair, a role he filled until he was succeeded by Henry Bienen in 2008. What Bowen "wanted to do after retiring from Mellon." Guthrie reflected, "was to keep working. Not to earn a salary, but to research, analyze data, consider new technologies, and whatever other work that he thought would make a positive impact on higher education's ability to fulfill its mission. He wanted to keep having impact and he was eager to find a way to continue that work and have some support in doing so." That meant "a place to work and some staff assistance." Bowen drew no salary, but he kept an office at ITHAKA as long as it was in the building on Sixty-First Street; when ITHAKA moved downtown in 2014, he transferred his office to the ITHAKA space in Princeton Junction. ITHAKA hired research assistants for him, and Bowen's

1 Interview with Alan B. Krueger, Sept. 14, 2018, Princeton, NJ.
2 Interview with Mary Ellen Bowen, July 20, 2018, Princeton, NJ.
3 This discussion of ITHAKA is based on interviews with ITHAKA staff, board chairs, and board members, in particular: Kevin M. Guthrie, Nov. 11, 2018, Princeton, NJ, and, by telephone, Oct. 1, 2021; Henry S. Bienen, Nov. 5, 2018, Chicago; Judith R. Shapiro, Oct. 31, 2018, Rosemont, PA; Michael H. Schill, by telephone, Feb. 7, 2020; Johanna Brownell, Oct. 3, 2021, Princeton, NJ; Mamphela Ramphele, by telephone, Feb. 4, 2022; Paul A. Brest, by telephone, Feb. 4, 2022; W. Drake McFeely, by telephone, Feb. 15, 2022.

executive and research assistant Johanna Brownell was on the ITHAKA payroll.[4]

Bowen was accustomed to having such an immense amount of power, with the staff and infrastructure to accomplish his purposes. Now he still had power as a legacy of who he was and the connections he had forged. But he was no longer running a major institution, and it was not an uncomplicated adjustment. While Guthrie was clearly in charge, Bowen wanted to have a significant say in the governance and direction of ITHAKA. It had been many years since he had shared power, and he was not always good at camouflaging his frustration. ITHAKA had been his invention, after all, and he had definite ideas about what the organization ought to be doing, ideas he expressed with a forcefulness that sometimes made it challenging for Guthrie to exercise his authority to run the enterprise. Bowen and Guthrie were exceptionally close, and they saw eye to eye almost, but not quite all, the time. The ITHAKA board spent time in executive session making sure that Guthrie felt supported and was given sufficient space to do what he wanted to do, not just what Bowen wanted done.

The board was made up of people close to Bowen—they were his picks, and many of them, as Michael Schill (one of their number) put it, "could tell stories of how Bill Bowen influenced their lives." While they were all strong, opinionated, experienced individuals, many of them also owed some part of their career to Bowen, and they had outsize respect for him. That resulted in unusual deference, in a disinclination to challenge him. It was often the case in meetings for them to wait, before they spoke, to hear what Bowen had to say.[5] As had been the case at Princeton and Mellon, the board generally did Bowen's bidding. Paul Brest, the Stanford law dean then chairing the Hewlett Foundation, who was vice chair of the ITHAKA board during Bowen's tenure as chair, said that there were no real controversies; Bowen "never doubted that you were in agreement with him," and he would "have his

---

4 E-mail, Kevin Guthrie to Nancy Weiss Malkiel, Feb. 8, 2022.
5 Schill interview.

ducks lined up if there were any issues."[6] Drake McFeely, president at that time of the publisher W. W. Norton, said of board deliberations, "You came out where Bill hoped you would come out, but you didn't feel manipulated."[7]

ITHAKA focused initially on three projects of its own devising. The first, Aluka, involved the creation of an electronic repository of primary source materials for Africa, collected, digitized, and disseminated online, in three areas: Struggles for Freedom in Southern Africa, African Plants, and Cultural Heritage Sites and Landscapes.[8] The second project, Portico, involved the preservation and maintenance of an archive of electronic journals, providing archiving services to nonprofit and commercial publishers, and enabling libraries to save on costs through electronic-only subscriptions.[9] In the third project, ITHAKA incubated the National Institute for Technology and Liberal Education, initially funded by Mellon, which focused on the uses of technology for teaching and learning at small liberal arts colleges, a venture eventually spun off under the aegis of another institution.[10] Reflecting on the importance of Aluka and Portico to the developing world, Mamphela Ramphele, an ITHAKA trustee who had been vice-chancellor of the University of Cape Town, said that by providing scholars with low-cost access to data and journals, ITHAKA connected them to what was going on in the academic world, enabled them to participate

6 Brest interview.

7 McFeely interview.

8 Ithaka trustees, Jan. 28, 2004, 3–4; June 9, 2004, 4–5; Oct. 19, 2004, 2–4; Feb. 15, 2005, I-4 to I-7; June 15, 2005, I-2 to I-4; Oct. 20, 2005, I-5 to I-6; Feb. 16, 2006, I-4 to I-6; June 14, 2006, I-2 to I-3; Oct. 3, 2006, I-5 to I-6; June 30, 2007, I-5 to I-7; Nov. 8, 2007, unpaginated; Feb. 13, 2008, I-5 to I-6; June 4, 2008, I-E-4 to I-E-5.

9 Ithaka trustees, Jan. 28, 2004, 4; June 9, 2004, 3–4; Oct. 19, 2004, 5–8; Feb. 15, 2005, I-7 to I-8; June 15, 2005, I-5 to I-7; Feb. 16, 2006, I-8 to I-9; June 14, 2006, I-4 to I-5; Oct. 3, 2006, I-6 to I-8; June 30, 2007, I-7 to I-8; Nov. 8, 2007, unpaginated; Feb. 13, 2008, I-6 to I-7; June 4, 2008, I-E-6 to I-E-8; Mar. 30, 2009, I-A-2 to I-A-3; Mar. 20, 2014, I-B-2 to I-B-3; June 19, 2014, I-B-2; Oct. 23, 2014, I-B-3 to I-B-4; Mar. 18, 2015, I-B-1 to I-B-3; June 17, 2015, I-B-2 to I-B-3; Mar. 23, 2016, I-B-4 to I-B-5.

10 Ithaka trustees, Nov. 4, 2003, 3; Jan. 28, 2004, 2–3; Oct. 19, 2004, 4–5; Feb. 15, 2005, I-8; June 15, 2005, I-4 to I-5; Oct. 20, 2005, I-6 to I-7; Feb. 16, 2006, I-6 to I-7; June 14, 2006, I-3 to I-4; Oct. 3, 2006, I-4 to I-5; June 30, 2007, I-2 to I-4; Nov. 8, 2007, unpaginated; June 4, 2008, I-E-5 to I-E-6; Mar. 30, 2009, I-A-2.

more fully in that world, and significantly improved the quality of academic discourse and scholarship in Africa—all told, "an absolute revolution."[11]

In addition to these three projects, ITHAKA began to fashion a role in research and strategic services—research on topics in higher education of concern to Bowen, Guthrie, and the board, as well as strategic services to other entities that would pay ITHAKA to undertake studies for them. After some fits and starts, these functions came together in a new unit, ITHAKA S & R (strategy and research), that would become a centerpiece of the organization's continuing work.

Bowen saw ITHAKA as a vehicle for exploring the potential of online learning, both to deliver high-quality education and, importantly, to reduce costs. Here was an opportunity to experiment with ways to make education more cost-effective, to tilt against the seemingly unshakeable hold of cost disease, and Bowen took the lead in devising and superintending projects that ITHAKA could undertake.[12] He was particularly impressed by a study of learning outcomes associated with a statistics course developed by Carnegie Mellon University with funding from the Hewlett Foundation. The course, part of Carnegie Mellon's Online Learning Initiative, was "taught in hybrid mode," with one face-to-face question-and-answer session a week.[13] It took "advantage of feedback mechanisms, online tutors, and constant interactions between the software system and user."[14] The fact that it did not "mimic what is done in the classroom" made it particularly attractive. It used "animations, interactive diagrams, virtual laboratories and simulations to create a rich learning environment that takes full advantage of the online medium. Courses contain 'cognitive tutors' which are embedded within the content of the course. These embedded assessments prompt students to answer practice questions and provide targeted

11 Ramphele interview.
12 Bienen interview; Guthrie interview.
13 William G. Bowen, with Kelly A. Lack, *Higher Education in the Digital Age* (Princeton, NJ: Princeton University Press, 2013), 48–49.
14 Ithaka trustees, Mar. 16, 2010, I-A-6.

feedback based on the answers the students give—all at frequent intervals."[15]

Bowen asked if the board "would be comfortable with ITHAKA pressing ahead with a one year research project to explore proof of concept for Carnegie Mellon's online learning resource." It was agreed that Strategy & Research would work with Bowen and a group of campuses (in the end, they partnered with the State University of New York and the University System of Maryland) to conduct the research and would then draft a paper laying out the findings.[16] The "basic concept," Bowen said, was "to explore . . . whether effective stand-alone online courses in basic subjects could be used to reduce substantially the resource costs of teaching gateway courses at large public universities in fields such as math, science, and languages." It was "also conceivable," he said, "that sophisticated online teaching might reduce drop-outs, shorten time-to-degree, and reduce disparities in outcomes related to race and SES [socioeconomic status]."[17] Bowen's hope: Online learning, as undertaken at Carnegie Mellon, would give public universities "a way to lower costs, raise productivity, and improve learning outcomes."[18] Teaching online, Bowen hypothesized, would "reduce substantially the resource costs of teaching basic introductory courses," thus saving the institutions money. As well, reducing failure rates in "gateway 'killer courses' such as math [and] statistics" offered the promise of "rais[ing] completion rates and reduc[ing] time-to-degree." And, if Bowen was right that online teaching might work better with "groups subject to stereotype threat," the experiment also offered hope of "reduc[ing] disparities in outcome related to race and socioeconomic status."[19]

15 William G. Bowen, "Online Learning in Public Universities," [revised Jan. 30, 2010], Bowen Ithaka.

16 Ithaka trustees, Mar. 16, 2010, I-A-6 (source of the quote) to I-A-7; June 9, 2010, I-A-3 to I-A-5; Oct. 13, 2010, I-A-3; June 16, 2011, I-A-6; William G. Bowen, Ithaka / "Public University Online Learning Project: Interim Update on Where We Stand," Mar. 18, 2010, Bowen Ithaka.

17 Bowen, "Online Learning in Public Universities."

18 "A Research Project to Test New Online Learning Techniques," [Mar. 10, 2010], Bowen Ithaka.

19 William G. Bowen, "Agenda Topics for Possible Meeting on the Uses of Online Learning Initiatives in Public Universities," [Jan. 19, 24, 2010], Bowen Ithaka.

Bowen wrote about the study in his book *Higher Education in the Digital Age*: It "used a randomized trials approach, involving more than six hundred participants across six public university campuses, to compare the learning outcomes of students who took a hybrid-online version [of the statistics course] . . . with the outcomes of students who took face-to-face counterpart courses." The result? "*[N]o statistically significant differences in standard measures of learning outcomes*," a finding "*consistent not only across campuses but also across subgroups of what was a very diverse student population*."[20] That meant that there was potential for the gains Bowen was looking for: enhancing learning outcomes and containing costs.

The Carnegie Mellon study led to a second ITHAKA project that Bowen initiated, this time involving the teaching of introductory mathematics. Bowen's hypothesis was that "a robust, easy to use, and affordable adaptive learning platform [could] reduce costs and improve learning outcomes." ITHAKA mobilized a high-powered team to develop the project: Richard R. Spies, previously a senior administrator at Princeton and later at Brown, took the lead administratively, and the retiring chancellor of the University System of Maryland, William E. "Brit" Kirwan, himself a mathematician, signed on as an enthusiastic partner.[21] Lisa Krueger, a senior research analyst in the ITHAKA office who had been a high school mathematics teacher in Princeton, served as the mathematician on staff, taking responsibility for significant hands-on work in developing the project.

Bowen pushed the project aggressively. The work began in earnest in the last months of 2014. He conceptualized the effort as "a grand experiment" to "test whether technology can enhance educational outcomes *and* control costs." He had in mind "an avowedly

---

20 Bowen, with Lack, *Higher Education in the Digital Age*, 48–49. See also William G. Bowen, Matthew M. Chingos, Kelly A. Lack, and Thomas I. Nygren, *Interactive Learning Online at Public Universities: Evidence from Randomized Trials* (May 2012), as cited in Derek Bok, *Higher Education in America* (Princeton, NJ: Princeton University Press, 2013), 429n38.

21 Ithaka trustees, Mar. 18, 2015, I-B-3 to I-B-4; June 17, 2015, I-B-3; Oct. 21, 2015, I-B-2 (source of the quote) to I-B-3; Mar. 23, 2016, I-B-6; June 15, 2016, 3; Bienen interview.

audacious project intended to attack directly the most serious unsolved problem in American higher education—namely, how to enhance specific educational outcomes (raise completion rates, reduce time-to-degree, and reduce disparities in outcomes by socioeconomic status) without commensurate increases in cost."[22] This was classic Bowen. The decision to focus initially on introductory (foundational) mathematics reflected the fact that those courses most often tripped up beginning students and kept them from completing college degrees.[23]

The idea was to reengineer an introductory math course, taking full advantage of technology, adaptive learning, flipped classrooms (lectures delivered online, class time devoted to problem solving and interaction between students and instructor)—every innovation already being tried in educational experiments around the country, but developed very carefully to meet the objectives of the project. There was much work to be done, including identifying funders; finding a vendor capable of providing a platform that could be customized for the project; finding a university system to embrace the effort; identifying a college or university where the course could be tested; and developing a rigorous plan of evaluation. Those efforts occupied Bowen, Spies, Krueger, Kirwan, and others for the rest of Bowen's life.

Bowen pushed the work as actively as he could, given his deteriorating health. Always he reminded his colleagues that they had a two-part objective: improving education and containing costs. For the near term, he encouraged a "laser-like" focus on a single course and the development of a platform that, "with the right math/stats content embedded in it, can produce better learning outcomes for

22 Kevin M. Guthrie, William G. Bowen, and Richard R. Spies, "Thoughts on a Grand Experiment: Let's Test Whether Technology Can Enhance Educational Outcomes *and* Control Costs," Nov. 14, 2014, Bowen Ithaka. See also Martin Kurzweil and Richard Spies, "Proposal to Plan an Experiment in Technology-Enhanced Instruction in Mathematics—as a Start at Something Bigger," Mar. 12, 2015, Bowen Ithaka.

23 William G. Bowen addition to "Summary Description of Proposed Math Project," draft, Aug. 2015; e-mail, Bowen to Kevin Guthrie, Apr. 5, 2015; "Notes on Meeting Today [April 16, 2015] with Phillip Griffiths and Brit Kirwan," Bowen to Griffiths, Kirwan, et al., all in Bowen Ithaka; telephone interview with William E. "Brit" Kirwan, Mar. 9, 2022.

students of all kinds without . . . increases in cost." The course would be introductory statistics. It would need to be tested rigorously "to accumulate real evidence as to effectiveness." If it all worked, then, and only then, they would "really have something to market to both funders and other institutions."[24] The grand experiment might be realized later.

In the months before Bowen's death in October 2016, Acrobatiq was selected as the platform, and the University of Maryland and Montgomery College (Maryland's premier community college, with branches around the state) as institutional partners to design the statistics course and serve as institutional test beds for its delivery. No funders were particularly interested in cost control, so the focus of the effort shifted to the improvement of student learning outcomes; cost containment would be deferred to a later stage.[25]

Funded by the Bill & Melinda Gates Foundation, the project was implemented on multiple campuses in a pilot in 2017–19.[26] The results were inconclusive at best. The adaptive learning platform proved to have significantly less sophistication and capability than advertised. And there were important differences in what faculty could deliver at the two-year and the four-year institutions. At the community colleges, with a revolving cast of instructors who had little opportunity for training and limited commitment to the project, there was little or no impact on student learning. At the universities, with permanent faculty members embedded in their institutions, there was more of an impact, and the courses were still being taught well beyond the pilot. But overall, there were no significant differences in student learning outcomes "between the test group and the control group." And there the effort rested. Without Bowen to drive and focus the project, there was neither appetite nor support for further

24 E-mail, William G. Bowen to Richard Spies, Aug. 3, 2015, Bowen Ithaka.
25 "Status Report on the Math Project for the [Ithaka] Board Package," draft, Mar. 12, 2016, Bowen Ithaka; telephone interview with Richard R. Spies, Mar. 2, 2022.
26 [Richard R. Spies,] "Math Project, Project Work Plan—January 2017 through June 2019," draft, Nov. 15, 2016, Bowen Ithaka.

investigation.[27] Given the objectives Bowen started with, it would be hard not to count the project a failure.

Lessons Learned, Higher Education in the Digital Age, Locus of Authority

The first two Bowen books published after he left Mellon grew out of work that had already been done or was well under way before his departure. In 2008 came *The Board Book: An Insider's Guide for Directors and Trustees*, the revision of *Inside the Board Room*. And in 2009, as we have seen, came Bowen's book with Michael McPherson and Matthew Chingos, *Crossing the Finish Line*.

Bowen kept publishing books until the year he died, but none of them had anything like the impact of *The Shape of the River*, the two books on athletics, *Equity and Excellence*, or *Crossing the Finish Line*. The imperative to write was powerful, probably irresistible, and he had an enthusiastic publisher in Princeton University Press. Bowen's first "new" book following his retirement from Mellon was *Lessons Learned: Reflections of a University President*, published in 2010. It was short—just shy of 150 pages—and eminently readable. The book was intended for presidents, senior academic officers, and trustees of colleges and universities, as well as readers more broadly who were interested in higher education.

Bowen had never intended to write a memoir, but colleagues and friends had long been urging him to write about what he had learned about university leadership. "I'd been pressured for a long time to write something like this," he said, "and I never thought that I was quite ready to do it. But finally I decided that I should answer a recurring question, namely, 'What, if anything, did I learn in all those years I was in and around presidents' offices.'"[28] What

27 Jenna Joo and Richard R. Spies, "Aligning Many Campuses and Instructors around a Common Adaptive Learning Courseware in Introductory Statistics: Lessons from a Multi-year Pilot in Maryland," Ithaka S & R Research Report, Nov. 7, 2019, https://sr.ithaka.org/publications/adaptive-learning-courseware-introductory-statistics; Spies interview; Kirwan interview. The quote is from e-mail, Richard R. Spies to Nancy Weiss Malkiel, Mar. 1, 2022. I am indebted to Catharine Bond Hill for the research report.

28 Bowen quoted in Ruth Stevens, "Bowen's Advice to Leaders: Plan Well, Then Act Quickly," Princeton University news release, Feb. 21, 2011, https://www.princeton.edu

he said he learned sounds, in retrospect, to be less than profound, possibly even banal. "The most important lesson is to listen carefully, find the facts and then decide," Bowen told an interviewer. "Formulate the question correctly. Assemble the evidence you need to make an informed choice, and then make the choice. But do those things in that order." "There are times when it may not be obvious what to do, but you need to do something," he continued. "You can see if it works. If it doesn't, you can do something else. But just equivocating is not terribly helpful."[29]

Bowen recounted his failures as well as his successes—as he put it, "some of the most compelling lessons I learned grew out of mistakes that I made."[30] Princeton's embrace of coeducation, he said, was a good example of success, where "plan carefully, then execute rapidly" worked well. The decade-long run-up to the establishment of molecular biology, on the other hand, was a big mistake. "We took much, much too long," he told an interviewer. "I made the mistake of thinking it was possible to do such a profound thing incrementally. It wasn't. We first had to make a sufficiently big bet that it had a chance to succeed."[31]

For college and university presidents just starting out on administrative careers, the book offered invaluable guidance in laying out Bowen's approach to the challenges he had faced as a president. Michael Schill, president of the University of Oregon and then of Northwestern, said that *Lessons Learned* was "the best of the genre," with the specific examples Bowen gave and the account of how he dealt with them "so helpful" in showing a university president how to handle really tough issues.[32]

Bowen's next book, *Higher Education in the Digital Age*, published in 2013, grew out of the Tanner lectures that he gave at Stanford University in October 2012.[33] The president of Stanford,

/news/2011/02/21/bowens-advice-leaders-plan-well-then-act-quickly, accessed Oct. 15, 2021.

29 Ibid.
30 William G. Bowen, *Lessons Learned: Reflections of a University President* (Princeton, NJ: Princeton University Press, 2011), 2.
31 Bowen quoted in Stevens, "Bowen's Advice to Leaders."
32 Schill interview.
33 Bowen, with Lack, *Higher Education in the Digital Age*.

John Hennessy, knew Bowen's early work on cost disease, and he shared with Bowen a strong concern about rising college costs and an interest in exploring uses of technology to "bend the cost curve." The point was to reduce institutional costs and improve student learning outcomes, including completion rates and time to degree. Hennessy and Bowen were both data people, and they thought it was worth undertaking educational experiments the results of which could be analyzed rigorously. Bowen both "provoked a lot of experiments" through his own work and "contributed to the conversation" about such online educational initiatives as edX and Coursera. And the fact that he championed experiments, Hennessy said, "reduced people's hesitancy about proceeding," given "who he was and how influential he was."[34]

The common ground Hennessy shared with Bowen led naturally to the invitation to deliver the Tanner lectures, talks that, together with the formal commentaries on those addresses that Hennessey organized at Stanford, formed the basis for *Higher Education in the Digital Age*. Bowen addressed two central topics: costs and productivity in higher education. His main themes were, first, how judicious expansion of online learning might contribute to a solution to the problem of cost disease—that is, how it might help to rein in the rising costs of college education; and second, how "raising completion rates and lowering time-to-degree"— that is, "improving student learning outcomes"—would enhance productivity.[35]

Bowen had earlier been a skeptic about technology contributing to a reduction in costs, a view he had elaborated in 2000 in his Romanes lecture at the University of Oxford, "At a Slight Angle to the Universe: The University in a Digitized, Commercialized Age."[36] But as he explained at Stanford, he had come to change his mind. He was persuaded, in part, by the success of the statistics course at Carnegie Mellon. But as useful as the experiment was in terms of

34 Telephone interview with John L. Hennessy, Oct. 5, 2021; Bowen, with Lack, *Higher Education in the Digital Age*, xi.

35 Bowen, with Lack, *Higher Education in the Digital Age*, 7–9.

36 Republished in Kevin M. Guthrie, ed., *Ever the Leader: Selected Writings, 1995–2016, William G. Bowen* (Princeton, NJ: Princeton University Press, 2018), 3–29.

documenting learning outcomes, it provided little evidence with respect to cost containment.

All told, the early returns from online learning were not as promising as Bowen had hoped. He put online learning "out there almost as a hypothesis," Michael Schill said, and the very fact that he did that "gave it instant credibility." Maybe online learning would "bend the cost curve." Maybe it would "help universities deliver high-quality, affordable education." As the results started coming in, however, it became clear that it was "not a solution"—lower-income, less-well-prepared students "did less well with online education."[37] And Bowen's hope that with online learning, "it might be possible to save significant amounts of resources while actually improving outcomes" remained just that, a hope, still not realized at the time of his death.[38]

Higher Education in the Digital Age "changed the conversation" about online education, the labor economist Rebecca M. Blank said. Bowen "brought a dose of reality" into a conversation that "went from being uninformed euphoria to being a serious academic conversation about what online learning is good for."[39] Daniel Greenstein, the director of the Postsecondary Success division at the Bill & Melinda Gates Foundation, told Bowen, "Your work on online learning has helped give credibility (and evidence) to an innovation that shows enormous promise (perhaps uniquely amongst all of the ones I am aware of) for improving learning outcomes AND bending the cost curve in HE [higher education]."[40]

Bowen's penultimate book, *Locus of Authority: The Evolution of Roles in the Governance of Higher Education*, published in 2015, had a narrower purpose, and, likely, a narrower audience.[41] It focused on faculty governance, a theme Bowen had raised briefly in *Higher Education in the Digital Age*. Bowen wrote the book with

37 Schill interview
38 William G. Bowen, Apr. 2010 typescript of foreword to Taylor Walsh, *Unlocking the Gates: How and Why Leading Universities Are Opening Up Access to Their Courses* (Princeton, NJ: Princeton University Press, 2011), Bowen Ithaka.
39 Telephone interview with Rebecca M. Blank, Aug. 29, 2019.
40 E-mail, Daniel Greenstein to William G. Bowen, Sept. 19, 2016, Bowen Ithaka.
41 (New York: ITHAKA; Princeton, NJ: Princeton University Press, 2015).

Eugene N. Tobin, who had coauthored the more consequential *Equity and Excellence* in 2006. Bowen had a gift, Tobin said, for "seeing the question that was worth asking, that was hiding in plain sight."[42] Here the question was how century-old governance structures might be impeding the effective functioning of America's colleges and universities in the twenty-first century. Bowen believed that the historic system of governance, which depended so much on independent faculty authority, made it much more difficult for those institutions to respond to the pressing issues of the time, from the enrollment of low-income, first-generation college students, to time-to-degree and college completion, to the containment of spiraling costs of higher education. In the face of "new demands for more cost-effective student learning," Bowen wanted to establish a new system of "shared governance" to address "decisions about deployment of technology, about new approaches to teaching at least some kinds of content, and about the reallocation of teaching resources."[43] With a "more effective, nimble and collaborative approach to institutional decision-making," colleges and universities, he thought, would have their best shot at "adapt[ing] to a changing landscape."[44]

Finding His Place in a World He No Longer Dominated

Bowen's later years brought a raft of health challenges. The most straightforward was knee replacement surgery at the Hospital for Special Surgery in New York in January 2009. Then there were two trip-and-falls in 2011, both resulting in serious injuries. The first, in Princeton in January, came when Bowen got up during the night to go to the bathroom and tripped, badly fracturing his ankle and tearing his deltoid ligament, which resulted in surgery at the Hospital

---

42 Eugene N. Tobin remarks, Mellon Foundation memorial event, Lotus Club, New York City, Mar. 9, 2017, courtesy of Eugene N. Tobin.

43 Bowen and Tobin, *Locus of Authority*, 4, 175, 184, 208, 210.

44 Colleen Flaherty, "'Locus of Authority,'" *Inside Higher Ed*, Jan. 5, 2015 ("effective, nimble"), https://www.insidehighered.com/news/2015/01/05/new-book-argues-more-effective-collaborative-methods-shared-governance, accessed Oct. 15, 2021; Tobin remarks, Mellon Foundation memorial event.

for Special Surgery and weeks of recuperation. The second came when Bowen fell off the roof porch at the house in Avalon in July. The roof—the perch, they called it—had been designed as a kind of open-air porch in the sky, affording a wonderful view of the ocean. The Bowens and their guests often gathered there after dinner, drinking wine and enjoying the ocean and the evening sky. The roof was accessed by a steep outdoor staircase with narrow steps, really more like a ladder. One night, Bowen tripped while descending the staircase. With a broken clavicle, broken ribs, and a concussion, he had to be airlifted to the intensive care unit at a hospital in Atlantic City. He came home, finally, after rehab at the St. Lawrence Rehabilitation Center in Lawrenceville.

The most frightening of these many medical events was a fierce infection in Bowen's back in the spring of 2013. Possibly originating from a cut in his foot, the infection could not be controlled at the hospital in Princeton, which led to Bowen being transferred to the Hospital for Special Surgery. After many weeks of treatment there, including having his replaced knee "washed out" to make sure that the infection had not traveled there, Bowen again did a stint at St. Lawrence and finally returned home to Princeton, still under heavy medication.[45]

And there were other challenges, related not to health but to finding his place in a world he no longer dominated. It was hard not to be in charge, increasingly so. "If you are used to being in charge and running things and derive a sense of self from being recognized as such," his friend Mike Blumenthal reflected, "when you're no longer in that position," it "requires an adjustment. For some people it's a jarring experience." Bowen's friends noted that he was consuming more alcohol. He gained a lot of weight. Never exactly a sharp dresser, he began to look sloppier, less put together. The tight discipline that had characterized his life gave way. He "let himself

45 On the various medical issues, see e-mails from Johanna Brownell to a group of Bowen's friends—Jan. 21, 2009, July 15, 25, 2011, May 10, 15, July 25, 2013, and an e-mail from Bowen to a group of friends, Jan. 5, 2011, all in Bowen Ithaka, as well as e-mail, Mary Ellen Bowen to Nancy Weiss Malkiel, May 15, 2013; e-mail, William G. Bowen to Malkiel, Nov. 4, 2014; e-mail, Brownell to Malkiel, Jan. 17, 2022; and e-mail, David Bowen to Malkiel, Feb. 5, 2022.

go," Blumenthal said, and "suddenly began to age."[46] On at least one occasion, Bowen spoke plaintively to the dilemma of relevance. At a seventieth birthday celebration for his friends Joan Girgus and Alan Chimacoff in 2012, Bowen—not especially mobile—and Mary Ellen were seated in a living room full of people. At one point in the evening, another friend overheard him say to Mary Ellen, "I don't understand, nobody's coming to talk to me."[47]

Fewer commitments, however, meant more time for some other things. There were visits from grandchildren—from Scarsdale, David's three daughters, Sarah, Katie, and Ellie; from Antwerp, Karen's two sons, Hans and Adriaan. Hans came to Princeton to explore opportunities for further schooling after high school, and he matriculated at the Lawrenceville School for a postgraduate year just as it became clear that his grandfather was terminally ill. Family visits to Princeton invariably included dinner in the kitchen at the Homestead Inn. As it turned out, both Sarah and Hans would later graduate from Princeton.

There was more time for visits to Avalon with friends and family. The Bowens traveled from Princeton to Avalon, as always, by car, with Mary Ellen driving so that Bowen could use the time to work. The Bowens' guests understood that Avalon meant defined activities at specified times—breakfast together, whether on the pier or with breakfast sandwiches Bowen would bring back to the house when he went to get the newspapers; time for work for Bowen and time on their own for guests; time for lunch and the beach, perhaps with Bowen and Mary Ellen; more time for work; dinner at home with Bowen barbecuing at the grill or boiling lobster, or dinner out at informal Italian or seafood restaurants in Avalon or at the more elegant 410 Bank Street in Cape May, where the Bowens were as much family to the owners as was true at the Homestead Inn. There was also time for organized house projects—clearing brush, planting, repairing some part of the now-two adjacent houses—projects that engaged guests as well as Bowen. If the visit

46 Interview with W. Michael Blumenthal, July 17, 2018, Princeton, NJ.
47 Interview with Paolo Cucchi, Aug. 22, 2018, Princeton, NJ.

to Avalon happened to coincide with a major sporting event, like Wimbledon, television-watching would be part of the routine. And there was always time for wine on the roof, with relaxed conversation and enjoyment of the view. There, and over meals, Bowen would "draw people out" and "drive and shape the conversation." He found "comfort and enjoyment in people he had invited," reflected Legrome Davis, Princeton '73, US District Court Judge for the Eastern District of Pennsylvania, who was a frequent visitor. And for his guests, there was pleasure at the opportunity "to be with real, genuine, good people, people committed to social ideas that matter, people who shared the same life values."[48]

As well, there were special celebrations. To take just two examples, a weekend extravaganza for the Bowens' fiftieth wedding anniversary in August 2006 brought dozens of friends and family members to Avalon for a pig roast at the Bowens' and a dinner at 410 Bank Street, among other activities. An eightieth birthday celebration in Avalon for Jerome and Legrome Davis's father in February 2009 brought all of his living siblings from New York and Pittsburgh; Legrome and his wife, Sue, from Philadelphia; and Jerome and his daughter, Kamille, from New York City for what their father insisted until the day he died was "the 'best birthday ever.'"[49]

There was time, too, for more personal connections with people with whom Bowen had previously had more limited opportunities to interact. Beatrijs Stikkers, who lived with the Bowens in Lowrie House during her years as a graduate student in the Woodrow Wilson School, was engaged in foundation work in the Netherlands. While Bowen was still at Mellon, she would visit the foundation annually and have dinner with him and Mary Ellen in New York. Now it was possible to spend more time with him in Princeton. He was "freer," she said, "more mellow, less tightly scheduled"—a "different Bill Bowen" than the one she had always known. As

48 Interview with Legrome Davis, Sept. 17, 2019, Princeton, NJ. See also telephone interview with Michael S. McPherson, Aug. 20, 2020; interview with Taylor Reveley, Sept. 4, 2018, Princeton, NJ.
49 E-mail, Jerome Davis to Nancy W. Malkiel, Mar. 7, 2022.

the pressure of his work diminished, there was "more space for his desire to connect personally." As always, he wanted to help with her foundation work, to connect her to people who might be useful to her, to assist her in thinking carefully about her priorities and taking the next step in her career.[50]

And there was also time for Bowen's unorthodox sense of humor and appreciation of whimsy (his friend and colleague Joan Girgus called it his "crazy streak")—telling stories, swapping jokes and *New Yorker* cartoons with good friends, sending specially selected Christmas presents to the dogs of some of his friends, naming each of the stuffed animals and fabric creations that populated the downstairs rooms of the houses in Princeton and in Avalon.[51]

In 2014, Bowen learned that he had colon cancer that had spread, undetected, through his abdomen. It came as a surprise, both to Bowen and to his physician in Princeton, Fong Wei. Bowen had no family history of colon cancer, nor a personal history of frequent polyps; with no apparent need for unusual surveillance, he had followed the normal protocol for periodic colonoscopies. But now there was a tumor, fast-growing and highly aggressive.[52] Bowen's longtime friend Kenneth Offit, a medical oncologist at Memorial Sloan-Kettering Cancer Center in New York City, connected Bowen to his colleague Leonard Saltz, a medical oncologist who specialized in colorectal cancer. Saltz determined that the cancer was inoperable, but devised infusions of chemotherapy, given every two weeks, to keep the disease at bay. The principal goal was to prevent the tumors from growing or spreading, and thus keep Bowen comfortable and extend his life as much as possible. A related objective—to shrink the tumors to make them operable—turned out to be unachievable.[53]

50 Telephone interview with Beatrijs Stikkers-Muller, Dec. 12, 2019.

51 Interview with Joan S. Girgus, Sept. 12, 2018, Princeton, NJ; Legrome Davis interview; telephone interview with Daniel H. Weiss, Sept. 17, 2020; interview with Lois Shepetin, Feb. 8, 2022, West Palm Beach, FL.

52 Interview with Fong Wei, May 20, 2019, Princeton, NJ.

53 Zoom interview with Kenneth Offit, June 2, 2021; e-mail, William G. Bowen to Nancy Weiss Malkiel et al., Nov. 11, 2014.

Haverford, Sweet Briar, Cooper Union, Lesson Plan

Sick as he was in those years, Bowen rallied to take on challenges that he could just as easily have avoided. It was part and parcel of what his friend Paul Benacerraf characterized as "need[ing] always to have something he felt was constructive to do"—without that, Benacerraf observed, "he would have felt diminished"—"it was as if he thought he would disappear" if he did not keep writing and speaking.[54]

The Haverford College commencement in 2014 offers a case in point. Bowen was slated to receive an honorary degree. The commencement speaker, another honorand, was to be Robert Birgenau, a physicist who had, until 2013, been chancellor of the University of California at Berkeley. Birgenau was well known for his support for undocumented and minority students, and he was going to speak about that in his address. He stood for things that would normally have won him plaudits from Haverford students, including support for the rights of gays and lesbians to marry; more funding for social services in California, including higher education; and the reinstitution of affirmative action in California's public colleges and universities. But some Haverford students took umbrage at the use of force by Berkeley campus police officers during some protests on campus in 2011, and they set nine conditions for Birgenau's appearance at Haverford, including apologizing publicly for police conduct at Berkeley, supporting reparations for victims, and writing a letter to Haverford students about his position on the events at issue and what he had learned from them. Deeply upset at the students' attack, Birgenau withdrew from delivering the commencement address.[55] Bowen, already scheduled to speak briefly as an

54 Interview with Paul Benacerraf, July 17, 2018, Princeton, NJ.
55 Susan Snyder "Haverford Mired in Its Own Commencement Speaker Controversy," *Philadelphia Inquirer*, May 7, 2014, https://www.inquirer.com/philly/education/20140508 _Haverford_mired_in_its_own_commencement_speaker controversy.html#AFjxWld 8Vv4wtS8x.01, accessed Oct. 16, 2021; Scott Jaschik, "Debate at Haverford over Speech by Ex-chancellor of Berkeley," *Inside Higher Ed*, May 9, 2014, https://www.insiderhighered .com/quicktakes/2014/05/09/debate-haverford-over-speech-ex-chancellor-berkeley#sthash .SaAhSIOG.dpbs, accessed Oct. 16, 2021; Scott Jaschik, "Commencement Speaker Withdraws at Haverford," *Inside Higher Ed*, May 14, 2014, https://www.insidehighered

honorand, asked the president of the college, Daniel H. Weiss, to allow him some extra speaking time to give additional remarks in Birgenau's stead. Bowen roundly criticized the students for their actions in blocking Birgenau's appearance. Taking issue with one protestor's characterization of Birgenau's withdrawal as "a 'small victory' for the college," Bowen said, "It represents nothing of the kind. I regard this outcome as a *defeat*, pure and simple, for Haverford—no victory for anyone who believes, as I think most of us do, in both openness to many points of view and mutual respect." The protestors, Bowen said, "should have encouraged [Birgenau] to come and engage in a genuine discussion, not to come, tail between his legs, to respond to an indictment that a self-chosen jury had reached without hearing counter-arguments." "It is my hope," Bowen concluded, "that this regrettable set of events will prove . . . to be a true 'learning moment,' and that Haverford will go forward . . . as a great liberal arts college committed, as always, to both the principle of non-violent protest and to the enduring values of openness and respect for diverse views."[56]

Another way in which Bowen engaged during those years was to publish long essays in the popular educational press, sometimes to raise key themes from his latest book, sometimes to address some of the widely reported, highly controversial educational issues of the day. Writing a long essay in the *Chronicle of Higher Education* to draw attention to the themes of the latest book was something Bowen had been doing for years.[57] Now there were new

.com/quicktakes/2014/05/14/commencement-speaker-withdraws-haverford#sthash
.iatSE3sF.dpbs, accessed Oct. 16, 2021; Doug Lederman, "The Substitutes Speak Out," *Inside Higher Ed*, May 19, 2014, https://www.insidehighered.com/news/2014/05/19/substitute-commencement-speakers-say-everyone-lose-out-protests, accessed Oct. 16, 2021.

56 Bowen quoted in Lederman, "The Substitutes Speak Out." For the full text of Bowen's remarks, see "Enduring Values: Openness and Mutual Respect," May 18, 2014, in Guthrie, ed., *Ever the Leader*, 40–43.

57 See, for example, James L. Shulman and William G. Bowen, "How the Playing Field Is Encroaching on the Admissions Office," *Chronicle of Higher Education*, Jan. 26, 2001, https://www.chronicle.com/article/how-the-playing-field-is-encroaching-on-the-admissions-office, accessed Aug. 25, 2020; William G. Bowen and Sarah A. Levin, "Revisiting 'The Game of Life': Athletics at Elite Colleges," *Chronicle of Higher Education*, Sept. 19, 2003, https://www.chronicle.com/article/revisiting-the-game-of-life-athletics-at-elite-colleges, accessed Aug. 25, 2020.

essays supporting *The Board Book, Crossing the Finish Line, Lessons Learned, Higher Education in the Digital Age*, and *Locus of Authority*.[58]

Writing about current educational controversies was also something Bowen had been doing for many years. His earlier essay with Neil Rudenstine on the uses of race in college and university admissions, published in 2003 as the Supreme Court prepared to hear oral arguments in *Gratz* and *Grutter*, is a case in point.[59] Now Bowen partnered with Lawrence Bacow, serving as a senior adviser at ITHAKA between his presidencies of Tufts and Harvard, to write about the controversies involving Sweet Briar College, a women's college in the foothills of the Blue Ridge Mountains in Sweet Briar, Virginia, and Cooper Union for the Advancement of Science and Art in New York City, an institution focusing on programs of instruction in art, architecture, and engineering. At Sweet Briar the issue was the uproar that ensued after the board, together with an acting president, took the decision in March 2015 to close the college as a consequence of low and declining enrollment, inadequate tuition revenue, a fast-declining endowment, and unpromising prospects for fund-raising, a decision countered when outraged alumnae, staff, and students protested; a "Saving Sweet Briar" group was formed; and the state attorney general brokered a settlement to

58 William G. Bowen, "The Successful Succession," *Chronicle of Higher Education*, Mar. 28, 2008, https://www.chronicle.com/article/the-sucessful-succession, accessed Aug. 25, 2020; William G. Bowen, Matthew M. Chingos, and Michael S. McPherson, "Helping Students Finish the 4-Year Run," *Chronicle of Higher Education*, Sept. 8, 2009, https://www.chronicle.com/article/helping-students-finish-the-4-year-run, accessed Aug. 25, 2020; William G. Bowen, "To Craft Higher-Education Policy, Start by Finding the Facts," *Chronicle of Higher Education*, Jan. 16, 2011, https://www.chronicle.com/article/to-craft-higher-education-policy-start-by-finding-the-facts, accessed Aug. 25, 2020; William G. Bowen, "Walk Deliberately, Don't Run, toward Online Education," *Chronicle of Higher Education*, Mar. 25, 2013, https://www.chronicle.com/article/walk-deliberately-dont-run-toward-online-education, accessed Aug. 25, 2020; William G. Bowen and Eugene M. Tobin, "Toward a Shared Vision of Shared Governance," *Chronicle of Higher Education*, Jan. 5, 2015, https://www.chronicle.com/article/toward-a-shared-vision-of-shared-governance, accessed Aug. 25, 2020.
59 William G. Bowen and Neil L. Rudenstine, "Race-Sensitive Admissions: Back to Basics," *Chronicle of Higher Education*, Feb. 7, 2003, https://www.chronicle.com/article/race-sensitive-admissions-back-to-basics, accessed Aug. 25, 2020.

keep the college open, with new leadership and financial contributions from Saving Sweet Briar.

Cooper Union, operating throughout its history on the mandate of its founder not to charge tuition, was in an impossible situation financially. The institution was running major operating deficits and drawing down unrestricted assets to cover budgetary shortfalls. When the Cooper Union board announced in the spring of 2013 that it would begin to charge tuition, students, faculty, and alumni erupted in outrage at the departure from the institution's fundamental identity and commitments. Intra-board conflicts, litigation, the intervention of the state attorney general, and the firing of the president made it extremely difficult to stabilize the university.

Bacow and Bowen argued that Sweet Briar and Cooper Union were bellwethers of the significant challenges to financial viability that were going to force a number of colleges and universities to make "painful decisions" about their futures. They underscored the responsibility of boards to steer clear of internecine conflicts and political pressures in order to live up to their fiduciary responsibilities by making the hard choices necessary to shape the future of their institutions.[60]

Characteristically, amidst his health challenges, Bowen also had one more book that he wanted to write. *Lesson Plan: An Agenda for Change in Higher Education*, published a year after *Locus of Authority*, laid out his prescriptions for fixing what was wrong with higher education.[61] He wrote it with his longtime friend and colleague Michael S. McPherson, his senior coauthor on *Crossing the Finish Line*. Bowen felt that he was "running out of time," and he wanted a partner whom he could trust to speak for the book for the longer run. "The level of urgency" on the project was "higher

---

60 Lawrence S. Bacow and William G. Bowen, "The Painful Lessons of Sweet Briar and Cooper Union," *Chronicle of Higher Education*, Sept. 24, 2015, https://www.chronicle .com/article/the-painful-lessons-of-sweet-briar-and-cooper-union, accessed Aug. 25, 2020; Bacow and Bowen, "The Real Work of 'Saving' 2 Colleges Has Yet to Be Done," *Chronicle of Higher Education*, Sept. 8, 2015, https://www.chronicle.com/article/the-real-work-of -saving-2-colleges-has-yet-to-be-done, accessed Aug. 25, 2020. See also the longer essay, Bacow and Bowen, "Double Trouble: Sweet Briar College & Cooper Union," Sept. 2015, Ithaka S + R Issue Brief.

61 (Princeton, NJ: Princeton University Press, 2016).

than usual," McPherson said. Princeton University Press, in a herculean effort, produced the book by spring 2016, intent on getting it into print before Bowen's health deteriorated precipitously.[62]

Bowen and McPherson made their agenda known at the outset of the book: American higher education had "lost its premier place" worldwide in educational attainment. It "needs to do much better than it is doing at present in meeting pressing national needs, especially achieving higher levels of educational attainment at the undergraduate level and reducing what are now marked disparities in outcomes related to socioeconomic status." As well, there was an urgent need to control the costs of higher education without diminishing educational quality.[63]

As for attainment, the rates of college completion in the United States were "simply too low to ensure the success of this country in a rapidly evolving global economy, and too low to give many Americans the improved life chances that they deserve." And in terms of outcomes with respect to socioeconomic status, American higher education, "once seen as the engine of social mobility in a land of opportunity, now serves at times, however inadvertently, to perpetuate gaps in outcomes related to socioeconomic status."[64]

Bowen and McPherson offered various prescriptions for how to address these problems. College completion was more likely to be accomplished if students enrolled in four-year rather than two-year colleges, and in the most demanding, most selective institutions to which they could win admission. And it was more likely to happen if colleges and universities rethought the foundational courses— especially in mathematics—that too often tripped students up. There was promising evidence that "adaptive learning"—with an emphasis on judicious use of information technology—combined with face-to-face instruction, could help in the latter assignment. One of the ways to improve instruction was to recognize reality: A large share of teaching was now being done by non-tenure-track faculty, and professionalizing the teaching corps would both give

---

62 Telephone interview with Michael S. McPherson, Aug. 20, 2020.
63 Bowen and McPherson, *Lesson Plan*, vii.
64 Ibid., 21, vii.

them the status they deserved and position them to invest more successfully in effective instruction, especially of gateway courses. With respect to cost containment, Bowen and McPherson offered a number of suggestions: targeting federal and state funding more efficiently; allocating funds for financial aid on the basis of need, not merit; cutting out lower-ranked doctoral programs; reducing ever-growing institutional investments in big-time athletics. And they affirmed the importance of strong leadership to enable colleges and universities to do the jobs they needed to do.[65]

Reporting on the book, a writer for *Inside Higher Ed* underscored the authors' emphasis on achieving academic rigor and enhancing graduation rates, not on the many quick fixes being bandied about for the supposed crises in higher education.[66] One reviewer called the book "a concise, compelling, and, at times, courageous analysis of the ways in which institutions of higher education are failing to provide equal opportunity" and credited the authors with laying out "an ambitious . . . agenda" for reform.[67] Another called it "a short, yet disarmingly rich and precise, primer on higher-education policy and its compelling relevance for the future of our economy and democracy."[68] Michael Schill thought it was "the single best thing to read about the waterfront of higher education" and gave a copy to every member of his board at the University of Oregon.[69] That was the kind of attention Bowen had hoped for.

On April 7, 2016, Bowen gave the keynote address for a presidential symposium on the future of higher education, part of Rutgers University's 250th anniversary celebration. His topic was

65 Ibid., passim.

66 Scott Jaschik, "Authors Discuss New Book on Higher Education's Problems, Real and Imagined," *Inside Higher Ed*, Mar. 22, 2016, https://www.insidehighered.com/print/news/2016/03/22/authors-discuss-new-book-higher-educations-problems-real-and-imagined, accessed Oct. 17, 2021.

67 Glenn L. Altschuler, "What's Really Wrong with Higher Education and How to Fix It," *The Blog, HuffPost Contributor*, May 12, 2016, https://www.huffpost.com/entry/whats-really-wrong-with-h_b_9928380, accessed Oct. 17, 2021.

68 Clayton Spencer, "America's Higher-Education Agenda," *Harvard Magazine*, Sept.–Oct. 2016, https://www.harvardmagazine.com/print/53835?page=all, accessed Oct. 17, 2021.

69 Schill interview.

"Issues Facing Major Research Universities at a Time of Stress and Opportunity," the content drawn significantly from *Lesson Plan*. He spoke about presidential leadership; disparities in educational outcomes and financial aid policies; educational costs, teaching methods, and technology; creation of a professionalized teaching corps; shared governance—all classic Bowen. His overall theme: how public universities could best deliver on their promise. "What those of us in academia do really matters," he concluded. "We should be unabashedly proud of having chosen what is indeed a noble calling."[70] It was the last time he would appear at any public event.

Illness and Death

Bowen's cancer treatments continued for more than two years. For a time, the infusions worked. But by the late fall of 2015, the significant build-up of fluid in the peritoneum in Bowen's abdomen came to require periodic draining to keep him comfortable.[71] Most often the procedure—paracentesis—was done in a radiology facility. In the summer of 2016, a special shunt was installed to permit continuous draining of fluid from the peritoneum to the veins, but it did not work, and the draining still needed to be done by a physician, as it had been before.[72]

Bowen thought—hoped—that the draining could be continued for some time. But the repeated fluid build-up signaled a reality that he resisted acknowledging: the efficacy of the treatments was coming to an end. He maintained a resolutely positive stance: "We are pressing on!" he wrote to a friend in June and again in July; and, in August, "We press on."[73] In fact, however, his condition had worsened markedly.

70 "Issues Facing Major Research Universities at a Time of Stress and Opportunity," Guthrie, ed., *Ever the Leader*, 258–74. The quote is on 274.

71 See, for example, "Radiology Post Procedure Discharge Instructions," Aug. 17, 2016, following paracentesis (draining the abdomen of peritoneal fluid), Bowen personal.

72 E-mail, William G. Bowen to Nancy Weiss Malkiel, July 31, 2016; e-mails, Johanna Brownell to Malkiel, Aug. 22, 2016, Jan. 17, 2022.

73 E-mail, William G. Bowen to Nancy Weiss Malkiel, June 28, July 31, Aug. 24, 2016.

Late in the afternoon of September 13, 2016, Bowen sent an e-mail to a group of family and friends. He and Mary Ellen and their son, David, had met that morning with Dr. Saltz to review the latest test results. "We have known from the start of this saga," Bowen reported, "that at some point the news was almost sure to turn negative." That time had come. "Unfortunately," Bowen reported, "the tumors are growing and spreading." Saltz concluded, he said, "that while the chemo has done wonders for over two years, it is no longer working." It was time, Saltz believed, "to allow the disease to run its course," keeping Bowen "as comfortable as can be." "The goal," Bowen said, was "as many good days as can be managed and to finish a few key tasks." "I am ever so grateful for having been given so many good years and so many wonderful friends—as well of course as a superb wife and family. So, no regrets, and my thanks once again for your unremitting support."[74]

For the next five weeks, Bowen was at home, save for brief hospitalization to alleviate pain. He had hospice nurses and a live-in caregiver, Jade Robinson. There were modest tasks to finish, but he lacked the energy to do more. He spent as much time as he could with Mary Ellen—"she is my light," he told Robinson.[75]

Bowen engaged with friends and colleagues as he could—early on, some dinners at the Homestead, later, brief visits to 87 College Road West or phone calls and e-mail exchanges. People wanted to find a way to tell him what he had meant to them and to say goodbye. John Hennessy, the president of Stanford, wrote, in a representative message, "I cannot think of anyone in my memory that has had such a broad and deep impact on higher education." He added, "you have been an inspiration to me, giving me courage to try things and create change. You have been a boon to those who are wise enough to examine your many contributions."[76] Bowen's friend of more than a half century, Mike Blumenthal, who had been teaching at Princeton when Bowen arrived as a graduate student, and who later served on the Princeton board, wrote more personally:

74 E-mail, William G. Bowen to Dirk Imhof-Karen Bowen et al., Sept. 13, 2016.
75 Interview with Jade Robinson, Aug. 6, 2021, Princeton, NJ.
76 John Hennessy to William G. Bowen, Sept. 24, 2016, courtesy of John L. Hennessy.

"You are among those few I have encountered in my life that I have always truly admired. You have done so much that will leave a lasting mark and you have done it so well. That should give you well-deserved satisfaction. As for us, I am one of the many whose life you touched and enriched more than once. I will always be grateful to you for that, for your confidence in me and for your friendship." Bowen's response: "I have been blessed by both opportunities and friends beyond my imagining. You are of course right at the top of the list."[77] Taylor Reveley, who had shared so much with Bowen—family visits to Avalon, the Princeton board, the Mellon board, the Rockefeller Trust Committee, and more—wrote, "I can count on one hand the people who have meant the most to me, and you are there along with my parents and Helen [his wife]. It is wrenching to think of life without you."[78]

Bowen was matter-of-fact about the reality of his situation. "You play the hand you're dealt," he told his Denison friend and fellow trustee Don Shackelford when Shackelford phoned.[79] Barbara Paul Robinson, who had been the lawyer for the Rockefeller Trust Committee, visited several days before he died. "He sort of lit up," she said—despite his pain and limited energy, he was "funny, lively, telling stories" from days gone by.[80] Bowen's friend Ken Offit, the medical oncologist at Memorial Sloan-Kettering, also visited shortly before he died. "He was in the best of form that day," Offit said, "eyes twinkling at Mary Ellen, and not at all looking like a patient."[81]

Bowen had continued throughout his last decade to do what he could to take care of people who might benefit from his help. When David Bayley's wife, Chris, developed lung cancer, the Bayleys turned to Bowen for help in obtaining a second opinion. The appointment for the second opinion, at Memorial Sloan-Kettering, was secured within eight hours. The oncologist at MSKCC told the

77 E-mail, W. Michael Blumenthal to William G. Bowen, Oct. 4, 2016; e-mail, Bowen to Blumenthal, Oct. 4, 2016, courtesy of W. Michael Blumenthal.
78 Quoted in e-mail, Taylor Reveley to Nancy Weiss Malkiel, Dec. 29, 2021.
79 Telephone interview with Don Shackelford, Aug. 23, 2018.
80 Telephone interview with Barbara Paul Robinson, Oct. 8, 2021.
81 E-mail, Kenneth Offit to Nancy Weiss Malkiel, Oct. 1, 2021.

Bayleys that "the treatment prescribed was right, that MSK couldn't do any better, and that medical facilities in Albany, NY, where [they] were living, were first class." The Bayleys "felt as if [they] had been holding . . . a balloon of anxiety. Bill punctured that at one stroke."[82] When "Brit" Kirwan's wife, Patty, was diagnosed with the multiple myeloma that eventually took her life, Bowen set up appointments for her at Sloan-Kettering and offered the Kirwans the use of the Bowens' New York apartment. "If you were in his orbit," Kirwan recalled, "there was nothing he wouldn't do for you."[83]

Now, increasingly, the caretaking focused on the children of people close to Bowen. That summer, Dennis Sullivan's son, Steve, ruptured his patella tendon while he was in the Adirondacks. Sullivan called Bowen, who called Thomas Sculco, the surgeon at the Hospital for Special Surgery who had done joint replacement surgeries for Bowen as well as Mary Ellen. Steve Sullivan had the necessary surgery at HSS that week. Bowen had "a deep sense of wanting to help people," Sullivan said, a commitment that was "there to the end."[84] A second example: Bowen had met Randy Kennedy's twins, Rachel and Thaddeus, and he knew that they were about to apply to college. In mid-September, Kennedy had a message from Johanna Brownell, Bowen's executive assistant: Please send information about the twins; Bowen would like to write letters of recommendation. "He was quite literally staring death in the face," Kennedy reflected. Writing for the twins "has to have been one of the last things he did."[85] And a third example: When Kevin Guthrie's eldest son, Jeffers, enrolled in September 2016 as a freshman at Princeton, he decided to try to walk on to the highly touted Princeton varsity lacrosse team. The roster was to be posted on Friday, October 14. On Friday night at 11:07, less than a week before Bowen died, hours before Mary Ellen checked him into the hospi-

82 David H. Bayley, remarks at the memorial service of William G. Bowen, Dec. 11, 2016, courtesy of David H. Bayley.

83 Telephone interview with William E. "Brit" Kirwan, Mar. 9, 2022.

84 Interview with T. Dennis Sullivan, Nov. 8, 2018, Princeton, NJ.

85 Interview with Randall L. Kennedy, July 26, 2018, Cambridge, MA; interview with Johanna Brownell, Oct. 3, 2021, Princeton, NJ.

tal in Princeton, he sent Guthrie an e-mail: "Did [Jeffers] make the lacrosse team? How about Jasper? (Jasper, who was also trying out, [was] the grandson of one of Bill's longtime friends.)" Guthrie replied "that the coach had decided to delay the final roster decisions, but that both boys would be traveling with the team for an exhibition game over the weekend." Bowen's response, the last communication Guthrie had from him: "Encouraging."[86]

Bill Bowen died at home in Princeton late in the evening of Thursday, October 20. It was Mary Ellen's eighty-third birthday.

86 Kevin M. Guthrie remarks, William G. Bowen memorial service, Princeton University Chapel, Dec. 11, 2016, courtesy of Kevin M. Guthrie.

18

Afterword

The Bowen Legacy

Bill Bowen was a singular figure in American higher education in the late twentieth and early twenty-first centuries. As provost and president of Princeton, he offered a case study in leadership, demonstrating how vision, strategy, political and organizational savvy, and sophistication about governance can enable leaders to deal with pressing problems and elevate the stature and efficacy of major institutions. The Bowen example shows us how one can remake such an institution, step by step, theme by theme, to produce an outstanding result, so that it is effectively transformed in the leader's hands—better organized, better governed, more inclusive, of demonstrably higher quality than it had been before.

The Bowen example also illustrates the generative power of boundless energy, high intellect, and "capacity to attend," in Taylor Reveley's words, "to many things at once," "to do everything quickly," and to press forward, determined, always, to reach for the next goal. Bowen juggled so many demanding responsibilities at once; he simply did not know the meaning of slowing down, trimming sails, settling for a less challenging set of objectives.[1]

The Bowen story shows us, too, how leadership can involve elaborate control, with the most intricate and detailed planning at every stage—the leader leaving nothing to chance, painstakingly orchestrating every step in a complex process. Such careful control can ensure the best, most positive outcomes. Unless one is scrupu-

1 E-mail, Taylor Reveley to Nancy Weiss Malkiel, Dec. 29, 2021.

lous in observing boundaries, however, it can affect the balance between collegiality and cooperation, on the one hand, and manipu-
lation on the other.[2]

The Bowen case shows us the power of learning. At Princeton
he had an important but carefully circumscribed field of vision; the
university was unique in many ways and not necessarily representative of many other institutions of higher education. When Bowen
went to Mellon, he expanded that visual scope to encompass other
elite private universities, liberal arts colleges, and, later, public institutions. He came "to appreciate [their] needs and demands" and
his programmatic initiatives and scholarship reflected that broadened perspective. Bowen wrote about and invested in elite institutions because he believed, correctly, that they carried outsize
influence—that other institutions watched them and followed what
they did. He invested in liberal arts colleges in significant measure
because of the great importance to him of his own college experience at Denison. And he came to appreciate over time the particular role that public institutions play in the overall scheme of higher
education in the United States. In his final tranche of scholarship
and in the initiatives he promoted at ITHAKA, public institutions
came finally to assume a central place.[3]

As stated in the preface, Bowen had a big impact in taking on
the biggest, most challenging problems that bedeviled American
higher education in the half century 1966 to 2016. He had a remarkable gift for identifying those problems, for seeing around
corners to forecast the challenges to come. And he offered well-
thought-out roadmaps to address them.[4] As provost and president
of Princeton, president of the Andrew W. Mellon Foundation,
founding board chair of ITHAKA, and as the author of some twenty
books in American higher education, he wrote about and promoted
initiatives to address central problems such as cost disease, inclusion, affirmative action, college access, college completion, and
online learning. He laid out both a scholarly case and a practical

2 I am indebted to Eva Gossman for this formulation.
3 Jonathan Cole, reader's report for Princeton University Press, May 2022.
4 I am indebted to Eva Gossman for this formulation.

blueprint that could be used and adapted by other leaders of his own and subsequent eras.

It was in his writing that Bowen had his most significant impact. Bowen, Harold T. Shapiro said, was "the most thoughtful researcher dealing with important issues in higher education at the turn of the [twenty-first] century."[5] Hanna Holborn Gray made a related point: "His was . . . above all an intellectual and scholarly influence rather than one that concretely shaped policy and practice elsewhere."[6] Stanley N. Katz called Bowen's work "engaged scholarship"—"serious scholarship on the problems of the university," in which Bowen tried "to think systematically about where higher education was, what the major problems were, and what a responsible institution should do about them."[7] Caroline Hoxby remarked on his unusual combination of talents: "to be a great university president" and, at the same time, "to be analytic about what it meant to be the leader of a university"—about the challenges to take on, the problems to address, the initiatives to be attempted.[8] Daniel H. Weiss noted the ways in which Bowen's model of leadership—original in his own time—"has become something of a gold standard": "His combination of serious engagement with substantive issues, a data-driven scholarly approach, collaboration always, and ambitious modes of outreach (serious books especially) represents an ideal now widely recognized."[9]

Bowen had an unusual ability to better the situations of the institutions and the people he touched. The institutions he led were demonstrably stronger, more influential, more efficacious, more impactful than they had been before he took over. That was clearly true of Princeton; it was true of Mellon as well. Moreover, Bowen built from scratch institutions that made a major difference in the world of academic scholarship and teaching; one has only to think of JSTOR as a prime example.

5 E-mail, Harold T. Shapiro to Nancy Weiss Malkiel, Dec. 4, 2021.
6 E-mail, Hanna Holborn Gray to Nancy Weiss Malkiel, Oct. 17, 2021.
7 Interview with Stanley N. Katz, July 18, 2018, Princeton, NJ.
8 Telephone interview with Caroline Hoxby, Oct. 26, 2021.
9 Princeton University Press reader's report, May 2022.

As for the people he touched, Bowen had a profound impact on so many individuals. He did that in part by creating and strengthening programs—academic programs as well as financial aid programs to provide access to life-changing educational opportunities. But he also did it by touching personally so many people—young people just starting out, mature individuals on the cusp of new opportunities—for whom a conversation with Bowen, or a recommendation from Bowen, resulted in a reset of professional direction with access to new possibilities never previously imagined. He was exceptionally generous in trying to help people; his concern for other people, from the most accomplished to the least advantaged, was genuine. As Morton Schapiro put it, "He invested heavily in people he trusted and admired."[10] At the same time, however, Bowen could be relentlessly self-referential, even self-absorbed, convinced that whatever he needed in order to be able to pursue the important work at hand took precedence over any staff member's private life, over any family member's competing desires.[11]

Bowen focused on advancing the fortunes of groups peripheral to the power structure in American society: Jews, Blacks, women. He elevated individuals to positions of opportunity and positions of leadership. And he advanced policies that made a material difference in the standing of groups previously overlooked or discriminated against in the sorts of institutions he led. Jews were prominently represented among the people Bowen recommended for college and university presidencies at a time when such appointments were still unusual. He was responsible directly for exceptional career outcomes for a number of Blacks in the academy—the Mellon Mays Undergraduate Fellowship Program, for example, prepared a notable fraction of the African American scholars and administrators now occupying senior positions at leading colleges and universities. And Bowen himself advocated for senior leadership roles in Fortune 500 companies for two African Americans who became chief executive officers, two of the

10 E-mail, Morton Schapiro to Nancy Weiss Malkiel, Dec. 27, 2021. The insights in this paragraph come also from David Cannadine and Eva Gossman.
11 I am indebted for this insight to Eva Gossman.

very small number of such individuals in corporate leadership roles at the highest levels in the first two decades of the twenty-first century. As for women, Bowen made senior administrative appointments of women at Princeton beginning in the 1970s, with Adele Smith Simmons as dean of students, Nina Garsoian as dean of the graduate school, and Joan Girgus as dean of the college, all appointed well before most of Princeton's peer institutions were ready to make such moves. And at Mellon he surrounded himself with exceptionally strong senior women—Hanna Holborn Gray as board chair, Pat McPherson, Harriet Zuckerman, and Tish Emerson as members of the senior staff—creating a model for other institutions where women later began to assume important roles.

All of that is part of the Bowen legacy. So is the broad and lasting impact of Bowen's initiatives in areas such as affirmative action—as followed or adapted by other colleges and universities, as evidenced in federal policy (the *Bakke* and *Grutter* decisions in the United States Supreme Court), as generalized at Mellon. At a moment when so much of what Bowen accomplished is under threat in American society, one cannot help but note the urgent need for the kind of vision and leadership that he provided. Some of what Bowen championed may be rolled back—the possibility as this book goes to press that the Supreme Court may outlaw affirmative action in college and university admissions is the most pressing example—but the directions he charted will still endure in one form or another as templates for future college and university leaders.

And Bowen's influence on current leaders persists. Upon being named president of Northwestern University, effective in September 2022, Michael H. Schill said, "Bill left an indelible mark on me," as he did on "so, so many" others.[12] Lawrence S. Bacow, president of Harvard University from 2018 to 2023, put it this way: "Through-

---

12 E-mails, Michael H. Schill to Nancy Weiss Malkiel, Aug. 12, 17, 2022. As Morton Schapiro has pointed out (e-mail to Nancy Weiss Malkiel, Dec. 27, 2021), Schill, who succeeded Schapiro as president of Northwestern on Sept. 12, 2022, became the third Northwestern president in a row (the first being Henry Bienen) whom Bowen either placed or greatly influenced. The same would have been true of Rebecca M. Blank, originally designated to succeed Schapiro, who was forced to resign as president-elect in July 2022 because of a diagnosis of an aggressive form of cancer.

out my time here I have often asked myself, 'What would Bill do?' He continues to be a presence in my life as I suspect he is for many of us."[13] The lessons about leadership, about values, about the purposes of higher education that Bowen imparted have had notable staying power and are likely to continue to hold currency as the current generation of college and university presidents seeks to chart the future course of their own institutions.

13 E-mail, Lawrence S. Bacow to Nancy Weiss Malkiel, June 9, 2022.

Abbreviations:
Manuscript Collections and
Oral History Transcripts

Throughout this volume, any underscoring that was used in the following material to indicate emphasis has been silently changed to italics.

Manuscript Collections

Bowen federal government	William G. Bowen Collection on the Federal Government and Princeton University, AC196, Princeton University Archives, Department of Special Collections, Princeton University Library
Bowen Ithaka	William G. Bowen correspondence, 2006–16, housed on the ITHAKA server, courtesy of Johanna Brownell
Bowen miscellaneous	Courtesy of Marcia H. Snowden, Lawrenceville, NJ
Bowen personal	William G. Bowen Personal Papers, courtesy of Mary Ellen Bowen
Bowen president	Office of the President Records, William G. Bowen, AC187, Princeton University Archives, Department of Special Collections, Princeton University Library
Bowen provost	Office of the Provost Records, William G. Bowen, AC195, Princeton University Archives, Department of Special Collections, Princeton University Library
Bressler Commission	Commission on the Future of the College Chairman's Records, AC186, Princeton University Archives, Department of Special Collections, Princeton University Library

CAP	Concerned Alumni of Princeton Records, AC305, Princeton University Archives, Department of Special Collections, Princeton University Library
Dean of the College	Office of the Dean of the College Records, AC149, Princeton University Archives, Department of Special Collections, Princeton University Library
Dean of the Faculty	Office of the Dean of the Faculty Records, AC118, Princeton University Archives, Department of Special Collections, Princeton University Library
Denison	Denison University Archives & Special Collections, Denison University Libraries, Granville, OH
Faculty Files	Faculty and Professional Staff Files, AC107, Princeton University Archives, Department of Special Collections, Princeton University Library
Goheen	Office of the President Records, Robert F. Goheen, AC193, Princeton University Archives, Department of Special Collections, Princeton University Library
Hackney	Office of the Provost Records, Sheldon Hackney, AC195, series 2, Princeton University Archives, Department of Special Collections, Princeton University Library
Ithaka trustees	Trustee minutes, 2003–16, courtesy of Kevin Guthrie
Kelley Committee	Special Committee on the Structure of the University Records, AC044, Princeton University Archives, Department of Special Collections, Princeton University Library
Kuhn	Harold Kuhn Papers on the Committee on the Structure of the University, AC391, Princeton University Archives, Department of Special Collections, Princeton University Library
Morrison	Toni Morrison Papers, C1491, Department of Special Collections, Princeton University Library
Offit	Papers in possession of Kenneth Offit, New York City, courtesy of Kenneth Offit

Princeton publications | Princeton University Publications, AC364, Princeton University Archives, Department of Special Collections, Princeton University Library

Princeton trustees | Board of Trustees Records, AC120, Princeton University Archives, Department of Special Collections, Princeton University Library (select content also available online at http://arks .princeton.edu/ark:/88435/w66343618)

Rees and Rudenstine provost | Office of the Provost Records, Albert Rees and Neil Rudenstine, AC195, series 3, Princeton University Archives, Department of Special Collections, Princeton University Library

Rockefeller | Laurance S. Rockefeller Papers, Rockefeller Archive Center, Sleepy Hollow, NY

Wyoming | Wyoming Historical Society, Wyoming, OH

Oral History Transcripts

Blumenthal oral history | W. Michael Blumenthal *53, *56 interview, June 12, 2014, Princeton, NJ, Princetoniana Committee Oral History Project Records, AC259, box 4, Princeton University Archives, Department of Special Collections, Princeton University Library

Borsch oral history | Frederick H. Borsch '57 interview, May 16, 2013, Philadelphia, Princetoniana Committee Oral History Project Records, AC259, box 2, Princeton University Archives, Department of Special Collections, Princeton University Library

Bowen oral history | William G. Bowen interviews, June 9 and 25, July 21, and Sept. 18 and 28, 2009, Princeton University Presidents Oral History Collection, AC318, series 3, Princeton University Archives, Department of Special Collections, Princeton University Library

Brombert oral history | Victor Brombert interview, Feb. 19, 2013, Princeton, NJ, Princetoniana Committee Oral History Project Records, AC259, box 2, Princeton University Archives, Department of Special Collections, Princeton University Library

Goheen oral history

Robert F. Goheen interviews, Oct. 21 and 26 and Nov. 4, 2004, and Jan. 6, 2005, Princeton University Presidents Oral History Collection, AC318, series 1, Princeton University Archives, Department of Special Collections, Princeton University Library

Katz oral history

Stanley N. Katz interview, Jan. 14, 2013, Princeton, NJ, Princetoniana Committee Oral History Project Records, AC259, box 4, Princeton University Archives, Department of Special Collections, Princeton University Library

Kuhn oral history

Harold Kuhn *50 interview, June 15, 2011, New York City, Princetoniana Committee Oral History Project Records, AC259, box 3, Princeton University Archives, Department of Special Collections, Princeton University Archives

Rawson oral history

Robert H. Rawson Jr. '66 interview, June 2, 2007, Princeton, NJ, Princetoniana Committee Oral History Project Records, AC259, box 3, Princeton University Archives, Department of Special Collections, Princeton University Library

Rudenstine oral history

Neil Rudenstine '56 interview, Mar. 20, 2009, Princeton, NJ, Princetoniana Committee Oral History Project Records, AC259, box 3, Princeton University Archives, Department of Special Collections, Princeton University Library

Whitman oral history

Marina Whitman interview, Oct. 26, 2013, Princeton, NJ, Princetoniana Committee Oral History Project Records, AC259, box 4, Princeton University Archives, Department of Special Collections, Princeton University Library

Zaharko oral history

Wendy Zaharko '74 interview, May 13, 2009, Princeton, NJ, Princetoniana Committee Oral History Project Records, AC259, box 4, Department of Special Collections, Princeton University Library

Interviews

Joel Achenbach, Jan. 9, 2019, by telephone
Franklin P. Agnew, June 29, 2018, by telephone
Bruce Alberts, Aug. 27, 2020, by telephone
Nicholas W. Allard, Sept. 11, Nov. 14, 2019, Princeton, NJ
Danielle Allen, July 20, Oct. 22, 2021, by telephone
Orley C. Ashenfelter, Oct. 3, 2018, Princeton, NJ
Jane Kenney Austin, Aug. 29, 2019, by telephone
Lawrence S. Bacow, Sept. 3, 2020, by telephone
Elizabeth E. Bailey, Jan. 14, 2019, by telephone
J. Scott Ballenger, June 21, 2021, by telephone
Jon Barfield, Jan. 14, 2019, by telephone
Thomas A. Barron, Aug. 27, 2019, by telephone
David H. Bayley, July 31, 2018, by telephone
Rachel N. Bellow, Sept. 11, 2018, New York City
Paul Benacerraf, July 17, 2018, Princeton, NJ
David A. Benjamin, Sept. 10, 2019, Skillman, NJ
Arnold Berlin, Sept. 5, 2018, by telephone
Ben Bernanke, Oct. 11, 2019, by telephone
Lewis Bernard, Aug. 11, 2020, by telephone
Louise H. Bessire, June 11, 2019, by telephone
Henry S. Bienen, Nov. 5, 2018, Chicago
Leigh B. Bienen, Nov. 5, 2018, Chicago
Rebecca M. Blank, Aug. 29, 2019, by telephone
W. Michael Blumenthal, July 17, 2018, Princeton, NJ
Halcyone H. Bohen, Sept. 10, 2018, by telephone
Derek C. Bok, June 20, 2018, Cambridge, MA
Lee C. Bollinger, Sept. 21, 2021, by telephone
David Bowen, Sept. 29, 2018, Princeton, NJ
Karen Bowen and Dirk Imhof, Aug. 12, 2018, Princeton, NJ
Mary Ellen Bowen, June 13, 22, 25, July 9, 20, 30,
    Sept. 19, 2018, Princeton, NJ
Thomas D. Boyatt, June 24, 2018, Princeton, NJ
William W. Bradley, Sept. 10, 2019, by telephone
Paul A. Brest, Feb. 4, 2022, by telephone
Charles Brickman, Sept. 12, 2020, by telephone
Victor and Beth Brombert, Aug. 20, 2018, Princeton, NJ
J. Anderson Brown, Oct. 30, 2019, Princeton, NJ
Johanna Brownell, Oct. 3, 2021, Princeton, NJ
Timothy C. Callard, June 18, 2018, by telephone
David Cannadine, May 16, 2019, Princeton, NJ
Philip Cannon, Jan. 14, 2019, by telephone
Nancy Cantor, Oct. 1, 2021, by telephone
David Card, Aug. 27, 2019, by telephone
Peter J. Carril, July 17, 2018, by telephone

Hodding Carter, July 24, 2018, by telephone
Gerhard Casper, Feb. 19, 2020, by telephone
Kenneth I. Chenault, Jan. 8, 2020, by telephone
Matthew M. Chingos, June 1, 2021, by telephone
Raymond J. Clark, July 12, 2018, Princeton, NJ
Janet Morrison Clarke, June 1, 2018, Princeton, NJ
Leonard Coleman Jr., Feb. 10, 2020, Palm Beach, FL
Edward C. Cox, Aug. 26, 2019, Princeton, NJ
Paolo Cucchi, Aug. 22, 2018, Princeton, NJ
Anthony M. Cummings, Mar. 22, 2019, Princeton, NJ
Stacy Berg Dale, June 15, 2021, by telephone
Mark Dalton, Sept. 15, 2020, by telephone
Robert C. Darnton, Aug. 26, 2019, by telephone
Jerome Davis, Nov. 19, 2021, by telephone
Legrome Davis, Sept. 17, 2019, Princeton, NJ
Natalie Zemon Davis, June 21, 2018, by telephone
Joseph J. Dehner, Jan. 14, 2019, by telephone
Elizabeth A. Duffy, Aug. 30, 2018, Princeton, NJ
Robert K. Durkee, July 9, 2018, Princeton, NJ
Christopher L. Eisgruber, Dec. 6, 2019, Princeton, NJ
Richard H. Ekman, Sept. 17, 2020, by telephone
Georgia Elliott, Sept. 7, 2019, by telephone
Alice F. Emerson, Oct. 31, 2018, Bryn Mawr, PA
Mary Tabor Engel, Jan. 20, 2019, by telephone
Richard Evans, Sept. 8, 2018, by telephone
Jacqueline Ewenstein, Oct. 13, 2021, by telephone
Edward Feld, Sept. 5, 2019, by telephone
T. Aldrich Finegan, Sept. 5, 2018, by telephone
Paul B. Firstenberg, June 28, 2018, by telephone
Joel L. Fleishman, July 16, 2021, by Zoom
John V. Fleming, Mar. 25, 2019, Princeton, NJ
Sally B. Frank, Aug. 3, 2020, by telephone
Kenneth C. Frazier, Sept. 9, 2020, by telephone
Ulrica Fredsvik-Konvalin, Aug. 6, 2020, by telephone
James C. Freund, Jan. 11, 2019, by telephone
William H. Frist, Sept. 28, 2020, by telephone
Ira H. Fuchs, July 20, 2018, Princeton, NJ
Mimi Gardner Gates, Nov. 2, 2021, by telephone
Robert L. Geddes, Sept. 13, 2018, Skillman, NJ
Joan Gilbert, Jan. 28, 2022, by telephone
William Y. Giles, Aug. 2, 2018, by telephone
Joan S. Girgus, Sept. 12, 2018, Princeton, NJ
Patricia Albjerg Graham, July 25, 2018, Cambridge, MA
Hanna Holborn Gray, Sept, 18, 2018, New York City;
    Oct. 19, 2021, by telephone
Vartan Gregorian, Aug. 11, 2020, by telephone
Robert C. Gunning, Aug. 26, 2019, Princeton, NJ
Kevin M. Guthrie, Nov. 11, 2018, Princeton, NJ;
    Oct. 1, 2021, by telephone
Jean McClung Halleran, Sept. 30, 2019, by telephone
William R. Hambrecht, Jan. 15, 2019, by telephone
Aaron Harber, Jan. 10, 2019, by telephone

Margaret M. Healy, Oct. 31, 2018, Rosemont, PA
James A. Henderson, Oct. 18, 2018, by telephone
John L. Hennessy, Oct. 5, 2021, by telephone
Carol P. Herring, Oct. 23, 2018, Princeton, NJ
Catharine Bond Hill, Feb. 1, 2022, by telephone
Ellen Porter Honnet, July 26, 2018, Cambridge, MA
David J. Hooker, Sept. 10, 2020, by telephone
John J. Hopfield, Oct. 14, 2019, Princeton, NJ
Charles Howard, Aug. 26, 2020, by telephone
Caroline Hoxby, Oct. 26, 2021, by telephone
Michael D. Iseman, Jan. 11, 2019, by telephone
Juanita T. James, Feb. 20, 2019, by telephone
Robert A. Kasdin, Aug. 25, 2020, by telephone
Stanley N. Katz, July 18, 2018, Princeton, NJ
Edmund L. Keeley, Sept. 3, 2019, Princeton, NJ
Michael J. Kelly, Feb. 7, 2019, by telephone
Randall L. Kennedy, July 26, 2018, Cambridge, MA
Nannerl O. Keohane, Apr. 23, 2019, Princeton, NJ
Marc W. Kirschner, Aug. 5, 2020, by telephone
William E. "Brit" Kirwan, Mar. 9, 2022, by telephone
Dale T. Knobel, Sept. 14, 2020, by telephone
Amie Knox, Sept. 9, 2019, by telephone
Marvin Krislov, June 28, 2021, by telephone
Alan B. Krueger, Sept. 14, 2018, Princeton, NJ
Martin A. Kurzweil, June 4, 2021, by telephone
Hanns Kuttner, Sept. 5, 2019, by telephone
Kelly A. Lack, May 25, 2021, by telephone
Eric S. Lander, Mar. 19, 2019, by telephone
Paul LeClerc, July 1, 2021, by telephone
Eva Lerner-Lam, Feb. 8, 18, 2019, by telephone
Richard C. Levin, Sept. 20, 2019, New Haven, CT
Arnold J. Levine, Aug. 7, 2018, Princeton, NJ
Marsha Levy-Warren, Aug. 13, 2018, New York City
Deborah Longino, Jan. 31, 2022, by telephone
Eugene Y. Lowe Jr., Nov. 6, 2018, Evanston, IL
Colin Lucas, Aug. 14, 2020, by telephone
Richard G. Lugar, Aug. 22, 2018, by telephone
Carolyn Makinson, Feb. 15, 2022, by telephone
Deanna Marcum, Feb. 1, 2022, by telephone
Sally Maruca, Aug. 15, 2018, Lawrenceville, NJ
Walter E. Massey, Aug. 13, 2020, by telephone
John W. McCarter, Jan. 11, 2019, Aug. 17, 2020, by telephone
W. Drake McFeely, Feb. 15, 2022, by telephone
Mary Patterson McPherson, Aug. 8, 2018, Rosemont, PA;
    Oct. 20, 2021, by telephone
Michael S. McPherson, Aug. 20, 2020, by telephone
June Mei, June 30, 2022, by telephone
Jack Meyers, June 15, 2018, by telephone
Martin Michaelson, July 1, 2021, by telephone
Luther T. Munford, Aug. 30, 2019, by telephone
Michele Tolela Myers, June 26, 2020, by telephone
Andrew P. Napolitano, Sept. 1, 2020, by telephone

Nancy J. Newman, Nov. 11, 2018, by telephone
Cynthia Nitta, Aug. 31, 2019, by telephone
Lee T. Nolan, June 27, 2018, Princeton, NJ
Thomas I. Nygren, May 27, 2021, by telephone
Kenneth Offit, June 2, 2021, by Zoom
James C. Parham Jr., July 16, 2018, by telephone
Gerald W. Parsky, Jan. 22, 2019, by telephone
Nancy Peretsman, Aug. 13, 2018, New York City
Susanne Pichler, Feb. 20, 2022, by telephone
Susanna Badgley Place, Sept. 6, 2019, by telephone
Elizabeth Plater-Zyberk, Jan. 11, 2019, by telephone
Alan G. Preucil, Aug. 28, 2018, by telephone
Emily Rauh Pulitzer, Sept. 7, 2020, by telephone
Richard E. Quandt, July 18, 2018, Princeton, NJ
Mamphela Ramphele, Feb. 4, 2022, by telephone
Don M. Randel, Aug. 5, 2020, by telephone
Robert H. Rawson, Oct. 22, 2018, by telephone
W. Taylor Reveley III, Sept. 4, 2018, Princeton, NJ
Eric Richard, Jan. 15, 2019, by telephone
Robert J. Rivers, Aug. 29, 2018, Princeton, NJ
William R. Robertson IV, Sept. 2, 2020, by telephone
Barbara Paul Robinson, Oct. 8, 2021, by telephone
Jade Robinson, Aug. 6, 2021, Princeton, NJ
Alysa Christmas Rollock, Oct. 3, 2019, Princeton, NJ
Lawrence Rosen, Aug. 21, 2019, by telephone
Karen Rosenberg, Sept. 27, 2019, Princeton, NJ
Henry Rosovsky, Mar. 11, 2020, by telephone
Neil L. Rudenstine, July 22, 2018, New York City
Jocelyn Russell, Jan. 21, 2019, by telephone
Morton O. Schapiro, Aug. 19, 2020, by telephone
Michael H. Schill, Feb. 7, 2020, by telephone
Mark S. Schlissel, Sept. 30, 2019, by telephone
Griffith Sexton, Oct. 8, 2019, Princeton, NJ
Donald B. Shackelford, Aug. 23, 2018, by telephone
Harold T. Shapiro, June 19, 2018, Princeton, NJ
Judith R. Shapiro, Oct. 31, 2018, Rosemont, PA
Thomas E. Shenk, July 31, 2018, Princeton, NJ
Lois Shepetin, Feb. 8, 2022, West Palm Beach, FL
Seth Shepetin, Feb. 23, 2022, by telephone
Elaine Showalter, Aug. 22, 2019, by telephone
James L. Shulman, May 30, 2018, Princeton, NJ;
    June 25, 2021, by telephone; Dec. 9, 2021, by Zoom
Adele Simmons, July 6, 19, 2018, by telephone
Ruth J. Simmons, Oct. 4, 2019, Princeton, NJ
Jonathan Smolowe, Feb. 6, 2019, by telephone
Marcia H. Snowden, June 25, 2018, Lawrenceville, NJ
Hugo F. Sonnenschein, Jan. 31, 2020, by telephone
Julie Ann Sosa, June 15, 2021, by Zoom
Susan Savage Speers, June 16, 2018, by telephone
Richard R. Spies, July 24, 2018, Princeton, NJ;
    Mar. 2, 2022, by telephone
Margaret Stengel, Sept. 19, 2018, Princeton, NJ

Beatrijs Stikkers, Dec. 12, 2019, by telephone
T. Dennis Sullivan, Nov. 8, 2018, Princeton, NJ
Sarah Levin Taubman, June 1, 2021, by telephone
Samuel O. Thier, July 30, 2021, by telephone
Carol and Dennis Thompson, July 26, 2018, Cambridge, MA
Robert L. Tignor, Sept. 24, 2019, Princeton, NJ
Shirley M. Tilghman, July 8, 2021, Princeton, NJ
Eugene M. Tobin, Sept. 18, 2020, by telephone
Nicholas A. Ulanov, Sept. 18, 2019, by telephone
P. Roy Vagelos, Oct. 1, 2018, Bedminster, NJ
Paul A. Volcker, July 13, 2018, New York City
Judith B. Walzer, July 5, 2018, Princeton, NJ
Michele Warman, Mar. 18, 2022, by telephone
Donald J. Waters, Feb. 17, 2022, by telephone
Armistead J. Webster, Mar. 19, 2019, by telephone
Fong Wei, May 20, 2019, Princeton, NJ
Daniel H. Weiss, Sept. 17, 2020, by telephone
Peter C. Wendell, Sept. 28, 2019, Princeton, NJ
Charles F. Westoff, July 3, 2018, Oct. 1, 2019, Princeton, NJ
R. Elton White, Oct. 31, 2019, by telephone
Marina von Neumann Whitman, June 26, 2018, by telephone
James Wickenden, June 22, 2018, Princeton, NJ
Van Zandt Williams Jr., July 12, 2018, Princeton, NJ
John F. Wilson, Jan. 30, 2019, by telephone
Patricia T. Woodford, Aug. 17, 2020, by telephone
Thomas H. Wright Jr., June 29, 2018, Princeton, NJ
Gordon Y. S. Wu, Aug. 20, 2020, by telephone
Timothy Wu, Jan. 11, 2019, by telephone
Wendy Zaharko, Sept. 1, 2018, Princeton, NJ
Froma I. Zeitlin, Aug. 21, 2019, Princeton, NJ
Ezra K. Zilkha, Aug. 1, 2018, by telephone
Theodore J. Ziolkowski, Oct. 4, 2019, Princeton, NJ
Harriet Zuckerman, Sept. 11, 2018, New York City

Index

Page numbers in *italics* denote figures.

Barron, James, 11
baseball idiom, 242
basketball, 15–16, 90–91, 230–31, 236, 307–8
Baumol, William J., xix, 28, 34–37. *See also* "cost disease"; *Performing Arts: The Economic Dilemma* (Baumol and Bowen)
Bayley, Chris, 381–82
Bayley, Connie, 22, 24
Bayley, David H., 20–22, 24, 381–82
Bayley, Frank, 21, 24
Beadle, George, 9, 42
behavioral sciences: Center for Advanced Study in the Behavioral Sciences, 72, 108–9, 238, 326n3
Bellow, Rachel N., 255, 258–59
Beloved (Morrison), 99, 108
Benacerraf, Paul, 9, 46, 50–51, 373
Bendheim Hall, 240
Bergman, Jed, 270–71
Berkeley, University of California at. *See* University of California at Berkeley
Berlin, Arnold, 211
Bernanke, Anna, 106
Bernanke, Ben, 100, 106–7
Berry, George P., 124
bicker process, 175, 184–86, 188–89, 191; and "dirty bicker," 175
Bienen, Henry S., 347, 349, 351, 356, 388n
Biggs, John H., 342
biochemistry/biochemical sciences, 122–50 passim; Special Committee on Biochemistry, 141–43
biological sciences, 128, 135, 142, 149–50. *See also* biochemistry; molecular biology
Birgenau, Robert, 373–74
Black administrators at Princeton, 165
Black faculty at Princeton, 53–54, 99, 107–8, 164–65
black horse story, 93
Black middle class, 300
Black Power movement, 52
Black students at colleges and universities, 52–54, 72, 300, 322; Association of Black Collegians, 55, 153, 163. *See also* minority students
Black students at Princeton, 52–54, 162–64; active recruitment of, xvi, 53, 163; Bow-

en's relationship with Black student leaders, 54; Third World Center (TWC), 164. *See also* minority students at Princeton
Blank, Rebecca M., 301, 320–21, 348n18, 353, 367, 388n
Blue and the Gold, The: A Personal Memoir of the University of California, 1949–1967 (Kerr), xxi
Blue Key Honor Society, 20
Blumenthal, W. Michael, 93–94, 209–12 passim, 369–70, 380–81
boards of directors and trustees, 341–42; *The Board Book: An Insider's Guide for Directors and Trustees* (Bowen), 341–42, 364, 374–75; Bowen as director and trustee, 325–42, 326n3 (*see also* American Express; Center for Advanced Study in the Behavioral Sciences; Denison University; Merck; National Cash Register; *Reader's Digest*; Rockefeller Trust Committee; Smithsonian Institution; Teachers Insurance and Annuity Association and College Retirement Equities Fund Boards of Overseers); for-profit, 341–42; *Inside the Boardroom: Governance by Directors and Trustees* (Bowen), 333, 341–42; Mellon Foundation (*see* under Mellon Foundation: working with the board); Princeton University (*see* Princeton University board of trustees)
Boesky, Ivan, 182
Bok, Derek, xxi, 28, 108, 218, 236, *289*, 353n, 354, 361n20. See also *Shape of the River, The* (Bowen and Bok)
Bollinger, Lee, 294, 301–4, 344, 346n13, 347; *Gratz v. Bollinger*, 297–98, 301–2, 375; *Grutter v. Bollinger*, xxiii, 266n, 294, 297–98, 301–6, 375, 388
Bonner, John, 129
books by William G. Bowen. See Bowen, William G., books/writings of
Borsch, Frederick H., 89–90, 173, 176–79, 181
Bossidy, Lawrence A., 332, 334
Bowen, Albert, 12–13, 15–17
Bowen, Bernice Pommert, 12–15, 18
Bowen, David, xxiv, 30, 86, 89, 228–30, 370, 380
Bowen, Ellie, 370
Bowen, Joseph G., 12

medical education, 123–24. *See also* professional schools

Mei, June, 278n27

Mellon, Andrew W., 246. *See also* Mellon Foundation

Mellon, Paul, 246, 262–63, 275–76

Mellon, Timothy, 263

Mellon Foundation, xvii–xxi, 11, 240–322; arts and culture, 248–50, 275–81 (*see also* Artstor); Dunhuang project/Mellon International Dunhuang Archive, 276–79; endowment of, 247–48, 253, 257; environment under Bowen, 255–59; fellowship programs, 266, 269, 271–73, 387; the Graduate Education Initiative, 269–70; grant-making, approach to, 251; and higher education/studies of higher education, 246, 266–75 (*see also* College and Beyond database) ; interest in humanities, 248–51, 267–70, 272; and public affairs, 281–83; recruiting philosophy, 259; and research, four elements of, 267–68 (*See also* College and Beyond database); research arm ("Bill Bowen's sandbox"), xviii, 291; and shaping the Mellon agenda, 266–87; women in senior ranks at, 388; working with staff, 249–63; working with the board, 263–65. *See also* Artstor; College and Beyond database; ITHAKA Harbors; JSTOR; Randel, Don M.; Rudenstine, Neil

Mellon Mays Undergraduate Fellowship Program (MMUF) (originally Mellon Minority), xviii, 266, 271–73, 387

Memorial Sloan-Kettering Cancer Center, 123, 146, 372, 381–82

Menand, Louis, 313

Menendez, Erik, 309

Menendez, José, 308–9

Menendez, Lyle, 308–9

Merck & Co., Inc.: Bowen's directorship at, 265, 326n3, 327, 330–36; and Vioxx, 330–35

merit aid, 349

Merton, Robert K., 226–27, 260

Mestres, Ricardo, 41

Metropolitan Museum of Art, 249, 347, 353

Mexican American students, 163

Michaelson, Martin, 297

Middlebury College, 193

middle class, 13; Black, 300. *See also* socioeconomic status

Miller, George A., 140–41

Miller, J. Roscoe "Rocky," 9

minority faculty members, Princeton. *See* faculty at Princeton University: minority members of

minority groups. *See* affirmative action; *by description*; diversity/inclusion; race

minority students at colleges and universities, 167–71, 173, 300, 303, 305, 318, 353, 373; and College and Beyond database, 297–98, 300; Mellon Mays Undergraduate Fellowship Program (MMUF) (originally Mellon Minority), xviii, 266, 271–73, 387. *See also* affirmative action; Black students; *by description/ minority group*; diversity/inclusion

minority students at Princeton, xvi–xvii, 55, 162–64, 167–71, 176; recruitment of, xiv, 53, 151, 163; Third World Center (TWC), 164. *See also* Black students at Princeton; *and by description/minority group*

mismatch theory, 305

mistakes, lessons from, 148–51, 365; *Lessons Learned* (Bowen), 272n9, 288, 364–65, 374–75, and passim

MIT. *See* Massachusetts Institute of Technology

MMUF. *See* Mellon Mays Undergraduate Fellowship Program

Moffett Biological Laboratory, 124, 129, 131, 142, 145–46

Molé, Harvey, 212

molecular biology department, Princeton University, 95, 102, 126, 135, 139–50, 240, 365; Lewis Thomas Laboratory, 147, 202, 240; rise of, 141–50. *See also* Levine, Arnold J.; Shenk, Thomas E.; Tilghman, Shirley M.

Montgomery College, 363

MOOCs (open online courses, *e.g.*, Coursera), 366

Morrison, Toni, 99, 107–8

Mullaney, Harvey, 14

Muller, Steven, 170

Murphy, Walter, 171

Murray-Dodge Hall, 180

Museum of Modern Art, 275, 279

museums, xvii, 249, 251, 275, 277–80. *See also by name*